ISLE OF MAN TT & MGP MEMORIAL

All profits from the sale of this book
will go to charities connected with the Isle of Man TT & MGP

Researched by Paul Bradford

Isle of Man TT & MGP Memorial 1907-2007
Published by Paul Bradford
ISBN 978-0-9560151-0-5
Printed by The Copy Shop – 01624 622697
© Paul Bradford July 2008

ISLE OF MAN
TT COURSE

Schoolhouse Corner
Parliament Square
Cruickshank's Corner
May Hill
23
24
Waterworks Corner
Milntown
Pinfold Cottage
22
Tower Bends
25
Gooseneck
Stella Maris
Hairpin
21
26
Glentramman
Guthrie's Memorial
20
Kerrowmoar
Ginger Hall
27
Sulby Bridge
19
Sulby Straight
28
18
Quarry Bends
Mountain Box
29
17
Ballaugh Bridge
Black Hut
Alpine Corner
Verandah
16
30
Bishopscourt
Graham Memorial
Rhencullen
Bungalow
31
15
Birkin's Bend
Hailwood Rise
Brandywell
Kirk Michael Village
Douglas Road Corner
Westwood
32
14
Cronk Urleigh
Windy Corner
13
Barregarrow Hill
33
12
34
Keppel Gate
Creg ny Baa
Kate's Cottage
Handley's Corner
11
Drinkwater's Corner
35
Cronk y Voddy
Sunny Orchard
Brandish
1m
10
Lambfell
Hillberry
36
Cronk ny Mona
Sarah's Cottage
Signpost
37
Glen Helen
Bedstead
The Nook
Black Dub
Governor's Bridge
9
Laurel Bank
Union Mills
Doran's Bend
Ballaspur
Greeba Bridge
Greeba Castle
Highlander
Bray Hill
8
1
Ballacraine
Ballagarey
Quarterbridge
7
Gorse Lea
Appledene
6
5
Crosby Village
Glen Vine
4
Ballahutchin Hill
3
2
Braddan Bridge

3

Long may they be remembered

This book is dedicated to those competitors who have paid the ultimate price in pursuit of their chosen sport, motorcycle racing on the Isle of Man TT course.

Victor Surridge astride the Rudge on which he was to ride in the 1911 Senior TT

At an early hour on the morning of Tuesday 27th June 1911, Victor John Surridge, one of the riders for the Rudge-Whitworth team, set off from the team headquarters at the Glen Helen Hotel. He was riding a Rudge motorcycle bearing the race number 8 and his intention was to complete two practice laps of the mountain course in preparation for the Senior Tourist Trophy Race, which was scheduled to take place on the 3rd July. This was the first year the mountain course was used whereas in previous years a much shorter course commencing at St. Johns and travelling via Ballacraine, Glen Helen, Kirk Michael and Peel had been used.

Shortly after 5.30am, Victor Avison Holroyd, the Managing Representative of the Rudge team and Frederick Clarke, a mechanic, were standing at the hotel gates watching the machines go by when they saw Surridge approaching. He had made a safe and speedy negotiation of the course and was travelling at a terrific speed with another machine approximately ten yards ahead of him. As the two machines negotiated the sharp left hand corner at the foot of the hill, Surridge, possibly too intent on passing the machine ahead of him, drifted to the right. His machine went into the roadside ditch and struck the earth bank. He fought to regain control of the Rudge but was unable to do so before colliding heavily with the rock face and was thrown from the saddle into the roadway. The gravely injured rider was picked up and carried down to the hotel where attempts were made to revive him with water and brandy but without success. A telephone call was made to Dr. Lionel Woods who was stationed at the Quarter Bridge in Douglas. He rushed to Glen Helen to render first aid but on his arrival he found that the unfortunate rider was dead and concluded that death had probably been instantaneous.

The inquest was held at the scene of the accident later that morning and the jury made a recommendation that the Auto-Cycle Union should shorten the course on any future occasion, as they thought there were so many bends on the course the riders could not possibly think them out. The Coroner, Mr J.M. Cruickshank of Cronkbrae, Ramsey, pointed out that this bend was in fact part of the old course and was within yards of where the rider had been living for the previous week.

Victor John Surridge, a single man, was 19 years of age. He was the son of a cycle agent and a resident of Ongar, Essex. He had ridden for the Rudge-Whitworth Company since October 1910 and had accomplished several speed records. On the 25th May, at Brooklands, he made a new record, covering 60 miles 783 yards in the hour and his fastest lap at Brooklands was at the speed of 66.47 miles per hour. He was subsequently banqueted at the Savoy Hotel, London, and presented with a gold watch as a memento of the record.

His funeral service was held at Ongar Church and then the procession marched slowly to the cemetery with an advance guard provided by the Territorial Company of the 4th Essex Battalion of which Surridge had been a member. A bearer party of soldiers carried the coffin on which were the cap, bandolier and sidearms of the deceased. After the body had been committed to the ground, a firing party fired three volleys, the buglers sounded the Last Post and the ceremony was over. A total of 51 wreaths were spread out at the head of the grave. His parents and 18 year old brother Aubrey Surridge, a sailor, received over 150 letters and telegrams of condolence.

Frederick Richard BATEMAN

(By kind permission of Manx National Heritage)
Frank Bateman pushes off to recommence the 1913 Senior TT on the second day

Unlike the previous two years, the 1913 Senior Tourist Trophy Race was held over two days. The first three laps from a total of seven were held on Wednesday 4th June. The start line was situated near to the house "Woodlands" on Quarterbridge Road, Douglas and this gave the competitors the advantage of a short downhill section on which to start their machines. Riding for the Rudge-Whitworth Company was "Frank" Bateman, riding a 499cc Rudge machine bearing the race number 52 and he was the second man to set off. He was the first to complete the three laps but on corrected time he was lying in second place overall, four minutes behind the race leader, Tim Wood riding a Scott machine.

On the Thursday night considerable amounts of broken glass were found scattered on the course at Kirk Braddan, Pear Tree Cottage (Greeba) and Bray Hill. On the hill between Glen Helen and Sarah's Cottage, nails had been placed on the road. It was suspected that the militant "Suffragettes" were responsible for the outrage but there was no evidence to substantiate this theory.

There was a cold wind blowing on the morning of Friday 6th June as the competitors gathered to complete the final four laps of the race. The first man, Tim Wood, set off at 10.00am followed 30 seconds later by Frank Bateman who again was the first to arrive at Ballacraine. On completion of the lap Bateman led the race by seven seconds. Tim Wood had lost three minutes at Ballacraine where he had to repair a water joint. At about 11.30am, on his fifth lap overall, Bateman was seen approaching Keppel Gate in close company with A.H. Alexander who had been holding second place. Just before the bend Alexander overtook Bateman then, as the two men travelled down towards the Creg ny Baa Hotel at an estimated 70mph, Bateman moved over to the right in an attempt to overtake Alexander which brought a loud cheer from the spectators. Suddenly the Rudge became caught in a rut and went out of control. He recovered momentarily but the machine then hit a bump, which put him back into the rut, and at that moment the rear tyre burst. Bateman was pitched over the handlebars and was thrown to the left side of the road. The unconscious and gravely injured rider was attended to immediately then carried by stretcher to the hotel before being conveyed by waggonette to Noble's Hospital where he succumbed to his injuries at 9.40pm the same day.

The race was won by Tim Wood with a mere five seconds advantage over second place man A.R. Abbott (Rudge) and A.H. Alexander (Indian) in third place.

Frank Bateman was 23 years of age. (Born 12th May 1890). He was a motorcycle tester by occupation and a resident of Coventry where he lived with his wife Laura and their five-month-old son, Frederick C. Bateman. He had been in the employ of the Rudge-Whitworth Company for two years having previously been engaged as a chauffeur. He was an experienced rider and at the Brooklands Easter meeting he had finished second in two races then at the BARC meeting at Brooklands on Whit-Monday he had secured first place in the long distance handicap. His funeral service was held at Allesley Church near Coventry and the chief mourners were his widow, mother and father together with his brothers and sisters. Over 30 floral tributes were received from friends and relatives of the deceased.

6

Frederick James WALKER

Fred Walker – total commitment during the fateful 1914 Junior TT

The starting point for the 1914 Tourist Trophy Races had been moved to the top of Bray Hill in Douglas and an enclosure for officials and spectators had been assembled on the site of the proposed new secondary school. The judges' box was situated a few yards away on Ballanard Road and this was to be the official finishing point of the race. The procedure of holding the races over two days as in 1913 had been abandoned.

The weather on the morning of Tuesday 19th May was dull but dry, although there were reports of thick mist on the mountain section of the course. At 9.30am prompt the forty nine competitors for the Junior Tourist Trophy Race were dispatched at half minute intervals and among those taking part in the race was Fred Walker, a newcomer to the Island, riding an Enfield machine bearing the race number 25 and it was soon his turn to set off down Bray Hill followed thirty seconds later by Jimmie Veasey, number 26 on a Levis machine. First to complete the opening lap was the previous years winner, Hugh Mason riding a NUT machine. However, on corrected time, Walker led the race by 45 seconds and it was announced that he had completed the fastest circuit in any Junior Race so far. On completion of the second lap Walker still led the race but his advantage had been reduced to 28 seconds. During his third circuit he suffered tyre problems, which caused him considerable loss of time, and he dropped from the leaderboard but by the end of the fourth lap he had made up ground rapidly and was now in sixth position.

As he negotiated Hillberry Corner on his fifth and final lap of the race his machine mounted the grass bank on the left and he was thrown onto the road. He crawled on his hands and knees to where his machine lay, remounted and set off again. At Cronk ny Mona he turned right and followed the course down to the junction with Ballanard Road but as he approached the sharp left hand corner he fell from the machine again when both wheels locked and skidded on the road surface. Without assistance he remounted and continued along Ballanard Road to finish the race in third place behind Eric Williams and second place man Cyril Williams both on AJS machines. However, after passing the judges box he failed to turn right onto Bray Hill where the official examination of machines was to take place. At high speed and with his head down he continued straight on past St.Ninian's Church and collided heavily with a wooden barrier, which had been placed across the road to keep traffic off the course. The unfortunate rider was hurled from the saddle and came to rest, unconscious, in the roadway where he received immediate care from a doctor. He was conveyed by motorcar to Noble's Hospital for treatment but despite emergency surgery he succumbed to his injuries at 6.00am on Sunday 24th May. His mother and the young lady to whom he was engaged to be married were at the hospital when he passed away.

Frederick James Walker was 28 years of age. He was a Milliner by occupation and a resident of Kingstown, County Dublin. Although this was his first appearance in the Isle of Man races he had for some years been a prominent rider in Irish reliability trials and was a former secretary of the Dublin and District Motor Cycling Club.

His funeral service was held on Wednesday 27th May and followed by interment at Glasnevin Cemetery, Finglas Road, Dublin.

James Henry Herbert VEASEY

Jimmie Veasey – image taken from memorial report

The overnight boats arriving in the Isle of Man were packed on the morning of Friday 15th June 1923 and the volume of traffic heading around the TT course was quite unprecedented. At 9.00am, the sounding of the Klaxon at the start area on Glencrutchery Road in Douglas signalled that the competitors for the Senior Tourist Trophy Race were able to claim their machines. Half an hour later the weather broke and the rain began to fall. At 9.45am the Klaxon sounded again and the machines were wheeled to the start line. At eight minutes to ten the Governor and Lady Fry arrived to the strains of the National Anthem during which the spectators stood bare headed and the riders stood to attention. On the stroke of ten, with reports of thick mist on the mountain section, the race commenced with Alec Bennett riding a Douglas machine being the first away. The remainder of the field followed at half-minute intervals. Amongst them, making his first appearance since 1914, was Jimmie Veasey, riding a Douglas machine bearing the race number 28, but as he left the start line his machine caught fire. However, without the rider stopping or slowing down, all danger was averted as firemen quickly extinguished the flames with Pyrene.

Veasey had safely made his way through Union Mills and Glen Vine when he was seen approaching the left hand bend at Greeba Bridge. He took an unusually wide course as he negotiated the bend and as a result he ran onto the footpath just beyond the cottage on the exit of the bend. Later, as he rounded the right hand bend close to the home of the late High-Bailiff Cruickshank in Ramsey, he mounted the footpath again and almost crashed but was able to recover control of the machine. The crowds of spectators cheered him and he gave them a wave of acknowledgement. It was becoming evident that he was not taking the corners as well as he might. At about 11.15am, Veasey was on his second circuit when he was seen approaching Greeba Bridge at an estimated 60mph with the engine of the Douglas running perfectly. An observer noted that, as on his first circuit, he appeared to be taking a wide course for the corner but then he began to wobble and was unable to make the turn. The machine went off the road and travelled the full length of the grass patch in front of Mrs. Craine's cottage on the right before colliding heavily with a thorn tree and a stone wall. The unfortunate rider came to rest lying on top of his machine. He had been killed instantly. The medical officer on duty at Ballacraine, Doctor Hampton, was quickly conveyed to the scene of the accident on the carrier of a motorcycle but there was nothing he could do to revive him. The inquest into his death was held the following day at the Hawthorn Inn, Greeba, a short distance from where the incident occurred.

Jimmie Veasey was 29 years of age. (Born 29th June 1893). He was a motorcycle agent by occupation and was a resident of Barnstaple, Devonshire where he lived with his wife Nan and their 2-year-old daughter, Pat. During the war he had served in the Motor Transport Service and was reputed to possess considerable inventive genius in relation to motor mechanics. Prior to travelling to the Isle of Man he had been triumphant against 81 other riders in the Yeovil and Lands End competition riding a Douglas machine that had previously belonged to the Duke of York.

His funeral service was held on Wednesday 20th June at Newport Parish Church and followed by interment at Barnstaple Cemetery.

Edward Caesar BREW

Ned Brew – pictured in his police uniform

Despite the difficulties following the end of the First World War, the TT Races had resumed in 1920 but had become dominated by factory machines ridden by professional works riders. The Manx Motor Cycle Club proposed a race over the Mountain Circuit for amateur riders on standard machines and the Manx Government had granted permission for such an event to take place in September 1923. Thirty-five entries were received and Councillor A.B. Crookall, Mayor of Douglas, presented a magnificent trophy for the 500cc race, whilst the proprietors of the magazine "The Motor Cycle" donated the trophy for the best 350cc.

On the morning of Saturday 15th September 1923 competitors were taking advantage of a practice session for the race and amongst them was "Ned" Brew, riding an Italian built 500cc Frera machine bearing the race number 25. This was the only foreign machine entered in the race. He had taken part in all the early morning practice sessions since they began on the Wednesday and had done so well that he was considered a likely winner. At about 7.20am, he had almost completed a circuit of the course when he was seen negotiating Hillberry Corner, which was almost within sight of his own home, "Glendhoo Cottage". At this point he saw his sister, Gertrude Victoria Brew, aged 19, standing at the top of the Glendhoo Road on his right. He smiled at her and lifted his right hand off the handlebars to wave to her. Almost immediately, his machine began to wobble and he was thrown into the roadway about thirty yards beyond the junction. The young girl ran to his side and called his name but he had sustained a serious head injury and was deeply unconscious. Moment's later, competitor number 15, Captain Charles Vere Bennett, having been overtaken by Brew after passing the Creg ny Baa, came upon the incident and stopped. He found Brew lying in the road on his back with his machine resting on one of his legs. Bennett pulled the machine to the side of the road and then lifted Brew onto the footpath and unfastened his crash helmet. A doctor attended the scene of the incident and had the gravely injured rider removed to Glendhoo Cottage where he received medical treatment. He was then conveyed by ambulance to Noble's Hospital where, at 11.00am that same morning, he succumbed to his injuries. Former TT winner, Thomas Mylchreest Sheard, later examined the slightly damaged Frera and found nothing to suggest that a mechanical failure had been responsible for the accident. He had in fact ridden the machine on several occasions and had found it to be very fast and steered perfectly.

The Inaugural Amateur Road Race was held on Thursday 20th September and Len Randles, riding a Sunbeam machine, won the race in a time of 3 hours and 34 minutes, an average speed of 52.77mph over the five laps. Ken Twemlow, riding a New Imperial, was second and Arthur Marsden, riding a Douglas, finished third. Captain Bennett, who had assisted Ned Brew after his accident, began the race but failed to finish.

Ned Brew, a single man, was 21 years of age. He was formerly a member of the Royal Irish Constabulary but had during the past season been driving a motor coach, "The Highlander" for a Douglas proprietor. His funeral service was held on Tuesday 18th September at the Douglas Borough Cemetery and among those present were a considerable number of the competitors entered for the race. The flags at the grandstand were lowered to half-mast and Brew's number on the scoreboard was covered with black ribbon.

James Thomas Arthur TEMPLE

Jimmy Temple pictured at Brooklands astride a side-valve 490 Norton

There were reports of misty conditions over parts of the TT course on the morning of Monday 31st August 1925 as competitors prepared to take part in the first official practice session of the meeting for the Amateur TT Motorcycle Race. Amongst them was Jimmy Temple, riding a Norton machine bearing the race number 11. He had completed eighteen unofficial circuits of the course prior to this practice session and on the previous Saturday he had lapped in less than 40 minutes despite having to stop and open all the gates on the mountain. Shortly before setting off, at around 5.30am, he had been heard joking about having had to pump up a soft tyre on his machine.

Having safely made his way round the course as far as Glentramman he began to negotiate the left hand bend known as Water Trough Corner but it appears that on the exit of the bend he drifted to the right and struck the stone hedge before colliding heavily with the base of a telegraph pole which stood about a foot out from the hedge. The force of the impact knocked the pole several inches out of plumb, loosening the foundations and bringing down the wires leading to the next pole. The crumpled front wheel of the Norton had been pushed back almost to the frame. A fellow competitor, Arthur Marsden, came upon the scene of the accident and found the unfortunate rider lying in the roadway beside his machine. He stopped and summoned assistance. Dr. Templeton, who had been on duty at the Town Hall Square in Ramsey, received a telephone message to proceed to Glentramman and arrived there at about 6.30am. He found Temple being supported by Arthur Marsden but on examination it was found that he had sustained severe injuries to the right side of his chest and was beyond help. He had been killed instantly.

The following morning, at the same location, another rider, Len Randles, race winner of the previous two years, was put in danger when a black and white sheepdog flew out at him. With some difficulty he managed to avoid the animal but it was later surmised that the same animal may have confronted Temple the previous day and caused him to swerve into the hedge.

Jimmy Temple, a single man, was 21 years of age. (Born in London on 29th May 1904). Engineering was to have been his profession and he had just completed a three-year course at Pembroke College, Cambridge where he had been a student with his close friend "Archie" Birkin. He was a fine swimmer and had put up records just before leaving Cambridge. Described as a brilliant motorcyclist, he was well known at Brooklands and had, for three years in succession, won the Inter Varsity Hill Climb. He had travelled extensively, having been to Australia and to Switzerland where he took part in the winter games every year. He had also visited India where his stepfather had an interest in jute plantations.

His funeral service was held on the afternoon of Wednesday 2nd September at Lezayre Church and followed by interment. He was laid to rest almost within a stone's throw of where he had lost his life. His mother and stepfather, Mr. & Mrs Ainslie, had spent part of the summer with him in Biarritz before he travelled to the Island. They had received the tragic news by cable in Port Said, but despite making their way with all haste they had been unable to reach the Isle of Man prior to the funeral taking place.

Charles Archibald Cecil BIRKIN

(By permission of Mortons Media Group Ltd)
Archie Birkin pictured astride the McEvoy at a morning practice session for the 1927 Senior TT

Shortly before 5.00am on Tuesday 7th June 1927, competitors for the Tourist Trophy motorcycle races gathered at the "Start" on Glencrutchery Road in Douglas ready to participate in a practice session. Amongst them was "Archie" Birkin, riding a 500cc McEvoy machine bearing the race number 10 and entered in the Senior Race. He had recently obtained a controlling interest in the McEvoy Company. The roads were not closed to traffic during practice and all riders had been warned that traffic might be met on the roads. At 5.03am he set off towards Bray Hill with his McEvoy team mate George William Patchett alongside him but by Crosby he had left Patchett well behind him.

All went well for Birkin through to Kirk Michael village where he overtook a Wolsley motor car, the passenger of which noted that his back stand was trailing and leaving a shower of sparks behind him. On reaching the right hand bend at Rhencullen he was confronted with a grey coloured Ford motor van travelling in the opposite direction. He swerved to avoid a collision but, travelling at an estimated 80 mph, he could do nothing to avert disaster. The machine mounted the sod hedge on the left before ploughing through some bushes and colliding with the corner of a small wooden hut. The unfortunate rider was thrown from the machine and came to rest in the centre of the road. His crash helmet had come off during the accident and was lying on the left side of the road while the McEvoy lay against the hedge on the right hand side of the road. Within a few seconds, the occupants of the aforementioned Wolsley motor car came upon the scene and stopped, one of them pulled the lifeless rider to the side of the road while the other warned other approaching motorcyclists. There was nothing that could be done for Archie Birkin. He had been killed instantly. The driver of the motor van, George Albert Teare of Ballaugh Glen, did not stop. He later admitted that he had seen the motorcycle swerve slightly but had been unaware that the rider had crashed, he had therefore continued on his journey to Peel to collect herrings.

Archie Birkin, a single man, was 22 years of age and the son of Sir Thomas and Lady Birkin of Ruddington Grange, Nottingham. He was a former student of Cambridge University where he had been a good friend of the late Jimmy Temple who had been killed during practice for the Amateur TT in 1925. His first appearance on the TT course was in September 1924 when he took part in the Amateur TT but retired on the fourth lap when lying in fourth place. Using the pseudonym "Cantab" which is short for Cantabrigia the Latin word for Cambridge, he returned the following year and again rode in the Amateur TT but retired with mechanical problems during the second lap. In 1926 he took part in the TT proper but crashed on the mountain during the Senior Race and sustained serious internal injuries, which kept him in Noble's Hospital for a long period of time. He was a well known and popular figure in the sport and invariably appeared clad in a black silk shirt.

Following his death the Road Closing Act was amended to ensure roads were closed, not only on race days, but during practice sessions as well.

His funeral service was held on 13th June at Wilford Hills Cemetery, Nottingham following which he was laid to rest in the family vault. To this day the bend where he lost his life is known as Birkin's Bend.

John COOKE

(National Motor Museum)

Jack Cooke at Ramsey Hairpin during the fateful 1927 Lightweight TT

Although the weather was fine on the morning of Wednesday 15th June 1927 there were gale force winds blowing across the Isle of Man. Not the best of racing conditions for the 29 competitors gathered on Glencrutchery Road in Douglas waiting to participate in the Lightweight Tourist Trophy Race. Amongst them was John "Jack" Cooke, riding a 249cc Dot machine bearing the race number 27. At 10.00am the race commenced and C.W. "Paddy" Johnston was the first away with the following riders being dispatched at one-minute intervals. At 10.26am it was the turn of Jack Cooke to begin his race against the clock but in his eagerness to get away he almost missed his saddle. On completion of the first circuit it was Wal Handley who led the race from Alex Bennett in second place and the Italian rider Luigi Archangeli third. Jack Cooke had completed his opening lap in 39 minutes and 40 seconds. There were reports of very strong winds on the mountain section of the course.

At around 11.30am Leonard Higson, who had started one minute after Cooke, was riding his Montgomery machine across the mountain section of the course on his second lap of the race. As he negotiated the left hand bend at the East Snaefell Gate he was confronted by the body of Jack Cooke lying face down in the centre of the road and almost ran over him. He stopped immediately and dragged the unconscious rider to the side of the road. With no spectators at that point he had to summon the help of some people about 200 yards away before proceeding to the Bungalow where he stopped and informed a marshal of the incident. A group of spectators including two doctors and a nurse set off towards Ramsey with a stretcher and bandages. Meanwhile the people gathered at the scene of the accident were becoming furious at the delay in medical assistance arriving. Doctor Rentoul who was on duty at the Creg ny Baa received instructions to attend the incident and made his way by car via the back road to Windy Corner then continued on foot. At a point beyond the Bungalow he came upon the stretcher party returning with the gravely injured rider. Arrangements were made to convey him by electric car to Laxey and then by ambulance to Noble's Hospital where he was admitted at 2.30pm. However, at 9.30pm that same day, with his fiancée, sister and brother by his side, he succumbed to his injuries. It was later surmised that he might have lost control of his machine after being hit by a strong gust of wind.

Wal Handley from Birmingham won the race from Luigi Archangeli (Guzzi) in second place. Cecil T. Ashby (O.K. Supreme) and Syd Crabtree (Crabtree J.A.P.) finished third and fourth respectively. Leonard Higson went on to finish the race in 10th place.

Jack Cooke was 35 years of age. He was a resident of Birkenhead and a motor mechanic by profession, being a partner in a motor agency. His racing debut on the Isle of Man came in 1923 when, riding an Edmund, he competed in the Lightweight TT but retired on the 5th lap. In 1924, riding a Dot, he finished 3rd in the Lightweight TT and in 1925, again riding a Dot, he finished fourth in the Lightweight. He rode a Calthorpe in the 1926 Junior TT but retired on the third lap. He frequently took part in the motorcycle races on the Southport sands and was well known at reliability trials organised by the Liverpool and Stalybridge clubs.

His funeral service was held at St. Bartholomew's Church, Thurstaston, Wirral and followed by interment.

Cecil Thomas ASHBY

(National Motor Museum)

Cecil Ashby at Ramsey Hairpin during the fateful 1929 Junior TT

Following the heavy showers the previous evening it was fresh and sunny on the morning of Monday 10th June 1929 and the roads around the TT course were dry. On Glencrutchery Road in Douglas there were forty-three competitors gathered in preparation for the Junior Tourist Trophy Race. Amongst them was Cecil Ashby, riding a New Imperial machine bearing the race number 42. Just before the race commenced Ashby bid farewell to his wife and remarked to a friend, "I have not had a great deal of luck in past TT races but perhaps after winning last year in Germany (Austria), I have now reached the turning point and I am going all out. All I want is a little luck".

On the stroke of ten, the firing of a gun announced the start of the race and as each rider set off towards Bray Hill the Union Flag was dipped by Boy Scouts. Parkinson and the Twemlow brothers were wearing spotless white leather suits that stood out in stark contrast to the rest of the riders who were predominantly dressed in black. Cecil Ashby was one of the last to leave the start line followed by Freddie Hicks.

On completion of the first circuit it was Jimmy Simpson who led the race with a mere two seconds advantage over Stanley Woods in second place. Freddie Hicks was holding third. Simpson and Woods experienced mechanical problems during the second lap, which allowed Hicks to move up into first place ahead of Alex Bennett and Wal Handley. Then, during the third lap, Handley moved up into second place ahead of Bennett.

On the fourth lap of the race, Cecil Ashby was seen approaching the right hand corner at Ballacraine but then, as he began to negotiate the corner, the footrest or exhaust caught the road surface which caused the back end of the machine to rear up. He put his foot to the ground in an effort to regain control but was suddenly thrown over the handlebars and landed heavily in the roadway. He was quickly attended to and carried, unconscious, into the yard of the Ballacraine Hotel where he received medical attention from Dr. Lane who had been on duty at that point. He called for an ambulance, which arrived within half an hour and conveyed the gravely injured rider to Noble's Hospital where, at about 5.00pm that same day and with his wife at his bedside, he succumbed to his injuries.

Of the 43 competitors that began the race just sixteen finished. The race winner, Freddie Hicks, set new records with a race average speed of 69.71mph and a record lap of 70.95mph. Wal Handley finished second and Alec Bennett took third.

Cecil Ashby was 32 years old. He was a motorcycle dealer by occupation and a resident of Kingston, Surrey where he lived with his wife, Mary. They had only married the previous year. He was a racing motorcyclist of great experience and had won the 250cc German GP at the Nurburg-Ring in 1925. In 1928 he won the 250cc Swiss GP in Geneva and the Austrian GP in Vienna. His first appearance on the Isle of Man was in 1924 but his best result in the TT came in the 1927 Lightweight Race when he finished in 3rd place.

His funeral service was held at 11.30am on Saturday 15th June and followed by interment at Putney Vale Cemetery, London

George Douglas Forbes LAMB

Douglas Lamb in the paddock with his Senior Norton at the 1929 TT

The early burst of sunshine on the morning of Friday 14th June 1929 had been deceiving as rain began to fall heavily 20 minutes before the start of the Senior Tourist Trophy Race. Amongst the 48 competitors lined up along Glencrutchery Road was Douglas Lamb, riding a Norton machine bearing the race number 32. Earlier in the week he had competed in the Junior TT but had been forced to retire at Kirk Michael with engine trouble.

At 10.00am the race commenced with Charlie Dodson (Sunbeam), exercising his right as winner of the previous year's race, being the first man away with the following riders being dispatched at half-minute intervals.

On the opening lap, Wal Handley, number 15, approached Greeba Bridge and began to reduce speed in order to negotiate the left hand bend but when about thirty yards from the bridge his AJS machine skidded on the wet road and he was thrown into the roadway. With assistance, he quickly recovered the machine and moved it into a side road where he began to carry out repairs. A few minutes later, at 10.16am, Douglas Lamb approached the bridge fast and as he banked over to take the corner his machine went into a skid. He was unable to regain control before the machine crashed heavily into the right hand kerb on the exit of the bend. The unfortunate rider was hurled into a thorn hedge followed by his machine, which crashed on top of him. He was carried, unconscious, to a bungalow nearby for medical treatment. Minutes later, another rider, number 42, Jack Amott, riding a Rudge Whitworth machine, crashed at exactly the same place and sustained a fractured right arm. Then shortly after he was carried clear, yet another rider, number 48, Jimmy Simpson, riding a Norton machine, crashed and suffered concussion. The doctor on duty at Ballacraine, Dr. Lane, attended Greeba Bridge and found Lamb's condition to be serious. He asked for an ambulance to be sent to the nearest point in relation to the bridge and at one o'clock he was informed that the ambulance was at Crosby railway station, about two miles away. He then made the decision that it would be better to wait until the roads were opened rather than carry the injured rider for that distance on a stretcher. The ambulance arrived at Greeba following the race and Lamb was conveyed to Noble's Hospital where he was admitted at 3.10pm, some five hours after his crash. At 8.50pm that evening, he succumbed to his injuries.

Charlie Dodson (Sunbeam) went on to win the race at an average speed of 72.05mph. Alex Bennett (Sunbeam) was second with H.G. Tyrrell-Smith (Rudge-Whitworth) third.

Douglas Lamb, a single man, was 22 years of age. He was a motor engineer by occupation and a resident of Coventry. He had first come into prominence as a motorcyclist of note when he won the Syston Park road race on a privately owned Norton when he was barely 18 years of age. He put up some excellent times on this machine and won other Midland amateur events. This was his second TT meeting; he had taken part in the 1928 Senior Race but failed to finish following a crash with Wilmot Evans on the mountain section of the course in which he sustained a sprained ankle.

Following his funeral service he was laid to rest in the London Road Cemetery, Coventry.

Frederick George HICKS

Freddie Hicks negotiates Ramsey Hairpin on his AJS during the fateful 1931 Senior TT

Rainfall in the early morning of Friday 19th June 1931 had left the roads around the TT course wet and treacherous. Grim conditions for the fifty-six competitors assembled on Glencrutchery Road in Douglas waiting to participate in the seven lap Senior Tourist Trophy Race. Amongst them was Freddie Hicks, riding an AJS machine bearing the race number 19. Earlier in the week he had competed in the Junior TT and had been lying in third place until mechanical problems forced him to retire on the 3rd lap. Just a few weeks before travelling to the Isle of Man he had won the 500cc Grand Prix of Nations at Monza in Italy.

At 10.00am, with the roads beginning to dry, the race commenced and it was soon the turn of Freddie Hicks to set off towards Bray Hill. On completion of his opening circuit he was lying in fifth place, just 19 seconds behind Jimmy Guthrie, the race leader. He put up a new lap record of 77.46mph on his second lap but this was soon beaten and he remained in fifth place. By the end of the third lap he had moved up to fourth place and Jimmy Simpson was now leading the race. However, Simpson came off at Ballaugh Bridge on the fourth lap and Tim Hunt took up the lead. On pulling into the pits to refuel at the end of the fourth lap Hicks learned that despite the magnificent lap times he was putting up he was not placed in the first three. He was in fact still holding fourth place.

He set off on his fifth lap and made his way through to Union Mills but on the exit of the right hand bend at the Railway Inn he had to veer to the right to avoid hitting the wall on the left. This action took him off the normal racing line and across the road to the right. By now he was leaning heavily over to the left in an effort to get back onto the racing line but his rear wheel then hit a drain near to the junction with the Strang Road. He was thrown from the machine and collided heavily with the stonework surrounding the front door of the village stores. He was quickly attended to and found to be unconscious. On hearing of the incident the Clerk of the Course gave instructions for a doctor to attend from the grandstand and for the ambulance train to proceed to the scene from St. John's. On his arrival at Union Mills the doctor found that the unfortunate rider had succumbed to his injuries.

Tim Hunt went on to win the race from Jimmy Guthrie and Stanley Woods. All three riders mounted on Norton machines. Only thirteen of the fifty-six riders completed the race.

Freddie Hicks was 29 years of age. He was the Experimental Manager of the AJS Company and lived with his wife Eva Rosalie in Birmingham where they had named their home "Laurel Bank". He was a rider of great experience and had won the 350cc French GP along with the 350cc Dutch TT in 1929. In 1930 he won the 350cc French GP for a second time. His debut on the Isle of Man came in the 1928 Junior TT and he finished in 5th place. The following year he won the Junior TT in record time and finished 6th in the Senior Race.

Several days prior to the fateful race, his wife had a narrow escape from death when the motorcar she was driving crashed and overturned on Richmond Hill.

His funeral service was held on Tuesday 23rd June at Shirley Churchyard and followed by interment.

15

Frank Augustus LONGMAN

Frank Longman on his Excelsior JAP entered in the 1933 Lightweight TT

Conditions were ideal for racing on the morning of Wednesday 14th June 1933. The weather was fine, visibility was clear and the roads around the TT course were dry. Welcome news for the twenty-eight competitors assembled on Glencrutchery Road in Douglas waiting to participate in the Lightweight Tourist Trophy Race. Amongst them was race veteran Frank Longman, riding an Excelsior JAP machine bearing the race number 22. This was to be his last motorcycle race as he had recently joined the ranks of car racing drivers and had already enjoyed success in this sport at Monte Carlo and Hastings. Once the race commenced it was soon the turn of Longman to begin his race against the clock. He made his way round the course to a point between Brandish and Hillberry where he pulled in and stopped as he had been having plug trouble. He made adjustments then set off again to complete the lap.

At Braddan Bridge on his second lap he pulled in again and stopped by the old church. He informed a marshal that the spring on his front forks had broken. The marshal wrote out a retirement form for him to sign but Longman said "You're not getting my autograph today". He then produced some insulating tape with which he tied the spring to the forks. He tested the repair by bouncing the front wheel then set off again. Moments later, at Union Mills, he pulled in and stopped at the Railway Inn. When asked if he was going to retire, he said, "I think I'll chance it". He then coasted down the road to restart the engine and rode away.

A short time later he was seen approaching Glentramman Corner at full racing speed, then, as he leaned his machine over to negotiate the left hand bend the footrest or exhaust caught the road surface and this lifted both wheels off the ground. The machine then travelled broadside across the road to the right and collided heavily with the stone wall on the exit of the bend. The unfortunate rider was thrown from the machine and came to rest, semi conscious, in the roadway. He was picked up and placed on the footpath on the left side of the road where he was examined by a qualified first aid man who had been on duty nearby. He was then carried by stretcher back along the road to the junction with Garey Road where he was further examined by a doctor who had been summoned from Ramsey. The doctor ordered his removal to nearby "Glentramman House" then returned to Ramsey where he arranged for an ambulance to attend via the back roads. The gravely injured rider was conveyed to Ramsey Cottage Hospital where, shortly after his admission, he succumbed to his injuries.

Sid Gleave (Excelsior) went on to win the race with an average speed of 71.59mph. Charlie Dodson (New Imperial) finished second with Charlie Manders (Rudge) third.

Frank Longman was 39 years of age. He was a motor engineer by occupation and a resident of Hounslow, Middlesex where he lived with his wife and two young daughters. He was a very experienced racing motorcyclist having won the 1924 350cc French GP; the 1926 350cc Belgian GP; the 1927 350cc French GP; the 1928 350cc Ulster GP; the 1929 250cc Ulster GP and the 1929 250cc Grand-Prix d'Europe held in Spain. His debut on the Isle of Man was in 1921 and he had entered every TT since. He had podium finishes in 1925, 1926 and 1929 but his best result was in 1928 when, riding an OK Supreme, he won the Lightweight TT.

His funeral service was he held in London and followed by interment at Acton Cemetery.

16

Arthur PILLING

HUDDERSFIELD DAILY EXAMINER, THURSDAY, AUGUST 31, 1933

LINDLEY RIDER'S FATAL
GRAND PRIX PRACTICE
CRASH

SKULL FRACTURED IN CORNERING
DISASTER

MAN AND MACHINE THROWN SIX FEET
INTO THE AIR

HIS FIRST BIG ROAD
RACE

* *

Arthur Pilling's death as headlined in his local newspaper

Weather conditions were fine on the morning of Thursday 31st August 1933, as competitors congregated in the area of the Grandstand on Glencrutchery Road in Douglas waiting to take advantage of a practice session for the Manx Grand Prix. Amongst them was Arthur Pilling, riding a Norton machine bearing the race number 56 and entered in the Senior Race. He had arrived on the Island the previous Saturday and had completed three official practice laps in total, one on the Monday morning and two on the Tuesday morning.

Once the session was under way, Pilling safely made his way round the course and was just two miles away from completing his lap when he was seen, alone on the road, approaching Hillberry Corner but he was wide of the normal racing line. As a consequence, when he leaned over to negotiate the right hand bend the exhaust pipe of his machine began scraping the ground, leaving a shower of sparks in its trail. In attempting to recover control he drifted wide on the exit of the bend and the footrest caught the grass banking just beyond the entrance to Hillberry Farm on the left. Both rider and machine were thrown into the air then tumbled along the road together for a distance of seventy yards. The unfortunate rider came to rest lying face down on the left hand side of the road while his extensively damaged Norton came to rest a further twenty yards beyond him. A police officer and marshals, posted at Hillberry, quickly attended to the unconscious rider and rendered what first aid they could until the arrival of a doctor and ambulance at 7.15am. The gravely injured rider was then conveyed to Noble's Hospital where he was admitted at 7.30am. Without regaining consciousness, he succumbed to his injuries later that same morning.

Arthur Pilling was 31 years of age. Although a single man, he was engaged to be married. He was an electrician by occupation, employed by Huddersfield Corporation and was a resident of Lindley near Huddersfield where he lived with his sister Gladys. He was an experienced trials rider but this was his first appearance on the Isle of Man roads and was to be his first really big road race. He was probably better known in Huddersfield sporting circles as a cyclist.

He had actually sent in his entry form for the races when he was lying in Huddersfield Infirmary, recovering from injuries sustained to his left knee and thigh following a motorcycle accident in Huddersfield when he swerved to avoid colliding with a young boy. He was discharged just three weeks before travelling to the Isle of Man and several of his friends tried to persuade him not to go. He confided to one of his friends that he had a premonition and felt he would not come back alive but could not give up the idea of entering the races. During the inquest at Douglas Court House his fiancée Miss Gwendolen Dack broke down and was in a very distressed state as she was led from the courtroom weeping bitterly.

His funeral service was held at East Street Methodist Chapel, Lindley on Monday 4th September and was followed by interment. His close friend F. Butterworth and five of his colleagues from the electricity department at Huddersfield Corporation were bearers. Among the many floral tributes was a wreath from the riders and officials of the Manx Grand Prix 1933, inscribed "With sincere regrets in the loss of a great sportsman".

Sydney Alfred CRABTREE

Syd Crabtree on the Excelsior entered in the 1934 Lightweight TT

Thick mist, on the morning of Wednesday 13th June 1934, enveloped the mountain section of the TT course along with the east coast of the Island, including Douglas. Daunting conditions for the twenty-four competitors congregating on Glencrutchery Road waiting to participate in the Lightweight Tourist Trophy Race. Amongst them was Syd Crabtree, the highly experienced race veteran, riding an Excelsior machine bearing the race number 23.

At 10.00am prompt the race commenced with a wave of the Manx flag from the official starter and the first man to push away was Paddy Johnston, riding a Cotton. A short time later it was the turn of Syd Crabtree to begin his race against the clock and he set off towards Bray Hill. By this time news was coming through from the Bungalow that visibility was down to less than 20 yards on the mountain road.

Paddy Johnston was the first man to complete the first circuit but on corrected time he was in 6th place overall. Charlie Dodson (New Imperial) led the race by almost 40 seconds from Ernie Mellors (Excelsior). Stanley Woods (Guzzi) went through and gave the "thumbs down" signal to his pit crew. Jimmy Simpson (Rudge), lying in fourth place, called at his pit and changed his dew covered goggles before heading off again.

Officials at the grandstand were becoming increasingly concerned for the welfare of Syd Crabtree as he had gone missing somewhere between the Mountain Box and the Bungalow. It was known that he had passed the Stonebreakers Hut (Black Hut) at 10.40am and in response to a telephone request a spectator at that location began walking towards the Bungalow in an effort to locate the rider. At 11.15am he found the body of Syd Crabtree lying on the grass verge on the left side of the road at the Verandah. It was evident that after travelling 25 yards along the grass verge the unfortunate rider had struck an iron post then collided head on with a heavy iron gate post. There was nothing that could be done for him. He had been killed instantly. His fiancée had been watching the race from the grandstand in Douglas.

Just eight riders completed the seven-lap race and the winner, Jimmy Simpson, declared that it had been "One of the most trying rides of my life". Simpson recorded a race average speed of 70.81mph and finished over three minutes ahead of his Rudge team mates Ernie Nott and Graham Walker who were second and third respectively.

Syd Crabtree, a single man, was 31 years of age. He was a motorcycle agent by occupation and a resident of Altrincham, Cheshire. Between 1926 and 1930 he had been highly successful in Europe, winning the French GP four times, the Belgian GP three times and the German GP twice along with victories in the Ulster GP, the Swiss GP and the Dutch TT. He made his debut at the Isle of Man TT in 1922 and became a regular visitor to the races. His best result came in 1929 when, riding an Excelsior, he won the Lightweight TT. In July 1933, driving an MG Midget motorcar bearing the race number 19, he took part in the fifty lap Mannin Beg car race around Douglas but crashed out on his 18th lap.

His funeral service was held at Altrincham Cemetery, Hale. On his coffin was the crash helmet he had been wearing when he was killed and this was buried along with him.

18

John Charles GILBERT

A catalogue image of a Velocette similar to that ridden by John Charles Gilbert during the 1934 MGP

Following a night of heavy rain the roads around the TT course on the morning of Monday 3rd September 1934 were wet and greasy. This offered treacherous conditions to the seventy eight competitors gathered at the Grandstand in Douglas waiting to take advantage of the opening practice session for the Manx Grand Prix races to be held the following week. Amongst them was John Charles Gilbert, a newcomer to the TT course, riding a 348cc Velocette machine bearing the race number 35 and entered for the Senior Race.

Once the session was under way it was not long before Gilbert set off along Glencrutchery Road towards Bray Hill to commence his first ever official lap of the course. He safely completed his first circuit in 36 minutes, giving him an average lap speed of 62.9mph.

At Sulby the bright rising sun was beginning to cause problems for the riders, especially on the approach to the bridge. The senior marshal at that location sent another marshal 300 yards back along the road towards Sulby Glen with the instruction to wave the green (caution) flag to every rider who approached.

At about 7.00am, having safely negotiated his way through nineteen miles of the course on his second lap of the morning, Gilbert was seen approaching Sulby Bridge but with the sun in his eyes he didn't appear to notice the green flag being shown by the marshal. Without reducing speed, he continued straight on, making no apparent effort to slow down for the right hand bend until he suddenly realised his position. He immediately shut off the power and jammed on the brakes but it was too late, he continued in a straight line and collided heavily with a large wooden board, portraying an arrow, which had been positioned there to warn riders that the road turned to the right. Both rider and machine ploughed through the hedge behind the board and came to rest in the field below the roadway. Marshals quickly attended to the unfortunate rider and found him lying on his back; he was unconscious and had sustained serious injuries. Doctor Templeton was summoned from Ramsey and together with the ambulance made all possible haste to Sulby. Within minutes of his arrival at the scene he ordered Gilbert's immediate removal to the Ramsey Cottage Hospital where, shortly after 9.00am that morning, he succumbed to his injuries.

The use of a dark green flag as a warning was a curio of the Manx Race Regulations and did not apply to race meetings in the south of England where Gilbert came from. The red flag was for stop and the blue flag for danger. However, prior to the meeting, all the riders had received written information containing instructions regarding the significance of each flag.

John Charles Gilbert, a single man, was 25 years of age. He was a butcher by occupation and a resident of East Dulwich, London where he lived with his widowed mother. He was captain of the Sydenham Motor Club and was a successful competitor at the Crystal Palace speedway races and on a number of grass tracks, notably at Brands Hatch where he held the "Silver Star" and in former years at Layham's Farm.

His funeral service was held at Streatham Cemetery, London on Monday 10th September and was followed by interment.

John Pritchard WILLIAMSON

Johnny Williamson on the Rudge he rode in practice for the 1934 Senior MGP

Other than the odd patch of mist on the mountain section of the TT course on the morning of Thursday 6th September 1934, the weather conditions were quite good. Welcome news for the competitors gathered at the Grandstand on Glencrutchery Road in Douglas waiting to take advantage of a practice session for the Manx Grand Prix races. Amongst them, making his second appearance at these races was Johnny Williamson, riding a Rudge machine bearing the race number 31 and entered in the Senior Race. On the first three days of the week he had completed a total of four laps and on the Tuesday his time of 35 minutes (64.8mph) made him the sixth fastest man in the Senior Class on that day. On Wednesday he completed a lap of the course in 34 minutes 27 seconds.

Shortly after 6.10am, Williamson pushed off from the Start and headed towards Bray Hill to commence his opening lap of the morning. About fifteen minutes later he was just over thirteen miles into the lap when he entered Kirk Michael village in close company behind Robert Edwards, a newcomer to the TT course, riding a Norton. He followed Edwards through the village then, on the approach to the left hand curve known as Vicarage Corner, he moved to the right and began to pass the slower machine. However, at almost the same instant, Edwards also moved to the right in order to take a racing line through the bend and the two machines collided. The Rudge skidded across the road to the right and scraped along the boundary wall of Whitehouse Cottages before colliding heavily with a gatepost. The unfortunate rider was thrown into the roadway. Edwards also came off his machine but escaped with minor injuries to his fingers. John Pattison, riding a Norton machine, had been travelling about forty yards behind the two men when they collided and narrowly avoided becoming involved in the accident. Williamson was quickly attended to but there was nothing that could be done for him. He had been killed instantly.

The following week Robert Edwards, a 22-year-old haulage contractor from Dewsbury, took part in the Junior event and finished in 24th position. He also took part in the Senior event but failed to finish the race. Pattison, from Inverkeith, Fife, also competed in the Senior but he too, failed to finish. Neither rider was to race on the Isle of Man again.

Johnny Williamson, a single man, was 20 years of age. He was a motor engineer by occupation and the son of Councillor and Mrs J. Williamson of Middlewich, Cheshire. From the time he could first sit astride a motorcycle the sport had been his chief pleasure. He was frequently seen at grass track meetings and had also ridden in the sand races at Southport and on the Oswestry Park Hall circuit as well as the Lancaster Speedway. As a member of Fodens Motorcycle Club in Sandbach he made his debut on the TT course when he entered the Senior MGP in 1933. Despite experiencing engine problems with his Rudge during the race, he finished in 12th place with a race average speed of 69.28mph and just missed out on a replica.

His funeral service was held in Cheshire on Saturday 8th September and followed by interment at Middlewich Cemetery, Cheshire.

John Angus MACDONALD

Angus MacDonald at Parliament Square, Ramsey during the fateful 1935 Junior TT

Observers around the TT course on the morning of Monday 17th June 1935, reported clear visibility and dry roads. Ideal racing conditions for the seven lap Junior International Tourist Trophy Race. The original entry of thirty-seven competitors had been reduced to thirty-one, mostly due to injuries sustained during practice. The principal alteration to the regulations for this year's races was that competitors were allowed to "warm up" the engines of their machines prior to the start of the race. Previously, having been locked up overnight the machines were started from cold. Therefore, at 9.30am, half an hour before the start of the race the usual murmur at the grandstand was shattered a roar as riders started their engines and prepared their mounts for racing by riding back and forth between the grandstand and Governors Bridge on Glencrutchery Road in Douglas.

With fifteen minutes to go, another innovation, the Grand March Past began and the riders, in their starting order paraded to the starting grid, accompanied by Boy Scouts carrying the flag of each country represented. Amongst the competitors was Angus MacDonald, riding a Norton machine bearing the race number 24. He had taken part in the Senior Manx Grand Prix the previous year and finished 13th with a race average speed of 68.9mph.

The race commenced at 10.00am with Jimmie Guthrie being the first rider to set off towards Bray Hill. The following riders started at half-minute intervals and shortly after 10.10am it was the turn of MacDonald to begin his race against the clock. He successfully completed his first two laps of the race and was not quite three miles into his third lap when he was seen, travelling at full racing speed, approaching the right hand bend at the Railway Hotel in Union Mills. However, as he negotiated the bend the Norton drifted wide on the exit and struck the stone wall on the left before travelling across the road where it collided heavily with the kerb on the right. The unfortunate rider was thrown and lost his crash helmet as he tumbled along the roadway together with his machine. He came to rest against the kerb on the right hand side of the road. Marshals went to his immediate assistance but there was nothing they could do for him. He had been killed instantly.

Having led from start to finish, the race was won by Jimmy Guthrie with a race average speed of 79.14mph. Walter Rusk was second, J.H. White third and Doug Pirie fourth

John Angus MacDonald was 24 years of age and just three days away from celebrating his first wedding anniversary. His wife Nancy had been watching the race from the grandstand. He began motorcycle racing at the age of 16, competing in dirt track events before moving up to circuits such as Brooklands. He had been instrumental in founding the Herts & Essex Aero Club, with whom he became a pilot. A few months before travelling to the Island he had become the licensee of the "Rose Inn", Plumstead, Essex.

His funeral service was held at Peter & Paul Church, Ilford on Friday 21st June and followed by interment at St. Patrick's Cemetery, Leytonstone. The hearse carried wreaths in the shape of an aeroplane and motorcycles and his coffin had been draped with the Civil Aviation Pilots flag.

Douglas Joseph PIRIE

Doug Pirie with the Velocette on which he finished fourth in the 1935 Junior TT

Thick mist on the mountain section of the TT course on the morning of Wednesday 19th June 1935 looked certain to dampen any hopes of fast racing. However, undeterred by the conditions, no less than twenty seven competitors collected their machines and warmed them up on Glencrutchery Road in readiness for the Lightweight Tourist Trophy race. Amongst them was Doug Pirie, riding a New Imperial machine bearing the race number 10 and which was to have been ridden by Syd Gleave who had been injured during practice. In the Junior TT two days earlier, Pirie had finished in fourth place with a race average speed of 77.69mph.

On the stroke of ten the race began with Les Archer being the first rider away and the rest of the field followed at half-minute intervals. During the race, cameramen were positioned at Parliament Square and the Hairpin in Ramsey, taking shots of the race that were to be included in the film "No Limit" in which George Formby was to star. Stanley Woods completed the first lap with a lead of over 30 seconds and had extended this to over a minute and a half at the end of the second circuit. By the end of the fourth lap Woods still held a comfortable lead and Doug Pirie had made his way up through the field into sixth position.

At about 1.00pm, during the fifth lap of the race and with visibility down to 15 yards on parts of the mountain section, Doug Pirie was seen approaching the left hand bend at the 33rd Milestone. However, he then appeared to make no attempt to negotiate the bend but went straight on across the road and collided heavily with the concrete posts situated along the right hand side of the course. The unfortunate rider was thrown over the wire fencing before coming to rest amongst a mass of boulders on the grassland below the road. Marshals and spectators quickly attended to him and found that he had been gravely injured. After first aid was rendered they used a gate as a makeshift stretcher to carry him to the Shepherds hut at Keppel Gate. Meanwhile, the doctor on duty at the Creg ny Baa received information that the accident had occurred at Windy Corner and made his way to that location via the back road. Finding no sign of an accident he then walked along the course until he reached Keppel Gate where he found Pirie unconscious and with serious injuries. After the race he was conveyed by ambulance to Noble's Hospital where he was admitted at 3.15pm but half an hour after admission, he succumbed to his injuries.

Stanley Woods went on to win the seven lap race with an average speed of 71.56mph. His teammate Omobono Tenni went out on the fifth lap when he crashed at the Creg ny Baa and collided with the flag marshal. Both men sustained minor injuries.

Doug Pirie, a single man, was 28 years of age. He was an architect by occupation and a resident of Old Southgate, London. He made his debut on the TT course in 1929 when he took part in the Amateur TT and was highly placed in both races. He returned in 1930, the birth of the Manx Grand Prix, and won the Junior Race. The following year, despite injuries sustained during practice, he won the Junior MGP once again. In 1934, with a race record speed of 79.19mph, he won the Senior Manx Grand Prix riding a Norton.

His funeral service was held during a thunderstorm and torrential rain at Christ Church, Southgate on Tuesday 25th June and followed by interment at Southgate Cemetery.

John MOORE

Jack Moore astride the Norton on which he was to compete in the1938 Junior TT

Brilliant sunshine graced the Isle of Man on the morning of Monday 13th June 1938, which was excellent news for the large numbers of spectators around the TT course and for the forty two riders competing in the seven lap Junior Tourist Trophy Race. Amongst them was "Jack" Moore, riding a Norton machine bearing the race number 28. Although he was a newcomer to the Island he was no novice to road racing as he had recently won the Senior Race at the Northwest 200 in Ireland.

At 10.50am, heralded by a fanfare of trumpets and escorted by Boy Scouts carrying the unfurled flags of the nations represented, the competitors brought their machines to the start line on Glencrutchery Road where the Lieutenant Governor met and shook hands with each rider, wishing them good luck. On the stroke of eleven, two maroons were fired to mark the start of the race and the first rider received his signal to commence racing. On completion of the first lap, Stanley Woods had recorded an average speed of 83.75mph and led the race by 11 seconds from Ernie Mellors with Freddy Frith holding third. By the end of the second lap Woods had increased his lead to 50 seconds.

During the third lap, having safely made his way round the course through Ramsey and up onto the mountain, Jack Moore was seen approaching the East Snaefell Gate (Mountain Box) in close company with Maurice Cann, race number 33, who was slightly ahead of him. Just before they negotiated the left hand bend Moore passed Cann on the left but this action put him off the usual racing line. As a consequence he drifted wide on the exit of the bend and collided heavily with several concrete fence posts situated along the right hand side of the road. He was thrown from the machine and came to rest in the roadway without his crash helmet, which had come off during the incident. Maurice Cann narrowly avoided becoming involved in the accident by passing through on the left side of the road. Marshals went to the immediate assistance of the unfortunate rider and moved him to the side of the road but there was nothing they could do for him. He had been killed instantly.

Stanley Woods (Velocette) went on to win the race, securing his ninth TT success, at an average speed of 84.08mph. Ted Mellors (Velocette) took second place, just two seconds ahead of Freddy Frith (Norton) in third place. Maurice Cann, winner of the 1937 Junior and Senior Manx Grand Prix Races retired at Sulby on his fourth lap when his Norton developed engine problems.

Jack Moore, a single man, was 29 years of age. He was a motor haulage contractor by occupation and a resident of Cheadle, Manchester. He had only taken up the sport of motorcycle racing four years earlier and had been described as a most promising rider. He was well known around the circuits and had enjoyed considerable success at Donington Park and in Ireland at the North West 200 and the Ulster Grand Prix where he had finished 2nd in the 1937 Senior Race. He was also a renowned competitor in sand racing at Southport and Wallasey.

His funeral service was held at Manchester Crematorium on Friday 17th June. A memorial headstone can be found at Cheadle Cemetery, Cheshire.

Percival Henry Bernard PRITLOVE

Percy Pritlove on his Vincent HRD entered in the 1938 Senior MGP

Rain was falling and visibility was poor on the mountain section of the TT course on the morning of Monday 12th September 1938. Unwelcome news for the sixty five competitors gathered at the Grandstand on Glencrutchery Road in Douglas waiting to participate in the concluding practice session for the Manx Grand Prix Races. Amongst them was "Percy" Pritlove, a newcomer to the Island, riding a 500cc Vincent HRD machine bearing the race number 21 and entered in the Senior Race. On hearing the warning about the poor conditions he joked with the race official, saying, "Righto, I'll go quietly". During practice he had completed four laps of the course from the Grandstand and several other laps starting and finishing at Ballacraine. He had fulfilled all the necessary qualifications to enable him to start in the Senior Race.

Once the practice session commenced it was soon the turn of Percy Pritlove to head off towards Bray Hill on his opening lap of the morning. He safely made his way through Quarterbridge and Braddan Bridge and was just under three miles from the start when, at about 6.40am, he was seen at Union Mills. He was alone on the road and travelling at racing speed on the approach to the right hand bend at the Railway Inn. However, as he negotiated the bend he drifted wide on the exit and went very close to the stone wall opposite the entrance to the railway station. He was now off the usual racing line for the following left hand bend and as a result he drifted to the right and, at a point about thirty yards Peel side of Green's stores, his machine grazed the black and white painted kerbing for a distance of twenty one feet. As he fought to regain control of the machine it suddenly veered diagonally across the road and struck a wooden post before crashing heavily with the four foot high boundary wall surrounding Mr Slater's house, which was situated on the left hand side of the road. The unfortunate rider was thrown over the wall and came to rest on the gravelled garden path. The upper portion of his crash helmet had become detached and was lying beside him while the inner lining and chinstrap were still fastened to his head. His Vincent machine had been extensively damaged and a large amount of masonry had been dislodged from the wall.

A police officer and marshals on duty at that point went immediately to his aid and a request was made for a doctor and ambulance to attend the scene but the gravely injured rider succumbed to his injuries five minutes before they arrived.

Percy Pritlove was 26 years of age. Although a single man, he was engaged and his fiancée had been in the area of the grandstand at the time of the accident. He was an electrician by occupation, employed at the Locomotive Depot of the LNER (London & North Eastern Railway) and a resident of March, Cambridgeshire. Described as a good rider with four years racing experience, he had raced at Donington, Brooklands and Louth. While on the Island he had been staying at "The Smithy", Cronk y Voddy.

His funeral service was held at Douglas Borough Cemetery on Thursday 15th September and followed by interment. Just two hundred yards away, competitors entered in the Senior Manx Grand Prix were making their final preparations before the start of the race.

Karl GALL

Karl Gall prepares for a practice session during the 1938 TT

From a spectator's point of view, conditions were perfect for racing on the evening of Friday 2nd June 1939. However, the setting sun would be troublesome for the competitors taking advantage of a practice session for the Tourist Trophy Races. Amongst them, having only arrived on the Island the previous evening, was the top German rider Karl Gall, riding a BMW machine bearing the race number 29 and entered in the Senior Race. During the 1938 TT meeting he had completed several laps of the course during official practice but a crash at the Gooseneck on open roads had left him with serious head injuries and a fractured arm, which had confined him to the Ramsey Cottage Hospital for several weeks.

Once the session was under way Gall, in company with his BMW team mate Jock West, set off along Glencrutchery Road on his first official practice lap of the meeting. A short time later, between Quarterbridge and Braddan Bridge, they were both overtaken by Freddie Frith on his Senior Norton. The BMW riders tacked on behind him but West soon eased off, as the speed was a little too brisk for him considering it was his first time out. However, Karl Gall continued to trail the Norton and tried to keep Frith within sight. Having safely made his way along the course and through Kirk Michael he was seen approaching Ballaugh Bridge at racing speed and attempting to pass another machine. This action had placed him on the left hand side of the road whereas he should have been on the right so as to avoid the wall at the entrance to the Glen Road after jumping the bridge. At the last moment he appeared to realise the danger and leaned over to the left but in doing so he came off his machine. He came to rest in the roadway where marshals went to his immediate assistance and found that he had sustained serious injuries. He was carried to the side of the road and first aid was administered until the arrival of a doctor who had been summoned by telephone to attend the scene from Ramsey. The doctor examined the unfortunate rider then immediately sent for the Ramsey ambulance and stayed with him until it arrived. Dr. Bergermann, the BMW team doctor, also attended the scene and accompanied the gravely injured rider in the ambulance to Ramsey Cottage Hospital where it was established that an operation would be necessary in order to save his life. The operation was performed by Dr. Bergermann the following day and appeared to be successful as Gall began to show signs of recovery. However, despite further surgery by Dr. Bergermann, his condition began to deteriorate and on the afternoon of Tuesday 13th June, he passed away. His wife Elisabeth, who had flown from Germany, was at his bedside.

Karl Gall was 37 years of age. He was an automobile engineer by occupation and a resident of Munich, Germany. He had a wealth of racing experience and was one of Germany's premier road racing men, having been crowned road racing champion of Germany in the 500cc class in 1937. He had secured a number of victories including the 250cc Austrian TT in 1925, the 500cc Austrian TT in 1928, the 1000cc Austrian GP in 1928; the 500cc Dutch TT in 1937; the 500cc Hungarian GP in 1937 and the 500cc German GP in 1937. It had been his intention to retire from the sport at the end of the 1939 season.

His funeral service was held in Germany and followed by interment at Waldfriedhof (Forest Cemetery) in Munich. In 1964 a bronze memorial in his name was attached to the boundary wall of a house opposite the hotel in Ballaugh Square.

25

Arthur Walter Frederick JOHNS

Arthur Johns pictured on his road going Norton

The weather conditions across the Isle of Man on the morning of Monday 26th August 1946 were fine. The roads around the TT course were dry and visibility was clear on the mountain section. Welcome news for the ninety one competitors gathered at the Grandstand in Douglas waiting to take advantage of the opening practice session for the Manx Grand Prix as racing returned to the Isle of Man for the first time following the war years. Amongst them was Arthur "Johnnie" Johns, a newcomer to the Island, riding a brand new 490cc Norton machine bearing the race number 34 and entered in the Senior Race. On his arrival in the Isle of Man he had been given the ultimatum to resign from the Amateur Motor Cycle Association of which he was the Press Secretary and to join the Auto Cycle Union before being allowed to compete in the races. After much deliberation he reluctantly agreed to do so.

Prior to 1939, a warning letter was sent to newcomers regarding the difficulties of the TT course generally and especially to the rising sun to be faced on the Ballaugh to Ramsey section. However, with no races held during the war, the organisers decided to send a warning to all competitors, old and new. Furthermore, riders starting late for morning practices were to be warned verbally of the rising sun on the Sulby section of the course. Most of the old hands had inspected the course beforehand and agreed that the road surface was better than pre-war, except the part between Brandish and Hillberry, which was bumpy.

One of the first to set off along Glencrutchery Road was Arthur Johns and he negotiated his way round the course in a time of 34 minutes 25 seconds, averaging almost 66mph. On his second circuit of the morning he safely made his way through Union Mills, Glen Helen and Ballaugh then, at about 6.45am, he was seen approaching the slight right hand bend at Ballavolley (Quarry Bends) just before the Sulby Straight. A marshal on duty at that location, Flying Officer Joseph Orbin, stationed at Jurby, saw him put his left hand up to shield his eyes from the very strong rising sun but then as he attempted to negotiate the bend the front wheel of his machine hit the kerb on the left. The Norton then travelled along the gutter for 43 feet before mounting the footpath and colliding with the hedge. The unfortunate rider was thrown from the machine and came to rest on the footpath where he received immediate assistance but there was nothing that could be done for him. He had been killed instantly.

Arthur Walter Frederick Johns, a single man, was 36 years of age. He was a laundry work's manager by occupation and a resident of Small Heath, Birmingham. When war broke out, his work precluded him from joining the services so he organised the dispatch riders at the Midland Regional Headquarters of the Ministry of Home Security. Among their duties was to escort ambulances into Coventry after the blitz. As a prominent member of the Moseley Motor Cycle Club he took it upon himself to write newsletters to send out to club members serving abroad and to those in Prisoner of War camps. He was an all rounder with regard to motorcycling and had won the 250cc class in the first AMCA North Devon Trial in 1938. He was known as a man of infectious good humour and had a flair for practical joking.

His funeral service was held on Saturday 31st August and followed by interment at Witton Cemetery, Birmingham.

Peter Michael AITCHISON

Peter Aitchison at Quarterbridge during the 1946 Senior MGP

There was a thick blanket of mist over the Isle of Man on the morning of Thursday 5th September 1946 and rain was falling in Ramsey. Atrocious racing conditions for the competitors lined up along Glencrutchery Road in Douglas waiting to participate in the six lap Senior Manx Grand Prix. Amongst them was Peter Aitchison, riding a Norton machine bearing the race number 38. Two days earlier, riding a Norton, he had finished second in the six lap Junior Manx Grand Prix with a race average speed of 73.89mph. As the flag dropped to begin the race the first man away was Albert Moule. Then, once all the competitors had been dispatched, the crowds on the Grandstand stood in silence as the Rev. R.H. Reid, paid fitting tribute to those sportsmen who had given their lives in World War II. By this time the mist was now thickening over Douglas and from the Grandstand it was difficult to discern the tower of St. Ninians Church.

On completion of the first circuit Ernie Lyons led the race, thirty seconds ahead of Ken Bills in second place. Having completed his opening lap at an average speed of 74.60mph, Peter Aitchison was holding third position and trailing the race leader by just over one minute. On completion of the second circuit the first three positions remained unchanged. At about 12.30pm, during the third lap of the race, Aitchison was seen on the mountain section of the course and approaching the left hand bend at the 33rd Milestone. At this time it was pouring with rain and thick mist had reduced visibility down to 20-30 yards. He was then seen to take his hand off the handlebar as if to wipe his goggles but as he did so he suddenly seemed to realise he was travelling too fast for the bend. He braked hard but in doing so his machine went out of control and slid sideways before crashing into concrete fence posts situated along the right hand side of the road. The unfortunate rider was thrown from the machine and came to rest in the roadway. He was immediately attended to and found to have sustained serious injuries. A doctor was summoned to the scene and a stretcher party carried the gravely injured rider almost a mile back along the course to Windy Corner from where an ambulance would collect him immediately after the race. However, at about 1.55pm, with the doctor still in attendance, he succumbed to his injuries.

Ernie Lyons, a 32 year old farmer from County Kildare, riding a prototype Triumph machine, went on to win the race from Ken Bills in second place and Harold Rowell third.

Peter Michael Aitchison, a single man, was 29 years of age. He was an optician by occupation and a resident of Kings Langley, Hertfordshire. He had extensive racing experience before the war having competed at Donington, Brooklands, Crystal Palace and the Isle of Man, first in the 1937 Senior Manx Grand Prix then again in 1938 when he finished 3rd in the Senior Race. In addition to motorcycle racing he was a great skiing enthusiast and had won many honours for Britain in this sport.

His funeral service was held on Tuesday 10th September at St. Barnabas Church, Bexhill-on-Sea and among the chief mourners were Mr E. Cooper, whose machines Aitchison had been riding and Harold Rowell, representing the Manx M.C.C.. Among the many wreaths were floral tributes from Norton Motors Limited, Sir Malcolm Campbell's Bluebirds and the Ski Club of Great Britain.

Benjamin Buckley RUSSELL

Benjy Russell negotiates Quarterbridge during the 1947 Lightweight MGP

Gale force winds swept across the Isle of Man on the morning of Tuesday 9th September 1947 and this made conditions around the TT course less than ideal for racing. Undeterred, forty competitors braved the cold and assembled on Glencrutchery Road in Douglas, ready to participate in the Lightweight Manx Grand Prix. Amongst them was "Benjy" Russell, a newcomer, riding a Moto Guzzi machine bearing the race number 144. This was the same machine on which Manliff Barrington had won the Lightweight TT three months earlier. Russell was a firm favourite as he had unofficially broken the lap record during practice.

The Junior and Lightweight races were run concurrently and once the Junior machines had all departed from the start line it was the turn of the smaller machines to tackle the six laps of the mountain course. By the time the riders flashed past the Grandstand to complete the first lap it was apparent that the Moto Guzzi's of both Russell and Austin Munks were going well but the official times showed that Russell was in second place, five seconds behind the race leader, Freddie Hawken. On completion of the second circuit, Benjy Russell had moved into first place, 45 seconds ahead of Hawken. His lap time of 31 minutes and 52 seconds was 42 seconds outside the lap record but remarkably good in view of the high winds that were slowing down the small machines. At the end of the third lap, Hawken coasted into the pits to refuel and was away again smartly just as Russell was pulling in to refuel. Continuing to ride in brilliant fashion, Russell had knocked ten seconds off his previous lap time and had increased his lead to over a minute. By the end of the fourth lap Munks had moved up into second place and was now just seventeen seconds behind Russell.

During the fifth lap of the race, Russell was seen travelling at racing speed on the approach to the left hand bend at Crossags Lane (Schoolhouse Corner) on Lezayre Road in Ramsey. Then, as he began to negotiate the bend his left footrest caught the road surface and the Guzzi went out of control. For sixty yards he fought to regain control of the machine but was unable to avoid colliding heavily with the right hand hedge on the exit of the bend. The unfortunate rider was thrown from the machine and came to rest in the roadway, without his helmet and goggles, which had come off during the incident. He was immediately attended to but there was nothing that could be done for him. He had been killed instantly.

Austin Munks from Boston, Lincolnshire went on to win the race and in doing so made Manx Grand Prix history by becoming the first man to have won all three races. He had won the Senior and Junior events in 1936.

Benjy Russell, a single man, was 29 years of age. He was an insurance official by occupation and a resident of Kilternan, County Dublin. He was a friend and race pupil of the great Stanley Woods who, having viewed the scene of the incident, expressed his opinion at the inquest that according to marks he had seen on the road, Russell's line of approach to the corner was perfect but he had maintained that line for two or three yards too long, with the result that he was too far out from the left hand side on the apex of the bend.

His funeral service was held at Kilternan Church, Dublin on the afternoon of Thursday 11th September and followed by interment.

Johan Erik van TILBURG

Bob Van Tilburg on the mountain section shortly before his accident

Conditions were described as just about perfect for racing on the evening of Friday 28th May 1948. Splendid news for the seventy five competitors lined up on Glencrutchery Road in Douglas waiting to take advantage of the third practice session for the Tourist Trophy Races. Amongst them was Johan Erik "Bob" Van Tilburg, riding a new 348cc AJS "Boy Racer" machine bearing the race number 3 and entered in the Junior Race. He was one of South Africa's four representatives in the races and had completed one official lap of the course during the practice session that morning.

Shortly after 6.30pm the session began and Jock West, riding his Senior AJS, was the first man away. A short time later Bob Van Tilburg set off towards the daunting drop of Bray Hill on his opening lap of the evening. Within thirteen minutes all the riders had been dispatched and it wasn't long before the first reports of casualties were received. Among them was the South African Jack Rowland who dropped his Norton at Ballaugh and sustained a broken leg.

Bob Van Tilburg safely negotiated his way round the course and up onto the mountain section then, at about 7.20pm, he was seen rounding Windy Corner with another rider, Tommy McEwan, on his Senior Norton, in close company behind him. As the two men approached the slight left bend approximately 500 yards beyond Windy Corner McEwan moved to the right and began to overtake but as he was doing so Van Tilburg also moved over to his right and his handlebar caught McEwan's left arm. Both machines went out of control but while McEwan was able to avoid crashing Van Tilburg was not so fortunate, his machine struck two or three concrete fence posts situated along the right hand side of the road and he was thrown from the machine. The unfortunate rider came to rest in the roadway while his wrecked machine lay a short distance further on. McEwan stopped and ran back to help the injured rider. With the assistance of a spectator he gently moved him to the grass verge on the right where a police officer and a nurse attended to him. He was carried by stretcher to the tent at Windy Corner where, shortly afterwards; he was examined by a doctor. Due to the seriousness of his condition the practice session was suspended and an ambulance rushed him to Noble's Hospital where he was admitted at 8.15pm. He underwent surgery later that evening but throughout the following day his condition slowly deteriorated and at 1.15am on Sunday 30th May he succumbed to his injuries.

Johan Erik van Tilburg was 33 years of age. He was a motor mechanic by occupation and a resident of Durban, South Africa where he lived with his wife Laura and their two young sons, Alfie aged 8 and Johnny aged four. During the war years he had served as a Petty Officer with the South African Naval Forces and in November 1941 was seriously wounded by shellfire in Tobruk Harbour. After the war he had become one of the top riders in South Africa and was described as an unassuming man whose personal charm endeared him to all those with whom he came in contact with, be it in business, social or sporting activities.

At the request of his widow, his remains were cremated in Liverpool and his ashes returned to South Africa. Following a service attended by a large number of mourners, his ashes were interred at Stellawood Cemetery in Durban, South Africa.

Thomas Robert BRYANT

Tommy Bryant astride his Velocette in the paddock

Cold winds swept across the Isle of Man on the morning of Thursday 3rd June 1948, but there was clear visibility and dry roads around the TT course as 103 competitors assembled at the Grandstand in Douglas waiting to take advantage of a practice session for the Clubman's Tourist Trophy Races. Amongst them was Tommy Bryant, riding a 248cc Velocette machine bearing the race number 10 and entered in the Lightweight Clubman's Race scheduled for Wednesday 9th June. Although a newcomer to the TT course he had been showing promise during practice, returning the fastest time in his class on Monday evening and second fastest on Tuesday morning.

After a short delay the session began at 5.00am and it was not long before Tommy Bryant set off along Glencrutchery Road towards Bray Hill on his opening lap. He safely negotiated his way round the course, through Ramsey and over the mountain section down to the Creg ny Baa. At 5.45am, he was just two miles from the Grandstand at the end of his lap when he was seen travelling at racing speed on the approach to the tricky left hand bend known as Brandish Corner which is situated mid way between Creg ny Baa and Hillberry Corner. As he rounded the bend he went wide on the exit and collided heavily with the grass bank on the right. He fought to regain control of the Velocette but it struck the hedge a second time and he was thrown into the roadway, losing his crash helmet in the process. Marshals ran to his immediate assistance and found him lying face down and unconscious in the middle of the road. He was lifted to the side of the road then carried into a nearby field. There, a trainee nurse from St. George's Hospital in London, who had been spectating at that location, administered first aid treatment. At someone's suggestion, the gravely injured rider was placed in a marshal's private car, which was then driven along the course to the Grandstand. Meanwhile, the police officer on duty at Hillberry Corner had made his way across the fields to the scene of the incident and arrived too late to stop the car being driven onto the course. The car arrived safely at the Grandstand where a doctor examined the unfortunate rider before he was removed by ambulance to Noble's Hospital. His parents had been on the Grandstand at the time of the incident and they accompanied him in the ambulance. He was admitted at 6.25am and placed in the male medical ward but his condition deteriorated and 25 minutes later, he succumbed to his injuries.

At his inquest, the Coroner Mr. Howard Lay, remarked that everyone had acted in what they thought was the best interests of the rider and showed initiative and enterprise. They did their best to get the injured man to hospital as quickly as possible and whether or not a car should be on the course is not a matter that in any way affected the cause of death.

Tommy Bryant, a single man, was 23 years of age. He was a motor engineer by occupation and a resident of Parkstone, Dorset. He had served in the Royal Navy as a Petty Officer during the war. Although this was to be his first major road race he had competed in other events, most notably grass track races and scrambles.

His funeral, which was attended by many friends and representatives of his local motorcycle clubs, was held at St. Aldhelm's Church, Branksome, on Monday 7th June, followed by interment at Parkstone Cemetery.

Neil CHRISTMAS

Noel Christmas at Ballaugh Bridge during practice for the 1948 Senior TT

Thick mist, on the morning of Friday 11th June 1948, had reduced visibility on the mountain section of the TT course and was down to 50 yards at the Bungalow but reports from Windy Corner suggested that the mist was slowly clearing. Fifty four of the original sixty nine entrants lined up along Glencrutchery Road in Douglas waiting to participate in the "Battle of the Giants", the seven lap Senior Tourist Trophy Race. Amongst them was Neil "Noel" Christmas, riding a 499cc Norton machine bearing the race number 34 and which had been entered by Francis Beart of Byfleet, Surrey. Days earlier, whilst participating in the Junior TT, Christmas had been forced to retire from the race when the frame of his machine cracked.

At 11.00am the flag dropped and the race began with the riders setting off individually and at ten second intervals. By this time the damp roads around the course were beginning to dry. The Italian rider Omobono Tenni (Guzzi) blitzed his way round on the opening lap and led the race. However, after a long pit stop at the end of the second lap, he lost the lead to Les Graham but then regained the lead during the third lap after Graham retired at Ballig.

On completion of his third lap, all appeared to be going well for Noel Christmas as he pulled into the pits to replenish his machine with fuel and oil before setting off again to resume the race. However, at about 1.10pm, on his fifth lap of the race and holding ninth position, he was seen approaching Douglas Road Corner, Kirk Michael in close company with another competitor who was just slightly ahead of him. Both riders were wide of the usual racing line with Christmas on the outside as if attempting to overtake but while the other rider was able to negotiate the sweeping right hand corner Christmas was wide on the exit of the bend and collided heavily with the unprotected hedge on his left. He was thrown from the machine, and came to rest on his back in the roadway with his extensively damaged machine beside him. Dr. W.M. Robertson of Ramsey had witnessed the incident and gave the severely injured rider immediate treatment before arranging his removal by special train to Ramsey and from there by ambulance to the Cottage Hospital. Over the following 24 hours, his condition slowly deteriorated and at 6.15pm the following day he succumbed to his injuries.

Mechanical problems later in the race saw Tenni fall back to finish in 9th place. Artie Bell went on to win his first TT while Bill Doran finished in second position and Jock Weddell third. All three men mounted on Norton machines. Less than three weeks later Omobono Tenni was to lose his life whilst practising for the Swiss Grand Prix.

Noel Christmas, a married man, was 39 years of age. His wife had been among a party of people from Surrey watching the race. He was a motor garage proprietor by occupation and a resident of Woking, Surrey. Before the war he had been a regular competitor at Brooklands and was a rider with a wealth of experience having raced in France, Belgium and the Ulster Grand Prix. He made his debut on the Isle of Man in 1933 when, riding a Scott, he took part in the Senior Manx Grand Prix. In 1934 he finished 7th in the Junior MGP then moved on to the TT. In 1947, riding a Norton, he finished 7th in the Senior TT.

His funeral service was held in St. Mary's Church, Douglas on Tuesday 15th June and followed by interment at Douglas Borough Cemetery.

Reuben Thomas DRINKWATER

(By permission of Mortons Media Group Ltd)

Ben Drinkwater pushes away from the start line during the 1949 Junior TT

Weather reports on the morning of Monday 13th June 1949 suggested it would be sunny all day on the Isle of Man but there would be a cool moderate breeze. The TT course was in perfect condition and the stage was set for the seven lap Junior Tourist Trophy Race. To the sounds of stirring music at the Grandstand in Douglas the grand parade of one hundred riders assembled on Glencrutchery Road. This was a record entry for the race and amongst them was race veteran Ben Drinkwater, riding a 348cc Norton machine bearing the race number 87. As winner of the 1948 Junior, Freddie Frith, riding a Velocette, had the privilege of being the first man away and for the first time, the remaining riders were dispatched in pairs at twenty second intervals. On completion of the first circuit, Les Graham (A.J.S.) led the race from Bill Doran (A.J.S.) with Freddie Frith holding third position. However, on the second lap of the race Les Graham went out with clutch problems and by the end of the third lap Doran and Frith still held the first two positions with Artie Bell and Ernie Lyons joint third.

At about 12.50pm, on the fourth lap of the race, Ben Drinkwater was seen approaching the right and left hand bends at the 11th Milestone in close company with two other competitors. One rider was slightly ahead but the other rider and Drinkwater were almost side by side as they began to negotiate the right hand bend at an estimated 85mph. At this point Drinkwater braked hard and to witnesses it appeared that he was attempting to give way to the rider alongside him. This act of sportsmanship cost him dearly as he quickly found himself in difficulties and on the exit of the bend the side of his machine struck the grass bank on the left. The Norton skidded across the road and just as it seemed possible that he would regain control, the front wheel struck the kerbstone on the other side of the road. The force of the impact collapsed the front wheel and in an instant the machine collided heavily with a dry stone wall and hedge. The unfortunate rider was thrown into the roadway and his machine crashed down on top of him. Marshals went to his immediate assistance but there was nothing they could do for him. He had been killed instantly.

Bill Doran later retired at the Gooseneck with gearbox problems. Freddie Frith went on to win the race with an average speed of 83.15mph. Ernie Lyons finished in second place and Artie Bell took third position.

Ben Drinkwater was 39 years of age. He was a garage proprietor by occupation and a resident of Rochdale where he lived with his wife Ruth and their three young daughters, Doris, Ruth and Jean. A fourth daughter, Mary, was born less than two months after his death. His debut on the Isle of Man was in the 1937 Lightweight Manx Grand Prix but he retired during the race. In 1938, despite a soft rear tyre on his Excelsior, he finished 6th in the Lightweight MGP. Following the war years he returned to the Island in 1946 and after leading the Lightweight Manx a damaged oil pipe on his Excelsior cost him time and he eventually finished in second place. At the North West 200 in 1947 he was leading the Lightweight Race but electrical problems saw him limp home in second place. At the TT the same year he finished 3rd in the Lightweight. Then, in 1948, riding a Moto Guzzi he finished 4th in the Lightweight TT. He had also raced in Holland and Belgium.

His funeral service was held on Friday 17th June and followed by interment at Bacup Cemetery.

32

TWO KILLED IN T.T. PRACTISING

Crashes at Handley's Corner and the Keppel

RIDERS DIE FROM INJURIES

INQUESTS were held at Douglas on Wednesday and yesterday on Charles Albert Makaula-White, a 24-years-old miner, of Forge House, Eyethorne, near Dover, and Thomas Alan Westfield, a 20-years-old engineer, of Roxby Road Garage, Winterton, near Scunthorpe, Lincs., who died from injuries received when practising for next week's T.T. Races.

Makaula-White, who crashed at Handley's Corner, Ballamenaugh, Kirk Michael, on Monday evening on his first practice lap, had entered for the Senior Clubman's event, and Westfield, an entrant for the Senior International Race, crashed at Keppel Gate on Tuesday morning.

Verdicts of "Misadventure" were returned in each case, and at the close of Wednesday's proceedings, the Coroner (High Bailiff Lay) commented that motor-cycle racing was a fine sport, but by its nature it entailed a certain amount of danger which the riders were prepared to face.

Isle of Man newspaper headlines 1950 TT

Rain began to fall just as the roads were closing around the TT course on the evening of Monday 29th May 1950. However, most of the competitors gathered at the Grandstand in Douglas were already heavily wrapped up in waterproof clothing as they prepared to take advantage of a practice session for the Clubman's Tourist Trophy Races. Amongst them was John Makaula-White, riding a 500cc Triumph machine bearing the race number 71 and entered for the Senior Clubman's Race scheduled for the following week. He was a newcomer to the Isle of Man and this was to be his first official lap of the course.

With the race officials seeking shelter from the rain, the practice session commenced with each competitor receiving the signal to proceed and it was soon the turn of John Makaula-White to set off towards St. Ninians crossroads and Bray Hill on his opening lap. At about 7.00pm and with the rain still falling, Makaula-White had safely negotiated the first eleven miles of the course and was seen approaching Handley's Corner, but he was on the wrong racing line as he began to negotiate the first bend. Realising his situation, he braked hard but the Triumph went out of control and collided with a stone pillar at the entrance to Ballamenagh Cottage. It then scraped along the stone wall for some yards before shooting across the road and colliding with a thicket hedge on the left. Both rider and machine were thrown into the air and came to rest in the roadway. Marshals went to his immediate assistance and found he was unconscious and seriously injured.

On hearing of the incident, the Deputy Clerk of the Course ordered an ambulance to proceed along the back roads from Ballacraine to Cronk y Voddy. Practicing was then suspended for approximately half an hour in order for the ambulance to travel along the course to the scene of the accident. At about 7.40pm word was received that the ambulance, with the gravely injured rider onboard, had left the course at Barregarrow crossroads and was making it's way to Nobles Hospital via Injebreck. The unfortunate rider was admitted to hospital at 8.45pm but his condition deteriorated and he succumbed to his injuries at 1.30am the following morning.

Victor Anstice, Scrutineer for the Auto-Cycle Union, later examined the Triumph and found damage, which indicated that following impact the machine had travelled upside down for some distance. He found no evidence to suggest that a mechanical failure had contributed to this accident.

John Makaula-White was 24 years of age. Although a single man he was engaged to Miss Rose Page. He was a miner by occupation and employed at the Tilmanstone Colliery. He did not have a great deal of racing experience but had always wanted to race on the Isle of Man course and had been entered for the race by the Folkestone Motor Cycle Club. He had been a keen junior footballer at Eyethorne and had also gained prizes for dancing.

His funeral service was held at All Saints Church; Waldershare on Saturday 3rd June and among the very many wreaths was those from the Dover & District Light Car Club, Tilmanstone Colliery and friends from the Palm Tree Inn, Eyethorne.

Thomas Alan WESTFIELD

Alan Westfield at Cronk ny Mona during practice for the 1950 Senior TT

Strong winds were blowing across the Isle of Man on the morning of Tuesday 30th May 1950 and the roads around the TT course were wet. To make matters worse, it was reported that visibility on the mountain section was down to 100 yards in places. However, these miserable conditions had not deterred the competitors gathered in the area of the Grandstand in Douglas waiting to take advantage of a practice session for the Tourist Trophy Races. Amongst them was Alan Westfield, riding a Triumph machine bearing the race number 59 and entered in the Senior Race scheduled for Friday 9th June. Just a few weeks earlier, he had finished second in the 500cc race at the Silverstone circuit.

Once the session was under way, Westfield set off along Glencrutchery Road towards Bray Hill and safely negotiated his way round the course to complete his opening lap of the morning. He then commenced his second circuit and made his way through Union Mills, Glen Helen, Ballaugh and into Ramsey before making the climb up onto the mountain section. At about 6.30am, race veteran Johnny Lockett, riding a Senior works Norton, rounded the tricky left hand bend at Keppel Gate and came upon Alan Westfield, lying unconscious in the roadway with his machine beside him. Fortunately, Lockett was able to find a way through and stopped at the Creg ny Baa where he reported the incident to the police officer on duty at that location. Marshals went to the assistance of the gravely injured rider and carried him to Mr. Tate's house (now know as Kate's Cottage) before he was collected by ambulance and conveyed to Noble's Hospital where he was admitted at 7.20am. However, at 6.25pm that same day, he succumbed to his injuries. His father, Sidney Charles Westfield, had been on the Island with him to act as his pit attendant.

Marks at the scene of the accident indicated that Westfield had negotiated the left hand bend too fast and on the exit of the bend his machine had mounted the low grass verge on the right. Having run along the verge for a distance of 96 feet both rider and machine were then thrown back into the road and slid along for a further 55 feet before coming to rest. It was surmised that the unfortunate rider had come into contact with one of the iron posts situated at the side of the road.

On the following Monday, Johnny Lockett took sixth place in the Junior Race and on the Friday, riding his works Norton in the Senior Race, finished in third place with a race average speed of 90.37mph.

Alan Westfield, a single man, was 20 years of age. He was a motor mechanic by occupation and resided at Roxby Road Garage, Winterton near Scunthorpe, Lincolnshire. He had built up a wide experience of motorcycle racing over the previous three and a half years and had enjoyed success at Cadwell Park and Silverstone. His first appearance on the Isle of Man was the 1948 Junior Clubman's TT when, riding a Norton, he finished in sixth place only to be disqualified after it was found that the engine of his machine was oversized.

His funeral service was held near his home on Saturday 3rd June and followed by interment at Winterton Cemetery.

34

Alfred BENT

Alfred Bent at Ballaugh Bridge during the Thursday afternoon practice session

Reports from around the TT course on the morning of Friday 8th September 1950 indicated that the roads were dry and visibility was clear. Welcome news for the competitors congregating at the Grandstand in Douglas waiting to take advantage of a practice session for the Manx Grand Prix Races. Amongst them was Alfred Bent, a newcomer to the Isle of Man, riding a 350cc Velocette machine bearing the race number 49 and entered in the Junior Race to be held the following week. During earlier practice sessions he had completed eight official laps of the course at times of between 30 and 31 minutes.

Once the session began Bent set off along Glencrutchery Road towards the daunting drop of Bray Hill on his opening lap of the morning. Then, at about 6.30am, with 15 miles of the course behind him and having safely made his way through Union Mills, Glen Helen and Kirk Michael village, he was seen approaching Birkin's Bend at Rhencullen. He was alone on the road and travelling at racing speed but was on the left side of the road whereas he should have been on the right, which was the usual racing line for the bends. As a result of his positioning he went wide on the right hand bend, his machine touched the kerb on the left then shot diagonally across the road for a distance of 175 feet before mounting the grass bank on the right. Both rider and machine travelled along the bank for a further 45 feet before colliding heavily with an electricity pole. The unfortunate rider was thrown from the machine and came to rest in the roadway while the Velocette skidded back across the road and came to a stop near to the kerb on the left. A marshal summoned the assistance of Leo Starr, who was the next competitor to arrive and together they carried the unfortunate rider to the side of the road. Starr then continued to Ballaugh Bridge where he reported the incident to the marshals at that location. Albert Moule, a travelling marshal, was dispatched from the grandstand and arrived at the scene of the incident just over five minutes ahead of a doctor who had been summoned to attend. On examination of the young rider the doctor declared that there was nothing that could have been done for him. He had been killed instantly.

The Velocette machine was later examined by Douglas Brown the official Scrutineer for the races and he found extensive damage down the right side. The front wheel was broken and the tyre had burst. The machine was in third gear but he could not definitely state that it was in this gear at the time of the accident, although it probably was. He found no evidence to suggest that a mechanical failure had been a contributory factor in the incident.

Alfred Bent, a single man, was 18 years of age. He was a farmer by occupation and a resident of Hale near Liverpool. Although he had competed in short circuit events he did not have a great deal of road racing experience and all his racing had been done on his Velocette. His brother, Herbert Bent, was also competing in the Manx Grand Prix for the first time but he had crashed his 350cc AJS machine at The Nook on the Monday morning and was lying in Noble's Hospital having sustained a broken ankle. Herbert did return to the Island the following year and competed in the Senior MGP. He continued to compete on the Isle of Man up to and including 1960 when he took part in the Junior MGP.

Alfred's funeral service was held at St. Mary's Church in Hale village and followed by interment.

Leonard Cedric BOLSHAW

1950 - Len Bolshaw at Quarterbridge on a 249cc Triumph during the Lightweight Clubman's TT

Fine weather, dry roads and clear visibility around the TT course on the evening of Tuesday 29th May 1951 provided perfect racing conditions for the 145 competitors gathered at the Grandstand on Glencrutchery Road in Douglas waiting to take advantage of a practice session for the Tourist Trophy Races. Amongst them was Len Bolshaw, riding a 500cc Triumph machine bearing the race number 55, which was entered for the Senior Clubman's Race to be held the following week.

The session was well under way when, at about 7.10pm, Stanley Cooper, riding a Douglas machine which had been entered for the Junior Clubman's Race, was seen negotiating the series of left bends at the 32nd milestone on the mountain section of the course with Len Bolshaw in close company behind him. As Cooper came out of the last bend and onto the short straight before Windy Corner he was travelling at about 85mph and was positioned only about one yard from the wire fencing on the right when Len Bolshaw made an attempt to pass between him and the fence. However, as he was doing so, the handlebars of the two machines locked together momentarily before Bolshaw's right handlebar became entangled in the fencing. In a cloud of dust and debris, both rider and machine crashed through the wire fence, snapping off four concrete posts at ground level, before tumbling across the adjoining grassland and coming to rest. A marshal manning the telephone in the caravan at Windy Corner witnessed the incident and immediately alerted the duty doctor who had been sitting in his car, which was parked nearby. With his case in hand the doctor quickly made his way on foot to the grass area where Bolshaw was lying. The marshal followed behind with a hot water bottle and blankets. Although reaching the unfortunate rider within three or four minutes of the incident, the doctor found that there was nothing that could be done for the unfortunate rider. He had been killed instantly. Stanley Cooper had managed to maintain control of his machine and continued. He took part in the Junior Clubman's Race the following week and finished in 7th position.

Vic Anstice, official Scrutineer for the Auto-Cycle Union, later examined the Triumph machine and found that it had sustained considerable damage to the front offside and to the rear end, consistent with the accident. It was found to be in second gear. The brakes were in order, although the controls of the rear brake were damaged during the incident. There was no evidence to suggest that the accident had been as a result of mechanical failure.

Leonard Bolshaw was 42 years of age. He was a farmer and cattle dealer by occupation and a resident of Holmes Chapel, Cheshire where he lived with his wife Pat and their three children. He was one of the oldest entrants in the race and had stated that on account of his age he would retire from racing after the event. For most of his life he had been a keen motorcyclist and had raced as far back as 1929, the year he won his first trophy. Riding a Triumph in the 1949 Lightweight Clubman's Race, which was held over two laps of the TT course, he finished in 5th place with a race average speed of 64.21mph.

His funeral service was held at the Methodist Church, Knutsford Road, Holmes Chapel and followed by interment at Holmes Chapel Cemetery.

John Patrick O'DRISCOLL

John O'Driscoll about to take part in a practice session for the 1951 Lightweight TT

Conditions were ideal for racing on the evening of Thursday 31st May 1951. The weather was fine, the roads around the TT course were dry and visibility was clear on the mountain. Welcome news for the competitors congregating at the Grandstand in Douglas waiting to take advantage of a further practice session for the Tourist Trophy races. Amongst them was John O'Driscoll, a newcomer to the Isle of Man, riding a 249cc Rudge machine bearing the race number 17, which was entered for the Lightweight Race to be held the following week. He had completed about a dozen laps of the course during earlier practice sessions and had in fact qualified for the race on the second day.

Once the session was under way it was not long before O'Driscoll was given the signal to commence his opening lap of the evening and he set off along Glencrutchery Road towards Bray Hill. He safely made his way round the course to complete his first circuit then pulled into the pits where his mechanic, Victor Sidney White, made some minor adjustments to the machine. Once these had been completed he set off again, making his way round the course through Glen Helen, Ballaugh and Ramsey before making the climb up onto the mountain section of the course for the second time that evening.

At about 8.00pm, with the setting sun in his eyes, John O'Driscoll was alone on the road and travelling at a relatively slow speed as he approached the sweeping left hand bend at the 33rd Milestone. A spectator, John Edward Barnes, the well known photographer, noted that the engine of the Rudge did not sound right. At this point, for some unknown reason, the Rudge began wobbling badly and drifted to the right hand side of the road where, at an estimated speed of 50mph both rider and machine collided heavily with the concrete fence posts situated along the side of the road. The unfortunate rider was thrown over the handlebars and came to rest in the roadway without his helmet, which had come off during the incident. His wrecked machine lay beside him. A spectator at the scene ran to his assistance and tried to make him as comfortable as he could but feared there was nothing that could be done for him. Meanwhile, a doctor was summoned to attend from Windy Corner and on his arrival he confirmed that John O'Driscoll had succumbed to his injuries and had probably been killed instantly.

Vic Anstice, an official Scrutineer for the Auto-Cycle Union, carried out an examination on the Rudge. He found that the front wheel and tyre were badly damaged and there was little left of the inner tube. The rear mudguard stays had broken and the exhaust was detached from the machine. There was no evidence to suggest that either the engine or gearbox had seized. However, O'Driscoll's mechanic could not understand what had happened to the front forks of the machine as the front spindle had apparently come out of the forks.

John O'Driscoll was 41 years of age. He was a motor trader by occupation and a resident of Forest Hill, London where he lived with his wife Eileen and their four children, Patricia aged 20, Anne aged 6, John aged 5 and Desmond aged 3. He was described as a cautious rider with several years experience in grass track and aerodrome racing.

His funeral service was followed by interment at Hither Green Cemetery, Lewisham.

John Thomas WENMAN

Tom Wenman about to participate in a practice session for the 1951 Junior TT

The all important weather forecast on the morning of Tuesday 4th June 1951 stated that the fine weather over the Isle of Man was unlikely to deteriorate. Welcome news for the large crowds of spectators positioned around the TT course and the 98 competitors lined up along Glencrutchery Road in Douglas waiting for the Junior Tourist Trophy Race to commence. Amongst them, riding a Norton machine bearing the race number 56, was Tom Wenman whose intention was to retire from racing at the end of the season.

At 8.55am, those watching from the Grandstand stood to attention for the arrival of his Excellency the Lieutenant Governor. At 9.00am three blasts from the siren signalled the commencement of the warming-up period and for fifteen minutes the machines were then ridden up and down the upper end of Glencrutchery Road as the riders brought the stone cold engines to life. Shortly before the race commenced, as the Lieutenant Governor moved among the riders, an announcement was made warning the riders to "Take care at Greeba Bridge, the tar is a bit troublesome".

At 9.30am the first man was sent on his way towards Bray Hill. Moments later there was a unique incident as E. Barrett, the fourth man to set off from the grid, became the first retirement - with possibly the shortest ride in TT history to his credit. Within 20 yards of leaving the start line the connecting rod on his AJS machine snapped and split the crankcase.

At about 10.30am, during the second lap of the race, Tom Wenman was travelling at racing speed towards the bottom of Rhencullen Hill, Kirk Michael when the engine of his machine suddenly locked solid. The Norton skidded in a straight line for 135 feet then fell over onto its side, dragging the unfortunate rider along with it for a distance of 93 yards before both rider and machine came to rest in the roadway. Marshals at the scene quickly carried the gravely injured rider onto the footpath and Dr. R.B. Jones was called to the scene from Ballaugh Bridge. On his arrival, the doctor examined Wenman then instructed that he should be removed to the nearby house, "Lyndhurst". He could not be moved to hospital other than on the main roads in an ambulance and as the race was proceeding it was decided to remove him at the conclusion of the race. However, by the time the ambulance arrived at Rhencullen, Tom Wenman had succumbed to his injuries. An examination of the Norton later confirmed that the accident had been caused by engine seizure.

Geoff Duke went on to win the race, setting new lap and race records. Johnnie Lockett was second and Jack Brett third. All three riding Norton machines.

Tom Wenman, a married man, was 46 years of age. He was a builder's foreman by occupation and a resident of Stanford Vale, Berkshire. His wife had been a spectator at the Grandstand during the race. He made his debut on the Isle of Man TT course in the 1947 Senior Clubman's TT but retired during the race. In 1948 he finished 24th in the Senior Clubman's and in 1949 he came 27th in the Junior Clubman's.

His funeral service was held in the Isle of Man and followed by interment at Douglas Borough Cemetery.

Douglas Lionel PARRIS

Parris pictured at Hillberry during practice for the 1951 Junior Clubman's TT

Bright sunshine, clear visibility and dry roads around the TT course on the afternoon of Tuesday 4th June 1951 provided near perfect racing conditions for the seventy five competitors assembled on Glencrutchery Road in Douglas waiting to participate in the four lap Junior Clubman's Tourist Trophy Race. Amongst them was Douglas Lionel Parris, a newcomer to the TT course, riding a Douglas machine bearing the race number 76. He had completed seven official practice laps of the course.

At 2.30pm the race commenced with riders being sent on their way in groups of three and at fifteen-second intervals. Within eight minutes they had all been dispatched from the start line. Parris was among the last to leave and headed off towards the daunting descent of Bray Hill then safely negotiated his way round the course, through Union Mills, Glen Helen and Ramsey before making the climb up onto the mountain section of the course.

Shortly after 3.00pm Parris was thirty miles into his opening lap of the race when he was seen travelling at racing speed, on the approach to the tight left hand bend immediately before the electric tram crossing at the Bungalow Hotel. To indicate to competitors the severity of the bend a warning board, displaying a directional arrow, had been positioned a short distance before the corner and on the road surface there was another arrow, painted in red. As he was negotiating the bend he ran wide and drifted onto the grass verge, narrowly missing two verge marker posts. He continued along the verge until the front wheel of his machine dropped into a gully and he was thrown off, tumbling across the tram lines before coming to rest, unconscious, in the roadway. Marshals went to his immediate assistance and on finding that his condition was serious they carried him by stretcher to an electric tramcar, which then conveyed him from the Bungalow down to Laxey village where a doctor and ambulance were waiting to carry him to Noble's Hospital. He was admitted within forty minutes of the incident but despite the best efforts of the medical staff his condition slowly deteriorated and he succumbed to his injuries at 8.00pm that same day.

The race had continued and on completion of the first circuit, having broken the lap record set by Brian Jackson the previous year, Ken James held a 22 second advantage over the gold coloured Douglas machine of B.J. Hargreaves in second place with Brian Purslow third.

During the second lap of the race, Ken James stopped at the Hawthorn and Hargreaves retired at Ballaugh. Eighteen year old Brian Purslow brought his BSA home in first place, setting a new race record time with an average race speed of 75.36mph. G.E. Read finished in second place and D.J. Draper finished third. Both mounted on Norton machines.

Douglas Lionel Parris, a single man, was 23 years of age. He was a toolmaker by occupation and a resident of Croyden, Surrey. The Sanderstead and District M & MC Club had entered him for the race.

His funeral service was held in the Isle of Man and followed by interment at Douglas Borough Cemetery.

Christopher HORN

Chris Horn about to participate in a practice session for the 1951 Senior TT

Record numbers of spectators positioned themselves around the TT course on the morning of Friday 8th June 1951. Unfortunately, the weathermen at Ronaldsway had forecast that the weather would probably remain cool throughout the day particularly on the mountain where some spectators had lit fires with bracken in an attempt to keep warm while waiting for the racing to commence. With 18 non-starters posted, there were 80 competitors assembled on Glencrutchery Road in Douglas waiting to take part in the Senior Tourist Trophy Race. Amongst them was Chris Horn, riding a Norton machine bearing the race number 36. Earlier in the week he had finished 36th in the Junior Race and 11th in the Lightweight Race.

At 10.30am the flag dropped and the race began with Geoff Duke, winner of the Junior Race, being the first to set off towards Bray Hill. On completion of the first circuit Geoff Duke led the race by 41 seconds from Bill Doran and Johnny Lockett who had recorded identical lap times. Amongst the early retirements was Frank Fry who had been forced out of the race with gearbox problems. On his second lap of the race Duke broke the lap record with an average speed of 95.22mph and was now well over a minute ahead of the second place man Johnny Lockett who in turn was just four seconds ahead of Doran.

During the third lap of the race, Chris Horn had safely made his way over the first nine miles of the course through Union Mills, Glen Vine and Ballacraine when he was seen approaching the bends just before Laurel Bank. As he was negotiating the bends his Norton clipped the kerb on the right and went out of control. The unfortunate rider was thrown from his machine and collided heavily with an ash tree situated by the roadside. Marshals went to his immediate assistance but there was nothing they could do for him. He had been killed instantly.

Geoff Duke went on to win the seven-lap race with a race average of 93.82mph adding to his Junior Race success to complete the "Double". Bill Doran finished in second place with Cromie McCandless third. A broken frame on his MV Agusta had forced Les Graham to retire during the third lap.

Christopher Horn, a single man, was 30 years of age. He was a welder by occupation and a resident of Whitley Bay, Northumberland where he lived with his mother who had been on the Island watching the race from another part of the course when the incident occurred. His first appearance on the Isle of Man was the 1948 Senior Clubman's TT when he finished eighth, a result which earned him a free entry in the Manx Grand Prix later that year and in which he finished 6th in the Junior Race. The following year, 1949, riding a Vincent HRD he broke the lap record in the Clubman's 1000cc Race and was leading by six minutes when forced to retire on the last lap. At the Manx Grand Prix that year, riding an AJS, he finished a lowly 35th in the Junior Race but went on to achieve a podium position in the Senior Race when, riding a Norton machine and with a race average speed of 82.83mph, he finished 3rd to Geoff Duke and Cromie McCandless.

Two hundred mourners attended his funeral service, which was held at Whitley Bay New Cemetery on Wednesday 13th June. Several months after his death motorcycle clubs in the North East subscribed to a memorial trophy to be competed for as a motorcycle trial.

John Morton CROW

Jim Crow exits Governors Dip during the 1951 Senior Manx Grand Prix

Apart from a brisk wind, conditions were almost perfect for racing on the morning of Friday 14th September 1951. The sun was shining and the roads were dry for the 93 competitors lined up along Glencrutchery Road in Douglas waiting for the start of the six lap Senior Manx Grand Prix, which had been postponed from the day before because of poor weather conditions. Among the riders was race veteran "Jim" Crow, riding a 500cc Norton machine bearing the race number 56. During practice he had crashed at Barregarrow when another rider had braked hard in front of him and he had been admitted to Ramsey Cottage Hospital with suspected fractured ribs but was discharged after an examination revealed that the injury was confined to bruising and he was out on the course again the following day. His intention was to retire from racing at the end of the season.

Once the race began it was not too long before Crow received his signal to commence his race against the clock and he set off towards Bray Hill on his opening lap. At the half way stage of the race he pulled into the pits, refuelled, then set off again to rejoin the race. By this time Dave Bennett was leading the race ahead of Don Crossley and Robin Sherry.

At about 12.50pm, having made his way safely through Union Mills, Glen Vine and Crosby on his fifth lap Jim Crow was seen negotiating the fast right hand bend at Appledene, the section immediately following Greeba Castle. The engine of his Norton was misfiring and he moved over to the left side of the road. He did not stop but continued towards Greeba Bridge at a greatly reduced speed and was seen fumbling under the fuel tank with his left hand. Then, as he rounded the next bend he struck the hedge on the left and was thrown from the machine. He came to rest just behind the hedge where Marshals quickly attended to him and an ambulance was dispatched to the scene via a back road that joined the course at Cronk Breck, a short distance further along the course from where the unfortunate rider lay. He was conveyed to Noble's Hospital where he was admitted at 2.30pm and received emergency surgery a short time later. However, his injuries were found to be so grave that his recovery was deemed impossible and at 6.20am the following morning he succumbed to his injuries.

Dave Bennett went on to win the race, almost two minutes ahead of Don Crossley with Denis Parkinson taking third place ahead of Robin Sherry.

Jim Crow was 38 years of age. He was an agricultural engineer by occupation and a resident of Bourn, Cambridge where he lived with his wife Joan and their five children, Diana, Veronica, John, Virginia and Victoria. He was an accomplished trials rider and a pioneer of road racing in the Cambridge Centaur Motor Cycle Club. On the Isle of Man he had competed in the Manx Grand Prix since 1946 with his best results coming firstly from the 1949 Junior Race when, lying in third place behind Cromie McCandless and Geoff Duke, he came off his Velocette at the Quarterbridge on the fifth lap. He quickly remounted and finished the race in 7th position. Then in 1950, riding a Norton machine, he finished 5th in the Senior Race.

His funeral service was held in Cambridgeshire and followed by interment in Bourn Churchyard.

Frank William Alfred FRY

Frank Fry with his Velocette during a practice session for the 1952 Junior TT

Weather conditions were fine on the morning of Wednesday 4th June 1952 and the roads around the TT course were dry together with clear visibility on the mountain. Welcome news for the competitors gathered at the Grandstand on Glencrutchery Road in Douglas waiting to take advantage of a practice session for the Tourist Trophy Races. Amongst them was the race veteran Frank Fry, entered in the Senior Race scheduled for the following week. He was riding a Norton machine that he had borrowed from another competitor and on which he had placed his own racing plate, number 58.

Shortly after the practice session commenced Fry set off towards Bray Hill and safely made his way through Union Mills, Ballacraine and Glen Helen. He was then seen, travelling at racing speed and in close company with two other riders on the approach to Westwood Corner in Kirk Michael. He was the last of the three going into the sweeping left hand bend when suddenly, for no apparent reason, the rear wheel stepped out and the machine went from beneath him. The Marshals in that area were at a loss to account for the incident as he was clear of Ballalonna Bridge and had not touched either of the other two machines. The rider slid along the road together with his machine and collided heavily with the hedge on the right before coming to rest, unconscious, in the roadway. The Norton lay on its side nearby with the engine still ticking over. Marshals went to his immediate assistance and did what they could for him until a doctor arrived at the scene. An ambulance conveyed the gravely injured rider to Noble's Hospital where he was admitted at 7.45am and by this time he was conscious and lucid but suffering from severe shock. There was some improvement throughout the following day but his condition then slowly deteriorated and at 4.45am on Friday 6th June he succumbed to his injuries. His parents had been on the Island with him when the accident occurred.

An examination of the Norton machine by an official Scrutineer for the Auto-Cycle Union, found that there was no compression but otherwise the engine appeared to be in good order. The machine was in top gear. The fuel tank, front forks and front wheel had all sustained damage from the accident and the right handlebar and footrest had been torn off. There was no evidence to suggest that a mechanical failure had contributed to this accident.

Frank William Alfred Fry, a single man, was 35 years of age. He was a motorcycle agent by occupation and a resident of Feltham, Middlesex. During the war years he had served as a Flight Sergeant in the Royal Air Force. He was a very experienced rider and had distinguished himself at Blandford, Dunholme, Thruxton, Silverstone and many Continental events. His debut on the TT course was in 1938 when he finished twelfth in the Junior Manx Grand Prix. During practice for the TT in 1950, he sustained serious injuries when he lost control of his Velocette machine and crashed near to Hall Caine's Castle (Greeba Castle) but he had fully recovered and was racing as well as ever. One of the highlights of his racing career was at the Ulster Grand Prix in 1948 when he took third place in the Junior Race.

His funeral service was held in the Isle of Man and followed by interment at Douglas Borough Cemetery.

Brian Arthur JACKSON

Brian Jackson with the BSA on which he won the 1950 Junior Clubman's TT

Weather conditions were fine on the morning of Tuesday 2nd September 1952, visibility was clear and the roads around the TT course were dry. Perfect racing conditions for the competitors gathered at the Grandstand in Douglas waiting to take advantage of a practice session for the Manx Grand Prix. Amongst them was Brian Jackson, riding a 499cc "Featherbed" Norton machine bearing the race number 84 and entered in the Senior Race to be held the following week.

At about 7.00am, with the session well under way, Brian Jackson was negotiating the mountain section of the course and approaching Brandywell Corner in close company behind another competitor, Neville Ernest Buxton of Hull. Travelling at around 90mph, Jackson moved to the right and began to overtake him but at the same instant Buxton also moved to the right in order to take the racing line through the right hand bend immediately before the Brandywell road junction. With both riders committed to the same piece of road, there was a slight collision as the Norton caught Buxton's right leg and went out of control. Brian Jackson was thrown from the machine and came to rest lying face down in the centre of the road approximately fifty yards Ramsey side of Brandywell. Marshals went to his assistance and found that he had sustained serious injuries but there was little they could do for him other than carry him by stretcher to the marshals hut to await the arrival of a doctor. The collision had almost caused Buxton to lose control of his AJS but he managed to stay on and negotiate the following sweeping left hand bend. Realising that there must have been an incident with another competitor he pulled over to the side of the road and stopped. On walking back along the road he found the two marshals attending to Jackson. At this time the official car was being driven on its way round the course to open the roads and instructions were given for a doctor and ambulance stationed in Ramsey to be sent to Brandywell after the official car had passed. On arriving at the scene of the accident the doctor found that there was nothing that could be done for the unfortunate rider. He had succumbed to his injuries and had probably been killed instantly.

Brian Jackson, a single man, was 24 years of age. He was a surveyor and draughtsman by occupation, employed by British Railways and was a resident of Gobowen, Oswestry. He had travelled to the Isle of Man from his home the previous Saturday, intending to ride a 350cc AJS machine and the Featherbed Norton, both of which had been ridden by Roy Evans of Oswestry in the recent Ulster Grand Prix. He was physically fit and had several years riding experience, competing in trials and scrambles in addition to circuit racing. On the Isle of Man, riding a BSA machine, he had won the 1950 Junior Clubman's TT at a race average speed of 74.25mph and during the race he set a new lap record of 76.12mph. Later that same summer, riding a BSA, he had taken part in the Junior MGP only to retire with engine problems. In 1951, riding an AJS, he had been lying in fifth place at the half way stage of the Junior Manx before a leaking fuel tank forced his retirement. Riding in the Senior three days later, when lying in 6th place, a broken chain on his Norton ended his race on the fifth lap.

His funeral service, followed by interment, was held on Friday 5th September at the Preeshenlle Congregational Church, Gobowen where he had been an active church member. There were a large number of mourners at the service and over 130 floral tributes.

Ivor Kenneth ARBER   A.F.C.

Ivor Arber during the 1951 Senior MGP in which he retired on the 5th lap when lying in third place

Observers around the TT course on the morning of Tuesday 2nd September 1952 reported fine weather, dry roads and clear visibility. Excellent news for the 115 competitors gathered at the Grandstand in Douglas waiting to take advantage of a practice session for the Manx Grand Prix. Amongst them was Ivor Arber, riding a 500cc Norton machine bearing the race number 4 and entered for the Senior race to be held the following week. The racing season had started well for him as he had won the Senior Race at the North West 200 in Ireland but then in July he sustained serious injuries while racing at Skerries and had only been passed fit to race again in August.

Not long after the session commenced, Ivor Arber set off along Glencrutchery Road towards Bray Hill on his opening lap of the morning. Francis Beart, a motorcycle development engineer, owned the Norton he was riding and he had instructed him to take it slowly to Ballacraine and to check the "revs" at Sulby and again on the mountain mile. He safely made his way round the course and completed the lap in a time of approximately 28 minutes. On pulling into the pit area he reported that the machine was going well then went out again to commence his second circuit. At about 7.15am he was seen travelling at racing speed on the approach to Hillberry Corner but then, as he was negotiating the sweeping right hand bend, he appeared to glance towards the grandstand on the left. His machine then drifted on the exit of the bend and ran up the grass bank on the left for about four yards before dropping into a shallow roadside gutter. Arber had lost his grip of the handlebars and was leaning backwards on the machine as it travelled along the gutter for about twelve yards before swerving back across the road and colliding heavily with the stone wall at the entrance to Glen Dhoo Farm. The unfortunate rider was thrown from the machine and came to rest in the roadway. A doctor on duty at Hillberry was with him very quickly and gave stimulants in an effort to revive him but within minutes of the accident he had succumbed to his injuries.

Former TT rider and 350cc World Champion, Bob Foster, witnessed the incident. He stated that Ivor Arber approached the corner on the correct line and was still on the correct line when in the corner but it appeared as if he was not concentrating sufficiently to complete the turn at the speed he was travelling at.

Ivor Arber, a single man, was 35 years of age. He was a works manager by occupation and a resident of Kettering, Northants. During the war he had been a Flying Officer in the Royal Air Force Volunteer Reserve employed in No. 41 Group and was qualified to fly all types of land based aircraft. During March 1944 he undertook the dangerous task of ferrying damaged aircraft to places where repairs could be undertaken and as a result very considerable savings were made both in time and skilled man-hours. He was awarded the Air Force Cross, the Royal Air Force's highest decoration for non-combat services. On the Isle of Man he was an experienced and talented rider, having won the Senior Clubman's TT in 1951.

His funeral service was held at All Saints Church, Douglas on Friday 5th September, with the chief mourners being his father and brother together with Francis Beart. Interment followed at Douglas Borough Cemetery where the rider had expressed a wish to be buried should anything happen to him while racing on the Island.

Kenneth Richard Vidal JAMES

Ken James at Cronk ny Mona during practice for the 1952 Junior MGP

Low cloud had reduced visibility on the mountain section of the TT course on the morning of Friday 5th September 1952 and in contrast there was a risk that the rising sun would be troublesome to riders on the approach to Sulby and then through to Ramsey. Not the best of conditions for the competitors gathered at the Grandstand in Douglas waiting to participate in a practice session for the Manx Grand Prix. Amongst them was Ken James, riding a 350cc Norton machine bearing the race number 81 and entered in the Junior Race scheduled to be held the following week. This machine was owned by the development engineer Francis Beart and was to have been ridden in the Junior Race by Ivor Arber who had lost his life during morning practice three days earlier when he lost control of his 500cc Norton at Hillberry Corner.

Once the session had commenced he set off along Glencrutchery Road and completed two laps of the course, setting what was to be the fastest Junior circuit of the morning, recording a time of 27 minutes 9 seconds (83.40mph). He then began his third lap and safely negotiated his way round the course and over the mountain down to the Creg ny Baa where he pulled in and stopped. He did not get off the machine but kept the engine running as he glanced at the back wheel. A few seconds later, before anyone could speak with him, he set off once more and continued along the course at racing speed.

Meanwhile, the Marshals at Signpost Corner experienced a slight shower of rain lasting just a few minutes and a short time later, a competitor from New Zealand, Douglas Francis Jenkins, skidded and came off his machine at the corner. He had been unaware of the rain shower and was not prepared for the roads being greasy, as they did not appear wet. Minutes later, Ken James was negotiating the sweeping left hand bend at Cronk ny Mona when he suddenly lost control of the Norton and collided heavily with the stone wall on his right. Within seconds, another competitor, Thomas Walter Swarbrick, riding a 348cc AJS machine, race number 70, rounded the corner at a speed estimated at 90mph and came upon the accident scene. He was unable to avoid colliding with the Norton machine, which had come to rest in the roadway and was thrown over the wall into the field on his right as both machines caught fire. Marshals went to the immediate assistance of the two men and found Ken James lying at the side of the road but there was nothing they could do for him. He had been killed instantly. Swarbrick was relatively uninjured but badly shaken. He was conveyed by ambulance to Noble's Hospital for treatment.

Ken James, a single man, was 25 years of age. He was a salesman by occupation, employed by Bob Foster and a resident of Parkstone, Dorset. He was an experienced racing motorcyclist and in June he had finished second in the Junior Clubman's TT and third in the Senior Clubman's TT. He had been successful in circuit racing at Thruxton, Silverstone and Ibsley, where, in July, just a few weeks before travelling to the Isle of Man, he was badly shaken up after a spectacular crash on Court Corner. He had spent the previous winter on a working holiday in Australia, travelling 10,000 miles on a Triumph "Thunderbird".

His funeral service was held in Dorset and followed by interment at Parkstone Cemetery.

Michael RICHARDSON

Mike Richardson moments before his accident at the foot of Bray Hill during the 1952 Senior MGP

With an almost cloudless sky on the morning of Thursday 11th September 1952 and perfect visibility on the mountain section of the TT course, conditions were ideal for racing. At the Grandstand in Douglas the flags fluttered lazily as the eighty three competitors for the six lap Senior Manx Grand Prix prepared their machines for the start of the race. Amongst them was Mike Richardson, riding a 348cc AJS machine bearing the race number 31. Two days earlier, riding the same machine, he had been competing in the Junior Manx Grand Prix and on his approach to the Quarterbridge he had been confronted with another rider who had taken a spill and rather than run into the fallen rider, he had thrown himself bodily from his machine. On getting to his feet he found that the strain had been too much for the handlebars of the AJS and he was forced to retire from the race.

Travelling marshal Albert Moule returned to the grandstand to report that all was well round the course and that there were large crowds of spectators everywhere, including some former MGP stars such as Peter Romaine, Don Crossley, Cromie McCandless and at the Stonebreaker's Hut, Geoff Duke. At 10.45am the race began with the riders being dispatched at ten second intervals. Five minutes later, it was the turn of Mike Richardson to begin his race against the clock and he headed off along Glencrutchery Road towards Bray Hill on his opening lap. Moments later, he was seen travelling down Bray Hill and at the foot of the hill he was on the correct racing line, passing close to the kerb on the right hand side of the road when suddenly, at an estimated speed of 100mph, his machine developed a slight wobble and drifted towards the left. He tried to correct this but the machine continued towards the left hand side of the road and collided with the hedge of Mr Hinton's gardens, which ran up to the junction with Brunswick Road. The unfortunate rider was thrown and then dragged along beneath the AJS for about ten yards before they parted company, leaving him lying in the road as the machine crashed into the kerb on the right hand side of the road. The gravely injured rider was carried into Brunswick Road where two nurses arrived with a stretcher and he was moved into Queenscliffe Nursing Home. A doctor acting as medical officer at the Grandstand was sent to the scene of the incident and on finding the rider unconscious and in poor condition he ordered his immediate removal to hospital. Richardson was admitted to Noble's Hospital at 11.25am but succumbed to his injuries ten minutes later. The young rider's father had been watching the race from Kate's Cottage and had been contacted immediately after the incident occurred. Using the back roads, he was taken to the hospital but arrived a short time after his son had died.

An examination of the machine revealed that the handlebars were loose, the method of retention was most unsatisfactory as parts of two metal bushes and soft alloy sheeting had been used as packing. However, the force of the impact may have loosened the handlebars.

Mike Richardson, a single man, was 19 years of age. He was a farmer by occupation and a resident of Swaton near Sleaford, Lincolnshire.

His funeral service was held on Monday 15th September at St. Michael's Church, Swaton, which was packed with mourners. More than 60 beautiful floral tributes had been sent and most of these were conveyed to the church on a trailer drawn by a tractor.

Harry Lace STEPHEN

Harry Stephen with his Norton ready to take advantage of a practice session for the 1953 Junior TT

Unlike the mist and rain of the previous few days, there was bright sunshine across the Isle of Man on the morning of Monday 8th June 1953. Apart from a slight breeze, conditions were almost perfect for racing which was good news for the ninety nine competitors lined up along Glencrutchery Road in Douglas waiting to take part in the Junior Tourist Trophy Race. Amongst them was Harry Stephen, riding a Norton machine bearing the race number 69.

The race commenced at 10.00am and it was soon the turn of Harry Stephen to head off from the start line on his opening lap of the race. He safely made his way round the course, through Glen Helen and Kirk Michael village before negotiating Birkin's Bends at Rhencullen in close company with two other riders, one in front and one behind. Moments later, travelling at almost 100mph they were rounding the right hand bend at the foot of Rhencullen Hill when Stephen made an attempt to overtake the rider in front. He cut the bend more finely than the other two but as he did so his Norton drifted towards the leading machine and they touched. In an instant, Harry Stephen lost control of his machine as it ran along the grass bank on the right before colliding heavily with an electricity pole. Marshals went to the immediate assistance of the fallen rider but there was nothing they could do for him. He had been killed instantly.

On completion of the first circuit Rod Coleman from New Zealand, mounted on an AJS machine led the race, just a few seconds ahead of the Norton ridden by Ray Amm from Southern Rhodesia. Fergus Anderson was holding third place on a Guzzi. During the third lap Coleman retired at Glen Vine with a split oil tank and Amm moved into the lead ahead of his Norton teammate, the Australian rider, Ken Kavanagh with Anderson maintaining third spot. The fourth lap saw tragedy strike the race for a second time when 29 year old Thomas Walter Swarbrick, riding an AJS machine, race number 79, lost control of his machine and crashed at "Westwood House", Kirk Michael. The unfortunate rider from Inskip near Preston, Lancashire was killed instantly. By the end of the fourth lap Kavanagh led the race with a one second advantage over Amm and as the race continued there was never more than a few seconds between the two riders with both shattering the Junior lap record held by Geoff Duke since 1951. At the end of the seven laps, with a race average speed of 90.52mph, the race went to Ray Amm who finished 9.6 seconds ahead of Kavanagh with Anderson third.

Harry Stephen was 37 years of age. He was an estate agent by occupation and a resident of Coventry where he lived with his wife Edna and their three children, Michael aged 10, Malcolm aged 9 and Hilary aged 6. He had considerable experience in motorcycle racing having taken up the sport as a hobby with his friend Wilmot Evans. His first appearance on the Isle of Man was at the 1950 MGP meeting where, riding an AJS, he achieved 7th place in the Junior Race and was rewarded with a replica. He returned to the Island the following June and took 28th place in the Senior TT and 18th place in the Lightweight Race.

His funeral service was held in Coventry and was followed by cremation at Canley Crematorium. Although Harry had been born and bred in Manchester, his father was from Ramsey in the Isle of Man.

47

Thomas Walter SWARBRICK

Thomas Walter Swarbrick ready to participate in a practice session for the 1953 Junior TT

Unlike the mist and rain of the previous few days, there was bright sunshine across the Isle of Man on the morning of Monday 8th June 1953. Apart from a slight breeze, conditions were almost perfect for racing which was good news for the ninety-nine competitors lined up along Glencrutchery Road in Douglas waiting to take part in the Junior Tourist Trophy Race. Amongst them was Thomas Walter Swarbrick, riding a 350cc AJS machine bearing the race number 79. Geoff Duke, winner of the Junior Race in 1952 and the holder of the lap record, was a non-starter for the race due to problems with his AJS machine.

The race was to be marred by tragedy on the opening lap, when, at about 10.15am, 37 year old Harry Stephen, from Coventry, was killed instantly after his Norton touched another machine at the bottom of Rhencullen Hill then collided with an electricity pole.

At the end of the first lap New Zealander, Rod Coleman, on an AJS, led the race by a few seconds from Southern Rhodesian, Ray Amm, on a Norton with Fergus Anderson on board a Guzzi in third place. On completion of the third circuit, Coleman had retired at Glen Vine with a split oil tank and Ray Amm had moved into the lead ahead of his Norton teammate, the Australian rider, Ken Kavanagh with Anderson maintaining third place.

At about 11.30am, during the fourth lap of the race, Swarbrick was seen approaching the sweeping left hand corner at Ballalonna Bridge, Kirk Michael and although he was not travelling excessively fast for the corner he was wide of the conventional racing line taken by the riders. He was then seen to put his left foot down and this threw him even further off the racing line. The AJS machine mounted the footpath just beyond "Westwood House" on the right hand side of the road then struck a thorn hedge. A cloud of dust and debris shot up in the air and the unfortunate rider was thrown into the road. Marshals went to his assistance but there was nothing they could do for him. He had been killed instantly.

By the end of the fourth lap Kavanagh led the race with a one second advantage over Amm and as the race continued there was never more than a few seconds between the two riders who both shattered the Junior lap record held by Geoff Duke since 1951. At the end of the seven laps, with a race average speed of 90.52mph, the race went to Ray Amm who finished 9.6 seconds ahead of Kavanagh with Anderson in third place.

Thomas Walter Swarbrick was 29 years of age. He was a farmer by occupation and a resident of Inskip near Preston, Lancashire where he lived with his wife Alice and their four young children, Jennifer aged 6, Robert aged 3, Cathleen aged 2 and Rosemary aged 10 months. He made his debut on the TT course in 1949 when he finished 12th in the Lightweight Clubman's TT. Then in 1951 he finished 11th in the Senior Clubman's TT and returned a few months later for the MGP, riding an AJS he finished 8th and won a silver replica. During practice for the 1952 MGP he had escaped serious injury at Cronk ny Mona after his machine collided with the wrecked Norton of Ken James who had been killed there seconds earlier.

His funeral service was held at St. Peter's Church, Inskip on Thursday 11th June and followed by interment.

48

At the end of the opening lap Les Graham exits Governor's Dip during the fateful 1953 Senior TT

The final word from the weathermen on the morning of Friday 12th June 1953, promised that the beautiful sunshine would last all day and that the 10 knot wind would rapidly blow away the last wisps of cloud from the mountain. The Senior Tourist Trophy Race was expected to provide the tremendous crowds of spectators around the course with a race-long duel between the Norton's of Ray Amm and Ken Kavanagh against the Italian multi-cylinder Gilera's ridden by Geoff Duke and Reg Armstrong and the MV Agusta in the capable hands of Les Graham who had won the 125cc Lightweight TT the day before.

At 10.30am the first of the 77 competitors, the Australian Tony McAlpine, was sent on his way towards Bray Hill and the remainder of the field followed at ten second intervals. Programmes and handkerchiefs were waved as Les Graham, race number 18, streaked away from the start line on the bright red MV machine. At 10.45am, as the last man moved off, reports from Ramsey indicated that Les Graham had already passed a number of riders who had started ahead of him.

As the riders passed through on completion of the first lap, Les Graham was now the fourth man on the road and recorded an average lap speed of 93.83mph which, on corrected time, placed him in second position, half a minute behind Geoff Duke with Ray Amm holding third.

Moments later, as Les Graham came out of the dip at the foot of Bray Hill on his second lap, his machine left the ground as it hit the top of the rise opposite the junction of Brunswick Road. On landing, the front wheel developed a wobble and despite his best efforts to regain control, the wobble became worse and the machine mounted the pavement on the left side of the road. The left handlebar scraped along the garden wall of the house "Meersbrook" before the unfortunate rider was thrown over the front of the machine and came to rest near to the gate pillar of "Rookwood House" on the right hand side of the road while his machine came to rest in the roadway 80 yards further on and burst into flames. Marshals went to his assistance but there was nothing they could do for him. He had been killed instantly.

The race continued and the honours went to Ray Amm of Southern Rhodesia despite coming off his Norton machine at Sarah's Cottage on his last lap. Jack Brett brought his Norton machine home in second place with Reg Armstrong finishing in third place on the Gilera.

Les Graham was 41 years of age. He was a professional racing motorcyclist by occupation and a resident of Chislehurst, Kent where he lived with his wife Edna and their two sons, Stuart aged 11 and Christopher aged 7. He made his TT debut in 1938, finishing 12th in the Lightweight Race, riding an OK Supreme. During World War II he flew Lancaster bombers and was awarded the prestigious Distinguished Flying Cross. After the war, he returned to motorcycle racing and in 1949 went on to become the first 500cc World Champion.

His funeral service was held on Thursday 18th June at the Cemetery in Landican Lane, Birkenhead and followed by cremation. A considerable number of mourners were unable to find room in the small chapel and they formed a supplementary open-air congregation, keeping in touch with the service through the open church doors.

Geoffrey James WALKER

An action shot of Geoff Walker during the fateful 1953 Senior TT

The final word from the weathermen on Friday 12th June 1953, promised that the beautiful sunshine would last all day and that the 10 knot wind would rapidly blow away the last wisps of cloud from the mountain. The Senior Tourist Trophy Race was expected to provide the tremendous crowds of spectators around the course with a race-long duel between the Norton's of Ray Amm and Ken Kavanagh against the Italian multi-cylinder Gilera's ridden by Geoff Duke and Reg Armstrong and the MV Agusta in the hands of Les Graham who had won the 125cc Lightweight TT the day before.

The grandstand was completely full as the National Anthem greeted the arrival of the Lieutenant Governor. A minute later the siren signalled that the riders could take their machines from the storage marquee and for the following fifteen minutes Glencrutchery Road echoed to the sounds of machines being warmed up in readiness for the race. At 10.30am the first of the seventy-seven riders, Tony McAlpine, was sent on his way towards Bray Hill and the remainder of the field followed at ten second intervals. Amongst them was the Australian rider Geoff Walker, a newcomer to the TT course, riding a 500cc Norton machine bearing the race number 53.

On completion of the first circuit it was Geoff Duke who led the race, having broken his own two year old record by 17 seconds. Les Graham was in second place, 38 seconds behind Duke with Ray Amm third and Ken Kavanagh fourth. However, shortly after commencing his second lap of the race, Les Graham was killed instantly when he lost control of his machine on Quarterbridge Road. On the fourth lap, race leader Geoff Duke came off at the Quarterbridge and was unable to continue leaving Ray Amm to move into first place.

Geoff Walker had been safely negotiating his way round the course over the first three laps of the race and was just over half way round on his fourth lap when he was seen approaching the "S" bends at Kerrowmoar but then as he rounded the first bend, the left hander, the front wheel of his Norton began to wobble. In trying to regain control of the machine he drifted off the racing line for the right hand bend immediately following and as a result the Norton mounted the footpath on the left, hit the hedge and then collided heavily with a tree. Marshals went to the immediate assistance of the unfortunate rider who had come to rest in the roadway but there was nothing that could be done for him. He had been killed instantly.

The race continued and Ray Amm, despite falling from his machine at Sarah's Cottage on his last lap, went on to win from Jack Brett (Norton) in second place and Reg Armstrong on the Italian Gilera in third place.

Geoffrey James Walker, a single man, was 23 years of age. He was a surveyor by occupation and a resident of Launceston, Tasmania, Australia. Although still relatively young, he had already shown his ability by achieving a number of racing successes in Australia

During his time on the Island he had been staying at Mount Rule, Braddan and following his funeral service he was interred at the nearby Braddan Cemetery.

HOW T.T. RIDER DIED
No Blame on following Competitor

A 25 years old Bristol transport driver, who was killed at T.T. practice twelve days ago, was run over by an oncoming rider.

But he was already dead, according to medical evidence.

Headline from Isle of Man newspaper reporting on the inquest of Ray Ashford

Weather conditions on the Isle of Man were fairly miserable on the morning of Monday 7th June 1954, it was dull and overcast but the roads round the TT course were almost dry following the rain that fell the previous day. Not the best of reports for the competitors gathered at the Grandstand in Douglas waiting to take advantage of a practice session for the Clubman's TT Races. Amongst them was Ray Ashford, a newcomer to the Island, riding a 350cc BSA machine bearing the race number 63 and entered in the Junior Clubman's race to be held later in the week. The riders were warned of damp patches on the roads and that visibility on the mountain road was down to twenty yards in places.

The poor light delayed the start of the session for a short time but then at 4.55am the first two men headed off on their opening lap. Not long after their departure it was the turn of Ray Ashford to set off along Glencrutchery Road towards Bray Hill and he safely made his way round to complete two laps of the course in times of 35.50 and 35.08 before commencing his third lap of the morning. At about 6.15am, a Marshal saw Ashford approaching the bends immediately before Laurel Bank, he was alone on the road and travelling at racing speed when a loud shrieking noise was heard coming from his machine as if the engine was seizing. The BSA then skidded on the road surface for a distance of 123 feet before colliding heavily with the rock face on the left side of the road. Ashford was thrown off and came to rest in the roadway along with his machine. Seconds later, Fred Wallis, travelling at a speed of between 80 and 90mph, came upon the scene of the accident and was confronted with the fallen rider and machine lying across the road. He instinctively straightened up and went to pass on the left but at the same time he realised that his path was blocked. There was just one small gap available to him, between the motionless rider and the edge of the pavement on the right. He made the split second decision to make for the gap and banked over very hard to his right but, with the frame of his BSA scraping the road surface, he was unable to avoid colliding with the fallen rider. His machine went out of control and he was thrown into the road. Marshals went to the assistance of the two men and found that there was nothing they could do for Ashford. He had been killed instantly. As a result of the injuries he sustained Fred Wallis was unable to take part in the race three days later.

After all the facts were put before the Coroner of Inquests there were many questions left unanswered. As to whether the engine of the BSA had seized or not was left undetermined and as a result it was unknown if the accident was caused by mechanical failure or by an error of judgment by the unfortunate rider. A doctor suggested that he was probably dead when struck by the machine of Fred Wallis. The Coroner exonerated Wallis, saying, "You are in no way responsible for this man's death".

Raymond Jeffrey Ashford, a single man, was 25 years of age. He was a transport driver by occupation and a resident of Redland, Bristol. Although this was to be his first road race experience he had been racing since 1951 and had considerable short circuit experience at places such as Silverstone and Blandford.

His funeral service was held on Monday 14th June and followed by interment at Canford Cemetery, Bristol.

Simon Ernest Edward SANDYS-WINSCH

Simon Sandys-Winsch on his Velocette at Quarterbridge during the fateful 1954 Senior TT

Low cloud and mist on the morning of Friday 18th June 1954 had reduced visibility on the mountain section of the TT course but the weather reports suggested that this would clear within an hour or so. With this in mind, the decision was made to postpone the start of the Senior Tourist Trophy race until conditions had improved. As predicted, the mist cleared and shortly before twelve noon the field of eighty competitors lined up along Glencrutchery Road in Douglas waiting for the race to commence. Amongst them was Simon Sandys-Winsch, a newcomer to the TT course, riding a 348cc Velocette machine bearing the race number 27. Earlier in the week he had taken part in the Junior TT but had been forced to retire on the first lap due to clutch problems with his machine.

Once the race began it was not long before it was the turn of Sandys-Winsch to begin his race against the clock and he set off towards Bray Hill on his opening lap of the race. A few minutes later, having safely made his way through Union Mills, Glen Vine and Crosby, he was seen approaching the Highlander at racing speed but as his machine went over the "hump" in the road it developed a slight wobble. He fought to regain full control but just when it seemed he had been successful the machine suddenly veered off to the left and collided with the boundary wall of the bungalow "Killard". Having been thrown from the machine Sandys-Winsch came to rest in the centre of the road while the Velocette had disintegrated as it continued under its own momentum for a further 40 to 50 yards before coming to rest on the right hand side of the road.

Conditions at the scene were described as near perfect, there was little breeze, the roads at that point were dry and there was little or no sun to impede the rider's vision. The gravely injured rider was carried by stretcher back along the course to Crosby village and then conveyed by ambulance to Noble's Hospital where, on his arrival at 1.10pm, it was found that he had succumbed to his injuries during the journey from Crosby.

Geoff Duke led the race at the end of the first lap but his average speed of 88.18mph showed how poor the conditions had become. Ray Amm was second with Reg Armstrong in third place. On completion of the second lap Duke held a mere two second advantage over Amm, then, at the end of the third lap Amm took the lead as Duke pulled into the pits to refuel. Controversially, following reports that visibility on the mountain was back down to 20 yards, the race was stopped after just four laps and Ray Amm was declared the race winner.

Simon Sandys-Winsch, a single man, was 28 years of age. He was a Corporal with the Royal Air Force and was stationed at Swanton Morley, Norfolk. However, during the war he had served with the Royal Navy and for a time he had been the youngest midshipman in the service. He saw action in the Mediterranean and in the Atlantic. He had considerable experience of motorcycle racing on the Continent but one of his most memorable moments came during the 1951 Dutch TT meeting at Assen where, after a delayed start, he had made his way through the field to take fifth position in the 350cc race and was the first of the privateers to complete the race.

His funeral service was held at Hethersett Church, Norfolk and followed by interment.

Ronald BUTLER

Ron Butler at Hillberry during the fateful 1954 Junior MGP

Apart from some low cloud on the mountain, conditions were perfect for racing on the morning of Tuesday 7th September 1954. At 10.00am three strident blasts from the klaxons signalled that the roads were closed and a short time later the procession of 75 competitors and their machines arrived at the Grandstand on Glencrutchery Road in Douglas in readiness for the start of the Junior Manx Grand Prix. Among them was Ron Butler, a newcomer to the TT course, riding a 348cc AJS 7R machine bearing the race number 63. On the Thursday of practice week he had crashed this machine at Sarah's Cottage having gone into the corner too fast and on the wrong line. After mounting the low earth bank on the left he had come to rest below the road and within a few feet of a barbed wire chicken run. He commented to a marshal and spectator, "That wasn't very good, was it?" Declining offers of tea and blankets he enlisted their help to return the slightly damaged machine back to the road whereupon he completed the lap and then did another on his Triumph, which was entered in the Senior Race.

During the third lap of the six lap race, the Deputy Clerk of the Course received a report from a police sergeant at Glen Helen that Butler wobbled noticeably every time he passed that point, possibly due to faulty front suspension. Orders were sent to Ramsey for him to be stopped and the travelling marshal was to examine the machine. At 12.20pm, the travelling marshal reported back that he had inspected the machine and had found everything in order. He added that the front suspension was "a bit flabby", but this did not make the machine unsafe. On completion of his third lap of the race Butler stopped at the pits to refuel, he was in good spirits and had no complaints. At this time he was holding 15th position in the race.

At about 12.45pm, fifteen miles into his fourth lap of the race, Butler was seen approaching Birkin's Bends at Kirk Michael but he was on the wrong racing line, positioned on the right hand side of the road whereas he should have been tight on the left hand side. Travelling at racing speed, his machine struck the kerb on the left outside the house "Broomville" then shot across the roadway and collided heavily with the grass bank on the opposite side of the road. Butler was thrown from the AJS and came to rest in the roadway. A marshal pulled him to the side of the road to protect him from approaching machines but there was nothing more that could be done for him. He succumbed to his injuries within minutes of the incident.

The race was won by Derek Ennett (AJS), the first Manx born rider to win a Manx Grand Prix, and he set a new race record of 86.33mph. Dave Chadwick (Norton) was second and John Hartle (Norton) finished in third place.

Ron Butler was 36 years of age. He was a laboratory tester by occupation and a resident of Blacon, Chester where he lived with his wife and four children, Peter aged 12, Anne aged 7, Margaret aged 6 and Janette aged 3. He was a competent motorcyclist, having competed in short circuit races for several years. While on the Island, Butler had been staying at the Douglas Holiday Camp. When his friends there tried to make arrangements for Mrs. Butler to travel to the Island, the Camp authorities took the task off their hands and arranged for the provision of aircraft seats and a car to meet her at the airport.

His funeral service was held on Saturday 11th September at St. Chads Church, Blacon.

Eric William MILTON

Eric Milton during practice for the 1955 Senior MGP

Conditions were fine on the morning of Saturday 3rd September 1955 and reports from around the TT course indicated that the roads were dry. Welcome news for the 130 competitors congregating at the Grandstand in Douglas waiting to take advantage of a practice session for the Manx Grand Prix. Amongst them, in only his second season of motorcycle racing, was Eric William Milton, riding a 499cc BSA machine bearing the race number 84, which had been entered in the Senior Race to be held the following Thursday. He had already qualified for the race during earlier official practice sessions and had also completed several unofficial circuits of the course on a touring machine.

Shortly after 6.00am, Milton set off along Glencrutchery Road towards Bray Hill on his opening lap of the morning and safely made his way round the course back to Douglas. He appeared to be travelling well and gave no signals to his assistants as he crossed the line to commence his second lap.

At about 7.00am, having negotiated his way through Union Mills, Glen Helen and Kirk Michael village, he was seen approaching Birkin's Bends, fourteen miles into his second circuit. He was travelling at racing speed but well off the usual racing line as riders usually kept to the left side of the road by Ballarhennie Cottage but he was about three quarters of the way across the road near to the right hand hedge. He did not shut off but carried straight on and as a consequence, his machine drifted to the left and struck the kerb at the gable end of the house "Hazel Dene" then shot diagonally across the road and caught the opposite hedge with a glancing blow. As the BSA travelled along the hedge he struggled desperately to regain control but was unable to do so before the machine collided heavily with the low garden wall outside "Rhencullen Cottage". At this point he was thrown into the air and both he and his machine tumbled back across the road and collided with the wall on the Michael side of "Rhencullen House". The unfortunate rider came to rest close to the left hand kerb about fifteen yards beyond the entrance to the house. Marshals went to his immediate assistance but there was nothing they could do for him. He had been killed instantly.

W.L. Shimmin, Chief Public Service Vehicle Examiner for the Isle of Man Highway and Transport Board, later examined the wrecked BSA. He concluded that all the damage to the machine had been caused during the crash and nothing was found to suggest that a mechanical failure had been a contributory factor.

Eric William Milton, a single man, was 23 years of age. He was a maintenance engineer by occupation and a resident of Enfield, Middlesex. He had been riding motorcycles since he was eighteen and had almost two seasons experience of racing, mostly on short circuits in England such as Brands Hatch, Silverstone and Ringwood. Although he was a newcomer to the TT course he had competed on the Isle of Man the previous year when, as a passenger to Ernie Young in the Sidecar Race, which was held over the "Clypse" course, they had brought their Triumph powered outfit home in 15th place.

His funeral service was held in the Isle of Man and followed by interment at Braddan Cemetery.

James Watson DAVIE

James Davie pictured during the fateful 1955 Junior MGP

Blue skies and dry roads was the forecast for the Isle of Man on the morning of Tuesday 6th September 1955. Perfect racing conditions for the field of 103 competitors entered in the Junior Manx Grand Prix. They arrived at the start area on Glencrutchery Road in Douglas at 10.15am, having ridden in procession from the garage where the machines had been stored overnight. Before lining up for the start of the race they were engaged for about 15 minutes, ensuring that fuel tanks were topped up and dealing with any mechanical problems. Amongst them was James "Ginger" Davie, riding an AJS machine bearing the race number 115. He had set the fastest time in this class during practice and was a likely race winner. At 10.45am a maroon was fired and the first man was sent on his way towards the daunting descent of Bray Hill with the remaining riders following at ten-second intervals. It was a full fifteen minutes before Davie received his starting orders, beginning his race against the clock. Without penalty, Alan Holmes, number 42, was given permission by the Clerk of the Course to start last in order to give him more time to overcome a mechanical problem. On completion of the opening lap Davie had recorded an average speed of 85.57mph, which put him in fourth place, eight seconds behind Gavin Dunlop (AJS) and thirty three seconds behind the race leader Geoff Tanner (Norton).

Twenty-four miles into his second lap Davie had passed through Parliament Square in Ramsey and negotiated the Hairpin bend before beginning the mountain climb. About 150 yards ahead of him was another competitor, number 53, Lawrence Frederick Ivin, a BBC Engineer from Ludlow, Shropshire. Unseen by Davie, Ivin lost control of his machine on the exit of the left hand bend immediately before the Gooseneck and was thrown into the grass bank on his right. His machine struck the bank and bounced back into the roadway. Moments later, Davie negotiated the bend travelling fast but perfectly steady until confronted by Ivin's BSA machine lying across the road about twenty yards ahead of him. He attempted to swerve but was unable to avoid colliding with the fallen machine. He was thrown from the AJS and came to rest, unconscious, in the centre of the road where he was quickly attended to by Marshals and a doctor who had been on duty at the Gooseneck. The gravely injured rider succumbed to his injuries in the ambulance transporting him to Ramsey Cottage Hospital.

Geoff Tanner went on to win the race with an average speed of 88.46mph, a new race record. Alan Holmes, who had started at the rear of the field, finished in second place with fellow Manxman Jackie Wood (BSA) securing third place.

James Davie was 31 years of age (born 24.6.24). He was a public works plant fitter by occupation and a resident of Kelty, Fifeshire where he lived with his wife Lottie who had been on the Island at the time of the race. He had considerable racing experience, having started his career just after the war when he took up "trials" and "scrambles" but gave these up in 1947 in favour of speed racing. His numerous Scottish successes included the 350cc Scottish Championship in 1952. On the Isle of Man, he had finished 3rd in the 1954 Junior Clubman's TT and in September the same year he had finished 12th in the Junior MGP.

His funeral service was followed by interment at Abbots Hall Cemetery, Kirkcaldy.

David MERRIDAN

David Merridan in action on his BSA during practice for the 1956 Senior Clubman's TT

Weather conditions on the evening of Monday 11th June 1956 were almost perfect for racing, visibility was clear and the roads around the TT course were dry. Good news for those competitors gathered in the area of the Grandstand in Douglas waiting to take advantage of the second practice session for the Clubman's TT Races. Amongst them was David Merridan riding a newly purchased 499cc BSA Gold Star machine bearing the race number 32 and entered in the Senior Clubman's Race to be held the following week. Earlier in the day, following the morning practice session, he had remarked to his friend and mechanic, Albert Edward Jeffrey, that he had a tendency to over throttle at Ballaugh Bridge before the rear wheel touched the ground again.

At about 6.30pm he set off along Glencrutchery Road to commence his opening lap of the evening. At the end of the circuit he stopped at the pits to replace a plug then went out again to commence his second lap of the evening. Having safely negotiated his way round the course without any apparent problems, he went straight through the "start" area to commence his third circuit.

A short time later, at about 7.50pm, Merridan was seen approaching Ballaugh Bridge at an exceptionally fast speed. His line for the bridge was not the usual racing line; he was much too close to the north side of the bridge and consequently was passing over at its highest peak. This fact, together with his high speed, caused the machine to jump high into the air for a distance of 15 to 20 yards and when it landed on the front wheel it began at once to wobble with Merridan, who was still completely astride the machine, fighting hard to regain control but before he could do so, the machine crashed heavily into the straw bags at the front of Mr. J.J. Radcliffe's store which faced the bridge. The unfortunate rider was thrown against the unprotected part of the stone wall at the extreme outside edge of the shop and came to rest in the roadway. Marshals went to his immediate assistance but there was nothing that could be done for him. He had been killed instantly.

Following the incident, Mr. Tom Sheppard, a Scrutineer employed by the ACU, carried out an examination on the BSA machine. He found extensive damage to the forks and front of the machine but the brakes, steering and controls were in perfect order. He could find nothing that may have been a contributory factor as to the cause of the accident.

David Merridan, a single man, was 28 years of age. He was a milk roundsman by occupation and a resident of High Wycombe, Buckinghamshire. He had considerable experience of motorcycling and had taken up racing just over three years earlier, competing at Silverstone, Thruxton and Brands Hatch. On the Isle of Man, riding a Triumph, he was 20th in the 1955 Senior Clubman's Race, which was held on the Clypse Course. He had not raced on the TT circuit before but had visited the Isle of Man for the previous five or six years.

His funeral service was held at The Baptist Chapel, Little Kingshill, Great Missenden, Buckinghamshire and followed by interment.

Peter George KIRKHAM

Peter Kirkham at Union Mills during practice for the 1956 Junior Clubman's TT

There were mixed weather conditions across the Isle of Man on the morning of Thursday 14th June 1956. The sunshine was strong and yet clouds were building up over the hills and there was a cool breeze blowing. However, the roads were dry for the competitors lined up along Glencrutchery Road in Douglas waiting for the Junior Clubman's Tourist Trophy Race to commence. Of the original entry of 68 there were now 55 riders and amongst them was Peter Kirkham, riding a 350cc BSA Gold Star machine bearing the race number 1. He had completed eight official circuits of the course during practice.

There was an extremely poor attendance at the Grandstand with less than one hundred spectators gathered to watch as, on the stroke of 11.00am, the race began with riders being dispatched in groups of four and at thirty second intervals. Peter Kirkham was among the first group to receive the signal to begin the first lap of three and set off towards Bray Hill. A few riders met with difficulties on the start line due to having to use the kick-start and Fred Wallis, one of the leading men in practice, had to work on his BSA before he could get away.

Peter Kirkham safely made his way through Glen Helen, Kirk Michael and Ramsey before the climb up onto the mountain section of the course. Observers at Waterworks Corner, just short of 25 miles into the opening lap of the race, saw that Bernard Codd, riding a BSA, was the first man on the road then came Peter Kirkham followed by W.D. Fellows, also riding a BSA machine and bearing the race number 2. On leaving the tricky right hand corner, Kirkham was then seen travelling at racing speed as he began to negotiate the following fast left hander at Tower Bends but, on the exit of the corner, he found himself running tight against the wall on his right for a distance of 30 to 40 yards before colliding heavily with a roadside tree. The unfortunate rider was thrown from the machine and came to rest at the side of the road near to the tree while the BSA crashed through an open gateway and into a field. Moments later, Fellows rounded the corner and saw Kirkham in the roadway with the leaves still falling from the tree that he had struck. Marshals went to his aid but there was nothing they could do for him. He had been killed instantly.

Bernard Codd, making his first appearance on the Island, went on to win the race with an average race speed of 82.02mph. John Eckhart was the second man home with Alan Shepherd finishing in third place. The rider W.D. Fellows went on to finish in 25th place. Codd went on to make it a double, winning the Senior Clubman's Race later in the week. Having first started in 1947, this was to be the last year that the Clubman's Races were held.

Tom Shepherd, official Scrutineer for the Auto-Cycle Union, later examined Kirkham's BSA and found no evidence to suggest that a mechanical failure had contributed to the accident.

Peter Kirkham, a single man, was 24 years of age. He was a motor mechanic by occupation and a resident of Llanymynech, Montgomeryshire. He had considerable racing experience and had finished 18th in the Junior Clubman's Race over the Clypse Course in 1955.

His funeral service was held at Maesbrook Chapel near Llanymynech and followed by interment.

Maurice William SALUZ

Maurice Saluz during practice for the 1956 Senior MGP

Apart from the brilliant rising sun and a few damp patches on the roads around the TT course, conditions were almost perfect for racing on the morning of Friday 31st August 1956. At the grandstand on Glencrutchery Road in Douglas a total of 111 competitors gathered in readiness to take advantage of a practice session for the Manx Grand Prix. Amongst them was Maurice "Mog" Saluz, a newcomer to the TT Course, riding a 500cc Norton machine bearing the race number 98 and entered in the Senior race to be held the following Thursday. All competitors were warned prior to the commencement of practice that the sun might be troublesome, especially on their second laps. This was in addition to receiving a letter when they arrived on the Isle of Man, warning of these dangers.

Saluz set off towards Bray Hill and then safely negotiated his way round the mountain course back to Douglas and passed through the start area at 6.43am commencing his second lap of the morning. During the course of the session, because of the strong rising sun, the flagman at Sulby Bridge received instructions from the Practice Controller to position himself at a point approximately 300 yards before Sulby Bridge and to signal approaching riders with a yellow flag, which indicated "proceed with caution".

At about 6.55am, Maurice Saluz was on his second lap of the morning and just over half way round the course as he approached Sulby Bridge with the rising sun directly ahead of him and appeared to acknowledge the yellow flag by slightly raising his left hand. He was on the correct racing line as he drew nearer to the bridge but travelling far too fast to negotiate the tricky right hand corner. He seemed to realise his predicament and gave the impression that he was making for the escape road. Unfortunately, when about 30 feet from the slip road his machine skidded and went from beneath him. He held onto the machine as it slid along the roadway before colliding heavily with the stone pillar on the north side of the slip road. The wrecked Norton came to rest against the hedge just beyond the pillar while Saluz had been thrown back into the roadway. The police officer on duty at that location went immediately to his aid but there was nothing that could be done for him. He had been killed instantly.

W.A. Rowell, Scrutineer for the Manx Motor Cycle Club, later examined the machine and he found no evidence to suggest that a mechanical failure may have contributed towards this accident.

Maurice Saluz was 25 years of age. He was employed as a radial driller at the Leavesden factory of the De Havilland Engine Company and was a resident of Edgeware, Middlesex where he lived with his wife Babs. Although this was the first time he had entered the Manx Grand Prix, he had gained racing experience on short circuits in England such as Brands Hatch, Silverstone, Cadwell Park and Crystal Palace since he took up the sport in the spring of 1955. He had completed nine official practice laps of the TT course prior to his death. His wife had been watching the practices from the grandstand and collapsed when the news of her husband's death was broken to her.

His funeral service was held on 5th September and followed by committal at Golders Green Crematorium.

Charles Francis SALT

Charlie Salt at the foot of Bray Hill during the fateful 1957 Senior TT

Exceptionally large numbers of spectators positioned themselves around the TT course on the morning of Friday 7th June 1957, the final day of the Golden Jubilee TT meeting. The weather was fine, the roads were dry and visibility was clear for the seventy-nine competitors assembled on Glencrutchery Road in Douglas waiting to participate in the Senior Tourist Trophy race. Amongst them was race veteran Charlie Salt, riding a 500cc BSA machine bearing the race number 2. At 10.45am there was silence as the warming up period ended and the riders shut down their engines before lining up for the start of the race.

At 11.00am, the flag dropped and the first man to push away was Jack Brett followed ten seconds later by Charlie Salt. History was to be made at the end of the second lap when it was learned that Bob McIntyre, riding a Gilera, had recorded a lap at 101.03mph.

At about 2.05pm, on the eighth and final lap of the race, Charlie Salt, lying in 17th place, was seen approaching the right hand bend at "Gorse Lea" when, without warning, the engine of his BSA machine suddenly seized and the rear wheel locked solid. The rear tyre squealed on the road surface as he struggled to maintain control of the machine but it went from beneath him. He kept his grip on the handlebars as the machine slid along the road and collided heavily with a concrete post situated on the left. There was a cloud of dust and debris as the post was torn from the ground and the unfortunate rider was thrown over a low stone wall. Marshals went to his assistance and found him suspended between the wall and a beech tree while his BSA came to rest in the roadway a few yards further along the course. The gravely injured rider was found to be unconscious and was soon attended to by a doctor who had been called from Ballacraine. For a short time he regained consciousness and asked what had happened. At 2.45pm an ambulance collected him and conveyed him to Noble's Hospital where he was admitted at 3.30pm. However, by this time he was deeply unconscious and in severe shock. Despite strenuous efforts by medical staff, they were unable to save him and he succumbed to his injuries at 4.40pm that same day.

After three hours of racing, the flying Scot, Bob McIntyre, won the race with an average speed of 98.99mph. Second place went to John Surtees and Bob Brown took third spot.

Charlie Salt was 43 years of age. He was a motorcycle designer with BSA and a resident of Streetly, Staffordshire where he lived with his wife and their son aged 7 years. They had been watching the race from the grandstand. He had a wealth of racing experience since his first race in 1939 and his debut on the TT course came at the MGP in 1946 when, riding a Norton, he finished sixth in the Junior and ninth in the Senior. At the Manx the following year he was fourth in the Senior. Riding a Velocette in the 1948 MGP he finished fourth in the Junior but glory almost came his way in the Senior when, having set the fastest lap of the race, he was leading on the last lap until the engine of his Norton expired at Governor's Bridge. Rather than retire, he pushed the heavy machine along Glencrutchery Road to the finish line and took third place.

His funeral service was held at Loscoe Parish Church near Heanor, Derbyshire on Wednesday 12th June and followed by interment.

John Frederick ANTRAM

John Antram astride his AJS ready to take part in a practice session for the 1958 Senior TT

Undeterred by the high winds blowing across the Isle of Man on the evening of Monday 26th May 1958, more than eighty competitors gathered at the Grandstand in Douglas ready to take advantage of the second practice session for the Tourist Trophy races. Amongst them was the New Zealand rider John Antram, riding a 348cc AJS machine bearing the race number 81 and entered for the Senior Race to be held the following week. He had completed one official lap of the course during the opening practice session that morning.

First man away was Ewan McHaldane on his Senior Norton, closely followed by John Hartle and John Surtees on their Junior MV's. At Braddan Bridge Surtees had the Marshals jumping as he approached the bends too fast and took to the slip road. With a grin on his face he rejoined the course and set off again with the MV on full song. The grandstand had been full of spectators when the session began but showers of rain later sent them scurrying to the refreshments tents.

On receiving his signal to start, John Antram set off along Glencrutchery Road towards the daunting descent of Bray Hill on his opening lap of the evening. He safely negotiated his way round the course through Union Mills, Glen Helen, Sulby and then into Ramsey with 23 miles behind him. Just seconds after leaving Parliament Square and travelling at racing speed he was seen approaching the tricky right hand bend at Cruickshank's Corner situated at the foot of Mayhill. Some observers thought he was on the wrong racing line and others thought he had left it too late to peel off for the corner but for whatever reason his machine struck the kerb on the left and mounted the footpath outside the house "Cronk Brae" before both rider and machine struck the stone pillar of an unused gateway. The unfortunate rider was thrown from the AJS as it bounced back across the road, hit the opposite wall and burst into flames. As he lay in the roadway petrol blazed around his legs but did not set fire to his leathers. Though prompt action was taken by the flag marshals to warn other riders, a number of competitors could not pull up in time and rode through the wall of flames and smoke. Eventually, the red flag was shown to stop oncoming riders while officials extinguished the fire. The gravely injured rider was carried to the side of the road where a doctor administered artificial respiration in an effort to revive him before he was taken by ambulance to Ramsey Cottage Hospital. Sadly, shortly after admission, he succumbed to his injuries.

Angus Stanley Herbert, Chief Scrutineer for the Auto-Cycle Union, later examined the AJS and found no evidence to suggest that a mechanical failure had contributed to this accident.

John Frederick Antram, a single man, was 22 years of age. He was a painter and decorator by occupation and resident of Te Puke, New Zealand. He had been racing for three years and in 1957 had finished 5th in the 250cc class in the New Zealand TT. His principal successes had been in trials and scrambles in which he had collected 18 trophies. He was a keen photographer and enjoyed metalwork as a hobby.

His funeral service was followed by interment at St. Nicholas's Church, Brighton, England. The Antram family having a long association with that church before emigrating to New Zealand.

Desmond Douglas WOLFF

Des Wolff pictured during the opening lap of the fateful 1958 Senior TT

The rain that had been forecast failed to appear on Friday 6th June 1958 and from an original entry of eighty one there were seventy four competitors lined up along Glencrutchery Road in Douglas awaiting the start of the Senior Tourist Trophy Race. However, one competitor suffered gearbox problems just before the start, which further reduced the field to seventy three. Amongst them was Des Wolff, an experienced competitor but a newcomer to the TT course. He was riding a 500cc Norton machine bearing the race number 80. Four days earlier, he had taken part in the Junior TT but had been forced to retire during the race with engine problems.

The race began at 11.00am and they all got away well, with the exception of the Australian rider Bob Thompson, whose engine was misfiring. Much interest centred on John Surtees, the race favourite, riding the big red MV Agusta and Geoff Duke on the German BMW machine. Both men made impressive starts.

Des Wolff was one of the last to leave the start line and had safely made his way over the first twelve miles of the course, through Union Mills, Glen Helen and Cronk y Voddy when, at about 11.20am, he was seen approaching the bottom of Barregarrow Hill, Kirk Michael. He was on the correct racing line but on rounding the left hand corner at "Ivy Cottage" his machine wobbled slightly then shot across the road and mounted the footpath on the right. As he fought to regain control of the machine it travelled along the path for about thirty yards, then went back across the road and collided heavily with the roadside hedge and a wooden telegraph pole. The unfortunate rider came to rest on top of the hedge while his Norton machine came to rest in the adjacent field. Marshals went to his immediate assistance but there was nothing they could do for him. He had been killed instantly.

Mr Angus Stanley Herbert, official Scrutineer for the races, examined the Norton machine after the accident and found extensive damage to the left side but the engine was free and he found no mechanical defect likely to have caused the machine to go out of control.

John Surtees, having won the Junior Race four days earlier, went on to complete a brilliant "double" when he won the Senior Race with an average of 99.98mph and finished over five minutes ahead of second place man Bob Anderson (Norton) with Bob Brown (Norton) finishing in third place. Geoff Duke had retired during his second lap with front brake problems. John Hartle who had been holding second place retired during the fourth lap after his MV machine burst into flames on the exit from Governors Bridge and was destroyed.

Des Wolff was 31 years of age. He was an interior decorator by occupation and resident of Salisbury, Southern Rhodesia where he lived with his wife who was on the Island at the time of the incident. Having arrived on the Island on 12th May, he had covered a considerable number of unofficial and official laps of the course.

His funeral service was held in the Isle of Man and followed by interment at Douglas Borough Cemetery.

Maurice WASSELL

Maurice Wassell at the Quarterbridge during practice for the 1958 Junior MGP

Brilliant weather conditions graced the Isle of Man on the evening of Friday 5th September 1958 and the roads around the TT course were dry. Near perfect for those competitors assembled at the Grandstand on Glencrutchery Road in Douglas ready to take part in a practice session for the Manx Grand Prix. The riders were also pleased to note that there was sufficient cloud towards the western horizon to diminish any dazzle from the setting sun during the latter stages of the session. Amongst them was Maurice Wassell, riding a 250cc AJS machine bearing the race number 4 and entered in the Junior Race to be held the following Tuesday. He had completed 12 laps during practice, the fastest in 27 minutes 30 seconds, which gave him an average lap speed of just over 82 mph.

With his parents, sister and fiancée watching the proceedings from the grandstand, Maurice Wassell set off towards St. Ninians crossroads on his opening lap of the evening and safely negotiated his way round the course to complete his first circuit. Without stopping he commenced his second lap and made his way through to Ramsey then up onto the mountain section of the course.

At the 32nd Milestone competitor John William Deaville of Staffordshire, practising for the Senior Race, had stopped and retired after his Matchless developed mechanical problems. He was watching the other riders go by when, at about 6.45pm, he saw Wassell approaching from Brandywell at normal racing speed. However, he was too far over to the left, which was not the usual racing line to negotiate the slight right hand bend just before the series of left hand bends at the 32nd. At the last moment he realised his position and tried desperately to take the bend but his machine collided with the grass bank on the left. The unfortunate rider was thrown into the roadway where he came to rest without his helmet, which had come off during the incident. His AJS had come to rest 32 yards beyond him. Marshals went to his aid but found there was nothing they could do for him. He had been killed instantly.

William Shimmin, chief public service vehicle examiner for the Highway and Transport Board later examined the crashed machine and found no evidence to suggest that a mechanical defect had contributed towards this accident.

Maurice Wassell was 26 years of age and although a single man he was engaged to Margaret Cooke of Sheffield. He was an electrician by occupation and a resident of Rotherham, Yorkshire. He had his first motorcycle at the age of 16 and became a frequent competitor in the Rotherham and District Motor Club's grass track and hill climbing events but favoured road racing. His debut on the Isle of Man TT course was during the 1955 Manx Grand Prix when, riding a BSA, he competed and finished in the Junior Race. The following year, while on National Service with the Royal Corps of Signals he was recalled to duty due to the Suez Crisis and missed the Manx. He returned to the Island in 1957, riding an AJS, and finished in both the Junior and Senior races. He wore spectacles for everyday use and also wore them underneath his goggles.

His funeral service was held at Thrybergh Parish Churchyard on Wednesday 10th September and followed by interment.

John HUTCHINSON

John Hutchinson pictured during the fateful Junior Snaefell Race in 1958

Mist on the mountain section of the TT course on the afternoon of Monday 8th September 1958, led the race stewards of the Manx Motor Cycle Club to postpone the start of the "Snaefell Races" for one hour. The race, which had already been postponed from the previous Saturday due to miserable weather conditions, had been introduced for the first time this year and was only open to riders competing in the Manx Grand Prix for the first time. There were two races being run concurrently, the Senior Race, in which there were 26 starters and the Junior Race, in which there were 75 competitors, all ready to face four gruelling laps of the course. Shortly before 3.30pm came the news that, providing weather conditions did not suddenly deteriorate, the race would commence at 3.45pm. Following this information the competitors warmed up their machines and began lining up on Glencrutchery Road in readiness for the start of the race. Amongst them was John Hutchinson, riding a 350cc BSA Goldstar machine bearing the race number 91 and entered in the Junior class of the race.

Following reports that the mist seemed to be lifting from the mountain it was decided that the race would go ahead. The competitors received a last minute warning from the Clerk of the Course that fog flags might be used to indicate trouble ahead and drifting mist must be expected. They were also told of wet patches under the trees at Quarterbridge, Quarry Bends and Bedstead Corner. At 3.45pm the flag dropped and the entrants were sent off at ten second intervals. On completion of the first lap Gordon Bell led the Junior race by 48 seconds and by the end of the second lap he had increased his lead to over two minutes and his immediate followers were now Ginger Payne and Phil Read.

During the third lap of the race, a rider indicated to marshals at Windy Corner, pointing backwards along the course. Realising something was wrong two marshals made their way towards Brandywell. On reaching the right hand bend immediately before the 32nd Milestone they found part of the wire fencing across the road, then found John Hutchinson, lying face down, on the grassland below the road with his machine beside him, the engine still running. They went immediately to the unfortunate rider but found that there was nothing that could be done for him. He had been killed instantly. There had been no witnesses to the incident but marks at the scene indicated that he had collided with the sod hedge on the left before crossing the road and striking six concrete fence posts.

Gordon Bell went on to win the race, nearly three minutes ahead of Ginger Payne in second place and Phil Read third. Philip Richardson (Norton) went on to win the Senior class.

John Hutchinson was 33 years of age. He was a toolmaker by occupation and resident of Mossley Hill, Liverpool where he lived with his wife whom he had married in the Spring. They had only lived in their new home for two months and when they left for the Isle of Man on a motorcycle combination, the racing motorcycle was carried on the sidecar. He had never raced over the TT course before but had competed on the Clypse Course in 1955 when, riding a Douglas, he took part in the Junior Clubman's TT and finished in 32nd position.

His funeral service was held on Saturday 13th September and followed by interment at Ford Cemetery, Gorsey Lane, Ford, Litherland.

James Edward COATES

Jim Coates at Ballaugh Bridge during practice for the 1959 Junior MGP

Glare from the setting sun on the evening of Friday 4th September 1959 was likely to be troublesome on certain parts of the TT course but otherwise conditions were ideal for racing. A total of 118 competitors gathered at the Grandstand in Douglas waiting to take advantage of a practice session for the Manx Grand Prix. Amongst them was Jim Coates, riding a 350cc AJS machine bearing the race number 100 and entered in the Junior Race to be held the following Tuesday. He had bought the machine five months earlier and had only ridden in two or three races beforehand. During the week he had completed five practice laps at speeds that showed he was a very capable rider.

Before the session began the riders were warned to anticipate some sun dazzle during the course of the evening. Practice then commenced and it was not long before Jim Coates set off along Glencrutchery Road towards Bray Hill. He made his way round the course through to Ramsey then up onto the mountain section where, at about 6.45pm, marshals and spectators at the 33rd Milestone saw him approaching the sweeping left hand bend at racing speed. However, he was wide of the usual racing line and as he began to negotiate the bend the front wheel of his machine caught the grass verge on the right. He immediately lost control of the AJS as it careered along the verge and collided with several wooden fence posts before tumbling down the grassland below the road. Jim Coates had been thrown from the machine and came to rest in the middle of the roadway opposite the shelter. A marshal went to him immediately and removed him from the road, out of the path of oncoming riders while a spectator made his way back along the course to flag down approaching competitors. Within minutes of receiving the emergency call, the duty doctor arrived at the scene of the incident on the back of a travelling marshals motorcycle but on examination of the unfortunate rider he found that there was nothing that could be done for him. He had been killed instantly.

Mr. W.L. Shimmin, the Chief PSV examiner for the Isle of Man, later examined the machine and found no evidence to suggest that a mechanical failure may have been responsible for the accident.

Jim Coates was 27 years of age. He was a resident of Nelson, Lancashire where he lived with his wife Emma and their two children, Julia aged 4 and Marjorie aged 2. They had bought a house in the village of Foulridge, where he ran a small joinery business, and were almost ready to move in. On the Monday morning following his death Emma received a greetings postcard from him, which he must have posted shortly before taking part in the fateful practice session.

He had been racing since 1954 and had competed on numerous short circuits in England. On the Isle of Man he had competed in the Clubman's races in 1954, finishing 12th and again in 1956 when he finished 7th. Riding a Norton, he had also taken part in the Junior Manx Grand Prix in 1956 but was forced to retire during the race.

His funeral service was held on Monday 7th September at St. Michael and All Angels Church, Foulridge and followed by interment. This was the same church where he and Emma had married six years earlier.

John Desmond HAMILTON

John Hamilton pictured during his fateful opening lap of the 1959 Senior MGP

Fine weather, dry roads and clear visibility around the TT course on the morning of Thursday 10th September 1959 signalled perfect racing conditions for the 105 anxious competitors lined up along Glencrutchery Road in Douglas waiting for the Senior Manx Grand Prix to begin. Amongst them was John Hamilton, riding a 500cc Norton machine bearing the race number 93. Five minutes before the race was due to start, an urgent call came on behalf of the rider R.G.J. Maw of Middlesbrough, who had smashed his goggles and was desperately seeking the loan of another pair. Another competitor in trouble was Dan Shorey, his Norton had developed problems on the way to the Grandstand but he had made it to the start line.

At 10.45am the red and gold Manx flag dropped to signal the first rider away on his race against the clock over six laps of the TT course, a distance of 226 miles. Observers soon forwarded reports of superb riding by the competitors and first lap times from a standing start were remarkably good. There were a number of retirements on this first lap, including Mike Brookes, one of the favourites; he called it a day at Rhencullen, Kirk Michael, after his Norton developed engine problems.

Having safely made his way through Glen Helen, Kirk Michael, Ramsey and up onto the Mountain section of the course John Hamilton was seen travelling at racing speed on the approach to the sweeping left hand bend at the 33rd Milestone. However, he was wide of the usual racing line for the bend and as he negotiated the bend his machine drifted to the right. The front wheel of the Norton caught the grass verge and immediately went out of control, colliding with several wooden posts as it careered along the roadside verge before both rider and machine parted company and tumbled down onto the grassland below the road. Two doctors soon attended to the gravely injured rider and a stretcher party carried him to Windy Corner. From there, a doctor accompanied him in the Civil Defence ambulance that conveyed him to Noble's Hospital. However, his condition slowly deteriorated during the journey and ten minutes after his admission to hospital he succumbed to his injuries.

The race was won by the Manx based rider Eddie Crooks (Norton) with a record race average speed of 94.87mph. Tom Thorp (Norton) finished in second place with Ned Minihan (Matchless) in third place. R.G.J. Maw found some goggles and finished the race in 43rd place. Dan Shorey had not been so fortunate; his Norton expired as soon as he left the start line.

John Hamilton, a single man, was 26 years of age. He was a resident of Highfield, Southampton and a director of Hamilton Electronics Limited, a company of radio and television engineers. He was an experienced competitor and had won the Junior Clubman's event at Silverstone in 1958. He was second in the same event in 1959. He made his debut on the TT course in 1956 when, riding a BSA, he finished 39th in the Junior Clubman's TT with a race average speed of 71.82 mph. Riding an AJS at the 1957 Manx Grand Prix, he took part in the Junior Newcomers Race but failed to finish.

His funeral service was held on 14th September and followed by interment at South Stoneham Cemetery, Swaythling, Southampton.

John Thomas SAPSFORD

John Sapsford at Signpost Corner on his opening lap of the 1960 Senior MGP

Grey skies loomed over the Isle of Man on the morning of Thursday 8th September 1960. However, observers around the TT course were reporting that the roads were dry and visibility was good. Promising news for the 106 competitors lined up along Glencrutchery Road in Douglas waiting to participate in the Senior Manx Grand Prix. Amongst them was John Sapsford, a newcomer to the Island, riding a 500cc BSA machine bearing the race number 121. He had been out on each practice session and was satisfied with the performance of this machine at all times. It was his intention to take it steady during the race as he hoped to finish and receive a coveted replica.

As the flag dropped the process of dispatching the riders from the start line began. One of the last to receive his starting orders was John Sapsford and he safely made his way round the course to complete his first circuit. Phil Read, the 21 year old apprentice engineer from Luton flew round on his first lap and recorded a time of 23 minutes 40 seconds giving an average lap speed as 95.64mph which put him in first place on the leader board. Scotsman John Adam was holding second place with David Williams five seconds behind in third place.

At about 11.50am, just over thirteen miles into his second lap of the race, Sapsford was seen approaching the right hand bend at Cronk Urleigh, Kirk Michael, with another rider approximately 20 yards behind him. As he was negotiating the bend his machine drifted wide on the exit and collided with the hedging on the left. The unfortunate rider was thrown from the machine and came to rest, unconscious, in the middle of the road. Meanwhile, the rider behind him, Geoff Cowell, race number 119, had braked hard but his machine was already banked over to take the bend and began to slide before crashing into the hedging about ten yards behind where Sapsford had first hit. The two riders were quickly removed from the roadway by marshals while the doctor on duty at Kirk Michael was summoned to the scene. On his arrival the doctor examined John Sapsford and found that he had succumbed to his injuries, probably within a few minutes of the accident. Cowell had sustained leg injuries and was later detained in Noble's Hospital.

Phil Read of Luton who had led from the start and averaged 95.38mph over the six laps won the race. The total time taken by Read was 46 seconds faster than the performance of Eddie Crooks average of 94.87mph the previous year. John Adam finished in second place and Ray Mayhew edged his Matchless into third spot.

Pelham Chaplin, Chief Scrutineer for the Manx Motor Cycle Club, later examined both the BSA ridden by Sapsford and the Triumph/Norton ridden by Cowell. He found no evidence to suggest that a mechanical failure may have contributed towards the accident.

John Thomas Sapsford, a single man, was 26 years of age. He was a bricklayer's labourer by occupation and resident of Eltham, London. He was an experienced rider and had raced at Brands Hatch. This was the second season he had been racing his BSA.

His funeral service was held at Eltham Cemetery, Greenwich on Saturday 17th September and followed by interment.

Michael Thomas BROOKES

Mike Brookes pictured during practice for the 1961 Senior TT

Weather conditions were fine on the morning of Saturday 10th June 1961 as competitors gathered at the Grandstand in Douglas waiting to take advantage of the final practice session for solo machines and for many it was an opportunity to run in tyres and chains before racing commenced the following week. Amongst them was Mike Brookes, riding a 499cc Norton machine bearing the race number 45 and entered in the Senior Tourist Trophy Race to be held the following Friday.

At about 5.30am, with the session well under way, the Guatemalan rider, Louis Giron, came off his 250cc Yamaha at Water Trough Corner, Glentramman and sustained a fractured femur. As soon as this happened the flag marshal at that point displayed the yellow flag to warn approaching riders of the incident. Two other marshals, assisted by two spectators, cleared the roadway of the rider and his machine, then used gravel and grit to clear up excess oil. One of the marshals then tried to awaken the occupants of a nearby house in order to use the telephone but he was unable to raise the occupants. He therefore went off down the road to his own home some 500 yards away. The marshal had hardly left the area when Mike Brookes came upon the scene travelling at full racing speed and apparently failed to see the yellow flag despite it being prominently displayed at the Water Trough. As he negotiated the left hand corner the footrest of his machine caught the kerb and this caused it to veer straight across the road and into a stone wall - striking it with considerable force. The unfortunate rider was thrown into the roadway and came to rest just before the point where the other rider's machine had left oil on the roadway.

On his own initiative, the flagman immediately displayed the red flag to stop approaching riders, while the remaining marshal and the two spectators went to the aid of Mike Brookes. The flagman later estimated that the first twenty riders who approached the corner following the accident did not acknowledge the flag and carried on after slightly slackening speed. The twenty-first rider stopped and he was asked to report the accident at Parliament Square and to make sure they sent a doctor and an ambulance to the scene.

A doctor attended the incident within ten minutes and the gravely injured rider was then conveyed by ambulance to Ramsey Cottage Hospital where immediate resuscitation was carried out and emergency treatment given. However, despite an operation to save his life, he succumbed to his injuries at 2.30am the following morning.

Mike Brookes, a single man, was 27 years of age. He was a salesman by occupation and a resident of Shirley near Birmingham where he lived with his parents. He had a wealth of racing experience since he started in 1956 and in his first year he had wins at Aintree and Brands Hatch. On the Isle of Man, he competed in the 1956 Clubman's TT and in the Manx Grand Prix from 1957 to 1960. At the North West 200 in 1959, he achieved a 4th place finish and the following year; he achieved a 3rd place finish. At Aberdare Park, South Wales in 1961 he finished third in the 500cc race and fifth in the 350cc event.

His funeral service was held at Our Lady of the Wayside Catholic Church, Shirley at 9.45am on Friday 16th June and followed by interment at Robin Hood Cemetery.

Marie Laure Rosine LAMBERT

Claude and Marie Lambert at Quarterbridge during the opening lap of the fateful 1961 Sidecar TT

Although the weather was dull and overcast on the afternoon of Monday 12th June 1961 the roads around the TT course remained dry. Good news for the 32 sidecar crews lined up along Glencrutchery Road in Douglas waiting to take part in the International Sidecar Tourist Trophy Race. Amongst them, from Switzerland, were Claude Lambert and his passenger, Marie Lambert, his wife. Their bright red coloured sidecar outfit, bearing the race number 23, was powered by a 500cc BMW engine.

The race commenced at 12.30pm and the Lambert's safely made their way round the course to complete their opening lap in just over 30 minutes, which placed them in 13th position. At Ramsey Hairpin, on their second circuit, they were immediately behind the sidecar of Eric Vincent and Ray Harding, race number 20. Just after the bend they were able to overtake them but they remained in close company throughout the journey over the mountain section. Vincent had noted that the Lambert's machine appeared to be running normally. However, as they approached the Creg ny Baa on the descent from the mountain, he noticed that Claude Lambert's approach to the right hand corner was much more cautious than normal and he then saw Marie Lambert sit up in the sidecar and look back towards him for three or four seconds, which was much longer than he would have expected. Going away from the corner she got back down onto the floor of the sidecar. Moments later, at Sunny Orchard, on the approach to Brandish Corner, Vincent was 20 to 25 yards behind the Lambert's, travelling at about 100mph, when he saw their outfit begin to weave from side to side. This became progressively worse until the sidecar touched the grass bank on the left side of the road then rebounded between the hedges completely out of control before mounting the bank on the right and overturned, flying high into the air. At this point Vincent actually passed beneath the sidecar. Claude Lambert came to rest on the right hand side of the road and had sustained a fractured leg. Marie Lambert came to rest in the middle of the roadway and was quickly attended to but she succumbed to her injuries within minutes of the accident.

The Chief Scrutineer for the ACU later examined the outfit and found it to have sustained considerable damage and the fairing had been demolished. Although he could find no evidence of mechanical failure he did put forward a theory that one of the fairing supports may have fractured and become jammed in the steering.

Max Deubel and his passenger Emil Hoerner went on to win the race and set a new record with a race average speed of 87.65mph. Eric Vincent completed the race in 12th position.

Marie Lambert (nee Page) was 26 years of age. She was a professional racing motorcyclist by occupation and a resident of Geneva where she lived with her husband Claude aged 30. They had been married for two years. She had two years experience of racing all over Europe but this was her first race on the Isle of Man. Her husband, the 1959 Swiss Sidecar Champion, had competed in the 1960 Sidecar TT Race and finished in 20th place. He returned to the TT in 1962 and took 4th place in the Sidecar TT.

Her funeral service was held at Sainte-Jeanne-de-Chantal Church in Geneva on Tuesday 20th June and followed by interment in the Saint-Georges cemetery, Geneva.

68

Ralph Beverley RENSEN

Ralph Rensen at Signpost Corner during the fateful 1961 Senior TT

Dark clouds had formed over the Isle of Man on the morning of Friday 16th June 1961 but the roads around the TT course would remain dry for the 74 competitors lined up along Glencrutchery Road in Douglas in preparation for the start of the Senior Tourist Trophy Race. Amongst them was race veteran Ralph Rensen, riding a 499cc Norton machine bearing the race number 2. On the Monday he had taken 6th place in the 125cc race then on the Wednesday he had secured 3rd place in the Junior TT with a race average speed of 93.65mph. At 11.00am Lord Brabazon of Tara dropped the flag to begin the six-lap race and Rensen pushed off from the start line along with his starting partner Bob McIntyre. Rensen's machine fired up first and he led McIntyre as they roared off towards Bray Hill. The first man to complete the opening lap was Gary Hocking on the MV, with an average speed of 101.70mph, which put him in first place ahead of Mike Hailwood. Ralph Rensen was holding 7th position and by the half way stage he had moved up into 6th place with a race average speed of 99.01mph.

During the fifth lap of the race, having safely negotiated his way through the tricky Glen Helen section of the course, Ralph Rensen, still holding onto 6th place, was seen approaching the bends at the 11th Milestone. He cleared the right hand bend then began to negotiate the left hand bend and was hardly twenty yards past the apex of the curve, when, whilst he was still leaning over to his left, the whole back end of his machine dropped as if the rear suspension had collapsed. He was thrown from the Norton and the rear wheel flew off, smashing through a gate fifty yards further down the road. Pieces of the wrecked machine rained down as Rensen tumbled down the roadway before coming to rest. Marshals did what they could for him until a doctor arrived at the scene from Ballacraine but on examination of the unfortunate rider he found that he had succumbed to his injuries.

Hocking was to retire on the fifth lap, leaving Hailwood to notch up his third race win of the week. Bob McIntyre finished second and Tom Phillis third. All three mounted on Norton's.

An examination of the Norton, which was brand new, revealed that the nut, which attached the right footrest to the frame was missing and the footrest stud, which should have been attached, was out of its hole in the frame. That stud was also used for fixing part of the gearbox foot change mechanism and securing the exhaust. Therefore, it was very probable that the accident had been due to a mechanical defect. The nut had come unscrewed with the result that the exhaust, foot rest and gear change had been affected, causing the Norton to slip into a lower gear, throwing the rider completely off his racing line.

Ralph Rensen, a single man, was 28 years of age. He was a motor engineer by occupation and resident of Liverpool. He had a wealth of racing experience both in the United Kingdom and the Continent. He made his debut on the TT course at the 1953 MGP then in 1955 he moved on to the TT races. At the North West 200 in 1956 he finished second in the Junior race.

His funeral service was held in the Isle of Man on Monday 19th June and followed by interment at Douglas Borough Cemetery.

Geoffrey James GRIFFIN

Geoff Griffin at Ballaugh Bridge during practice for the 1961 Senior MGP

Conditions were described as near perfect for racing on the afternoon of Thursday 31st August 1961 as competitors gathered at the grandstand on Glencrutchery Road in Douglas waiting to take advantage of a practice session for the Manx Grand Prix. Amongst them was Geoff Griffin, riding an almost new 500cc Matchless G50 machine bearing the race number 100 and entered in the Senior Race to be held the following Thursday. He had completed four official laps of the course during earlier practice sessions with his best lap speed recorded at around 85mph.

On receiving the signal to start Geoff Griffin set off towards Bray Hill on his opening lap of the afternoon and safely negotiated his way almost completely round the course until he was back at Governor's Bridge. However, at about 3.35pm, as he emerged from the dip onto Glencrutchery Road he appeared to take a much wider turn than usual and as he straightened up the Matchless developed a slight wobble. The machine then brushed along the kerb on his left for a considerable distance before it mounted the footpath and collided heavily with a tree. He was thrown off and landed heavily in the roadway near to the entrance to "Ashfield House". Marshals, spectators and police officers went to his immediate aid and found him to be deeply unconscious. The gravely injured rider was conveyed by ambulance to Noble's Hospital where he was admitted at 4.00pm and over the following three hours he received blood transfusions. Despite this, his condition slowly deteriorated and he succumbed to his injuries at 8.40pm that same evening.

Pelham Chaplin, Chief Scrutineer for the races later stated that the Matchless machine had been examined prior to the practices and was declared to have been in a thoroughly roadworthy condition. On examination of the machine after the accident he could find no mechanical defect likely to have contributed to the crash. He added that in trying to reconstruct what had happened he was definitely of the opinion that the rider had got through the corner and had straightened out. However, he had been told since the accident that the rider was coming in for a plug check at the end of that lap, and it was likely, therefore, that he would "rev" up at that point. It was possible that the rider momentarily glanced at the "rev" counter and while doing so he has drifted into the kerb.

Geoffrey James Griffin, a single man, was 26 years of age. He was a resident of Isleworth, Middlesex and a Draughtsman by occupation, employed by a heating and ventilation firm at Ruislip, having recently completed studies at the National College for Heating and Ventilation Engineers. He was a member of the British Motor Cycle Racing Club and was an experienced rider, having competed in 40 to 50 meetings at circuits such as Crystal Palace and Silverstone. He knew the TT course well, having first entered the 1959 Manx Grand Prix but he broke a finger as the result of a spill during practising and this prevented him from starting in the race. In the 1960 Senior Manx Grand Prix, from a field of 106 competitors, he finished in 39th position with a race average speed of 80.92mph.

His funeral service was held in Hanworth, Middlesex on Thursday 7th September and was followed by cremation. A plaque in his name can be found on the memorial wall at Douglas Borough Cemetery.

Frederick Allan NEVILLE

Fred Neville at Quarterbridge during the fateful 1961 Junior MGP

There were grey skies over the Isle of Man on the morning of Tuesday 5th September 1961 and a bitterly cold wind as 100 competitors lined up along Glencrutchery Road in Douglas ready to participate in the Junior Manx Grand Prix. Amongst them was Fred Neville, riding a black and red coloured 350cc AJS machine bearing the race number 99. He had been fastest in practice with a lap of 92.38mph, which was twelve seconds inside the official record set during the 1960 Junior Manx. He was being strongly tipped to complete the "Double" and join the exclusive club of Eric Briggs, Geoff Tanner, Jim Buchan and Alan Holmes.

By the time the race commenced rain was already beginning to fall on parts of the course and low cloud was affecting visibility on the mountain. These conditions would handicap the riders, especially the quicker men. On completion of his first circuit Fred Neville was leading the race with a 27 second advantage over Frank Reynolds in second place. His time of 27.23 minutes was an indication of how bad the conditions were around the course. By the end of lap two Reynolds had reduced the advantage to twelve seconds and at the half way stage Reynolds was leading. However, on completion of the fourth circuit Fred Neville was back in front and 22 seconds ahead of Reynolds. Some riders were now retiring and complaining of the cold. Many were forced to make unscheduled stops at the pits just to change waterlogged goggles. Five AJS machines now held the top five places.

On the fifth lap, despite the terrible conditions, Neville made his bid to get clean away from the field and his lap of 85.22mph was to be the best of the day. It gave him a lead of just over two minutes with just one lap to go. Having made his way through Union Mills, Glen Vine and Crosby on his final lap he was seen approaching the bends at Appledene then his machine began to slide on the wet road surface. He corrected this but as he went into the next right hand bend the rear end began to slide away to the left. The unfortunate rider was unable to regain control of the machine and crashed heavily into the stone wall at "Meadowside Cottage". Marshals went to his immediate assistance and found that he had sustained serious injuries. A doctor was called to the scene and did what he could for him until the arrival of an ambulance. The doctor then travelled in the ambulance with the gravely injured rider as they headed for Noble's Hospital but his condition was deteriorating all the time and as the ambulance approached Braddan Bridge he succumbed to his injuries.

Frank Reynolds of Middlesbrough, unaware of the tragedy, swept on to victory. He averaged 81.28mph - 9mph slower than the winning speed in the 1960 race - and had to be lifted from his machine, utterly exhausted.

Fred Neville was 26 years of age. He was a motorcycle agent by occupation and a resident of Worcester Park, Surrey. He had a considerable amount of road race experience in England and Ireland and was tipped to become a TT Ace in the future. He made his debut on the TT course during the Manx Grand Prix in 1960 when he finished 9th in the Junior Race, an achievement that earned him the Newcomers Award.

His funeral service was held on Wednesday 13th September and followed by committal at North East Surrey Crematorium.

Thomas Edward PHILLIS

Tom Phillis pictured at Quarterbridge during the 1962 Junior TT

Weather conditions were excellent on the afternoon of Wednesday 6th June 1962, visibility was clear and the roads around the TT course were dry. Welcome news for the 73 competitors assembled on Glencrutchery Road in Douglas waiting to participate in the Junior Tourist Trophy Race. Amongst them was Tom Phillis, from Australia, riding a 285cc Honda machine bearing the race number 1. Earlier that day he had taken third place in the Lightweight 125cc Race with an average speed of 88.30mph. In the Lightweight 250cc Race on the Monday, he had finished third with a race average speed of 92.87mph.

At the drop of the flag the race began and Tom Phillis was the first man away as he set off towards Bray Hill on his opening lap. Gary Hocking on the MV Agusta was sixth on the starting grid and it was evident throughout the opening lap that he was setting the pace. As he passed the grandstand on Glencrutchery Road to complete his first lap he was leading the race, having broken his own lap record from the standing start, with an average speed of 100.90mph. Breathing hotly down his neck were Mike Hailwood, also on an MV Agusta, in second place with a lap of 100.03mph and Tom Phillis third at over 99mph. At about 2.00pm, during the second lap of the race, marshals and spectators positioned at the bend immediately prior to Laurel Bank Corner saw Hocking and Hailwood pass through, next came Tom Phillis but as he negotiated the corner he lost control of his machine and came off, sliding along the ground with the Honda following him rear end first before both rider and machine hit the stone bank at the side of the road. The gravely injured rider was carried to the Starvey Road and then conveyed by ambulance to Ballacraine where a doctor examined him and found that he had succumbed to his injuries.

On the sixth and final lap of the race, Mike Hailwood, who had started ten seconds ahead of Hocking moved back ahead of him on the road and by Ramsey Hailwood was 300 yards in front as they began the climb over the mountain. At the Grandstand stop watches were poised as Hailwood crossed the finishing line, then came Hocking, 15.6 seconds behind on the road and 5.6 seconds down on corrected time. Hailwood had taken the race and in do so he set up a new Junior lap record of 101.58mph. Frantisek Stastny took his Jawa into third place.

Tom Phillis was 28 years of age. He was a married man and the father of two children, Brenda Ann aged two and Thomas Braddan aged one. He was a professional racing motorcyclist by occupation and a resident of Sydney, Australia. His wife and children, along with his 81-year-old grandmother, were on the Island at the time of the accident. Quickly rising to stardom down under, he first came to Europe in 1957 with his wife, Betty, after they had sold nearly all they had to make the trip. Signed up by Honda in 1960, Tom scored a last-race win in the 1961 125cc Championship and finished second to Mike Hailwood in the 250cc table. He also became the first man to lap the Mountain Circuit at over 100mph on a push-rod engined machine during his third-place Senior ride on the new Norton "Domiracer" in 1961. At the time of his death he was the reigning 125cc World Champion.

His funeral service was held in the Isle of Man and followed by committal at Douglas Borough Crematorium. A plaque in his name can be found on the memorial wall in the cemetery.

Colin Thomas MEEHAN

Colin Meehan at Ballaugh Bridge during practice for the 1962 Junior TT

The weather conditions were ideal for racing on the afternoon of Wednesday 6th June 1962 and there were huge crowds of spectators lining the TT course for the International Junior Tourist Trophy race. The 73 competitors entered in the race included representatives from New Zealand, Australia, Southern Rhodesia, Canada and several European nations. Amongst them, making his debut on the TT course, was Colin Meehan from New Zealand, riding a 349cc AJS machine bearing the race number 63.

The machines were wheeled to the starting grid on Glencrutchery Road in Douglas and the race commenced with Tom Phillis being the first man away. Several minutes later it was the turn of Colin Meehan to begin his race against the clock and he set off towards Bray Hill. He safely made his way round the course and completed his opening lap with an average speed of 91.17mph, which put him in 32nd place. Gary Hocking led the race with an average lap speed of 100.99mph. Mike Hailwood was second and Tom Phillis was third

Eight miles out into the second lap of the race, Tom Phillis lost control of his Honda on the bends immediately before Laurel Bank and sustained injuries, which were to prove fatal. Colin Meehan had commenced his second lap without stopping at the pits and a couple of minutes later he was seen negotiating the right hand bend at the Railway Hotel in Union Mills but then as he positioned himself for the following sweeping left hand bend his machine developed a wobble. He fought hard to regain control but was gradually lifted out of the saddle and thrown into the roadway. The AJS tumbled along the road, mounted the footpath on the right just beyond the post office and dislodged several straw bales that had been positioned against the boundary walls of the adjacent houses, before bouncing back into the roadway. Eventually, the machine came to a halt outside Slater's Garage while the unfortunate rider came to rest in the roadway opposite number 2, Mill Cottages. Marshals and a police officer went to his immediate aid but there was nothing they could do for him. He had been killed instantly. An examination of the scene later revealed a tyre mark on the road surface measuring 143 feet and leading to the point where Meehan had been thrown.

The AJS was later examined by Angus Stanley Herbert on behalf of the Auto-Cycle Union and found that it had sustained extensive damage but there was no evidence to suggest that a mechanical failure had contributed to the accident.

There was a dramatic finish to the race following a tremendous spurt on the last lap by Mike Hailwood on his Italian MV Agusta, which enabled him to snatch victory by 5.6 seconds from the Southern Rhodesian rider Gary Hocking, also riding an MV Agusta. Third place went to the Czechoslovakian rider Franta Stastny, riding a Jawa machine.

Colin Meehan, a single man, was 28 years of age. He was a mechanic by occupation and a resident of Wellington, New Zealand but was temporarily staying at Belvedere, Kent. He had won the 500cc New Zealand Clubman's TT in 1960 and the 1961 race at Levin.

His funeral service was held in the Isle of Man and followed by interment at Douglas Borough Cemetery.

Thomas William PRATT

Billy Pratt pictured at Quarterbridge during the fateful 1962 Junior MGP

Rain was falling across the Isle of Man on the morning of Tuesday 4th September 1962 leaving wet roads around the TT course and with low cloud reducing visibility down to 25 yards in places on the mountain section, race officials made the decision to postpone the start of the Junior Manx Grand Prix for an hour. Amongst the 98 competitors assembled in the area of the Grandstand in Douglas waiting to participate in the race was Billy Pratt, riding a Norton machine bearing the race number 92. He had come off his machine at the Quarterbridge during practice week and had sprained his left shoulder but had been declared fit to take part in the race.

The weather began to brighten up and at 11.45am, an hour later than scheduled, the race commenced and several minutes after the first of the competitors had been dispatched from the start line it was the turn of Billy Pratt to begin his race against the clock and he set off along Glencrutchery Road towards Bray Hill on his opening lap. He safely made his way round the course and recorded a lap time of 26 minutes 43 seconds. As he passed the Grandstand to commence his second lap he was in close company with John Evans of Liverpool, riding an AJS (No.91) and Ernest Wooder of Romford, Essex, riding a Norton (No.95). In the vicinity of Union Mills, all three riders overtook John Farrer of Golborne near Warrington, riding a BSA (No.87). At about 12.35pm, as the group of riders approached Greeba Castle it began to rain. Moments later, at Appledene, Pratt was three or four yards ahead of Wooder when his rear wheel began to slide. He regained control momentarily but within a matter of yards the rear wheel broke away again and he crashed into the stone wall at "Meadowside Cottage". His machine bounced back into the road and brought Wooder off his machine. Evans tried to pull to the right but was unable to avoid colliding with one or both machines and also crashed. Farrer tried to get through on the right but collided with Pratt's machine, which was still sliding in the road and was thrown off. Marshals went to the immediate assistance of the four men and found that Wooder had sustained a fractured foot, Evans had sustained a leg injury and Farrer had escaped unhurt. However, there was nothing they could do for the unfortunate Billy Pratt. He had been killed instantly.

Robin Dawson of East Barnet, Hertfordshire, riding an AJS machine at an average lap speed of 89.02mph, won the race. Peter Darvill, also riding an AJS, finished the race in second place while Fred Fisher, riding a Norton, took third place on the rostrum.

Billy Pratt was 20 years of age, and although a single man, he had planned to marry his childhood sweetheart, 19-year-old Carole Scott of County Durham. She had pleaded with him to give up racing and he intended doing so but he wanted to ride in the Isle of Man first. Billy's father, younger brother and uncle were in the Grandstand and saw him set off. They had flown to the Island with the idea of surprising him when he finished his first race on the TT circuit. They watched him set off but then, an hour or so later; they were informed of the fateful crash. Billy was a close friend of the late Bob McIntyre and had borrowed the Norton from motorcycle agent, George Bell of Bedlington, Northumberland.

His funeral service was held in Rowlands Gill on Monday 10th September and followed by committal at West Road Crematorium, Newcastle.

Charles Edmund ROBINSON

Charlie Robinson exits Governors Dip at the end of his opening lap in the fateful 1962 Junior MGP

There was rain and a blanket of low cloud over the Isle of Man on the morning of Tuesday 4th September 1962 leaving wet roads and visibility down to twenty five yards in places on the mountain section of the TT course. These conditions led to the start of the Junior Manx Grand Prix being delayed for one hour. Not the best of news for the 98 competitors gathered at the Grandstand in Douglas waiting for the race to commence. Amongst them was Charlie Robinson, riding a 305cc Honda machine bearing the race number 36. Impressed by the possibilities of the Honda he had decided to have one last shot at a major event on the Island.

Within the hour, the weather had become brighter and the rider's pushed their machines out onto Glencrutchery Road ready to race. At 11.45am the flag dropped and the first riders were sent on their way towards Bray Hill followed three minutes later by Charlie Robinson. On completion of the first lap, Robin Dawson led the race with Dave Williams in second place and Peter Darvill holding third. As Charlie Robinson passed the pits at the end of his first circuit, he gave the "thumbs down" signal to his pit attendants and from the sound of the machine it appeared that he was having problems with the clutch.

Just over fifteen miles into his second lap Robinson was travelling through Bishopscourt with the Norton of Dave Williams behind and gaining rapidly on him. Approximately 75 yards from the sweeping right hand bend after the entrance to Bishopscourt Farm, Robinson began to turn into the bend but Williams, travelling at 120mph, had already lined up to pass him on the right and was now only 20 yards behind him. Realising the imminent danger of a collision, Williams sat upright and braked hard but his front wheel began to lock up so he made the split second decision to accelerate in an effort to try and pass Robinson on the inside before the apex of the bend. However, the two machines touched and the two riders came into contact with each other, shoulder to shoulder. In that instant Charlie Robinson lost control of his machine and collided heavily with the hedge on the right. He was thrown off and came to rest in the roadway while his machine finally came to a stop on the footpath on the left. A marshal had witnessed the incident and ran to Robinson's assistance, dragging him from the roadway and to the relative safety of the footpath but there was nothing that could be done for him. He had been killed instantly. Williams had been able to maintain control of his Norton and stopped two hundred yards further on and began running back towards the scene but on seeing that Robinson was being attended to he remounted his machine and rode to Ballaugh Bridge where he reported to the Police Officer on duty there "I've just touched another rider on the bend before Alpine. He has crashed and could be seriously injured". He then continued and eventually finished the race in seventh place.

Charlie Robinson was 39 years of age. He was a garage proprietor by occupation and resident of Market Rasen, Lincolnshire where he lived with his wife Rose and their two children, Paul aged 15 years and Jillian aged 14 years. He had built up a wealth of racing experience since the early 1950's both in the Isle of Man and on various English racing tracks. His best result on the Isle of Man came in 1950 when he took 5th place in the Junior Clubman's TT.

His funeral service was held on the Isle of Man and followed by interment at Douglas Borough Cemetery.

Geoffrey Charles PRENTICE

Geoff Prentice exits Governor's Dip during the fateful 1962 Junior MGP

Heavy rain was falling across the Isle of Man on the morning of Tuesday 4th September 1962, which was far from ideal racing conditions for the 97 competitors assembled in the area of the Grandstand in Douglas waiting to participate in the Junior Manx Grand Prix. Amongst them was Geoff Prentice, riding an AJS machine bearing the race number 35. With wet roads and low cloud reducing visibility down to 25 yards in places on the mountain section of the course, race officials made the decision to postpone the start of the race for one hour.

By 11.45am the weather was beginning to brighten and the race commenced, an hour later than scheduled. A few minutes after the first of the riders had been dispatched from the start line it was the turn of Geoff Prentice to begin his race against the clock and he set off along Glencrutchery Road towards Bray Hill on his opening lap. On completion of the first circuit, Robin Dawson held a five second advantage over second place man Dave Williams with Peter Darvill in third place. Tragedy was to strike during the second lap when Billy Pratt lost his life in an incident at Appledene involving four machines and at Bishopscourt Charlie Robinson lost his life following a collision with Dave Williams. Williams, who had been lying in second place, was able to continue but dropped from the leaderboard and eventually finished in 7th position.

At the half way stage, with pit stops coming in to play, Fred Fisher had taken the lead, eleven seconds ahead of Darvill with Dawson now in third place. Geoff Prentice pulled into the pits, refuelled, changed his goggles and told his pit attendant that everything was all right before setting off again to commence his fourth lap of the race. He safely made his way round the course and was seen approaching Birkin's Bends at Rhencullen with another rider close behind him. He was sitting upright on the machine and appeared to be touring. Observers gained the impression that his engine was not running and he was applying the brakes when suddenly, the rear wheel locked and although he put his right foot to the ground in an effort to steady the machine he was unable to prevent it colliding heavily with the boundary wall of "Brookville Cottage". Marshals went to the immediate assistance of the unfortunate rider but there was nothing they could do for him. He had been killed instantly.

Robin Dawson of East Barnet, Hertfordshire, riding an AJS machine, went on to win with a race average speed of 89.02mph. Peter Darvill finished second and Fred Fisher came third.

Geoff Prentice, a single man, was 24 years of age. He was a radio and television service engineer by occupation and a resident of Cheveley near Newmarket where he lived with his parents. However, he had been called up for National Service and was stationed in Germany with the Royal Signals. His debut on the TT course was in the 1959 Junior MGP when he finished 51st and in the same race the following year he finished 48th. He had saved up his army leave and earned extra money by working as a cinema projectionist in order to compete in the Manx Grand Prix again.

His funeral service was held at St. Mary's Church, Cheveley on Saturday 8th September and followed by interment. The service was attended by a large number of mourners and there were many floral tributes.

Keith Terrance GAWLER

Keith Gawler pictured on Bray Hill during the fateful 1962 Senior MGP

Overcast skies on the morning of Thursday 6th September 1962 brought a threat of rain but the roads around the TT course were dry and visibility on the mountain section was clear. Welcome news for the 94 competitors entered in the Senior Manx Grand Prix as they wheeled their machines onto Glencrutchery Road in Douglas ready to take part in the six lap race, a distance of just over 226 miles. Amongst them was Keith Gawler, a newcomer to the Isle of Man, riding a 499cc Norton machine bearing the race number 103.

At 10.45am the flag dropped and the race began with each rider setting off at ten second intervals. Because of his high start number it was several minutes before Keith Gawler could set off and he safely negotiated his way round the course to complete his first circuit. On his second lap he had made his way through Glen Helen, Ballaugh and Sulby when he was seen approaching "Pinfold Cottage" on roads that were still dry at that time. He was travelling at racing speed and on the usual racing line as he began to negotiate the right and left hand bends at that location when the rear wheel of his Norton suddenly began to slide away from beneath him. Twisting from one side to the other, he tried desperately to regain control but failed to do so and was thrown from the machine. Both rider and machine then collided heavily with the stone wall on the right hand side of the road. The Norton rebounded back across the road and struck a tree before coming to rest on the footpath. On hearing the crash from her home a State Registered Nurse ran to the scene of the incident and found the unfortunate rider lying in the middle of the road but there was nothing she could do for him. He had been killed instantly.

Pelham Chaplin, Chief Srutineer for the races, later made an examination of the Norton machine and found that it had sustained extensive damage. The rear wheel was buckled and the tyre deflated. On inspection of the inner tube fitted to the rear wheel he found a small hole, which was in line with an indentation mark on the rim of the wheel as though there might have been previous contact with a kerb. It was therefore surmised that the tyre had been deflating as Gawler was attempting to negotiate the right hand bend.

Dave Williams, the former race leader experienced gearbox problems during the second lap and as a result, Joe Dunphy overhauled him to take a four second lead. Fred Fisher held third place. At the half way stage of the race it began to rain and lap times dropped dramatically as a result. Dunphy retained his lead and went on to win the race with an average of 91.83mph. Second place went to Peter Darvill with Dave Williams third. Fred Fisher had retired at Rhencullen with gearbox problems on the last lap.

Keith Gawler, a single man, was 22 years of age. He was a scientific optical worker by occupation and a resident of Sidcup, Kent. He had two or three years racing experience at most of the circuits in the south of England including Silverstone and was a club member of "Gravesend Eagles". A friend described him as a man of cheerful disposition and in fact he was usually the life and soul of any party.

His funeral service was held on 14th September and followed by committal at Eltham Crematorium.

Raymond ROWE

Raymond Rowe at the foot of Bray Hill during the fateful 1963 Senior MGP

Strong winds were blowing across the Isle of Man on the morning of Thursday 5th September 1963 but the sun was shining, visibility was clear and the roads around the TT course were dry. Almost perfect racing conditions for the 84 competitors waiting to participate in the six lap Senior Manx Grand Prix. Amongst those lined up along Glencrutchery Road in Douglas was Raymond Rowe, riding a 499cc Norton machine bearing the race number 89.

At 10.00am the flag dropped and the race was under way. Several minutes after the first man had left the start line it was the turn of Raymond Rowe to begin his race against the clock and he set off towards Bray Hill. On completion of his third circuit he pulled in and stopped at the pits to take on fuel and told his pit attendant, Joseph Chapman, that everything was okay. They had known each other for four years. Two days earlier Rowe had acted as pit attendant for Chapman when he competed in the Junior race.

During the fourth lap of the race Rowe had safely negotiated his way round the course and up onto the mountain section when, on the approach to the Black Hut he passed Brian Smith of Preston, race number 53. Smith then followed him and moments later, he saw Rowe negotiating the series of right hand bends at the Verandah but he was off the usual racing line, being too far over to the left. Smith knew that if the corner was taken wide there was a tendency to drift to the left due to the camber of the road. Rowe was unable to regain the racing line and his machine drifted to the left and onto the grass verge where it collided heavily with several iron fence posts before tumbling down the grassland below the road. A spectator who had witnessed the crash made his way to the scene along with a race marshal and they found the unfortunate rider lying entangled in the wire fencing but there was nothing they could do for him. He had been killed instantly. Brian Smith had continued to the Bungalow where he reported the incident to a travelling marshal.

During the fifth lap of the race, Dave Williams, the race leader, came off his Norton after the engine seized. Then, on the final lap, the new leader, Roger Hunter, ran out of fuel at the Gooseneck, which left Griff Jenkins to claim the honours. Peter Darvill, winner of the Junior MGP two days earlier, was second with Jimmy Guthrie claiming third spot.

Raymond Rowe, a single man, was 24 years of age. He was an engineering draughtsman by occupation and a resident of Consett, County Durham. He was an experienced racing motorcyclist having competed on many circuits within the UK and most notably at Charterhall. His first appearance on the Isle of Man was during the 1962 Manx Grand Prix when he crashed at Ballaugh Bridge during the opening practice session and although he sustained minor injuries his machine had burst into flames and was destroyed. Through his insurers, a new Norton machine was rushed to him and he went on to finish 26th in the Senior Manx Grand Prix.

At the time of his death, his mother and father had been on the Isle of Man together with his girlfriend, Joan Smith and they attended his funeral, which was held on the Island and followed by committal at Douglas Borough Crematorium.

Brian William COCKELL

Tony Baitup and Brian Cockell at Quarterbridge during practice for the 1964 Sidecar TT

Light rain was falling on the evening of Tuesday 2nd June 1964 and this had left the roads around the TT course wet and greasy but this had not deterred the 47 sidecar crews congregating at the Grandstand in Douglas waiting to take part in the opening practice session for the International Sidecar Tourist Trophy Race. Amongst them were Tony Baitup, a 30 year old maintenance fitter from Tonbridge, Kent and his passenger, Brian Cockell. Both men were newcomers to the Isle of Man and were about to embark on their first ever official lap of the TT course. Their sidecar, powered by a Norton engine, was bearing the race number 43.

At about 6.35pm Baitup and Cockell set off on their opening lap and moments later as they negotiated the descent of Bray Hill they passed the sidecar outfit of Arsenius Butscher. A little more than a mile from the grandstand they rounded the right hand bend at the Quarterbridge Hotel and headed for Braddan Bridge with another outfit, race number 50, just ahead of them. On the immediate approach to the left hand bend at the bridge, the other rider reduced speed and positioned his outfit to the right hand side of the road in preparation for the bend. Baitup did not to slow down and passed the other sidecar on the left. Almost immediately he realised that he was going too fast to take the bend safely and tried to continue straight on into Strang Road, using it as a slip road. However, it was too late, the sidecar collided with the kerbing surrounding the "Jubilee Oak Tree" and both rider and passenger were thrown into the road. They came to rest on the footpath beside the boundary wall of "Bridge House" just inside the Strang Road. Cockell had collided heavily with the wall and sustained serious crush injuries to his left arm while Baitup sustained spinal injuries. Their sidecar had come to rest upside down in the gutter just beyond them.

The two competitors were conveyed by ambulance to Noble's Hospital where they were admitted at 7.05pm. Brian Cockell's condition quickly deteriorated as his body went into shock and despite emergency treatment and desperate attempts at resuscitation he succumbed to his injuries at 7.35pm. Tony Baitup survived the incident and returned to the Island to compete in the sidecar races in 1965 and for several years beyond that.

Chief Scrutineer, Robert James Havers, later examined the sidecar. He found that apart from the wrecked fairing the machine was relatively undamaged. No evidence was found to suggest that a mechanical failure had contributed to this accident.

Brian William Cockell, a single man, was 23 years of age. He was a panel beater by occupation and resident of Bexley Heath, Kent. He had been a solo competitor on various race circuits throughout England for four years prior to meeting up with Tony Baitup at Crystal Palace in 1963 where, after hearing over the tannoy that Baitup was without a passenger for the meeting, he volunteered to help out. Despite falling from the chair on leaving the start line for the first heat the pair went on to record a victory later in the day. They became a successful team and had won several races over the following twelve months.

His funeral service was held on Wednesday 10th June and followed by committal at Eltham Crematorium.

Peter Lawrence ESSERY

Norman Huntingford and Peter Lawrence Essery pictured during practice for the 1964 Sidecar TT

Fair weather conditions on the morning of Monday 8th June 1964 resulted in dry roads around the TT course and clear visibility on the mountain section. Perfect racing conditions for the 47 crews warming up their machines on Glencrutchery Road in Douglas ready to compete in the International Sidecar Tourist Trophy Race. Amongst them were Norman Huntingford and his passenger, Peter Lawrence Essery, riding a sidecar outfit powered by a Matchless engine and bearing the race number 49.

At 11.00am the flag dropped and the opening race of the week began. Four minutes after the first two machines were dispatched it was the turn of Huntingford and Essery to begin their race against the clock. They had made their way through Glen Helen and Kirk Michael when, at about 11.15am, they were seen approaching Ballaugh Bridge in close company behind two other sidecar outfits, numbers 40 and 50. Huntingford tried to pass number 50 on the right but as he did so he realised that he was on the wrong line to negotiate the bridge and began braking hard but was unable to prevent the front of the outfit colliding heavily with the low wall on the right hand side of the bridge. Both rider and passenger were thrown from the machine as it cartwheeled along the roadway before coming to rest in the centre of the road. Huntingford came to rest on the road at the mouth of the junction with the Glen Road while Essery came to rest, unconscious, in the middle of the course. Within seconds one of the following outfits caught the crashed machine with a glancing blow which caused it to slide a short distance across the road towards the hotel and directly into the path of number 33 ridden by Michael Potter who was unable to avoid a hefty collision which left him and his passenger Ronald Carroll lying in the roadway with their machine lying upside down beside them. Fortunately, they both escaped serious injury. The unfortunate passenger Essery was carried to the side of the road then conveyed by ambulance to Ramsey Cottage Hospital where he was admitted at 11.45am but he was suffering from multiple injuries and his condition slowly deteriorated. At 1.10am the following morning he succumbed to his injuries.

Max Deubel went on to win the race having led from the start. Florian Camathias had been holding second position but engine problems on the last lap caused him to lose time and Colin Seeley took full advantage to claim second place. Third place went to Georg Auerbacher.

Peter Lawrence Essery, a single man, was 30 years of age. He was an electrician by occupation and a resident of West Croyden where he lived with his parents. He had been a passenger to Huntingford for about nine or ten races since March that year and was a first time competitor in the Isle of Man.

His funeral service was held on Tuesday 16th June and followed by interment at Croydon Cemetery.

Norman Huntingford returned to the Isle of Man TT races in 1965 and with Ray Lindsay as his passenger, took his Matchless powered outfit to eighth place. Their achievement earned them bronze replicas. The following year, 1966, they crashed whilst competing in the Dutch TT and Huntingford sustained fatal injuries.

George Brian ARMSTRONG

Brian Armstrong pictured on his Triton at a race meeting in the UK

Dry roads and clear visibility round the TT course on the morning of Tuesday 1st September 1965 provided almost perfect racing conditions for the competitors gathered at the Grandstand in Douglas preparing to take advantage of a practice session for the Manx Grand Prix. Amongst them was Brian Armstrong, riding a Triton machine, a combination of a Triumph engine in a Norton frame, bearing the race number 39 and entered in the Senior Race to be held the following Thursday. He had completed two official practice laps of the course the previous evening.

Shortly after 6.00am, with the intention of completing two laps, Brian Armstrong set off along Glencrutchery Road on his opening lap of the morning and safely made his way round the course back to Douglas. Without stopping, he passed straight through the start area to commence his second circuit and gave the "thumbs up" sign to his brother, Ray Armstrong.

At about 6.30am, the flag marshal at Sulby Bridge saw that the rising sun was beginning to cause difficulty as some riders were lifting their hands to shade their eyes. A marshal was sent back along the course 600 yards from the bridge and displayed the large "Sun" warning flag, which carried the word "Sun" in large black letters on a white background. Riders on the Sulby Straight could see the flag from about half a mile away and most of them acknowledged that they had seen it by giving a wave.

At about 6.50am, despite the warning flag, Armstrong was seen approaching Sulby Bridge at a speed of between 70 and 80mph and it appeared to Marshals that he was being dazzled by the sun as he didn't seem to know he was at the corner until the last moment when he passed through a patch of shade about 30 yards from the bridge. Realising his position and being unable to make the tight right hand bend he stood up on his machine and braked hard, leaving a 68 foot long tyre mark on the road surface but it was too late and he was unable to avoid colliding with the wooden board that had been placed on the road to indicate the sharp bend to approaching riders. The unfortunate rider was thrown from his machine and came to rest in the field beyond and below the road. Marshals went to his immediate assistance but there was nothing they could do for him. He had been killed instantly.

The Chief Scrutineer, Ken Harding, later examined the extensively damaged Triton and found no evidence of mechanical failure having contributed to this accident.

Brian Armstrong was 31 years of age. He was a traffic manager by occupation and resident of Stokesley, Middlesbrough where he lived with his wife Dorothy who was carrying their first child and gave birth to their daughter, Julie, some months later. Brian had originally been a motorcycle scrambler and had a number of successes before turning his attentions to road racing, competing at circuits in the North of England and Scotland. Both he and his brother had competed in the Manx Grand Prix the previous year but Brian was forced to retire during the second lap of the Senior Race while Ray retired during the Junior Race.

His funeral service was held on the morning of Saturday 5th September and followed by committal at Middlesbrough Crematorium

Toshio FUJII

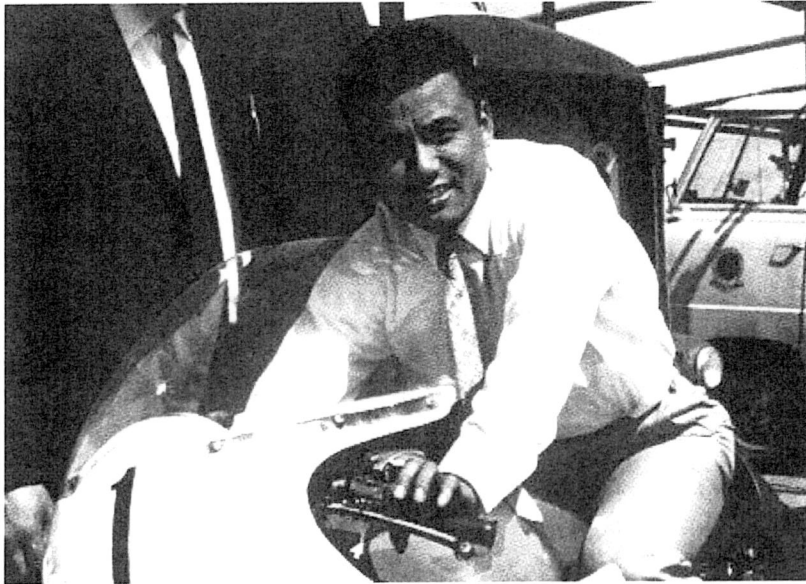

Toshio Fujii swaps his leathers for a shirt and tie in this photo taken in the UK

Threatened by a national seaman's strike, the 1966 TT meeting had been saved by a combination of wise heads and good co-operation between organisations. The races were postponed rather than cancelled and were held over a two week period at the end of August, immediately before the commencement of the Manx Grand Prix.

On the evening of Friday 26th August 1966, the weather conditions around the TT course were almost perfect for the competitors gathered at the Grandstand in Douglas waiting to take advantage of the final practice session for the Tourist Trophy Races. Amongst them was the ever cheerful Toshio Fujii of Japan, riding a grey coloured 125cc Kawasaki machine bearing the race number 44 which was entered in the International Lightweight 125cc Race to be held the following Wednesday. Earlier in the week he had experienced gearbox problems and had been unable to continue practising until this Friday evening when he was required to complete three laps of the course in order to qualify for the race.

Fujii left the grandstand at about 6.15pm and safely made his way round the first 23 miles of the course and through Parliament Square in Ramsey. He was then seen approaching Cruickshank's Corner at the foot of May Hill with another competitor riding a 50cc machine directly ahead of him. He chose to overtake the slower machine before the corner but on doing so he was unable to return to the correct racing line. Travelling at racing speed he attempted to negotiate the corner but his machine drifted wide and struck the kerb on the left side of the road. The unfortunate rider was thrown from the Kawasaki and slid along the pavement with his machine before colliding heavily with the stone wall at "The Mount", a total distance of 114 feet. Marshals ran to his assistance and found him lying unconscious on the pavement. The fuel tank had come away from the machine and was lying on his chest. A doctor attended to him and as he regained consciousness he was indicating that he had a pain in his lower chest. He was conveyed by ambulance to Ramsey Cottage Hospital where he received immediate treatment but at 9.10pm he suddenly collapsed and despite efforts to save him, he died fifteen minutes later.

The Chief Scrutineer, Robert James Havers, examined the Kawasaki machine at Ramsey Police Station the following day. He found that the front wheel, frame and forks had sustained extensive damage but there was nothing evident to suggest that a mechanical failure had contributed to this accident.

Toshio Fujii, a single man, was 25 years of age. He was a professional racing motorcyclist by occupation and resident of Tokyo, Japan. Before moving to Kawasaki he had ridden for the Suzuki works team for the previous five years and had gained a wealth of experience with race wins at Oulton Park and Silverstone where he won the huge Mellano Trophy in 1965 riding a 50cc Suzuki machine. This trophy was awarded for the ride, which comes closest to or breaks by the biggest margin the lap record for that class of machine and he won the race with a race average 7mph up on the old lap record.

His funeral service was held in Japan and followed by interment in Hachioji-shi, Tokyo.

Brian DUFFY

Brian Duffy pictured at Quarterbridge during practice for the 1966 Lightweight TT

A national seaman's strike in 1966 caused the postponement of the TT meeting from June to the August and the first races were held on Sunday 28th August. Following the International Sidecar Race came the 250cc Lightweight Tourist Trophy Race and conditions were described as near perfect for the 61 competitors lined up along Glencrutchery Road in Douglas waiting for the six-lap race to commence. Amongst them was race veteran Brian Duffy, riding a Yamaha machine bearing the race number 73.

At 2.00pm the flag dropped and the first of the riders were sent on their way towards Bray Hill on the opening lap. Several minutes later it was the turn of Brian Duffy to begin his race against the clock and safely made his way round the course to complete his opening circuit in 18th position. Mike Hailwood, riding a Honda, led the race by 40 seconds and his average speed of 104.29mph was more than four miles an hour faster than the previous 250cc record set by Jim Redman and nearly two miles an hour faster than his own 350cc record. By the end of his second lap Brian Duffy had moved up to 15th position. Phil Read who had been holding second place was forced to retire his Yamaha at the Ginger Hall Hotel in Sulby. On completion of his third circuit Brian Duffy made his pit stop and had a drink while his machine was refuelled. He told his pit attendant that he was very tired but was pleased with his lap times. He was lying in 16th position as he set off to commence his fourth lap of the race. Hailwood had also made his pit stop to refuel without any hitch or fuss. Holding second place was Stuart Graham but he lost time after his machine refused to restart after his pit stop. Brian Duffy recorded his fastest lap time during his fifth circuit and was up to 12th position as he began his final lap of the race. Watching the race from a point about 300 yards before the Mountain Box was competitor Larry Evans of Manchester who had retired his BSA there during the first lap. When he saw Brian Duffy pass by he noted that the engine of the Yamaha sounded "very rough" and felt that it had partly seized. Seconds later, as Duffy rounded the left hand bend at the Mountain Box the engine of his machine suddenly cut out and on losing momentum he drifted wide to the right and collided heavily with concrete fence posts situated at the side of the road. He was just eight miles from the finish line. Marshals went to his immediate assistance but there was nothing they could do for him. He had been killed instantly.

An examination of the machine revealed that although there was no evidence of mechanical failure it was still possible that there had been a seizure.

Mike Hailwood went on to win with a race average speed of 101.79mph and finished six minutes ahead of his nearest rival Stuart Graham with Peter Inchley in third place.

Brian Duffy, a single man, was 47 years of age. He was a sales representative by occupation and a resident of Solihull, Warwickshire. He had a wealth of racing experience and made his debut on the Isle of Man in 1951 when he competed in the Junior Clubman's Race.

His funeral service was held on 1st September and followed by interment at Landican Cemetery, Wirral. He was formerly from Wallasey and had worked for the GPO in Liverpool.

Alfred Evans SHAW

1962 - Alf Shaw sits astride a Norton during practice for the Junior TT

Sixty years after the first motorcycle TT races, the Isle of Man was celebrating its Diamond Jubilee TT meeting in 1967.

Weather conditions were fine on the morning of Saturday 10th June and the roads around the TT course were dry as competitors assembled at the Grandstand in Douglas waiting to take advantage of the final practice session for the Tourist Trophy Races. Amongst them was the race veteran Alf Shaw, riding a 499cc Norton machine bearing the race number 104 and entered in the Senior Race to be held the following week.

At 4.47am, Alf Shaw set off along Glencrutchery Road towards Bray Hill to commence his opening lap and safely made his way round the course, through Ramsey and up onto the mountain section. However, at about 5.10am, Kel Carruthers, from Australia, riding his Senior Norton, rounded the slight left hand bend just beyond the Mountain Box and came upon Alf Shaw lying face down and motionless in the centre of the road. As there was no one attending to the fallen rider he stopped his machine then ran back to where he was lying and found that he had sustained serious injuries. Carruthers made his way back along the course, slowing down and warning other riders on the way. On reaching the Mountain Box he notified the marshals and police officer on duty at that point and they returned with him to the scene of the incident. Shaw was carried by stretcher to the shelter at the Mountain Box to await the arrival of a doctor but his condition deteriorated and he passed away at 5.40am, just three minutes before the arrival of Dr. Paton from Ramsey. There had been no witnesses to the accident and although visibility was restricted to sixty yards on some parts of the course, visibility at the scene of the accident was perfect.

An examination of the Norton revealed no evidence of seizure to the engine or gearbox but the chain was very slack and a theory was put forward that a small stone might have become wedged between the teeth of the sprocket and the chain causing a temporary locking of the rear wheel. This was corroborated by a black tyre mark on the road surface at the scene of the accident, measuring 15 yards in length followed by 75 yards of scrape marks leading to the point where the Norton had collided with the grass bank on the left.

Alf Shaw, a married man, was 51 years of age. He was a salesman by occupation and a resident of Birkenhead, Cheshire where he lived with his wife Nancy. He was an experienced racing motorcyclist and had competed at the Manx Grand Prix both before and after the war. His best results being 10th in the 1937 Lightweight Race and 17th in the 1948 Junior. Then in 1949 he took part in his first TT but was forced to retire on the 4th lap of the Junior Race. In 1950 he won the 250 class at the Leinster "200" and a week later he came second in the 250 class at the NorthWest "200". In 1960, after an absence of many years, he returned to the TT and became a regular from then onwards, gaining a number of replicas and finishers awards.

His funeral service was held in Douglas and followed by committal at Douglas Borough Crematorium. A plaque in his memory can be found on the Memorial Wall in the Borough Cemetery.

Geoffrey PROCTOR

Geoff Proctor at Signpost Corner during the 1966 Lightweight MGP

Windy conditions were being reported at various points around the TT course on the morning of Tuesday 29th August 1967 but generally the weather was fine although there was a likelihood of damp patches beneath the trees in the area of Quarry Bends. Probably not the best of news for the competitors gathered at the Grandstand on Glencrutchery Road in Douglas waiting to take advantage of the third practice session for the Manx Grand Prix. Amongst them was Geoff Proctor, riding a 248cc Cotton machine bearing the race number 64 and entered in the Lightweight Race to be held the following Tuesday. This was the same machine that had taken him to 25th place in the Lightweight Manx the previous year and had been prepared for racing by one of his closest friends, Brian Ingram of George Collis Limited, the Southampton based motorcycle dealers.

Shortly before the session commenced at 6.20am Geoff told his mechanic John Husher not to bother timing him as he was going to take it steady for the first lap to run the engine in as this was the first time the machine had been used since it was prepared. The engine of the Cotton sounded healthy as he set off towards Bray Hill on his first lap of the meeting and safely made his way through Union Mills, Glen Helen and Kirk Michael village before he was seen approaching Birkin's Bends, fifteen miles into the lap. He was alone on the road and travelling at normal racing speed but as he passed the junction with the Orrisdale Road the rear end of his machine suddenly began to wobble from side to side and his right foot came off the footrest then his other foot came off the footrest as he struggled to regain control of the machine but at this point the Cotton appeared to start jumping about and mounted the footpath on the left. The unfortunate rider was thrown from the machine and came to rest in the roadway. Marshals went to his immediate assistance but there was nothing they could do for him. He had been killed instantly.

Ken Harding, Chief Scrutineer for the Manx Motor Cycle Club, examined the relatively undamaged Cotton at Ramsey Police Station and could find no evidence of engine seizure. The primary chain, clutch and gearbox were all in perfect condition. The braking system and suspension were in good working order. However, the nearside handlebar was broken at the point of attachment to the clip securing it to the fork stanchion. The brazing was not of good quality and there was a concern that the brazing may have failed before the accident, but this could only be speculated as the bar had sustained impact damage during the accident.

Geoff Proctor, a single man, was 24 years of age. He was a resident of Swaythling, Southampton and although a draughtsman by trade he was employed as a coachbuilder with Wimpson's of Southampton. He had moved to the south of England from his hometown of Stockton three years earlier. He was an experienced racing motorcyclist who competed about once a fortnight during the racing season.

His funeral service was held at Holy Trinity Church, Stockton on the afternoon of Monday 4th September and followed by interment at Oxbridge Lane Cemetery.

Kenneth Edwin HERBERT

Ken Herbert about to retire at Ballaugh Bridge during practice for the 1967 Senior MGP

Rain and wet roads around the TT course on the evening of Friday 1st September 1967 made grim racing conditions but this had not deterred those competitors congregating at the Grandstand in Douglas waiting to participate in a practice session for the Manx Grand Prix. Amongst them was Ken Herbert, riding a 499cc Manx Norton bearing the race number 77 and entered in the Senior Race to be held the following Thursday. At this stage he had still not qualified for the race.

With the session under way, Herbert set off along Glencrutchery Road to commence his opening lap and safely made his way through the first eight miles of the course. Then, at about 6.35pm, with the rain still falling, he was seen approaching the sweeping left hand corner known as Doran's Bend. On going into the bend his machine began to drift to the right and struck the kerb. The unfortunate rider was thrown from the machine and collided with four concrete fencing posts before coming to rest on the footpath. There were two marshals in the vicinity of the accident and one displayed the yellow flag to warn oncoming riders while the other ran back to Ballig Bridge to call for a doctor and ambulance to attend. Meanwhile, another competitor, Peter Ward, riding his Senior BSA, came upon the incident. Seeing that the fallen rider was not being attended to, he stopped his machine and went back to the scene. For the safety of other competitors he removed the crashed Norton from the roadway then attended to Ken Herbert. Moments later he was joined by a Travelling Marshal but there was nothing they could do for the fallen rider. He had been killed instantly.

Herbert had intended to use his 498cc Triumph/Norton in the Senior Race and had brought this with him to the Island. However, on the Monday evening practice session, he was unable to get it started and later found that the Magneto had failed. He therefore decided to prepare his Manx Norton for racing instead and purchased an exhaust system from Colin Seeley. The following day, he went to the Race Office and obtained permission to use the Manx Norton in the Senior Race. He took it out for the first time during the Wednesday morning practice session but only made it to Kirk Michael because the nut and bolt holding the swinging arm suspension had become loose. With the machine repaired, he went out again during the Thursday afternoon session but was forced to stop at Ballaugh with the same problem. He subsequently purchased a completely new swinging arm suspension unit from Colin Seeley and had prepared the machine for the fateful Friday evening practice session.

Ken Herbert, a single man, was 26 years of age. He was a motor mechanic with the GPO by occupation and a resident of Holloway, London where he lived with his parents. He was a member of the Greenwich Motor Cycling Club and the Louth Motor Cycling Club in Lincolnshire with racing experience on most of the short circuits in England. His first appearance on the Isle of Man was at the 1965 Manx Grand Prix but he did not take part in the races. He returned the following year but was forced to retire during the Senior Race.

His funeral service was held in London on Friday 8th September and followed by interment at Trent Park Cemetery, Cockfosters Road, Enfield.

Ian D`arcy VEITCH

Ian Veitch at Quarterbridge during the fateful 1968 Lightweight 250 TT

Weather conditions were fine on the afternoon of Monday 10th June 1968, visibility was clear and the roads around the TT course were dry as 81 competitors lined up along Glencrutchery Road in Douglas waiting to participate in the International Lightweight 250 Tourist Trophy Race. Amongst them was Ian Veitch of New Zealand, a newcomer to the Isle of Man, riding a Kawasaki machine bearing the race number 77. He had completed nine official laps of the course during practice.

Bill Ivy, the reigning 125cc World Champion set up a blistering pace on his Yamaha. From a standing start he completed his first lap in 21 minutes 27.4 seconds, which was breathtaking for it set up a new lap record of 105.51mph. His stable mate, Phil Read, was just over 14 seconds in arrears.

Ian Veitch went straight through at the end of his first lap and signalled to his pit attendant, Leonard Perry, that everything was okay. He then safely made his way through Quarterbridge, Braddan and Union Mills before making the climb up the Ballahutchin Hill towards Glen Vine. On the approach to the right hand bend at Ballagarey he was alone on the road and travelling at racing speed but as he began to negotiate the corner the front wheel of the Kawasaki clipped the kerb on the right, throwing the machine onto its right hand side. Both rider and machine then slid along the road for thirty to forty yards before colliding heavily with a stone pillar at the gateway to the house "Kufri". On impact with the pillar his helmet came off. The unfortunate rider rebounded back into the roadway while his machine slid back across the road before coming to rest near to the right hand kerb. Marshals went to his immediate assistance and found that he was not breathing. Gallant efforts were made to resuscitate him even while he was being carried by stretcher to a point where he could be transferred to an ambulance. He was then conveyed to Noble's Hospital in the hope that more could be done for him there but on his arrival it was confirmed that he was beyond human aid. He had succumbed to his injuries.

Ivy pulled in at the end of the second lap to refuel and it was learned that he had caught his right foot when cornering and had sprained his ankle and cut his toes. He gamely continued, having lost the lead to Phil Read. Then drama during the fourth lap, Read was out of the race having stopped at the Bungalow with a punctured rear tyre. Ivy raced by - back into the lead. After refuelling and making some adjustments to the front brake he went on to complete the six lap race and took the chequered flag two minutes and 12 seconds ahead of the Italian Renzo Pasolini (Benelli). The East German rider Heinz Rosner (MZ) finished third. Seventh place went to the Spanish rider Santiago Herrero (Ossa).

Ian Veitch, a single man, was 23 years of age. He was a motor mechanic by occupation and a resident of Gisbourne, New Zealand. He had raced for five years in New Zealand with considerable success, including a win in the New Zealand TT. He was on the Island to gain experience with a view to competing in the TT again the following year.

His funeral service was held on the Isle of Man and followed by interment at Douglas Borough Cemetery, within a stone's throw of the TT grandstand.

Peter RAY

Peter Ray at Ballaugh Bridge during the fateful 1968 Lightweight MGP

Dark grey clouds spreading over the Isle of Man on the morning of Tuesday 3rd September 1968 displayed a threat of rainfall later in the day. Not the best of outlooks for the 95 competitors assembled on Glencrutchery Road in Douglas waiting to participate in the Lightweight Manx Grand Prix. Amongst them was Peter Ray, a newcomer to the Island, riding an Aermacchi machine bearing the race number 29.

When the flag dropped and the race began the riders were sent on their way in pairs and at ten-second intervals. Shortly after the first riders had passed over Ballaugh Bridge on the opening lap it began to rain quite heavily and several riders were experiencing difficulty when braking on the approach to the bridge. The road had been recently resurfaced but the new surface did not begin until approximately 20 feet after the usual braking point. Therefore, riders were applying their brakes on the old and much smoother road surface, which would have been perfectly adequate had it not been raining.

At about 11.10am, on his third lap of the race, Peter Ray was seen approaching Ballaugh Bridge and as he applied his brakes his machine began to "snake" along the roadway then the front wheel suddenly slipped away to the left and the machine fell from beneath him. With the unfortunate rider still holding on, the machine slid along the road and glanced off a car parked on the garage forecourt on the left side of the road before colliding with the stone wall on the bridge. This impact caused the machine to be thrown back onto its wheels, the rider still onboard, it then ran along the side of the wall for a few yards before falling over onto its side again. At this point Peter Ray separated from the machine and collided heavily with the stone wall. Marshals went to his immediate aid but there was nothing that could be done for him. He had been killed instantly.

The lap record was broken during the race by Stanley Woods from Helsby, Cheshire who, from a standing start, recorded a time of 25 minutes and 1.8 seconds, chopping 16 seconds off the existing record. However, he was to run into mechanical problems on the last few miles of the last lap and eventually finished ninth. Frank Whiteway from Dalton-in-Furness went on to win the race with a record breaking average speed of 88.52mph.

Peter Ray was 22 years of age. He was an experimental engineer by occupation employed at the Ford Motor Company research centre at Dunton, and was a resident of Grays, Essex where he and his wife Susan lived with his widowed mother. Having taken up motorcycle racing approximately three years earlier he had only started competing seriously this year and had won several races at venues all over Britain. He was regarded as a competent rider of exceptional ability and his ambition was to become a professional racing motorcyclist.

A poignant feature of this accident was that on the morning of the race his 18-year-old wife Susan, entered a maternity hospital and a few hours after his death, unaware of the tragedy, gave birth to a baby girl, Laura.

His funeral service was held in England on 10th September and followed by committal at Upminster Crematorium.

Roger PERRIER

Roger Perrier pictured during practice for the 1968 Junior MGP

Wind and rain swept across the Isle of Man on the afternoon of Tuesday 3rd September 1968 and mist had reduced visibility on certain parts of the TT course. However, undeterred by the poor racing conditions were more than a hundred competitors lined up along Glencrutchery Road in Douglas waiting to take part in the Junior Manx Grand Prix. Amongst them was Roger Perrier, a newcomer to the Island, riding a Norton machine bearing the race number 17.

Within three minutes of the commencement of the race, the first retirement was posted when John Dallow of Wolverhampton slid off at Quarterbridge and damaged his machine. Leading at the end of the first lap by four fifths of a second was David Thomas from Buckley, Flintshire but he was forced to retire at the Quarterbridge during the third lap of the race when an inspection of his machine revealed a damaged seat. John Findlay of Bonnyrigg, Midlothian, who had been second, forged an eleven second lead at the half way stage over his nearest rival, Clive Brown of Harpenden, Hertfordshire.

At about 3.55pm, on the fifth lap of the race, officials at Douglas Road Corner, Kirk Michael saw two competitors, number 10, Maurice Jefferey from South Wales and number 17, Roger Perrier approaching the corner in close company. Jefferey changed down to third gear for the corner, and then saw his friend, Perrier; overtake him on the inside going into the right hand bend. However, on the exit of the bend, Perrier's machine went wide, struck the left hand kerb and mounted the footpath. The machine then travelled along the footpath, grazing a pebble dashed brick wall for a distance of 41 feet before both rider and machine collided heavily with a brick gate pillar situated at the entrance to the house "Borodail". The unfortunate rider was thrown back into the roadway and although he was quickly attended to there was nothing that could be done for him. He had been killed instantly. His Norton machine had continued for a further 69 feet before it dug into a sod hedge and rebounded back into the roadway, sliding for a further 380 feet before coming to a stop. Maurice Jefferey continued on to finish the race in 19th position, unaware that his friend had been killed.

During the last lap of the race, Nigel Warren who had been challenging Clive Brown for second place came off at Doran's Bend just beyond Ballig Bridge and was taken to hospital with a fractured leg. Brown was also forced to retire on the last lap after losing a footrest, which allowed Welshman Gordon Pantall to move into second place behind race winner John Findlay who recorded a race average speed of 89.85mph.

Roger Perrier was 29 years of age and a resident of Cardiff, South Wales where he lived with his 26 year old wife Eileen who had never seen him race because she found it too worrying. They had been married for about six years and had no children. He was a civil servant by occupation and formerly worked with the GPO as an engineer. Although the fateful race was his first on the Isle of Man he had been highly placed in national and club events at circuits such as Mallory Park, Cadwell Park and Oulton Park. He had also raced at Crystal Palace and Thruxton.

His funeral service was held on Tuesday 10th September and followed by interment at Thornhill Cemetery.

Edgar Arthur LAVINGTON

Arthur Lavington pictured on the mountain during practice for the 1969 Junior TT

Observers around the TT course on the evening of Friday 6th June 1969 confirmed fine weather, clear visibility and dry roads. Ideal conditions for the competitors assembled in the area of the Grandstand in Douglas waiting to take advantage of a practice session for the Tourist Trophy Races. Amongst them was the race veteran, Arthur Lavington, riding a 350cc Velocette machine bearing the race number 107 and entered in the Junior Race to be held the following week.

At about 7.45pm, sixteen miles out from the start line in Douglas, Arthur Lavington was seen approaching Alpine Corner in Ballaugh with another rider close behind him. He was travelling at racing speed and on the correct line for the sweeping right hand bend but the other rider was travelling much faster and began to overtake him on the right. However, there was insufficient room between the Velocette and the hedge for the other rider to pass and the two machines collided then became locked together for a short distance. As they separated Lavington was thrown from his machine and slid along the roadway before colliding heavily with the kerbstone of the footpath on the left. The other rider did not stop but continued on towards Ballaugh. Marshals went to the immediate assistance of the unfortunate rider and found him lying on his back in the road. He was unconscious and had sustained serious injuries. The Marshals carefully lifted him onto the footpath to await the arrival of an ambulance and the duty doctor from Parliament Square in Ramsey. Race officials suspended the practice session to allow an ambulance onto the course via Brough Jairg farm Road in Ballaugh. The gravely injured rider was conveyed to Ramsey Cottage Hospital where an emergency operation was carried out to assist his breathing but there was no improvement and his condition slowly deteriorated until 1.30pm on Sunday 8th June when he succumbed to his injuries.

Despite extensive enquiries by the police and the Auto Cycle Union, the other rider was not identified. Ken Shierson, secretary of the ACU and clerk of the course stated, "We questioned all the riders who were on that part of the circuit at the time. We are satisfied that none of them knew more than he told us or was holding anything back ".

Arthur Lavington was 52 years of age. He was a self employed motorcycle agent by occupation and a resident of Farnborough, Hampshire. He was a rider of great experience and had raced on the TT course many times, always on Velocette machines. His first racing appearance on the Island was the 1949 Junior Clubman's race, which was held over three laps of the TT course, but he was forced to retire during the second lap. In 1954 he began his long association with the TT races, winning a bronze replica in the Junior Race but retired during the second lap of the Senior. During the 1965 Junior Race he came off his machine at Greeba Bridge on the sixth and final lap of the race, sustaining cuts and abrasions to both knees and his left hand. With a number of race day retirements he had never achieved great success on the Island but he was described as one of the characters of the races whose enthusiasm and spirit was of the calibre which helped to make the TT races.

His funeral service was held in the Isle of Man on Thursday 12th June and followed by committal at Douglas Borough Crematorium.

Gordon Victor TAYLOR

Gordon Taylor pictured during practice for the 1968 Lightweight MGP

Those rising early on the morning of Monday 25th August 1969 were met with grey skies, a brisk wind and wet roads round the TT course. To make matters worse, mist between the Gooseneck and Brandywell on the mountain section had reduced visibility to 30 yards in places. These were the unwelcome conditions that faced the competitors gathered at the Grandstand in Douglas waiting to take part in the opening practice session for the Manx Grand Prix. Amongst them was Gordon Taylor, riding a 325cc Kawasaki machine bearing the race number 27 and entered in the Junior Race to be held the following week.

Shortly after 6.00am, as the first riders headed off along Glencrutchery Road the roads were beginning to dry out and the general weather conditions were slowly improving. Five minutes after the first men departed Gordon Taylor received the signal to commence his opening circuit and the Kawasaki fired up at the first time of asking. He set off along Glencrutchery Road and safely negotiated his way round the course back to the Grandstand, passing straight through without stopping. Stanley Speer, his pit attendant, had timed his lap at around 31 minutes, which indicated just how poor the conditions were around the course.

Meanwhile, at Alpine Corner a short distance before Ballaugh Bridge, a course marshal, Dick Reeves, who was on duty alone at that location, noticed that the rising sun was beginning to break through the clouds and several riders appeared to be blinded by the sun as they were coming out of the right hand corner. Some competitors were forced to brake or change down to a lower gear. In view of this danger, Reeves held up a yellow flag to warn approaching riders of the danger. In addition, there was a large "Sun" warning board at Kirk Michael and sun warning lights were also in operation along this stretch of the course.

At about 6.55am, sixteen miles into his second lap, Gordon Taylor was alone on the road as he approached Alpine Corner. He was on the correct racing line for the bend and travelling at racing speed. As he passed the marshal and began to negotiate the corner he went into a beam of bright sunlight, which almost certainly dazzled him because on the exit of the bend he drifted wide and his machine struck the kerb on the left side of the road. Machine and rider then shot back across the road and collided heavily with the hedge on the right. The unfortunate rider parted company from the Kawasaki and was thrown against a tree before coming to rest lying face down on top of the hedge. The marshal went to his immediate aid but there was nothing he could do for him. He had been killed instantly.

Gordon Taylor, a single man, was 30 years of age. He was a sheet metal worker by occupation and a resident of Rainhill near St. Helens. He made his debut on the Isle of Man in 1964 when he competed in the Lightweight MGP but was forced to retire his Cotton machine during the race. He returned every year following that appearance to contest the Lightweight Manx and his best result came in 1968 when, riding a Kawasaki, he took 8th place.

His funeral service was held on Saturday 30th August, followed by committal at St. Helens Crematorium. His ashes were scattered on the family grave at St. Ann's Church, Rainhill.

91

Michael Leslie BENNETT

Michael Bennett at Quarterbridge during practice for the 1969 Senior MGP

Very strong winds were blowing across the Isle of Man on the evening of Tuesday 26th August 1969 and swirling mist was reducing visibility down to 35 yards in various places on the mountain section of the TT course. Not the best of conditions for racing but at least the roads were dry for the competitors congregating in the area of the Grandstand on Glencrutchery Road in Douglas ready to take advantage of the fourth practice session for the Manx Grand Prix. Amongst them was Michael Bennett, riding a 350cc Yamaha machine bearing the race number 77, which was entered in the Junior Race scheduled for the following Tuesday. The previous evening, riding a 500cc Norton machine bearing the race number 10, he completed two practice laps for the Senior Race and had returned fast times.

The session commenced at 6.15pm and at some time within the next half hour he set off towards Bray Hill on his opening lap of the evening. He then safely made his way through the first nine miles of the course and into the tricky Glen Helen section where, at about 6.50pm, he was seen approaching the left hand bend immediately before the Glen Helen Hotel then, for some unknown reason he collided with the grass bank on the left hand side of the road. The Yamaha went down onto its left side and along with the unfortunate rider, slid along the roadway before coming to rest. A police officer and marshals stationed near that point went immediately to the crash scene and found Bennett lying on his back and unconscious on the right hand side of the road. He was placed on a stretcher and carried to the living room of the hotel where his crash helmet was removed and a doctor who had been conveyed to the scene from Laurel Bank examined him. Due to the serious nature of his injuries, instructions were issued by the Clerk of the Course for riders to be stopped at Ballacraine in order to allow an ambulance from the St. Johns Ambulance Brigade to proceed along the course to pick up the injured rider and to convey him to Noble's Hospital. The ambulance left Glen Helen at 7.20pm and arrived at the hospital fifty minutes later. However, despite emergency treatment in the intensive care unit, he succumbed to his injuries at around 11.30pm that same evening.

Michael Bennett was 31 years of age. He was a garage proprietor and a fully qualified mechanical engineer by occupation and was a resident of Towcester, Northamptonshire where he lived with his wife Ruth and their 12 month old son, Paul. Prior to setting off on his fateful lap, his wife Ruth had accompanied him to the grandstand but had to leave prior to his departure because the baby had fallen asleep in the pushchair. He was an experienced rider, having made his debut on the Island in 1963 when he finished 24th in the Senior Manx. He returned the following year and finished 11th in the Junior race. In the 1965 Senior, he was forced to retire during the race but in the 1966 Junior, after lying in 4th place after the first lap he eventually finished a creditable 8th from a field of 97 starters. His best performance came in 1967 when, from a grid of 99 riders he finished 4th in the Junior Race, which was won by John Wetherall. In the Senior Race two days later he had been holding third place until having to retire at Sulby on the fourth lap with a seized engine. He was the holder of three silver replicas, all gained from his Junior MGP results and all on Norton machines.

His funeral service was held at Whittlebury Church on Tuesday 2nd September and followed by committal at Milton.

Iain SIDEY

Iain Sidey pictured on the mountain during practice for the 1969 Senior MGP

Strong winds and damp patches would be encountered across the mountain section of the TT course on the afternoon of Thursday 28th August 1969. Not the best of conditions awaiting the competitors gathered at the Grandstand in Douglas waiting to take advantage of the seventh practice session for the Manx Grand Prix. Amongst them was Iain Sidey, riding a G50 Matchless machine bearing the race number 45, which had been entered in the Senior Race to be held the following Thursday. The previous evening he had been working on this machine, fitting a new big end to the engine and also fitting a five-speed gearbox, which he had borrowed. However, he had to work late into the evening after he discovered a fault with the new big end and had taken it back for some work to be done before it could be fitted.

Shortly before setting off along Glencrutchery Road to commence his opening lap he had told his wife Pat that he intended to take it easy for the first two laps so that he could get used to the new gearbox as he had never ridden a racing machine fitted with a five speed gearbox before. His intention was then to speed up during the third lap of the session.

Having completed two laps of the course with average lap speeds of between 87 and 88 mph, he passed straight through the start area to commence his third lap of the afternoon. He had safely made his way through St. Ninian's crossroad's and down Bray Hill when he was seen approaching the relatively slow right hand corner at the Quarterbridge. He took the usual racing line through the corner but as he let out the clutch after changing gear on the exit, the rear wheel of his machine suddenly slid away to the left. He instinctively steered to his left in an effort to correct the slide but was thrown over the front of the machine and landed heavily in the road. Marshals went to his immediate aid and found that his condition was serious. He was lifted onto a stretcher and carried to a safe place at the side of the road where first aid was administered before he was conveyed from the scene by ambulance to Noble's Hospital. However, on his arrival at the Hospital he was examined by the duty doctor and found to have succumbed to his injuries.

An examination of the machine by Ken Harding, Chief Scrutineer for the Manx Motor Cycle Club, revealed that it had been assembled by fitting a Matchless engine and gearbox to a Norton frame and because of the way it had been put together there was a dangerous amount of "chain snatch". He later gave a warning about the danger of racing on hybrid machines.

Iain Sidey was 26 years of age. He was a design draughtsman by occupation and a resident of Glasgow where he lived with his wife Pat and their two year old son David. They had travelled to the Isle of Man with him, intending to spend a fortnight's holiday while he competed in the races. He had competed in the Senior Manx Grand Prix on three previous occasions, the first being in 1965 when he was forced to retire his Triumph-Norton. The following year, riding a Matchless, he finished 28th and in 1967 achieved his highest placing when he finished 24th riding a Matchless.

His funeral service was held on 3rd September and followed by committal at Maryhill Crematorium, Glasgow.

Lester John ILES

1969 - Les Iles pictured on his Bultaco during practice for the Lightweight 125 TT

Conditions around the TT course on the morning of Monday 1st June 1970 were described as ideal for racing, which was welcome news for the competitors congregating at the Grandstand in Douglas waiting to take advantage of the opening practice session for the Tourist Trophy Races. Amongst them was race veteran Les Iles, riding a 125cc Bultaco machine bearing the race number 36 and entered in the Lightweight TT to be held the following week.

During the course of the session, which commenced at 4.45am, Les Isles set off on his opening circuit and safely made his way through to Ramsey then up onto the mountain section where, at about 5.50am, he was seen approaching Kate's Cottage. However, he was not on the usual racing line for the left hand bend and was only travelling at 40 to 50mph but looked to be struggling to maintain control of his machine. At a point just below the cottage the Bultaco collided with the grass bank on the right hand side of the course and on impact the unfortunate rider was thrown forward into a substantial hawthorn bush while his machine continued down the hill and hit the hedge a second time before eventually coming to rest on it's side in the roadway and with the engine still running.

There were two marshals on duty at that location and while one went to the assistance of the injured rider the other removed the crashed machine to the side of the road and then warned approaching riders with a yellow flag. A young spectator appeared on the scene and he was dispatched to the Creg ny Baa to summon assistance. On hearing of the accident, the medical officer on duty at Creg ny Baa, Dr. J.R. Daniel, Senior House Surgeon at Noble's Hospital, immediately made his way to the scene of the incident and following his examination he ordered the gravely injured rider to be carried by stretcher to the Creg ny Baa Hotel. From there he was conveyed by ambulance to Noble's Hospital where, on his arrival it was found that he had succumbed to his injuries.

Ernest Alfred Woods, Chief Scrutineer for the Auto-Cycle Union, later examined the Bultaco machine and found that the brake cable nipple had worked loose. He concluded that this mechanical failure might have been a contributory factor to the accident.

Les Iles, a single man, was 40 years of age. He was a machine setter by occupation and a resident of Henfield, Coalpit Heath, Bristol. He was a rider of considerable racing experience throughout the United Kingdom and on the Continent with top placings in Belgium and France. His made his debut on the TT course in 1963 when he competed in the Lightweight 125 TT. He returned in 1964 and again competed in the Lightweight 125 TT but during the second lap he came off his Bultaco on the bends immediately before Laurel Bank and sustained cuts and bruises. Undeterred, he returned to the TT in 1965 and 1966, gaining further finishers awards. During the opening practice session for the 1967 TT he met with an accident at Braddan Bridge and sustained injuries, which put him out of racing for some time. In 1969 he gained a bronze replica in the Lightweight 250 TT and four days later he gained a silver replica in the Lightweight 125 TT.

His funeral service was held in the Isle of Man and followed by interment at Douglas Borough Cemetery.

94

Michael COLLINS

Mike Collins pictured during practice for the 1970 Senior TT

Conditions were described as ideal for racing on the morning of Wednesday 3rd June 1970. The weather was fine, the roads around the TT course were dry and visibility was clear on the mountain section. Welcome news for the competitors assembled at the Grandstand in Douglas waiting to take advantage of the fifth practice session for the Tourist Trophy Races. Amongst them was Mike Collins, riding a 496cc Seeley machine bearing the race number 78 and entered in the Senior Race to be held on Friday 12th June.

The session commenced at 4.45am and prior to setting off Collins was spoken to by Colin Seeley who had semi-sponsored him at race meetings in the past. Seeley advised him to relax a bit as he thought he had been trying too hard. He also warned him to be wary of the rising sun on the approach to Sulby. When his turn came, Collins set off along Glencrutchery Road towards Bray Hill on his opening circuit and safely made his way round the course to complete the lap with an average speed of 92.88mph. He continued straight past the Grandstand to commence his second lap and somewhere near to Ballacraine he overtook the Italian rider Renzo Pasolini who was riding a Benelli. The Italian noticed that Collins was travelling fast and decided to follow him in order to study the way he was taking the bends.

Pasolini followed him through to Ramsey and up onto the mountain section of the course where, after negotiating the bends at the Verandah, Collins had positioned himself in the middle of the road but then began to slowly drift to the left. At first this seemed normal to Pasolini as they were approaching a very slight right hand bend immediately before the short straight on the approach to the Les Graham Memorial. However, he soon became concerned and began to slow down as Mike Collins continued to move slowly to the left. His first thought was that the rider was feeling unwell. At this point the Seeley went onto the grass verge and on doing so Collins reacted very strongly, trying desperately to get off the grass and back onto the road. Just when it seemed he would succeed his left handlebar hit a fence post and he was thrown from the machine as it demolished several concrete posts. Some of the debris flew back into the roadway and damaged the fibreglass fairing on the front of Pasolini's Benelli. Marshals had witnessed the incident and immediately made their way to the scene where they found the unfortunate rider lying on the grassland some 60 feet below the road. He had sustained serious injuries and while arrangements were being made to stop the practice session to allow an ambulance onto the course at Ramsey the gravely injured rider succumbed to his injuries.

Michael Collins was 26 years of age. He was a sheet metal worker by occupation and a resident of Crayford, Kent. He was an experienced rider, having raced for about five years and had done very well on the short circuit courses such as Snetterton and Mallory Park. Riding a Seeley, he made his debut in the Isle of Man at the Manx Grand Prix in September 1969 and won the Newcomer's Award after he finished 6th in the Junior Race.

His funeral service was held on Tuesday 16th June and followed by committal at Eltham Crematorium.

Renzo Pasolini was to lose his life whilst racing at Monza, Italy in May 1973.

Dennis BLOWER

Dennis Blower and Stuart Brown at Braddan Bridge during practice for the 1970 Sidecar TT

On the afternoon of Tuesday 2nd June 1970, Dennis Blower arrived on the Isle of Man to compete in the Sidecar Tourist Trophy races. He met up with his passenger, Stuart Brown and that evening they took part in the opening practice session for the Sidecar Tourist Trophy races. Their sidecar outfit bearing the race number 67 was powered by a 499cc BSA engine and entered in the 500cc race to be held on Wednesday 10th June. On stopping after their first lap the outfit was checked and only minor defects were found such as a loose fuel tank, which was easily remedied. They then went out and completed a second lap.

On Wednesday 3rd June 1970, they worked on the outfit all day, replacing the engine with the 654cc BSA engine that they intended using for the 750cc Sidecar TT to be held on Monday 8th June. They finished at around 4.30pm and returned to their hotel for a meal. At 6.30pm they were at the Grandstand when the evening practice session commenced and they waited for all the other sidecars to get away before they set off along Glencrutchery Road in ideal racing conditions. At the end of their first circuit they pulled into the pits and on checking the machine they found that they had to replace two screws in the top of the fairing. They cleaned their goggles, stretched their legs and then set off on their second lap of the evening.

They had safely made their way round the course through to Ramsey and up onto the mountain section when, at about 8.15pm, they were seen travelling at racing speed and on the usual racing line on the approach to the Mountain Box. Dennis Blower was seated correctly on the outfit and Stuart Brown was getting up from the floor of the sidecar in preparation for the sweeping left hand corner when, at a point approximately 150 yards before the corner, the front of the sidecar suddenly dipped. The machine then veered to the right and collided with the wire roadside fencing, bounced off, then went back into and through the fencing before coming to rest on the grassland below the road. Marshals went to the assistance of the two men and found Dennis Blower lying in the grass having sustained serious injuries while Stuart Brown was found on the grass verge at the roadside with his arms and legs entangled in the wire fencing but he had escaped serious injury. A doctor and ambulance were directed to the scene from Ramsey and both men were then conveyed to Noble's Hospital. At 9.30pm, a short time after admission, Dennis Blower succumbed to his injuries. Stuart Brown recovered from his injuries but was unable to recall anything about the incident.

Following an examination of the machine, the Chief Scrutineer advanced a theory that a nut securing the fork assembly came off the sidecar combination making it difficult to control.

Dennis Blower, a married man, was 23 years of age. He was a maintenance engineer by occupation and a resident of Mattersea, near Doncaster, Yorkshire. His wife of ten months, Anne, who was expecting their first child, had accompanied him to the Island and was waiting in the pits at the time of the accident. This was his second time at the TT, his first appearance in 1969 ended on 4th June after he was involved in a crash at Brandywell during practice, which put both he and his passenger, A. Skirrow, in hospital for several days.

His funeral service was held in England and followed by interment at Mattersea Cemetery, Rotherham.

Santiago HERRERO-RUIZ

Santiago Herrero leaves Parliament Square, Ramsey during the fateful 1970 Lightweight 250 TT

Bright sunshine on the afternoon of Monday 8th June 1970 provided dry roads around the TT course and clear visibility on the mountain section. Perfect conditions for the 71 competitors lined up on Glencrutchery Road in Douglas waiting to participate in the Lightweight 250 Tourist Trophy Race. Amongst them, currently leading the world championship in this class was Santiago Herrero of Spain, riding a 250cc Ossa machine bearing the race number 10.

At 1.30pm the flag dropped and the race commenced with the riders setting off in pairs and at ten second intervals. Forty seconds later it was the turn of Santiago Herrero to begin his race against the clock and he roared off from the line ahead of his starting partner Jack Findlay. On completion of the first circuit he was holding fifth place and maintained that position through to the end of the second circuit. During his third lap of the race, Herrero took the slip road at Braddan Bridge then fell from his machine when turning in the road to rejoin the course. With no apparent damage to the machine other than a broken Perspex windshield he remounted and continued the race. On completion of his fourth circuit he pulled into the pits for his second stop and changed his goggles while his machine was being refuelled. He then set off again to commence his fifth lap. Kel Carruthers was leading the race, Stan Woods was second and Rod Gould third, just two seconds ahead of Herrero now in fourth place.

During the fifth lap, Stan Woods had stopped at Glen Vine and lost a considerable amount of time while he fitted new plugs to his Yamaha. Eventually he was able to rejoin the race and as he set off again he was passed by Santiago Herrero who was now on his sixth and final lap of the race and holding third position as a result of Woods dropping from the leaderboard. By Greeba Bridge, Woods had caught Herrero on the road and kept in his slipstream through Glen Helen, Handley's Corner, Barregarrow and on to the sweeping left hand bend below the 13th Milestone. Then, as they were negotiating the bend Herrero's machine began to slide away to the right and although Woods tried to take evasive action the two machines collided. Both riders were thrown off and slid along the road together with their machines before crashing heavily into the thorn hedgerow just beyond the house "Westwood". Marshals went to their assistance and found that Woods had fractured both collarbones and an ankle but Santiago Herrero was unconscious and had sustained multiple injuries. He was conveyed by helicopter to Noble's Hospital where, despite emergency treatment, his condition slowly deteriorated and he passed away at 2.00pm on Wednesday 10th June.

Kel Carruthers of Australia went on to win the race, having led from start to finish. Rod Gould (Yamaha) was second and Gunter Bartusch (MZ) was third.

Santiago Herrero-Ruiz, a single man, was 28 years of age. He was a professional racing motorcyclist by occupation and a resident of Bilbao, Spain. He was an experienced rider and had been with the Ossa factory for four years. He was Spanish Champion in 1967, 1968 and 1969. On the Isle of Man he was 6th in the 1968 Lightweight TT and 3rd in the 1969 Lightweight TT. He finished 3rd in the 1969 World Championship.

His funeral service was held in Spain on 19th June and followed by interment at the cemetery in Vistalegre near Bilbao.

John Joseph WETHERALL

John Wetherall at Keppel Gate during the fateful 1970 Senior TT

With the TT course on the Isle of Man bathed in sunshine on the afternoon of Friday 12th June 1970 conditions were near perfect for racing. Good news for the 86 competitors lined up along Glencrutchery Road in Douglas waiting to take part in the Senior International Tourist Trophy Race. Amongst them was John Wetherall, riding a 499cc Norton machine bearing the race number 35. The riders about to race represented no less than eight countries.

At 1.30pm the flag dropped and the race commenced with Giacomo Agostini on the MV Agusta being the first away. Having won the Junior Race two days earlier he was aiming to win both races for the third year in a row. The new idea of setting the riders off in groups of nine had been abandoned on safety grounds. Therefore the riders would be dispatched in pairs and at ten second intervals. A little over two minutes following Agostini's departure it was the turn of John Wetherall to begin his race against the clock and he safely made his way round the course to complete his opening circuit with an average speed of just over 91mph, which put him in 30th position. As predicted, Agostini was leading from Peter Williams, Alan Barnett and Brian Steenson.

On completion of the second lap Agostini had maintained his lead and the only change in the top four came from Alan Barnett who had moved up into second place, just three seconds ahead of Williams. Brian Steenson had recorded an average lap speed of 99.86mph and held fourth place. John Wetherall completed his second lap six seconds quicker than his opening lap but had dropped one place to 31st.

Having made his way through Glen Helen, Kirk Michael and Sulby, John Wetherall was 22 miles into his third lap when he was seen, alone on the road and approaching the right hand bend known as Milntown Corner. After crossing the small bridge immediately before the bend he was on the usual racing line but then as he banked over to negotiate the bend his shoulder caught the stone wall on the right and he was thrown from the machine. The unfortunate rider came to rest on the left hand pavement and had sustained serious injuries. He was rushed to Ramsey Cottage Hospital by ambulance then conveyed by helicopter to Noble's Hospital where he was admitted at 3.45pm. However, despite emergency treatment, his condition slowly deteriorated and he succumbed to his injuries at 4.40pm that same day.

With an average race speed of 101.52mph Agostini won the race ahead of Peter Williams and Bill Smith. Alan Barnett had crashed at Ballig Bridge on the fourth lap and Brian Steenson had crashed at the Mountain Box, sustaining injuries that were to prove fatal.

John Wetherall was 30 years of age. He was a plumber by occupation and although originally from Reading he had, for the previous three years, been a resident of St. Julian, Malta where he lived with his wife Shelley. He was an experienced rider who had made his debut on the TT course at the 1964 MGP when, riding a Cotton, he finished 7th in the Lightweight Race. At the 1967 Manx Grand Prix, he won the Junior Race and finished third in the Senior.

His funeral service was held in England and followed by interment at Henley Road Municipal Cemetery, Caversham, Reading.

Robert William Brian STEENSON

Brian Steenson leaves Parliament Square, Ramsey during the fateful 1970 Senior TT

Sunshine beamed down on the Isle of Man on the afternoon of Friday 12th June 1970 as 86 competitors, representing eight countries, lined up along Glencrutchery Road in Douglas waiting to participate in the Senior Tourist Trophy Race. Amongst them was Brian Steenson, riding a 498cc Seeley machine bearing the race number 12. The previous Saturday, riding a BSA Rocket Three, he had taken part in the Production Machine Race and was lying in second place when he was forced to retire with mechanical problems during the fourth lap.

The race began at 1.30pm and the first man to leave the starting line was the Italian rider, Giacomo Agostini, riding an MV Agusta. Less than a minute later, with his father watching from the Grandstand, Brian Steenson set off towards Bray Hill on his opening lap and safely made his way round the course to complete the lap with an average speed of just under 99mph, which put him in fourth place. Agostini led the race and was over a minute ahead of his nearest rival, Peter Williams with Alan Barnett third. By the end of the second circuit Agostini was still well ahead but Barnett had moved up to second place. Steenson had put in a lap of 99.86mph and maintained fourth place.

During his third lap of the race Brian Steenson had safely negotiated his way through to Ramsey and up onto the mountain section of the course when he was seen approaching the Mountain Box. Then, as he banked over to take the left hand corner the rear wheel of his machine suddenly jumped off the ground and stepped out to the right. The unfortunate rider had no chance of recovering control and was thrown from the machine, sustaining serious injuries. He was conveyed by helicopter to the casualty department at Noble's Hospital where he was admitted at 3.15pm. Despite extensive medical treatment over the next few days, his condition slowly deteriorated and he succumbed to his injuries at 11.45am on Wednesday 17th June.

Also on the third lap of the race, John Wetherall from Malta crashed at Milntown near Ramsey and sustained injuries that were to prove fatal.

Agostini went on to win the race with an average speed of 101.52mph and was over five minutes ahead of Peter Williams. Alan Barnett had come off his machine at Ballig Bridge on the fourth lap and so third position went to Bill Smith. It was the third year in succession that the Italian world champion had won both the Junior and Senior events.

Brian Steenson, a single man, was 23 years of age. He was a mechanical engineer by occupation, employed by BSA of Birmingham and his home was at Crossgar, County Down, Northern Ireland. After leaving school he had studied for a degree in mechanical engineering at the Ashby Institute at Queens University in Belfast and later graduated with a BSc. He was a very experienced racing motorcyclist having raced on circuits in England, Northern Ireland and the Continent. His first appearance on the TT circuit was at the 1968 TT and riding an Aermacchi he secured 9th place in the Junior. He returned in 1969 and riding an Aermacchi in the Junior TT he took 2nd place behind Agostini and his MV.

His funeral service was followed by interment at First Presbyterian Church, Killyleagh, County Down.

George Robert Vivian COLLIS

George Collis at Signpost Corner during the fateful 1970 Lightweight 250 MGP

Although it was sunny and the roads around the TT course were dry on the morning of Tuesday 1st September 1970 there was a gale force wind blowing, which would be a concern for the 84 competitors lined up along Glencrutchery Road in Douglas waiting to take part in the Lightweight 250cc Manx Grand Prix. Amongst them was race veteran George Collis, riding a Yamaha machine bearing the race number 25.

At 10.00am the flag dropped and the race commenced with the first riders being sent on their way towards Bray Hill. It wasn't long before George Collis received the signal to begin his race against the clock and he safely made his way round the course to complete his first circuit with an average lap speed of 90.94mph, which made him the race leader with a 30 second advantage over Alan Steele in second place. However, by the end of the second lap the positions had been reversed and Steele now held an 11 second lead over Collis.

During the second lap, two competitors, James Ward and Robert Nicholson had both retired at Handley's Corner and were watching the remainder of the race from that location when they saw George Collis approaching on his third lap. He was travelling at racing speed and on the perfect racing line to negotiate the bends but as he was coming to the slight left hand bend he twice looked down at the left hand side of his machine and seemed to be tapping something on that side with his foot, probably the gear lever because both Nicholson and Ward agreed that his machine appeared to be out of gear. While he was trying to adjust his machine, it drifted over to the right hand side of the road. He seemed to realise this and immediately sat upright but by this time he was already through the left hand bend and off the racing line to negotiate the following right hand bend. As a consequence, on the exit of the bend his machine collided heavily with a thorn hedge on the left hand side of the road and he was thrown into the roadway. Marshals went to the immediate aid of the unfortunate rider and found that he had sustained serious injuries and was unconscious. They did what they could for him until he was conveyed by helicopter to Noble's Hospital where he was admitted at 11.32am. Fifty minutes later he was transferred to the Intensive Therapy Unit but his condition slowly deteriorated during the afternoon and at 3.10pm he succumbed to his injuries.

The race had continued and at about 11.40am it began to rain at the Bungalow, which caused further difficulties for the riders. Alan Steele went on to win the race at an average speed of 90.44mph with John Griffiths second and Les Trotter third.

George Collis was 35 years of age. He was a garage proprietor by occupation and a resident of North Baddesley, Hampshire where he lived with his wife Maureen and their two young sons, Geoffrey and Nicholas. He was noted for his achievements in long-distance races and for several years he had competed with some success in the Barcelona 24 hour race in Spain. In 1968 he and Maureen were travelling back home from Barcelona when their E-type Jaguar was involved in a road traffic accident in which they both sustained serious injuries. He was an experienced competitor on the Isle of Man, having taken part in seven previous Manx Grand Prix races since 1964 and had gained three coveted replicas.

His funeral service was held at St. Johns Church, Rownhams and was followed by interment.

Brian FINCH

(By kind permission of Manx National Heritage)
Brian Finch pictured on the mountain during practice for the 1971 Production Race

With fine weather and dry roads around the TT course on the afternoon of Wednesday 9th June 1971 conditions were ideal for the competitors assembled on Glencrutchery Road in Douglas waiting to participate in the Production Machine Race. Amongst them was Brian Finch, riding a Suzuki T500 machine bearing the race number 43. Earlier that day, riding a Yamaha, he had taken part in the in the Lightweight 250cc TT Race and finished in 24th place with an average speed of 87.35mph, which earned him a coveted silver replica.

The race was split into three classes, all commencing with a Le Mans style start with a three-minute delay between each class. Fifteen minutes before the race began, the machines were taken from the warming up enclosure to their allotted positions beneath the scoreboard opposite the Grandstand where handlers held them. With five minutes to go, the track cleared and the riders took their places in front of the Grandstand. At 2.00pm the flag dropped and the seventeen riders for the 750 class ran across Glencrutchery Road to their machines, started the engines and roared off towards Bray Hill. This action was repeated three minutes later as the seventeen riders for the 500 class, including Brian Finch, began their race. Three minutes after they had departed the fourteen men entered in the 250 class, including Barry Sheene, repeated the same process.

Brian Finch had safely made his way through Union Mills and Greeba on his opening lap when he was seen approaching Ballacraine in close company with several other competitors. They reduced speed then began peeling off into the right hand corner. However, Finch appeared to have missed his "peeling off" point and applied his brakes hard but with his rear tyre smoking he realised that he would be unable to make the corner and attempted to take the escape road but it was too late. The Suzuki went onto the forecourt of the Ballacraine Hotel and with Finch stood up on the footrests the machine struck the front steps of the hotel. The unfortunate rider was thrown against the front door frame and landed on some spectators who had been sitting on the steps. Despite receiving immediate medical aid he succumbed to his injuries within minutes of the accident.

Brian Finch was one week short of his 25th birthday. He was a motor mechanic by occupation and a resident of Denton, Lancashire where he lived with his wife Christine and their four-year-old son, Paul. Christine had not travelled to the Island to watch her husband race as they had planned another holiday later in the year. His mother and father had emigrated to Australia two years earlier and a family reunion had been planned for October. His first race on the Isle of Man was the 1968 Lightweight MGP when, riding a Greeves, he finished 10th. An example of his determination was shown in 1969, when, in poor weather conditions he was taking part in a morning practice session and had set the fastest lap before he came off his Yamaha machine in Parliament Square, Ramsey where marshals tried to persuade him to stop. However, he remounted and carried on but within half a mile, at Cruickshanks Corner, his machine slipped on the wet road and he came off again, this time cutting his hands and damaging the machine. Only then did he call it a day. Moving to the TT in 1970, riding a Velocette Thruxton, he finished 7th in the 500cc Production Race.

His funeral service was held on Tuesday 15th June and followed by committal at Stockport Crematorium. A memorial plaque can be found on the wall of the Ballacraine Hotel.

Maurice Arthur JEFFERY

Maurice Jeffery pictured during the fateful 1971 Senior TT

Unlike the previous day when deteriorating weather conditions caused the postponement of racing, the weather on the morning of Saturday 12th June 1971 was much more promising. The early morning mist was clearing and conditions looked good for the 66 competitors lined up along Glencrutchery Road in Douglas waiting to take part in the six lap Senior Tourist Trophy Race. Amongst them was Maurice Jeffery, riding a 499cc Norton machine bearing the race number 83.

After a thirty-minute delay, the flag dropped at 11.30am and the race was under way. Several minutes later it was the turn of Maurice Jeffery to begin his race against the clock and he set off on his opening lap towards the daunting drop of Bray Hill. He safely made his way through Braddan, Greeba and Glen Helen then, with fourteen miles behind him, he was one of three riders seen travelling in close company through Kirk Michael village. As they approached Birkin's Bend at Rhencullen, Jeffery was leading the trio with Robert Graham, race number 88, just behind him. Graham had just overtaken the third man, L. Williams, race number 80, and was looking for an opportunity to overtake Jeffery but noticed that he was positioned in the middle of the road, which was the wrong racing line for the sweeping right and left hand bends. Then, despite his attempts to correct his position Jeffery drifted wide on the exit of the bend and struck the kerb on the left. His Norton immediately went out of control and the unfortunate rider was thrown as it tumbled across the road, narrowly missing Graham as he passed by, before coming to rest on top of the grass bank on the right. Marshals and the duty doctor at that location went to his immediate assistance and although he was found to be unconscious he did appear to be coming round but within a short time of the incident, he succumbed to his injuries.

The race continued with Giacomo Agostini way out in front throughout. Attention centred on the riders sparring for the following places. Peter Williams on his Arter Matchless in fact held second place throughout the race, but for the first three laps John Williams, also on a Matchless, closely contended the position before retiring with engine problems on the fourth lap. Frank Perris, riding a Suzuki moved up into third place and held that position for the rest of the race. Having narrowly avoided a collision when Maurice Jeffery crashed on the first lap Robert Graham continued his race but was forced to retire his Norton during the third lap. L. Williams went on to finish in 25th place, which earned him a silver replica.

Maurice Jeffery, a single man, was 28 years of age and a resident of Rumney near Cardiff, South Wales where he lived with his parents. He was a joiner by occupation, employed by Minter (South Wales) Limited and over the previous four years had been working on the construction of the University of Wales Hospital in Cardiff. He was a very experienced rider and had been racing for several years in England and Wales. He had fractured his skull whilst racing in the late sixties and surgeons had used a metal plate to mend the fracture. His debut on the Isle of Man was the 1968 Junior Manx Grand Prix, when, riding a Norton, he finished in 19th position with a race average speed of 83.23mph.

His funeral service was held in Wales and followed by Committal at Thornhill Cemetery, Cardiff.

Gilberto PARLOTTI

(By kind permission of Manx National Heritage)
Gilberto Parlotti at Signpost Corner during the first lap of the fateful 1972 Lightweight 125cc TT

Despite the pouring rain on the morning of Friday 9th June 1972 and reports of thick mist on the mountain section of the TT course, there was a majority decision by the jury of the ACU to run the International Lightweight 125cc Tourist Trophy Race as scheduled. From an original entry of 45 there were 35 riders lined up along Glencrutchery Road in Douglas waiting to participate in the three-lap race. Amongst them was the Italian rider, Gilberto Parlotti, riding a Morbidelli machine bearing the race number 12. As this was his first appearance on the course he had made determined attempts to learn the course before practising had commenced. He was the current leader of the 125cc world championship.

The race began at 11.00am with Chas Mortimer being the first man to push away and his Yamaha fired up at the first time of asking. Fifty seconds later it was the turn of Parlotti to set off towards Bray Hill on his opening lap. By Ramsey, Parlotti was leading the race by 20 seconds from Chas Mortimer, but by the time they reached the Grandstand his lead had been reduced to 15 seconds. However, by Ramsey on the second lap of the race, Parlotti had increased his lead to 18 seconds on corrected time as he began the mountain climb for the second time. It had stopped raining by this time and the mist was lifting when Parlotti was seen negotiating the three right hand bends at the Verandah. Suddenly, the Morbidelli skidded sideways and struck the kerb on the left. The unfortunate rider was thrown as his machine went out of control and collided with concrete posts supporting the roadside fencing. A radio operator on duty at that location reported the incident immediately then went to the gravely injured rider and did what he could for him until the arrival of the rescue helicopter. He was conveyed to Noble's Hospital where, on arrival, it was found that he had succumbed to his injuries.

Chas Mortimer went on to win the race with a six-minute advantage over Charlie Williams in second place with Bill Rae taking third spot.

An examination of Parlotti's severely damaged Morbidelli machine revealed that the petrol filler cap was missing and the rear end of the machine was severely contaminated with a mixture of petrol and oil. It was the opinion of the chief scrutineer that this contamination would have caused loss of road adhesion and subsequent loss of control. The screw-on type filler cap fitted to the machine was unusual in modern machines and he considered it extremely unlikely that a threaded cap of this kind could have become undone in the impact of the accident. The filler cap was never found.

Gilberto Parlotti, a married man and the father of an eight-year-old son, was 31 years of age. He was a motor trade salesman by occupation and a resident of Trieste, Italy. He had been riding motorcycles since he was ten years old.

His funeral service was held in Trieste and followed by interment in the town cemetery. Among those attending the funeral were motorcycling personalities such as Angel Nieto, Giancarlo Morbidelli and his good friend Giacomo Agostini with whom he went round the TT course in a car the night before the race.

Christopher Michael CLARKE

Chris Clarke pictured at Keppel Gate during the 1970 Junior MGP

Glare from the setting sun was likely to cause problems for competitors travelling along the TT course between the Quarterbridge and Ballacraine on the evening of Monday 28th August 1972. Otherwise, conditions were good, the roads were dry and visibility was clear on the mountain section, which was welcome news for those riders gathered at the Grandstand in Douglas waiting to take advantage of the second official practice session for the Manx Grand Prix. Amongst them was Chris Clarke, riding a 250cc Yamaha machine bearing the race number 31 and entered in the Lightweight Race to be held on Tuesday 5th September.

Once the session was under way it was not long before he received the signal to commence his opening lap of the evening and he set off along Glencrutchery Road towards the descent of Bray Hill. He safely made his way through Union Mills and Ballacraine then into the tricky Glen Helen section of the course. Moments later he was seen travelling at racing speed on the approach to the left hand bend immediately prior to the Glen Helen Hotel. Then as he began to negotiate the bend he suddenly sat upright as his machine drifted to the right, struck the kerb and mounted the footpath. After travelling along the path for a distance of 90 feet the machine then collided heavily with the straw bales covering the low stone wall at the entrance leading to "Claddeeyn Cottage". The occupant of the cottage witnessed the incident and immediately made her way to the Glen Helen hotel via the back pathway shouting for help as she went. Meanwhile another competitor slowed down at the entrance to the hotel car park and indicated to the police officer on duty at that location that there had been an accident.

Accompanied by marshal's the police officer went immediately to the scene and found that the unfortunate rider had come to rest on top of the stone wall with his badly damaged Yamaha machine laying against the wall below him. His helmet had come off during the incident and was later found on the riverbank below the road along with a dislodged straw bale. The rider was lowered from the wall onto a stretcher and examined by a Red Cross Nurse and a State Registered Nurse but there was nothing that could be done for him. He had been killed instantly.

John Kenneth Harding, Chief Scrutineer for the Manx Grand Prix, later examined the Yamaha machine and found that it had sustained severe impact damage but there was no evidence of mechanical failure, which might have accounted for the accident. Witnesses had stated that the engine had still been running after the machine had crashed.

Christopher Michael Clarke, a single man, was 25 years of age. He was a cabinet maker by occupation and a resident of Rathfarnham, Dublin. He was an experienced competitor who had first competed on the TT course in 1969 when, riding an AJS machine, he took part in the six lap Junior Manx Grand Prix and from a field of 94 riders he finished in 26th place with a race average speed of 84.82mph. He returned to the Manx the following year but crashed his 349cc AJS machine at Hillberry during the Junior Race and was knocked unconscious. His injuries were to keep him out of racing throughout the 1971 season.

His funeral service was held in Ireland and followed by interment at Mount Jerome Cemetery, Harold's Cross, Dublin.

John Lawrence CLARKE

John Clarke leaps Ballaugh Bridge during practice for the 1973 Production TT

Although overcast on the afternoon of Saturday 2nd June 1973 conditions were generally good around the TT course, which was excellent news for the 68 competitors gathered at the Grandstand in Douglas waiting to participate in the International Production Machine TT. There were three different classes in the race, 750cc, 500cc and 250cc with each class having a "Le Mans" start and separated by a two-minute interval. Amongst those entered in the 250cc class was John Clarke, riding a 250cc Pell Suzuki bearing the race number 91.

The first to go would be the twenty-seven riders taking part in the 750cc class and as they lined up on the Grandstand side of Glencrutchery Road their machines were being held upright on the opposite side of the road. At 4.30pm, on receiving the signal to start they sprinted across the road, mounted their machines and roared off towards Bray Hill on the opening lap of four. The next to go were the fifteen 500cc competitors then the twenty six taking part in the 250cc class but John Clarke experienced difficulties with his machine and was held up for a couple of minutes before he could begin and by that time he was the last man on the road.

Meanwhile, at Union Mills, just minutes before the race commenced, it began to rain very lightly and the road surface was becoming damp in patches. However, the competitors had all made their way through the village without incident but a few minutes later John Clarke was seen, alone on the road, approaching the sweeping right hand bend by the Railway Inn but then, as he banked over to negotiate the bend, his Suzuki suddenly went from beneath him. Both rider and machine slid across the roadway, mounted the footpath on the left and crashed into a wooden gate opposite the house named "Slieu Rhee". The unfortunate rider came to rest in the field on the other side of the gate while his machine slid back across the road and came to rest against the kerb outside "Slieu Rhee". Marshals and the doctor on duty at Union Mills went to his immediate assistance but there was nothing that could be done for him. He had been killed instantly. He was carried from the field then conveyed by ambulance to Noble's Hospital where his death was confirmed by the duty house surgeon.

The 750cc class was won by Tony Jefferies with John Williams second and Dave Nixon third. All three mounted on Triumph machines. The 500cc class was won by Bill Smith (Honda) from Stan Woods (Suzuki) in second place and Keith Martin (Kawasaki) in third place. Charlie Williams (Yamaha) won the 250cc class with a race average speed of 81.76mph. The fastest lap of this class was 84.06mph, recorded by Eddie Roberts (Yamaha) who finished in second place ahead of Tommy Robb (Honda).

John Clarke, a single man, was 25 years of age. He was a machine tool fitter by occupation and a resident of Towcester, Northamptonshire. He had raced on short circuits all over England since 1967 and had never been involved in any serious accidents. On the Isle of Man he had competed in the 1971 Junior Manx Grand Prix riding a Norton machine and finished in 41st place. In the 1972 Senior MGP, again riding a Norton, he finished 42nd.

His funeral service was held on 11th June and followed by committal at The Counties Crematorium, Milton Malsor, Northampton.

Eric Ronald PINER

Eric Piner pictured at Braddan Bridge during the first lap of the fateful Lightweight 250 MGP

With the Isle of Man celebrating the 50th Anniversary of the Manx Grand Prix there were record numbers of spectators positioned around the TT course on Wednesday 5th September 1973. Unlike the previous day when poor weather had caused the postponement of the race, conditions were almost perfect for racing. Good news for the 88 competitors lined up along Glencrutchery Road in Douglas waiting to participate in the four lap Lightweight 250 Race. Amongst them was Eric Piner, riding a 250cc Yamaha machine bearing the race number 24.

At 10.00am the flag dropped and the race began with Hugh Mitchell and Tony Edwards being the first to set off. Less than two minutes later it was the turn of Eric Piner to receive the signal to begin his race against the clock and the engine of his Yamaha fired up at the first time of asking. He set off towards Bray Hill and then safely negotiated his way through Union Mills, Ballacraine, Glen Helen and the 13th Milestone before he was seen approaching the sweeping right hand bend at Douglas Road Corner in Kirk Michael village. He changed down a gear in order to drive through the bend but for some reason he had left it late, he was sixty yards beyond the usual point where riders changed down. Realising his predicament he tried to lean over further in an effort to negotiate the bend but on doing so his rear wheel drifted out to the left and the machine went from beneath him. Both rider and machine then slid along the road and mounted the footpath on the left. The Yamaha collided heavily with the stone wall, which was covered with straw bales while the unfortunate rider struck the gate pillar of the house "Tamarisk" before coming to rest on the opposite side of the road. A Police Officer and Marshals went to his immediate assistance and found that although conscious, he had sustained serious injuries and his condition was deteriorating. The gravely injured rider was conveyed by helicopter to Noble's Hospital where, shortly after admission, he succumbed to his injuries.

Dave Arnold, a sergeant in the Royal Air Force, had gambled on a non-stop ride on his 247cc Yamaha and this paid off as he smashed the lap record by nearly 15 seconds while his main rivals lost valuable seconds refuelling. However, this new record did not survive long as Paddy Reid, another RAF man, put in a fantastic last lap of 98.426mph. Arnold went on to win the race with a record race average speed of 97.232mph with Reid in second place and Vic Wright in third place.

Eric Piner, a single man, was 22 years of age. He was a commercial fitter by occupation, employed by AEC and a resident of Southall, Middlesex. He was regarded as an experienced racing motorcyclist having taken up the sport four years earlier and although this was only his second appearance on the Isle of Man he did have a good knowledge of the TT course. As a newcomer to the Island in 1972, he took part in the Lightweight MGP and won a replica after finishing 14th from a field of 85 competitors. Along with Dave Arnold and Paddy Reid, he was representing the Newmarket & District Motorcycle Club during that race and they carried off the team prize, the Bills/Harding Trophy.

His funeral service was held on Thursday 13th September at Breakspear Crematorium, Ruislip, Middlesex.

Peter Lingard HARDY

Pete Hardy and his twin brother Ron during their opening practice lap for the 1974 Sidecar 750cc TT

Fine weather and dry roads around the TT course on the evening of Monday 27th May 1974 offered perfect racing conditions for the competitors gathered at the Grandstand in Douglas waiting to participate in the opening practice session for the Sidecar Tourist Trophy Races. Amongst them were Pete Hardy and his passenger, Ron Hardy, his twin brother. They were riding a HTS (Hardy Twin Special) 750cc Imp sidecar outfit bearing the race number 29.

Once the session commenced it was not long before the Hardy brothers headed off along Glencrutchery Road towards Bray Hill on their opening lap. They safely made their way round the course and set what was to prove the fastest lap of the evening for the 750cc sidecar class. They continued straight past the Grandstand to commence their second lap and Pete gave the "thumbs up" signal to their pit crew. Meanwhile, shortly before 8.00pm, light rain began to fall in the area of Laurel Bank.

At about 8.05pm, having made their way through Union Mills and Crosby the two brothers were seen approaching Ballacraine, then, as they negotiated the right hand corner, the outfit began to slide but they were able to regain control of the machine and continued on their way towards Glen Helen. Ron Hardy later put this slide down to a little too much throttle. Moments later, they were seen approaching Laurel Bank at racing speed but then just as they were beginning to negotiate the right hand bend the outfit continued straight on. Pete Hardy immediately applied the brakes but was unable to prevent the front of the sidecar colliding heavily with a stone gate pillar at the entrance to a small field just a few yards beyond Ebenezer Lane. The outfit came to rest between the two gateposts with Pete Hardy, unconscious and seriously injured, still astride the machine. Ron Hardy had been thrown into the field and was lying a short distance from the outfit. He was also unconscious but came round within a minute or two of the accident and was relatively uninjured. Pete Hardy was examined by a doctor on duty at that location and was then carried by stretcher to the "Old Work Hut" near the foot of Ebenezer Lane but his condition was slowly deteriorating. He was conveyed by helicopter to Noble's Hospital where he was admitted at 8.34pm but it was found that he had succumbed to his injuries. Medical staff spent almost 40 minutes trying to revive him but without success.

An examination of the sidecar outfit by the Chief Scrutineer revealed that the throttle cable had broken. The effect of this defect would be that power would go off the machine and the driver would have no option but to brake hard and carry on in a straight line.

Peter Hardy, a single man, was 38 years of age. He was an electrician by occupation and a resident of Ashton-under-Lyne, Lancashire. He began racing solo motorcycles in 1962 then in 1967/68 switched to sidecar racing with his brother Ron as passenger. Since that time they had won championships at Darley Moor, Cadwell Park and Snetterton. They were experienced competitors on the Isle of Man having previously raced in 1969, 1970, 1971 and 1972 when they finished 14th in the 750cc race and gained silver replicas. In 1973 they were runners-up in the British Sidecar Championship.

His funeral service and was held on Monday 3rd June and followed by committal at Dukinfield Crematorium

David John NIXON

Dave Nixon on the Triumph Trident during the fateful 1974 Production TT

Miserable weather conditions on Saturday 1st June 1974, especially on the mountain section of the TT course, forced the jury of the Auto-Cycle Union to postpone the Production Machine Race to Tuesday 4th June. There were three different classes in the race, 1000cc, 500cc and 250cc with each class having a "Le Mans" start and separated by a three-minute interval. The first to go would be the 24 machines entered in the 1000cc class and as the competitors lined up on the Grandstand side of Glencrutchery Road their machines were being held upright on the opposite side of the road. On receiving the signal to start they sprinted across the road, mounted their machines and roared off towards Bray Hill on the opening lap of four. Amongst them was Dave Nixon, riding a 741cc Triumph Trident machine bearing the race number 20. Earlier in the year he had injured his arm in a crash whilst racing at Brands Hatch and the plaster cast had only been removed two weeks earlier.

On completion of the first circuit Mick Grant led the race by just under eight seconds from Darryl Pendlebury. Peter Williams was lying third, sixteen seconds ahead of Dave Nixon in fourth place. Just over nine miles into the second lap of the race Dave Nixon, having moved up into second place behind race leader Mick Grant, was seen approaching Glen Helen. However, as he negotiated the left hand bend immediately before the entrance to the Glen Helen Hotel the rear end of his machine began to slide away to the right. He fought to regain control but was unable to prevent the Triumph mounting the footpath before colliding heavily with a dry stone wall. The unfortunate rider was thrown from the machine and came to rest in the roadway. A police officer and marshals on duty near that location went to his immediate assistance and quickly removed the unconscious and gravely injured rider from the road. He was then conveyed by helicopter to Noble's Hospital where, five minutes after admission and without regaining consciousness, he succumbed to his injuries.

The cause of the crash remains a mystery as witness reports differed as to whether Dave Nixon was or was not on the correct racing line for the bend. A marshal who picked up the Triumph reported that there was oil on the rear tyre but Len Harfield, the Chief Scrutineer, was of the opinion that this oil had come from the breather pipe after the accident.

Mick Grant went on to win the race with an average speed of 99.72mph. German rider Hans-Otto Butenuth finished in second place almost forty seconds ahead of fellow German Helmut Dahne in third place.

Dave Nixon was 30 years of age. He was an engineer by occupation, employed by Piper Cams as a machine shop supervisor and was a resident of Ashford, Kent where he lived with his wife Vanessa and their three sons. He began racing motorcycles in 1965 and was an experienced competitor on the Isle of Man where he had enjoyed some degree of success in this particular race, the 750cc class of the Production TT, finishing 5th in 1971 on a Triumph Trident, 3rd in 1972 on a Triumph T150 and 3rd in 1973 again on a Triumph.

His funeral service was held in England on Thursday 13th June and followed by committal at Newcourt Wood Crematorium, Charing near Ashford, Kent.

Nigel John CHRISTIAN

Nigel Christian at Quarterbridge during practice for the 1974 Lightweight MGP

Despite the fine weather on the evening of Monday 26th August 1974 there were reports that the roads on the TT course between Douglas and Ballaugh were still damp, especially under the trees. Additionally, the setting sun was likely to be troublesome on certain parts of the course. Undeterred by the news and prepared to tackle these challenges were the competitors gathered at the Grandstand in Douglas ready to take advantage of a practice session for the Manx Grand Prix. Amongst them was Nigel Christian, riding a 250cc Yamaha machine bearing the race number 42 and entered in the Lightweight Race to be held the following week. As a newcomer to the Isle of Man he was required to wear a white coloured jacket over the top of his leathers to signify his inexperience on the course.

During the practice session Nigel Christian set off along Glencrutchery Road towards Bray Hill on his opening lap and despite the problems with the sun and damp roads he safely made his way through to Ramsey and up onto the mountain section. At about 6.55pm, as he rounded the left hand corner at Brandywell, the highest point on the course, he was being closely followed by two other riders. The last of the trio was another newcomer, Russell Webb, riding a 500cc Matchless Metisse. Moments later, on the exit of the bends at the 32nd Milestone, Christian began to reduce speed quite quickly and the rider behind had to flick his machine over to the left in order to avoid a collision. However, in that instant Webb was confronted with the rear of Christian's machine and immediately applied his front brake but was unable to avoid a heavy collision with the rear of the Yamaha. Webb was thrown from his machine and after sliding along the road for a short distance he jumped up and leapt over the fencing on the right before collapsing. The impact had caused the Yamaha to veer to the right where it demolished several concrete fence posts before coming to rest. Marshals and a police officer on duty at Windy Corner quickly attended to the riders. Christian was found lying beneath the fencing and was deeply unconscious. A stretcher party carried him to the hut at Windy Corner where first aid was rendered by a marshal. Due to the serious nature of the accident, other competitors were flagged down at the Bungalow and a doctor on duty at the Mountain Box was rushed to the scene on the pillion of a travelling marshals machine. On his arrival at the scene of the incident the doctor found that the unfortunate rider had sustained serious chest injuries and his condition was rapidly deteriorating. A few minutes later, at 7.20pm, he succumbed to his injuries. Russell Webb sustained leg and arm injuries and was conveyed by ambulance to Noble's Hospital.

Following the incident the practice session was abandoned and a huge convoy of riders who had been flagged down at the Bungalow were escorted back to the pits by travelling marshals. Russell Webb did not compete in the races the following week.

Nigel Christian, a single man, was 27 years of age. He was a television engineer by occupation and a resident of Peterborough where he lived with his parents. Although he had not previously raced on the TT course he did have experience on short circuits such as Mallory and Snetterton.

His funeral service was held at Peterborough Crematorium on Tuesday 3rd September.

David FORRESTER

Dave Forrester at Ballaugh Bridge during practice for the 1974 Junior MGP

Although the Island had been enveloped by mist and rain on the morning of Tuesday 3rd September 1974 conditions had improved by the afternoon, much to the relief of the 94 competitors lined up along Glencrutchery Road in Douglas waiting to participate in the Junior Manx Grand Prix. Amongst them was Dave Forrester, riding a Kirby Metisse machine powered by a 350cc AJS engine and bearing the race number 62. He had completed ten official laps on this machine during practice.

Once the race had commenced it was not many minutes before it was the turn of Dave Forrester to begin his race against the clock. His machine fired first time as he pushed off from the start line and headed for Bray Hill. He safely made his way through to Ballacraine then into the tricky Glen Helen section of the course. Just over nine miles into his opening lap, he was seen travelling at racing speed and in close company with a small group of riders negotiating the left hand bend immediately before the entrance to the Glen Helen Hotel. However, on the exit of the bend he began to drift towards the kerb on the right hand side of the road. Realising his predicament he sat upright on the machine but was unable to prevent it mounting the footpath and colliding heavily with a dry stone wall. The unfortunate rider was thrown against the wall and into the trees beyond while his machine slid back into the roadway. Marshals went to his immediate assistance and found him lying beneath the trees but there was nothing they could do for him. He had been killed instantly.

The machine was subsequently examined at Douglas Police Station by Ken Harding the Chief Scrutineer and he found that there was little or no damage to the nearside of the machine but there was damage to the offside where the brake lever and footrest were broken off and the megaphone crushed. The hydraulically operated front brake cylinder fitted to the offside of the machine had sustained slight impact damage and was found to be cracked and leaking. This could have been a contributory factor in the cause of the incident if this unit had failed whilst braking but due to the impact damage this could not be determined one way or the other.

Alan Jackson, race leader at the end of the first lap, retired from the race with a broken gear lever. Wayne Dinham, a newcomer to the Manx Grand Prix, was to upset the form books during the race and in fact led the race on his Yamaha for the next two laps without even knowing. Meanwhile, Bernard Murray had been gradually moving up the leader board and took the lead on the fourth and final lap of the race, finishing just over a minute ahead of Dinham. Third place went to RAF Technician John Goodall.

David Forrester was 27 years of age. He was a master builder by occupation and a resident of Greenwich, London where he lived with his wife Daphne and their two young children; Paul aged four years and Jill who was just two weeks old. He was an experienced rider and had competed in the 1973 Senior Manx Grand Prix when, from a field of over 100 competitors, he finished in 40th place.

His funeral service was held in London and followed by committal at Hither Green Crematorium, Verdant Lane, London SE6.

Peter McKINLEY

Pete McKinley pictured during practice for the 1975 International Senior TT

Conditions were perfect for racing on the evening of Wednesday 28th May 1975, the weather was fine, the roads were dry and visibility was clear. Welcome news for the competitors gathered at the Grandstand in Douglas waiting to take advantage of an official practice session for the Tourist Trophy Races. Amongst them was Pete McKinley. Riding his Junior machine he completed his first lap of the evening with an average speed of 102.03mph. He then changed to his 500cc Yamaha bearing the race number 9, which was entered in the International Open Classic Race to be held on Friday 6th June.

For the second time that evening he set off along Glencrutchery Road towards Bray Hill and quickly made his way round the course to Ballaugh Bridge where, on the approach, he overtook another competitor, Thomas Robinson who was also out on his second lap of the evening and riding a 350cc Yamaha. Robinson followed him out of Ballaugh and kept him in sight through Quarry Bends and along the Sulby Straight but McKinley was pulling away from him all the time. Around three miles further along the course, Pete McKinley was seen negotiating the left hand bend at the junction with the track leading to Skye Hill but on the exit of the bend his machine began to drift to the right and was within a foot or two of the grass bank when it began to wobble. He recovered control of the machine but by this time he was on the wrong racing line going into the bends at Pinfold Cottage and collided heavily with the hedge and stone wall near to the house "Glen Link" situated on the right hand side of the road. The unfortunate rider was thrown from the machine and came to rest on the left side of the road. His helmet had come off during the incident. The Yamaha came to rest almost opposite him on the right hand side of the road. Seconds later, Thomas Robinson came upon the scene but had reduced speed considerably as a result of being warned to slow down by someone at the roadside. He rode slowly through the debris in the road and alerted a group of marshals a short distance further along. The gravely injured rider was conveyed by helicopter to Noble's Hospital where he was admitted at 8.00pm but his condition slowly deteriorated and at 9.15pm that same evening he succumbed to his injuries.

The Chief Scrutineer later examined the Yahama machine and found no evidence to suggest that a mechanical failure may have contributed to the accident.

Peter McKinley was 26 years of age. He was a foreman mechanic by occupation and a resident of Batley, Yorkshire. He was an experienced competitor, having started his racing career in 1969 at Brands Hatch. He won his first race the following season at Snetterton but really began to make progress in 1971 when he met Peter and Don Padgett. He was later to become their workshop foreman at their premises in Bradford Road. Batley. Originally from Worcestershire, the bespectacled rider finished 1974 as Cadwell Park champion and was looking forward to competing in the 1975 Classic Races. In his first Grand Prix, the French, he finished 6th in the 500 race and 9th in the 350, both on Team-Padgett Yamahas. In the Isle of Man he was familiar with the TT course, having finished 6th in the Lightweight 250cc race and 8th in the Senior during the 1974 TT meeting.

His funeral service was held at St. Giles Church, Heightington on 4th June 1975 and was followed by interment.

Philip GURNER

(By kind permission of Manx National Heritage)

Phil Gurner at Quarterbridge during the fateful 1975 Senior TT

Overcast skies on the afternoon of Wednesday 4th June 1975 carried a threat of rain for the 75 competitors lined up along Glencrutchery Road in Douglas waiting to participate in the six lap Senior Tourist Trophy Race. Amongst them was Phil Gurner, riding a 351cc Yamaha machine bearing the race number 58. He had originally entered a 500cc Yamaha machine but this had caught fire and burnt out near the Nook during the Monday evening practice session.

The race began with Phil Carpenter and Charlie Williams being the first to set off towards Bray Hill with the following riders starting in pairs and at ten-second intervals. Just under five minutes later it was the turn of Phil Gurner to begin his race against the clock and he headed off on his opening lap along with his starting partner, Hans-Otto Butenuth. On completion of the first lap Chas Mortimer led the race with a thirteen second advantage over Mick Grant in second place. John Williams was holding third position. Phil Gurner had recorded a lap time of 23m36s and was lying in fifth position. He maintained this position through to the end of the third lap, the half way stage, when he pulled into the pits to refuel. His third lap time of 22m43s had been his fastest of the race. While his fuel tank was being filled and his visor cleaned his father asked him if he was all right, he nodded and put his thumb up before setting off again.

Approximately fifteen minutes later he was around twenty two miles into his fourth lap of the race when he was seen approaching "Pinfold Cottage", Lezayre but by now the roads in that area were wet following a shower of rain and as he began to negotiate the right hand bend the rear wheel of his machine stepped out to the left and despite all his efforts to regain control of the Yamaha he was thrown. The unfortunate rider came to rest in the roadway while his machine, which had mounted the footpath and collided with the hedge on the left, came to rest near to the centre of the road 20 to 25 yards beyond him. Marshals went to the immediate assistance of the gravely injured rider but there was little that they could do for him and he succumbed to his injuries within a very short time.

Mick Grant went on to win the race with a race average speed of 100.27mph. John Williams took second place and Chas Mortimer finished third.

Phil Gurner, a single man, was 22 years of age. He was a mechanic by occupation and a resident of Dinnington, Sheffield. He began road racing in March 1971 and since that time had competed in England, Europe and America. His debut on the TT course came during the 1972 MGP but an injury sustained during practice prevented him from racing. The following June he returned for the TT and competed in the Junior, Formula 750 and Senior races but failed to finish in any of them. However, in 1974 he showed his true potential when he took 3rd place in the Production 500 Race, 9th place in the Junior TT and 16th place in the Senior TT. In the days just prior to his death, paired with Dave Saville, he had competed in the ten lap Production Race and they achieved 29th place on their 499cc BSA. Then, in the Junior TT, he was forced to retire during his second lap due to a split fuel tank on his Yamaha.

His funeral service was held in Sheffield and followed by interment at Thurcroft Cemetery just outside Dinnington.

Robert Brian McCOMB

Brian McComb at the foot of Bray Hill during the opening lap of the fateful 1975 Lightweight MGP

The weather conditions across the Isle of Man on the morning of Tuesday 2nd September 1975 were ideal for racing. The roads around the TT course were dry and visibility was clear on the mountain section. Good news for the 74 competitors lined up along Glencrutchery Road in Douglas ready to take part in the Lightweight Manx Grand Prix, the opening event of the meeting. Amongst them was Brian McComb, riding a Yamaha machine bearing the race number 35. He had been lapping consistently at over 90mph during practice week and was expected to do well in the four-lap race covering a distance of just over 150 miles.

At 10.00am prompt the flag dropped and the first of the competitors were sent on their way towards Bray Hill and within a few minutes it was the turn of Brian McComb to begin his race against the clock. At about 10.15am, twelve miles into his opening lap of the race, he was seen approaching the left hand bend at the foot of Barregarrow Hill, Kirk Michael, one of the fastest sections of the course. He was alone on the road and travelling at an estimated 120mph as he negotiated the bend but on the exit his machine drifted to the right and the front wheel touched the kerb. The Yamaha immediately went out of control and veered across the road to the left where it collided with the grass bank and a tree. The unfortunate rider was thrown against a telegraph pole while his machine tumbled back across the road and finally came to rest near the gateway of "Cammal Farm". The police officer and marshals on duty at that location went immediately to his aid but there was nothing they could do for him. He had been killed instantly.

Ken Harding, Chief Scrutineer for the Manx Motor Cycle Club, later examined McComb's wrecked Yamaha machine and found no evidence to suggest that a mechanical failure had contributed to the accident.

Having led from start to finish, Alan Jackson, from New Longton, Lancashire, went on to win the race with an average speed of 96.59mph, 25 seconds ahead of Roger Cope. The final place on the rostrum went to Rich Burrows. All three men had been riding Yamaha machines. Lee Heeson who had topped the practice leaderboard retired at Ballig during the first lap and Steve Ward, one of the early contenders, had been forced to retire with electrical problems during the third lap of the race.

Brian McComb, a single man, was 24 years old and a resident of Ballynahinch, County Down, Northern Ireland. He was a motorcycle mechanic by occupation and was employed as a service manager at the Kawasaki Centre in Belfast. He was an experienced racing motorcyclist who had held a racing licence since 1969. He had competed on many occasions in major championship meetings in Ireland and had also ridden in the Manx Grand Prix since 1972 when, riding a Honda, he was forced to retire during the Lightweight Race. However, he returned to win replicas in 1973 when he finished 16th in the Lightweight and in 1974 when he finished 9th in the Lightweight.

His funeral service was held on Friday 5th September and followed by interment at Magheradroll Church, Ballynahinch, County Down.

Walter WÖRNER

Siegfried Maier and Walter Wörner at Quarterbridge during the fateful 1976 Sidecar TT

Fine weather on the afternoon of Monday 7th June 1976 provided dry roads around the TT course and clear visibility on the mountain section. These conditions were perfect for racing, which was good news for the competitors lined up along Glencrutchery Road in Douglas waiting in anticipation for the 500cc Sidecar Tourist Trophy Race to commence. Amongst them were Siegfried Maier and his passenger, Walter Wörner, riding a sidecar outfit powered by a 496cc Yamaha engine and bearing the race number 25. They were both newcomers to the Isle of Man and had qualified for the race despite problems during practice week when they had run out of fuel on one session and suffered engine problems on another.

The race began at 2.30pm and the first two of sixty-four outfits set off towards Bray Hill. The following sidecar crews were dispatched in pairs and at ten-second intervals. Two minutes after the first crews left the start line it was the turn of Maier and Wörner to begin their race and they set off towards Bray Hill together with their starting partners Alex and Russell Campbell who were also using a Yamaha powered sidecar.

Maier and Wörner had safely negotiated their way through Union Mills, Glen Vine and Crosby when they were seen approaching the bends at Greeba Castle, less than six miles into their opening lap of the race. However, travelling at an estimated 110-120mph, the wheel of the sidecar struck the wall on the left at a point approximately 60 yards Douglas side of the house "Fern Bank". Walter Wörner was instantly thrown into the roadway while Maier fought to regain control of the outfit but he was unable to prevent it drifting across the road and crashing into straw bales just beyond the telephone kiosk. At the point of impact the sidecar burst into flames, setting fire to the straw bales and several bushes. Marshals went to the immediate assistance of the two men and found Walter Wörner lying beside the kerb on the right hand side of the road but there was nothing they could do for him. He had been killed instantly. Siegfried Maier sustained serious arm injuries for which he was treated at Noble's Hospital.

The race was won by Rolf Steinhausen & Josef Huber, having led from start to finish on a Busch Konig machine, race number 1. Second place went to Dick Greasley & Cliff Holland (Yamaha) race number 10. Third place went to Mac Hobson & Mick Burns (Yamaha) race number 8. Fourth place went to Siegfried Schauzu & Wolfgang Kalauch (Aro) race number 9 and fifth place went to Jeff Gawley & Ken Birch (Yamaha) race number 24. Alex and Russell Campbell went on to finish in 8th place.

Walter Wörner, a married man and the father of a three-year-old child, was 22 years of age. He was a mechanic by occupation and a resident of Kreis Boblingen, West Germany. He began racing with Maier, who was from the same village, in 1973 and after a period of two years racing, he had a one-year lay off before starting again in 1976. On 30th May 1976, they pair were competing at Bremen in Germany, their last race before the TT, when Walter Wörner fell from the outfit but escaped injury and was able to remount and continue the race.

His funeral service was held in Germany and followed by interment at Schafhausen in the small town of Weil der Stadt.

Leslie Frederick KENNY

Les Kenny at Braddan Bridge during the fateful 1976 Lightweight 250 TT

Unlike the previous day when the poor weather had forced the postponement of racing, the weather was fine on the morning of Saturday 12th June 1976 and the roads around the TT course were dry. Welcome news for the 55 competitors lined up along Glencrutchery Road in Douglas waiting to participate in the Lightweight 250 Tourist Trophy Race. Amongst them was Les Kenny, riding a Yamaha machine bearing the race number 23. Four days earlier, together with competitor Len Carr, he had taken part in the nine lap 250cc International Production Machine Race and finished in 20th place. Kenny taking the 250cc Yamaha round for six of the laps and Len Carr taking the middle three laps.

At 11.00am the flag dropped and the race was underway as the first two riders, Chas Mortimer and Tony Rutter, were sent on their way. The rest of the field followed in pairs and at ten-second intervals. Less than two minutes later it was the turn of Les Kenny and his starting partner Noel Clegg to leave the starting line and they headed off towards the descent of Bray Hill. All but one of the race competitors were mounted on Yamaha's.

Within minutes of leaving the start and less than two miles into his opening lap, Les Kenny was seen approaching Snugborough, Union Mills and was travelling at racing speed when his Yamaha suddenly went from beneath him. The unfortunate rider was thrown into the roadway and collided heavily with the stone wall on the left while his machine came to a stop almost opposite him on the right hand side of the road. Denis Alfred Hamer, the Police Constable on duty at that location, witnessed the incident and together with a marshal he lifted the gravely injured rider clear of the road and rendered first aid until a doctor arrived on the scene and found that there was nothing more that could be done for him. He had succumbed to his injuries. Constable Hamer was to lose his life three months later when he was struck by a racing machine at Union Mills during the Junior Manx Grand Prix.

Derek Francis Brindley, the Deputy Chief Scrutineer, later examined the Yamaha at Police Headquarters in Douglas and found that the left hand piston showed signs of seizure, which would have caused the engine to lock.

Ulsterman, Tom Herron went on to win the race, adding to his Senior Race win three days earlier. Herron led throughout the four-lap race and set a record race average speed of 103.55mph and nearly broke the lap record set by the late Bill Ivy in 1968.

Les Kenny, a married man and the father of an eight-year-old daughter, was 30 years of age. Born in Sydney, Australia, he was a mechanic by occupation and a resident of Tonbridge, Kent. He had been racing for six or seven years, initially in Australia then in Europe. His first racing experience on the Isle of Man had been at the 1974 TT when, riding a 349cc Yamaha, he finished 28th in the Junior Race with a race average speed of 95.71mph and 23rd in a wet and windy Senior Race at 85.09mph. The following year he finished 10th in the Senior Race with a race average speed of 96.72mph.

His funeral service was held in the Isle of Man and followed by interment at Douglas Borough Cemetery.

David FEATHERSTONE

Dave Featherstone at Ballaugh Bridge during the fateful 1976 Junior MGP

Fine weather and dry roads around the TT course on the afternoon of Tuesday 7th September 1976 offered almost perfect racing conditions for the 100 competitors lined up along Glencrutchery Road in Douglas waiting for the Junior Manx Grand Prix to begin. Amongst them was Dave Featherstone, riding a Yamaha TZ 350cc machine bearing the race number 82. At the TT races three months earlier, along with John Goodall, he had taken part in the ten lap Production Race. Riding a 750 Moto Guzzi they finished in 26th place.

At 2.00pm the flag dropped and the riders were sent on their way in pairs and at ten second intervals. Within seven minutes of the first machines leaving the start line it was the turn of Dave Featherstone to begin his race against the clock and he set off towards Bray Hill. During the fourth lap of the race he overtook another competitor, Nigel Rigg from Warrington, Cheshire and for the following two laps, Rigg followed Featherstone at a close distance and could tell by his riding and his lines into all the corners that he was an experienced rider.

On the sixth and final lap of the race, Rigg was about twenty yards behind Featherstone going through the bends just before Alpine Cottage. He was in fifth gear, travelling at about 110mph and concentrating on the apex of the right hand bend at Alpine Cottage when he realised that Featherstone was to his left and definitely off line for the bend. He then saw that his right foot was down off the footrest and that he was sat upright on his machine heading straight for the kerb on the left hand side of the road, making no attempt to crank over for the corner. After mounting the kerb, both rider and machine crashed into some trees situated on the left side of the road immediately before Alpine Cottage. Marshals went to his immediate assistance but there was nothing they could do for him. He had been killed instantly.

An examination of the Yamaha revealed no evidence of seizure. However, it was found that at some stage, ordinary filler had been used to repair an area of the fuel tank where the fuel taps were attached. This filler had failed and allowed fuel to seep onto the rear tyre causing the compound to soften and lose adhesion with the road surface.

Having led the race for the first four laps, Dave Williams crashed out at the 11th Milestone. He had sustained serious injuries and was conveyed by helicopter to Noble's Hospital where he was detained in intensive care. Joe Lindsay, a 29 year old docker from Belfast went on to win the race with a record speed of 101.30mph. Second place went to Keith Trubshaw with Kevin Riley taking third. Nigel Rigg finished the race in 24th place and received a replica.

Dave Featherstone was 30 years of age. He was a Flight Lieutenant serving in the engineering branch of the Royal Air Force, stationed at RAF Abingdon, Oxfordshire where he lived with his wife Pat and baby son, Allan. He was a member of the RAF Motorcycle racing team and had ridden in the Manx Grand Prix on four previous occasions.

His funeral service was held in the Parish Church at Shippon and followed by interment at Spring Road Cemetery on Tuesday 14th September. At the graveside, a dozen airmen with rifles fired a volley as a last salute. A memorial plaque in his name can be found on the wall of the marshal's shelter at Alpine Corner.

Peter Rodney TULLEY

1976 - Pete Tulley pictured during the Junior MGP

There was fine weather, clear visibility and dry roads around the TT course on the evening of Tuesday 30th August 1977, providing perfect racing conditions for the competitors gathered at the Grandstand in Douglas waiting to take advantage of a practice session for the Manx Grand Prix. Amongst them was Pete Tulley, riding a 348cc Yamaha TZ machine bearing the race number 28 and entered in the Junior Race to be held the following week. His friend and fellow competitor, David John Hickman, was acting as his timekeeper.

Once the practice session commenced it was soon the turn of Pete Tulley to set off towards Bray Hill and he safely negotiated his way round the course to complete his opening lap then continued straight through the start area to begin his second circuit of the evening. At about 7.10pm, just over sixteen miles into his second lap, Tulley was alone on the road and travelling at racing speed as he approached the right hand bend at Alpine Corner. He changed down a gear then as he released the clutch the rear wheel "stepped out" to the left and the machine began to snake violently. He tried to regain control of the Yamaha but it drifted wide on the exit of the bend and collided with the kerb on his left. The unfortunate rider was thrown against the boundary wall of "Alpine Cottage" at a point six yards beyond the front gate and then hit by his machine, which then tumbled along the roadway for a distance of 70 yards before coming to rest six feet from the kerb on the left. Marshals went to the assistance of the gravely injured rider and lifted him from the roadway to the relative safety of the footpath where his crash helmet was removed in order to assist his breathing. He had sustained multiple injuries and the Marshals did what they could for him until the arrival of the emergency helicopter, which then conveyed him to Noble's Hospital. On his arrival at 7.45pm, immediate resuscitation measures were taken and emergency surgery carried out before he was placed in the Intensive Care Unit. However, at 1.20am the following morning, he succumbed to his injuries.

An examination of the Yamaha machine by the Chief Scrutineer, John Kenneth Harding, revealed that both engine and gearbox were free from seizure. Nothing was found to suggest that a mechanical fault was contributory to the incident.

Dave Hickman went on to win the Lightweight 250 race the following week and as he crossed the line he privately dedicated the win to Pete Tulley.

Pete Tulley, a single man, was 25 years of age (born 01.04.52). He had gained an HND in building and civil engineering at Southampton College of Further Education and was a quantity surveyor by occupation residing in Sherwood, Nottingham. He had been a keen rock climber until taking up motorcycle racing in 1974. In 1976 he suffered two bad crashes whilst racing at Croft in Yorkshire and Cadwell Park in Lincolnshire. His first appearance on the Isle of Man was at the Manx Grand Prix in 1976 when, despite encountering mechanical problems on his Yamaha during the Junior Race he went on to finish in 57th place and received a finisher's award. His last meeting before travelling to the Isle of Man was at Croft, for which he had rebuilt his machine and he was placed in the top six in three of the races.

His funeral service was followed by interment at Western Cemetery, Springbank, Hull.

Ivan John HOUSTON

Ivan Houston at Ballacraine during practice for the 1977 Lightweight 250 MGP

Although the weather was fine on the morning of Wednesday 31st August 1977 it was still dark under the overhanging trees and there were damp patches on the roads around the TT course. Not the best of conditions for the competitors assembled at the Grandstand in Douglas waiting to participate in a practice session for the Manx Grand Prix. Amongst them was Ivan Houston, riding a 250cc Yamaha machine bearing the race number 20 which had been entered in the Lightweight 250 Race to be held the following week. He was a newcomer to the Isle of Man and was therefore obliged to wear a white jacket over the top of his leathers to signify to other riders his inexperience on the course.

At about 6.15am he set off along Glencrutchery Road towards Bray Hill on his opening lap of the morning and safely made his way through Union Mills, Crosby, Ballacraine and then into the tricky Glen Helen section of the course. On the approach to the entrance of the car park at the hotel he had two competitors close behind him, David Allman from Grimsby, riding a 500cc Norton and Mike Davies from Oswestry, riding a 250cc Yamaha. The three riders began to climb Creg Willey's Hill together but near the top, travelling at 70-80mph, Houston appeared to be on the wrong racing line to negotiate the left hand bend situated approximately 80 yards prior to Lambfell Farm. As a consequence, his machine went straight on and collided with the kerb on the right hand side of the road. In an instant, both rider and machine were thrown against the grass bank before rebounding back across the roadway. Allman was able to pass between the fallen rider and his machine as they slid across the road in front of him and he went on to complete his lap. However, Davies was then suddenly confronted with the fallen rider coming to rest on the racing line and was unable to avoid him. Davies was thrown into the road and sustained a fractured collarbone. On getting to his feet he saw Houston lying at the side of the road and finding no marshals or spectators at the scene he ran back down the course to warn oncoming riders. Ivan Houston had sustained serious injuries and was conveyed by helicopter to Noble's Hospital where he was admitted at 6.50am but just over ten minutes later, he succumbed to his injuries.

Ken Harding, Chief Scrutineer for the Manx Motor Cycle Club, later examined both machines at Douglas Police Station. He found no evidence on either machine to suggest that a mechanical failure may have contributed towards this incident.

Dave Allman competed in the Senior Manx Grand Prix the following Thursday but was forced to retire during the race. Mike Davies was unable to compete in the Lightweight Race due to his fractured collarbone but did return the following year.

Ivan Houston, a single man, was 26 years of age. He was an auto-engineer by occupation and a resident of Ballymena, County Antrim. He had been racing in Ireland for several years and was a good consistent rider. He had enjoyed success on the Ulster short circuits where he rode for the Mid-Antrim Club.

His funeral service was held on 4th September and followed by interment at Broughshane New Cemetery, Ballymena, County Antrim, Northern Ireland.

Norman TRICOGLUS

Norman Tricoglus at Ballacraine during practice for the 1977 Senior MGP

Conditions were fine on the evening of Saturday 3rd September 1977, the roads around the TT course were dry and visibility on the mountain section was clear. Welcome news for the competitors congregating in the area of the Grandstand in Douglas waiting to take part in a practice session for the Manx Grand Prix. Amongst them was Norman Tricoglus and once the session began he went out to complete two laps on his Lightweight machine. He then changed to his 500cc Yamaha machine bearing the race number 45, which had been entered in the Senior Race to be held the following week. During practice he had set the second fastest time for the Lightweight and was high on the leaderboard for the Senior. However, he had told friends how difficult he found the winding Rhencullen section on the course and felt he was much slower than other competitors going through the bends just beyond Kirk Michael.

He set off along Glencrutchery Road on the Yamaha and had safely made his way through Crosby, Glen Helen and Kirk Michael village when he was seen approaching Birkin's Bends at Rhencullen. Marshals described his speed as being very fast as he began to negotiate the bends but as he did so the Yamaha developed a "tank slapper", the handlebars moving rapidly from side to side. In an effort to regain control of the machine he braked hard, leaving a 75 foot long tyre mark on the road surface, but was unable to prevent the machine colliding heavily with the gable end of the house "Cronk Steone" situated on the right hand side of the road at the top of Rhencullen Hill. The force of the impact caused the machine to disintegrate and the engine block hurtled across the road and struck the legs of a marshal, Mrs Carol Watney, aged 61 years, who had been sitting on top of the opposite hedge. Mrs Watney sustained a doubled fracture of the left leg and a smashed right kneecap. Marshals went to the immediate assistance of the unfortunate rider but there was nothing that could be done for him. He had been killed instantly. Mrs Watney was conveyed by helicopter to Noble's Hospital in Douglas for treatment.

Norman Tricoglus was 25 years of age. He was a car salesman by occupation and a resident of Acomb, North Yorkshire where he lived with his wife Celia. He was an experienced rider and a former North-East England Champion in the 500cc and 1000cc classes. In the Isle of Man, his first appearance on the TT course was at the Manx Grand Prix in 1973 and, riding a Yamaha, he was to achieve 10th place in the Lightweight Race with an average speed of 90.24mph. He returned to the Manx the following year and although he finished in 50th position in the Lightweight Race he went on to claim a podium position in the Senior Race when, riding a Walker Yamaha and with a race average speed of 93.24mph, he finished in second place, just over three seconds behind the race winner Bernard Murray. At the 1975 TT meeting, the Production Race had been increased to ten laps with two riders to each machine and Norman was paired with Phil Carpenter on a Honda 400 but they were to retire from the race on the eighth lap. A few months later Norman was back on the Island for the MGP but he was unable to compete after he sustained serious injuries when he crashed near to Greeba Castle during practice. Undeterred, he returned to the Manx the following year and secured another excellent result, finishing 6th in the Lightweight Race.

His funeral service was held at St. Andrew's Church, Heddon on the Wall, Northumberland and followed by interment.

Neil EDWARDS

Neil Edwards at Ballaugh Bridge during the fateful 1977 Junior MGP

Unlike the previous day, when poor conditions had caused the postponement of the race, the weather on the afternoon of Wednesday 7th September 1977 was fine and the roads around the TT course were dry. A column of almost one hundred competitors stretched back along Glencrutchery Road in Douglas ready to participate in the six lap Junior Manx Grand Prix. Amongst them, making his third appearance on the Isle of Man, was Neil Edwards, riding a 350cc Yamaha machine bearing the race number 21.

On completion of the first circuit, Yamaha mounted Kevin Riley, number 48, who had finished 3rd in the Junior Race the previous year, led by 30 seconds from Jim Heath with Mick Capper in third place and Ron Jones fourth.

Neil Edwards completed his first lap and without stopping went past the Grandstand to commence his second circuit. He safely made his way through to Parliament Square in Ramsey then headed for the mountain climb. Moments later, he was seen approaching Cruickshanks Corner at the foot of May Hill with the race leader, Kevin Riley a short distance behind him. He was travelling at racing speed and on the usual racing line but then appeared to leave it too late to bank over in order to negotiate the right hand bend. As a consequence his machine drifted wide and mounted the footpath on the left before colliding heavily with the straw bales covering a stone pillar on the boundary wall of the house "Cronk Brae". Both rider and machine were thrown back into the roadway, directly into the path of Kevin Riley who braked hard and changed down into first gear but as he weaved his way between the fallen rider and the crashed machine, part of his machine caught the fallen riders crash helmet with a glancing blow. He managed to maintain control of his machine and continued the race while marshals quickly carried the unfortunate competitor to the side of the road where a State Registered Nurse, attended to him. However, there was nothing that could be done for him. He had been killed instantly by the initial impact with the stone pillar and it was considered that the glancing blow from Kevin Riley's machine had no bearing on his death.

Kevin Riley went on to win the race, having led from start to finish on his twin cylinder Yamaha, with a fastest lap of exactly 105mph, only just short of the record set by David Williams in the same class in the 1976 MGP but his race average speed of 102.63 was way better than the old record held by Joe Lindsay from 1976 at 101.30mph. Ron Jones finished second with Ronnie Russell third. The first twelve riders were all mounted on 350 Yamaha machines. Kevin Riley took part in the Senior the following day but was forced to retire during the race.

Neil Edwards, a married man, was 26 years of age. He was a machine operator by occupation and a resident of Prescot, Lancashire. His wife Rosemary and his parents were on the Island to watch the races. His first appearance on the Isle of Man was the 1975 Junior Manx Grand Prix when, riding a Yamaha, he finished in 38th place. He competed in the same race the following year but was forced to retire during the race.

His funeral service was held on Friday 16th September and followed by committal at St. Helens Crematorium where his ashes were scattered in the garden of remembrance.

David Edward Stephen DAVIES

Steve "Snuffy" Davies at Quarterbridge during practice for the 1978 Senior TT

Weather conditions were hot and sunny on the afternoon of Thursday 1st June 1978 and dry roads around the TT course provided perfect racing conditions for the competitors gathered at the Grandstand on Glencrutchery Road in Douglas waiting to take advantage of a practice session for the Tourist Trophy Races. Amongst them was Steve "Snuffy" Davies, riding a 347cc Yamaha machine bearing the race number 60 and entered in the Senior Race to be held the following Monday. The previous year, riding a Yamaha, he had won the Senior Manx Grand Prix with a race average speed of 100.48mph.

At about 3.00pm, Davies was seen travelling at racing speed and on the correct racing line as he approached Glen Moar Mills in the tricky Glen Helen section of the course. On passing the Mills he banked over to negotiate the following left hand bend dropping into the "Black Dub" but as he did so it appeared that the footrest or some other part of the Yamaha dug into the road surface, which caused him to lose control of the machine. Both rider and machine slid and spun along the road before mounting the footpath on the right and colliding heavily with a telegraph pole. The unfortunate rider came to rest in the roadway and was immediately attended to by marshals and the duty medical officer at that location but there was nothing they could do for him. He had been killed instantly.

Leonard Charles Harfield, Chief Scrutineer for the Auto-Cycle Union, later examined the Yamaha machine and found it to be extensively damaged at the rear end. He dismantled the engine and found it to be in good condition with no signs of seizure. The same applied to the gearbox, which, despite the accident, could still be operated. Both brakes were out of operation due to accident damage. He was unable to find any evidence of a mechanical failure, which may have contributed to the accident.

During the same practice session, making only his second TT appearance, the American rider Pat Hennen, riding his 653cc Classic Suzuki, recorded an unofficial lap time of 19 minutes and 54 seconds (113.75mph), the first time a rider had gone round the course in under 20 minutes. During the 5th lap of the Senior Race four days later Hennen recorded 19 minutes and 53.2 seconds on his 500 Suzuki but a serious crash at Bishopscourt during the 6th and final lap almost cost him his life and put an end to his racing career.

Steve "Snuffy" Davies, a single man, was 25 years of age and had been given his nickname by his younger sisters when he was in his teens. He was a heavy goods vehicle driver by occupation and a resident of Colwyn Bay, North Wales. An experienced competitor on the Isle of Man having competed in the Manx Grand Prix in 1974, 1975, 1976 and 1977 when, despite having been up most of the night servicing his bike and having just two bars of chocolate for breakfast he went out and won the Senior Manx Grand Prix with a race average speed of 100.48mph. He was a popular character, known to his fellow competitors as "the joker of the paddock".

His funeral service was held at St. John's Methodist Church, Colwyn Bay on Tuesday 13th June and followed by interment at Bron-y-Nant Cemetery. A memorial service was held at Bethel Church, Old Colwyn on Sunday 25th June.

Malcolm HOBSON & Kenneth Maurice BIRCH

Mac Hobson and Ken Birch during practice for the 1978 Sidecar TT

Conditions were perfect for racing on the afternoon of Monday 5th June 1978, the sun was shining, the roads were dry and visibility was clear on the mountain section of the TT course. Welcome news for the 75 sidecar crews lined up along Glencrutchery Road in Douglas waiting to take part in the first leg of the Sidecar Tourist Trophy Race. Amongst them was the former British Sidecar Champion Mac Hobson and his passenger Kenny Birch on their red and white coloured outfit bearing the race number 6 and powered by a 750cc Yamaha engine. The pair were lying second in the world sidecar ratings and leading the British Championship.

At 2.30pm the flag dropped and the race began with the crews being set off in pairs and at ten second intervals. The first four had departed before Hobson and Birch moved up to the start line along with outfit number 5 manned by Rolf Biland and Ken Williams. Hobson had a perfect start and left Biland trailing behind. However, seconds later, having negotiated the bend at St. Ninians crossroads, Hobson positioned his machine for the descent of Bray Hill, but just below the top of the hill the sidecar hit a "bump" on the road surface near to a manhole cover. The outfit lifted off the ground then, on landing, veered sharply to the right, mounted the pavement and collided heavily with a garden wall. The sidecar disintegrated and scattered debris over the road. A police officer and marshals went to the assistance of the two men but there was nothing that could be done for either of them. They had both been killed instantly.

It is believed that the "bump" had developed following road works on Bray Hill during the previous winter. All competitors had been handed a written warning prior to the beginning of practices, warning of the dangerous bump. Additionally, a 95 foot long fluorescent yellow line had been painted on the road surface leading to the bump, which had also been daubed with the yellow paint. Furthermore, two warning boards had been placed on the approach.

With a race average speed of 101.75mph, Dick Greasley and Gordon Russell won the race. Second place went to Jock Taylor & Ken Arthur with Graham Milton & John Brushwood finishing third.

Mac Hobson was 47 years of age. He was a motor mechanic by occupation and a resident of Gosforth, Newcastle on Tyne where he lived with his wife Catherine and their three children, Philip, Paul and Nicola. He was an experienced competitor on the Isle of Man and with Mick Burns as passenger, had won the 1976 International 1000cc Sidecar TT with a race average speed of 97.77mph. The following year, with Stuart Collins as passenger, he won the second leg of the Sidecar TT with a race average speed of 99.74mph. His funeral service was held at All Saints Church, Gosforth followed by interment at Hollywood Avenue Cemetery.

Ken Birch, a single man, was 26 years of age. He was a fitter & turner by occupation employed by the North Killingholme engineers Fullcliff and was a resident of Scunthorpe, South Humberside. Although not a newcomer to the TT course, this was the first time he had partnered Mac Hobson on the Isle of Man. He had previously partnered Jeff Gawley and over a four year period the pair had twice finished second in the British Championship and had finished 5th in the World Championship. His funeral service was held on 12th June and followed by committal at Walton Lea Crematorium near Warrington.

Ernst TRACHSEL

Ernst Trachsel and Andreas Stager during practice for the 1978 Sidecar TT

Conditions were near perfect for racing on the afternoon of Monday 5th June 1978, the sun was shining, the roads were dry and visibility was clear on the mountain section of the TT course. Welcome news for the 75 sidecar crews lined up along Glencrutchery Road in Douglas waiting to take part in the first leg of the Sidecar Tourist Trophy Race. Amongst them were Ernst Trachsel and his passenger Andreas Stager, riding an outfit powered by a 499cc Suzuki engine and bearing the race number 15.

At 2.30pm the race began with the crews being set off in pairs at ten second intervals. Twenty seconds later it was the turn of Mac Hobson & Ken Birch to begin their race and they made a much cleaner start than the outfit beside them. However, seconds later as Hobson began the descent of Bray Hill his machine hit a bump in the road, went out of control and crashed into a wall. Both rider and passenger were killed instantly. Just over a minute later, unaware of the tragedy that had just occurred, Trachsel and Stager pushed off from the start line to commence their opening lap but they had difficulties with the engine and Stager had to jump out of the sidecar to push again. Eventually the engine fired up and they were on their way.

From his position in the sidecar Andreas Stager felt the outfit hit the same bump at the top of Bray Hill but he had experienced this before during practice. However, he thought that due to their bad start, Trachsel was eager to make up the lost time and they had hit the bump faster than they usually did. As the outfit lifted in the air it turned to the right and they lost control momentarily before continuing down Bray Hill, passing the scene of Hobson's crash. Moments later, spectators at the foot of Bray Hill saw Trachsel approaching on the usual racing line but now travelling noticeably slower than the other sidecars. As the outfit came out of the dip and passed the junction with Brunswick Road it suddenly went out of control and veered to the right, mounted the footpath and collided with a garden wall and a lamp post before bouncing back into the roadway. Both rider and passenger were thrown from the machine. Marshals went to the assistance of the two men but there was nothing they could do for Ernst Trachsel. He had been killed instantly. Stager sustained leg injuries and survived the incident.

An examination of the sidecar by the Chief Scrutineer revealed that the crash was probably caused by a fatigue fracture in the front suspension, which may have been present since manufacture but could only have been discovered by X-ray.

Dick Greasley & Gordon Russell on a 750cc Yamaha won the race. Jock Taylor & Kenny Arthur finished second with Graham Milton & John Brushwood third.

Ernst Trachsel, a single man, was 34 years of age. He was a garage proprietor by occupation and a resident of Heimberg, Switzerland. He was an experienced competitor and had been crowned Swiss Sidecar Champion four times. On the Isle of Man in 1976, he finished in 19th place in the 1000cc Sidecar TT.

Following committal at Douglas Borough Crematorium, his ashes were flown home to Switzerland for burial.

Michael ADLER

Mike Adler pictured during the fateful 1978 Schweppes Classic TT

Conditions were described as perfect for racing on the afternoon of Friday 9th June 1978, as 73 competitors lined up along Glencrutchery Road in Douglas awaiting the start of the Schweppes Classic Race, the final contest of this TT meeting. Amongst them was Mike Adler from New Zealand, a newcomer to the Isle of Man, riding a 350cc Yamaha machine bearing the race number 76. Earlier in the week, on the same machine, he had competed in the Senior Tourist Trophy Race and finished in a creditable 35th position with a race average speed of 95.99mph, only just missing out on a bronze replica.

The race commenced at 2.30pm with the riders starting in pairs and at ten-second intervals although the first man to leave, Joey Dunlop, was alone on the grid due to Tony Rutter being a non-starter. Also alone on the start line was Mike Adler and just over six minutes after Dunlop had left it was his turn to head off towards Bray Hill on his opening lap. One of the first to retire from the race was Mike Hailwood on the 750 Yamaha. By the end of the first circuit it was Mick Grant on the 750 Kawasaki who led the race with John Williams in second place and Alex George in third. Mike Adler recorded a lap speed of just over 98mph and was in 41st place. On completion of his second circuit he recorded an average lap speed of just under 100mph and had moved up to 36th place.

As he commenced his sixth and final lap of the race, Mike Adler had moved up to 26th place and was contending for a replica finish. He had safely made his way through Greeba, Ballacraine and then into the tricky Glen Helen section of the course, where, at about 4.40pm, he was seen travelling at racing speed with another rider just ahead of him on the approach to the left hand bend immediately before the entrance to the Glen Helen Hotel. He banked over to negotiate the bend but on doing so his machine drifted wide on the exit and struck the kerb on the right. In an instant the unfortunate rider was thrown from the machine and after striking several tree branches he came to rest on top of a roadside stone wall. Marshals went to his immediate assistance and found him to be gravely injured. He was carried to the emergency helicopter, which then conveyed him to Noble's Hospital where he was admitted at 5.00pm. However, at about 6.50pm, whilst undergoing emergency surgery, he succumbed to his injuries.

Mick Grant went on to win the race, having led from start to finish and breaking lap and race records in the process. He had set the new absolute lap record of 114.33mph on his second lap of the race. John Williams on a 496 Suzuki finished in second place with Alex George on board a 738 Yamaha in third place.

Mike Adler, a single man, was 27 years of age. He was a sales representative by occupation and a resident of Auckland, New Zealand. With ten years racing experience in New Zealand he had travelled to the Island in May to learn the course. He had left the Island briefly to compete in the North West 200 in Northern Ireland before returning to take part in official practising for the TT.

His funeral service was held in the Isle of Man and followed by committal at Douglas Borough Crematorium after which his ashes were later scattered on the TT mountain course.

Michael Leslie SHARPE

1976 - Mike Sharpe pictured at Ballaugh Bridge during the Junior MGP

Conditions were fine on the morning of Tuesday 29th August 1978, the roads around the TT course were dry and visibility was clear on the mountain section, which was good news for the competitors congregating at the Grandstand in Douglas waiting to take advantage of a practice session for the Manx Grand Prix. Amongst them was Mike Sharpe, riding a 347cc TZ Yamaha machine bearing the race number 88 and entered in the Junior Race to be held the following week.

With the session under way, Mike Sharpe set off along Glencrutchery Road to begin his opening lap and safely negotiated his way round the course to complete his first circuit of the morning. He then commenced his second lap and made his way through Union Mills, Kirk Michael, Sulby and Parliament Square in Ramsey before heading for the mountain climb. Moments later he was seen travelling at racing speed on the approach to Cruickshank's Corner at the foot of May Hill. However, as he went to negotiate the right hand bend he appeared to "peel off" too soon and as a result his Yamaha drifted wide on the exit of the corner and went perilously close to the kerb on the left. Realising his predicament he banked the Yamaha over further until the exhaust expansion box grounded on the road surface leaving a shower of sparks behind. As he was struggling to maintain control of the machine the rear end suddenly spun round and threw him across the road where he collided heavily with straw bales placed around the base of a telegraph pole situated on the right hand side of the road opposite the junction with Seamount Road. The unfortunate rider came to rest in the roadway with the detached fuel tank from his machine beside him. Marshals quickly removed him from the course and into a nearby garden but there was nothing they could do for him. He had been killed instantly.

The Yamaha machine had sustained very little damage and was later examined in the rear yard at Ramsey Police Station by John Kenneth Harding, Chief Scrutineer for the Manx Grand Prix. He found that the machine had been well maintained. He also found scrape marks underneath which indicated to him that the machine had banked over too far on a right hand bend and as a result the exhaust expansion box had touched the road surface which in turn would have caused the rear wheel to lift. He could find no evidence of mechanical failure likely to have been a contributory cause of the accident.

Michael Leslie Sharpe, a single man, was 28 years of age and a resident of Horsforth, Leeds. He was a company director by occupation, being a joint director of the Pudsey Motorcycle Company. He had been motorcycle racing for about eight years and had achieved successes at local meetings but he had also taken part in national meetings at venues such as Oulton Park and Mallory Park. His first venture on the Isle of Man TT course came in 1976 when he competed in the Junior Manx Grand Prix but he was forced to retire his 347 Yamaha during the race. He returned to the Manx the following year and took part in the practice sessions but was forced to pulled out of the race as his machine broke down on the race day.

His funeral service was held in the Isle of Man and followed by committal at Douglas Borough Crematorium. A plaque in his name can be found on the memorial wall situated in the Borough Cemetery.

Steve VERNE

Philip Williams and Steve Verne during practice for the 1979 Sidecar TT

Conditions were perfect for racing on the afternoon of Monday 4th June 1979, the weather was fine, visibility was clear and the roads around the TT course were dry as no less than 81 sidecar crews lined up along Glencrutchery Road in Douglas waiting to participate in the first leg of the Sidecar Tourist Trophy Race. Amongst them were Philip Williams and his passenger Steve Verne riding a silver coloured outfit bearing the race number 60 and powered by a 738cc Suzuki engine. Williams had raced on the Island before but this was to be Steve Verne's first TT race experience.

At 2.30pm the race began with the outfit of Dick Greasley and John Parkins being the first to set off towards Bray Hill. The remainder of the field followed, one at a time and at ten-second intervals. Nine minutes and forty seconds later it was the turn of Williams and Verne to push off from the start line. They enjoyed a wonderful start and with the machine running perfectly had a trouble free lap, recording an average lap speed of around 82mph.

At about 3.15pm, having safely negotiated their way through Union Mills, Ballacraine and Glen Helen, they were seen travelling at racing speed down Barregarrow Hill, twelve miles into their second lap of the race. In close company behind them was the much faster 750cc Yamaha outfit, number 75, manned by Jim Norbury and his passenger Bernard Wright. Norbury pulled out and began to overtake on the right but at that same moment Williams moved over to the right hand side of the road in preparation to negotiate the left hand bend at the foot of the hill. The two outfits touched and locked together momentarily with the exhaust pipe of the Suzuki having jammed into an air vent in the fairing of the Yamaha. A split second later the two outfits separated and while Norbury was able to maintain control of his sidecar Philip Williams had been unable to regain control of the Suzuki as the damaged exhaust system had been pushed forward and in effect had locked the steering. The outfit swerved to the right, mounted the footpath and collided with trees. As the dust and debris began to settle, a police officer and marshals went to the assistance of the two men. Williams had been thrown through the trees and into the adjacent field where he had come to rest having sustained cracked ribs. Steve Verne was found lying on the footpath near to the extensively damaged Suzuki. He had sustained serious injuries and was conveyed by helicopter to Noble's Hospital where he was admitted at 3.48pm. However, despite emergency treatment his condition slowly deteriorated and he succumbed to his injuries at 9.50pm that same evening.

Trevor Ireson & Clive Pollington won the race on a 750cc Yamaha machine with Dick Greasley & John Parkins in second place followed by Mick Boddice & Chas Birks taking third place.

Steve Verne was 24 years of age. He was a shipwright and diver by occupation and a resident of Havant, Hampshire where he lived with his wife Jane and their three year old son Daniel. An experienced sidecar passenger, he had been with Philip Williams for about 18 months prior to his appearance on the Isle of Man.

His funeral service was held on Tuesday 12th June and followed by committal at Portchester Crematorium, Fareham, Hampshire.

Frederick Walter John LAUNCHBURY

Fred Launchbury at Quarterbridge during the fateful 1979 Formula III TT

Weather conditions were fine on the morning of Friday 8th June 1979 and the roads around the TT course were dry. Welcome news for the 54 competitors lined up along Glencrutchery Road in Douglas waiting to participate in the Tourist Trophy Formula III Race. Amongst them was race veteran Fred Launchbury, riding a 245cc Maico machine bearing the race number 62. Two days earlier he had taken part in the Junior Tourist Trophy Race and from a field of 75 he finished in 44th position with a race average speed of 87.44mph.

The race commenced shortly after 11.00am with the first of the riders, Derek Huxley and Richard Hunter, being sent on their way. The remainder of the field followed in pairs and at ten-second intervals. Fred Launchbury left the start line in company with Les Trotter and they headed off towards Bray Hill on their opening lap. Former TT winner, Tommy Robb, riding a 398cc Suzuki, had left the start line ten seconds ahead of them. On completion of the first circuit, having recorded an average lap speed of around 90mph, Launchbury was lying in 12th place and was just two seconds ahead of his starting partner Les Trotter. He completed his second lap ten seconds quicker and maintained his 12th position.

During the third lap of the race Fred Launchbury was seen approaching the left hand bend known as Watertrough Corner at Glentramman in close company with Tommy Robb. The two riders had been together on the road from the 11th Milestone and remained close together as they began to negotiate the bend. Then, on the exit of the bend, the Maico struck the stone wall on the right and scraped along it for a distance of about 30 yards as the unfortunate rider fought to regain control but despite his best efforts he was thrown from the machine and his helmet came off as he collided heavily with a road sign and a telegraph pole. Marshals went to his immediate assistance and a short time later the gravely injured rider was conveyed from the scene by helicopter to Noble's Hospital where he was admitted at 12.50pm. Despite emergency medical treatment his condition deteriorated and he passed away at 3.15pm that same afternoon.

The Australian rider Barry Smith, who was making a return to the Island after an absence of ten years, won the race with an average speed of 97.82mph. Richard Hunter took second place while Malc Wheeler finished in third place. Tommy Robb continued his race after the incident with Launchbury and finished in 5th place. Les Trotter completed two laps before retiring from the race.

Fred Launchbury was 47 years of age and a resident of New Malden, Surrey where he lived with his wife Beryl and their 12-year-old daughter Sarah Jane. He was a mechanical engineer by occupation and was well known in his hometown through his motorcycle shop in West Barnes Lane. Having made his debut on the Isle of Man in 1963 he went on to compete in no less than 28 TT races and picked up four silver replicas. He had five top ten finishes, three in the Lightweight 125 TT and two in the Formula III.

His funeral service was held on Tuesday 12th June and followed by committal at Douglas Borough Crematorium. A plaque in his name can be found on the memorial wall situated within the Borough Cemetery.

Steven Robert HOLMES

Steve Holmes pictured during the 1978 Newcomers MGP

Conditions were ideal for racing on the evening of Monday 27th August 1979, the weather was fine and the roads around the TT course were dry as competitors assembled in the area of the Grandstand in Douglas waiting to take part in a practice session for the Manx Grand Prix. Amongst them was Steve Holmes, riding a 350cc Yamaha machine bearing the race number 104 and entered in the Senior Race to be held on Thursday 6th September. Roy Wilcock, owner of Sheffield Commercial Garage, had loaned the machine to him.

At about 6.25pm, with his father watching from the pit lane, Steve Holmes set off along Glencrutchery Road towards Bray Hill on his opening lap. He safely made his way round the course and completed the lap in a time of about 27 minutes then, without stopping, continued straight through to commence his second lap of the evening.

He made his way through Glen Helen, Kirk Michael, Sulby and on into Parliament Square in Ramsey before heading towards the mountain climb. Moments later he was seen approaching the right hand bend known as Cruickshank's Corner at the foot of May Hill in Ramsey with two riders in close company behind him. Tony Rennie, the rider immediately behind had intended to pass him on the inside of the corner but decided against this when he noticed that Holmes was not reducing speed and was well off the usual racing line. As a consequence, on attempting to negotiate the bend his machine drifted to the left, mounted the footpath and collided heavily with the straw bales covering the stone pillar of a disused gateway. The unfortunate rider was thrown from the Yamaha and came to rest against the kerb on the opposite side of the road. Rennie was also thrown from his machine after colliding with one of the several straw bales that had been dislodged during the impact and scattered across the road directly in front of him. Marshals went to the immediate assistance of the two men but there was nothing that could be done for Steve Holmes. He had been killed instantly. Tony Rennie had escaped with relatively minor injuries.

The Chief Scrutineer, John Kenneth Harding, later examined the Yamaha, which had sustained very little damage during the accident. It was evident that the machine had been well maintained and had been in good working order. He found no evidence to suggest that a mechanical failure had played a contributory part in the accident.

Steven Robert Holmes, a single man, was 22 years of age. He was a resident of Sheffield where he lived with his parents and was a maintenance fitter by occupation employed by the steel firm of Arthur Lee in Meadowhall, Sheffield where his girlfriend Mavis Newton also worked. He had been riding motorcycles since he was 16 and had raced all over Britain since he was 18 years old. In 1978 he competed for the first time in the Manx Grand Prix but, riding a Yamaha machine, was forced to retire in the Newcomer's Race. In the Senior Race he was mounted on a Norton Domiracer and finished the six-lap race in 56th position with a race average speed of 79.05mph.

His funeral service was held at Shiregreen Cemetery on Thursday 6th September and was followed by interment.

Alan TAYLOR

Alan Taylor pictured during the fateful 1979 Lightweight MGP

As a result of poor weather conditions across the Isle of Man on the morning of Thursday 6th September 1979, race officials for the Manx Grand Prix made the decision to delay the start of the Lightweight Race. Furthermore, the race was reduced from four laps of the TT course to three laps. Not the best of news for the 85 competitors gathered in the area of the Grandstand in Douglas waiting to participate in the race. Amongst them was Alan Taylor, riding a 246cc Yamaha machine bearing the race number 75.

Eventually, at 11.30am, an hour and a half later than the scheduled start, the race commenced and the riders were set off in pairs and at ten second intervals. Just over six minutes later it was the turn of Alan Taylor to begin his race against the clock and he headed off along Glencrutchery Road towards St.Ninian's crossroads and Bray Hill. He safely made his way round the course through Greeba, Glen Helen and Kirk Michael village then, fourteen miles into his opening lap, he was seen approaching Birkin's Bends at Rhencullen. He was travelling at racing speed and on the correct racing line but as he negotiated the first right hand bend, for no apparent reason, his machine drifted off line and struck the kerb on the left hand side of the road. The machine travelled along the kerb edge for a distance of 62 feet then shot back across the road and mounted the grass bank on the right. At this point the unfortunate rider parted company from the machine and was thrown against a telegraph pole that had two straw bales attached to its base. As his machine continued along the top of the bank he fell back into the roadway. Marshals went to his immediate assistance but there was nothing that could be done for him. He had been killed instantly. His helmet had come off during the accident and was found lying in a field on the left hand side of the road.

An examination of the Yamaha machine following the accident found that the fairing was shattered, the front forks were twisted and the front tyre deflated but no evidence was found to suggest that a mechanical failure had contributed to the accident.

Having led virtually from start to finish, Con Law from County Antrim won the race with a record average race speed of 101.78mph. Fellow Irishman Conor McGinn took second place and Bob Jackson of Cumbria took third place.

The race was watched by Prince Michael of Kent who later that day became the first member of the Royal Family to ride on closed roads around the TT Mountain Circuit. Following the Senior Race, the Prince climbed astride a 900cc Honda then, preceded by travelling marshal "Kipper" Killip and followed by the Roads Open car, he completed a circuit of the course.

Alan Taylor, a single man, was 38 years of age. He was an engineering turner by occupation and a resident of Radcliffe, Greater Manchester. His first race experience on the TT course was the 1970 Lightweight Manx Grand Prix and he became a regular competitor in this class with his best performance coming in 1978 when he finished the race in 21st place, winning a coveted replica.

His funeral service was held on Tuesday 18th September and followed by committal at Overdale Crematorium, Bolton.

Martin Bernard AMES

Marty Ames and Dave Innocents at Ballaugh Bridge during practice for the 1980 Sidecar TT

Although the rain had stopped falling on the evening of Saturday 31st May 1980 the roads round the TT course were still wet as competitors lined up along Glencrutchery Road in Douglas waiting for the first leg of the Sidecar TT race to commence. Amongst them were Marty Ames and his passenger Dave Innocents, riding a sidecar outfit powered by a 750cc Yamaha engine and bearing the race number 81. Although familiar with the TT course as a solo rider, this would be the first time that Marty Ames had raced a Sidecar on the course other than in practice.

The race began at 6.30pm, half an hour later than scheduled and the first Sidecar away was that of Mick Boddice and his passenger Chas Birks. The following outfits were set off individually and at ten second intervals. Just over thirteen minutes later it was the turn of Marty Ames and Dave Innocents to begin their race against the clock and they headed off towards Bray Hill. Meanwhile, Marshals had noticed several outfits "snaking" on the wet road surface as they came out of the "dip" at the foot of Bray Hill and onto Quarterbridge Road near to the junction with Brunswick Road.

Moments after leaving the start line, Marty Ames and Dave Innocents were seen descending Bray Hill on the correct racing line and travelling at the normal racing speed but as they emerged from the "dip" onto Quarterbridge Road the outfit began to slide. Ames was unable to regain control of the machine as it slid across the road, mounted the footpath and collided heavily with the wall and hedges on the right. Both rider and passenger were thrown from the machine and came to rest in a nearby garden while the Sidecar had come to a stop in the roadway near to the junction with Selbourne Drive. A police officer and marshals went to the immediate assistance of the two men. Dave Innocents had sustained serious injuries to his legs and Marty Ames was deeply unconscious. Both men were conveyed by ambulance to Noble's Hospital where they were admitted at about 7.00pm. After initial treatment Marty Ames was placed in the Intensive Therapy Unit. However, shortly after midnight on the morning of Wednesday 4th June, just over three days after the accident, his condition began to deteriorate and he passed away at 12.25am.

The race was won by Trevor Ireson & Clive Pollington, having led from start to finish on the home made 750cc Yamaha powered outfit which had given Ireson victories in both legs of the 1979 meeting. Second place went to Jock Taylor & Benga Johannson who were just six seconds adrift of the winners. Third place went to Dick Greasley & John Parkins.

Marty Ames was 29 years of age. He was an auto engineer by occupation and employed by Lockside Engineering Works of Castleford who were also his race sponsors. He was a resident of Sherburn-in-Elmet, Leeds where he lived with his wife of one year, Carol, who, along with his mother, had stayed by his bedside following the accident. Before turning his attentions to sidecar racing he had years of experience racing solo machines and had finished in 3rd place in the 1979 Senior Manx Grand Prix with a race average speed of 101.80mph.

His funeral service was held at All Saints Parish Church, Sherburn-in-Elmet, Leeds on Tuesday 10th June and was followed by interment.

Andrew Michael HOLME

Peter Williams and Andrew Holme at Quarterbridge during the fateful 1980 Sidecar TT

There were wet roads around the TT course on the evening of Saturday 31st May 1980 as competitors lined up along Glencrutchery Road in Douglas waiting to participate in the first leg of the Sidecar Tourist Trophy race. Amongst them were Peter Williams and his passenger Andrew Holme, riding a sidecar outfit powered by a Yamaha engine and bearing the race number 33. Williams had previous experience of racing on the Isle of Man but Holme was making his first appearance.

The race commenced at 6.30pm with Mick Boddice & Chas Birks being the first to set off towards Bray Hill on the opening lap. Just over five minutes later it was the turn of Williams & Holme to leave the start line and begin their race against the clock. They safely made their way round the course to complete the first circuit without problems but had been travelling much slower than they normally would because of the wet roads.

At about 7.20pm, having passed through Ballacraine, Kirk Michael and Sulby, they were twenty one miles into their second lap when, travelling at an estimated 120-130mph, they were negotiating their way through the bends between Glen Duff and Glentramman, Lezayre when Andrew Holme suddenly lost his grip and fell from the sidecar. He came into contact with a low stone wall on the right hand side of the road before coming to rest near to the house, "Yn Druin" on the left. Meanwhile, Williams had continued, unaware that he had just lost his passenger, and almost lost control of the outfit when the chair lifted as he negotiated the next bend. At this point he realised that Holme was missing. He stopped at the side of the road and ran back along the course to where he found his passenger being attended to by marshals. It was thought that Holme might have lost his grip on the sidecar due to his gloves being wet. He was conscious but had sustained serious injuries and was unable to speak. He was conveyed by helicopter to Noble's Hospital where he was admitted at 7.55pm. Despite emergency surgery his condition slowly deteriorated over the following days and he passed away in the Intensive Care Unit at 6.40pm on Thursday 5th June.

The race was won by Trevor Ireson & Clive Pollington, having led from start to finish on the home made 750cc Yamaha powered outfit which had given Ireson victories in both legs of the 1979 meeting. Second place went to Jock Taylor & Benga Johannson who were just six seconds adrift of the winners. Third place went to Dick Greasley & John Parkins. The race had been marred by tragedy on the first lap when Marty Ames & Dave Innocents crashed on Quarterbridge Road in Douglas. Ames was to succumb to his injuries four days later.

Andrew Holme was 29 years of age and married to Jenny. He was a mechanical engineer by occupation and a resident of Sutton Coldfield, West Midlands. His father Dr. Guy Holme, consultant radiologist at the Queen Elizabeth Hospital in Birmingham, had a premonition of disaster and had been worried about his son's first appearance on the Isle of Man. Williams and Holme were both experienced in solo and sidecar racing.

His funeral service was held at 12 noon on Friday 13th June and was followed by interment at Coleshill Church.

Roger William CORBETT

Roger Corbett at Braddan Bridge during the fateful 1980 Classic TT

Fine weather, clear visibility and dry roads around the TT course on the morning of Friday 6th June 1980 provided ideal racing conditions for the competitors lined up along Glencrutchery Road in Douglas waiting for the Classic Tourist Trophy Race to commence. Amongst them was Roger Corbett, riding a 984cc Kawasaki machine bearing the race number 41. Two days earlier, riding a 497cc Kawasaki in the Formula II Race, he had finished in 8th place with a race average speed of 89.67mph.

The race commenced at the rescheduled time of 11.00am and the first two men away were the Irishman, Billy Guthrie and the Australian rider Jeff Sayle. Almost three and a half minutes later it was the turn of Roger Corbett and the German rider Hans-Otto Butenuth to leave the starting line to begin their race against the clock. Race favourite, Charlie Williams, went out at Ballaugh on the opening lap leaving Yamaha mounted Joey Dunlop to take an early lead.

Roger Corbett completed his first circuit and had safely negotiated his way over nine miles into his second lap when he was seen approaching the sweeping left hand bend immediately prior to the Glen Helen Hotel. However, whilst negotiating the bend the Kawasaki drifted to the right, mounted the footpath and collided heavily with the straw bales covering the stone wall at the entrance to Glen Helen Cottage. The unfortunate rider was thrown from the machine as it tumbled back across the roadway and struck the grass banking on the left. A Police Officer, Marshals and the Medical Officer on duty at Glen Helen went to his immediate assistance and found him lying in the roadway. He had sustained serious injuries and was conveyed by emergency helicopter to Noble's Hospital where desperate attempts were continued in an effort to revive him but at 12.05pm he succumbed to his injuries.

The second lap of the race saw the retirements of Australian rider Graeme McGregor at Bishopscourt and the New Zealander, Graeme Crosby, at the pits. As the pit stops came into play, Mick Grant with a quick-filler took 12 seconds to refuel while Joey Dunlop with a standard filler took 43 seconds. Grant led by 1.2 seconds at the end of the fourth lap but Dunlop broke the lap record on the fifth lap to take a seven second lead. On the final lap, Dunlop raised the absolute record to 115.22mph to win from Mick Grant and Ron Haslam.

Roger Corbett was 38 years of age and ran his own haulage business, Corbett for Carrying Limited. He was a resident of Bishops Cleeve near Cheltenham where he lived with his wife Joan and their three daughters, Elaine aged eight, Diane aged seven and Lesley aged five. He was a very experienced competitor and had made his first appearance on the TT course at the Manx Grand Prix in 1965. However, an injury sustained when he came off at Stella Maris during practice week prevented him from competing. He returned to the Manx the following year and again in 1967 but without success. Turning to the TT Races he continued his association with the Island and in 1973, riding a Triumph, he finished 9th in the Production 750 Race. From that point on he became a regular top ten finisher at the TT.

His funeral service was held at St. Michael's & All Angels Church, Bishops Cleeve and followed by interment. A large number of mourners attended the service and there were almost one hundred floral tributes.

Kenneth Maxwell BLAKE

Kenny Blake at the Bungalow during the fateful rescheduled 1981 Senior TT

Due to deteriorating weather conditions on the mountain section of the TT course on Monday 8th June 1981 the Senior Tourist Trophy Race had been controversially abandoned during the third lap of the race and was declared null and void. The most disappointed rider being the race leader, Chris Guy, whose machine was bearing the race number 13. The race was rerun the following day, Tuesday 9th June 1981 and amongst those taking part once again was the Australian rider Kenny Blake who had set the second fastest lap time during practice. He was riding a 350cc Yamaha machine bearing the race number 26 but as the riders lined up along Glencrutchery Road for the start of the race Blake discovered that a float in the carburettor of his machine was sticking, causing the float chamber to overflow. This problem was eventually rectified and he was allowed to start at the rear of the field.

At the end of the first lap, Mick Grant led the race and by the end of the second lap he was 40 seconds ahead of Charlie Williams with Donny Robinson and George Fogarty holding third and fourth. With some riders taking pit stops after two laps, the leader board began to change and Fogarty was now second with Chris Guy in third place. The usefulness of the "dump" fillers proved their worth after three laps as Mick Grant refuelled in under 11 seconds while Chris Guy, without the use of a quick filler took over 50 seconds. Grant stretched his lead on the fourth lap, despite having lost the use of fourth gear. On the fifth lap of the race showers of rain had began to fall on the circuit and both Chris Guy and George Fogarty were forced to retire after dropping their machines at Braddan Bridge.

During the fifth lap Kenny Blake was seen approaching the right hand bend at Ballagarey in Glen Vine on roads that were saturated with rainwater. He was on the correct line to negotiate the corner but as he did so the rear wheel of his machine began to slide away to the left and he lost control. Both machine and rider collided with a stone pillar at the entrance to the house "Leafy Rise". The unfortunate rider was thrown into the air and came to rest on the other side of the road outside the house "High Riggs" while his machine came to rest outside the house "Cedar Rise". Although he received immediate assistance there was nothing that could be done for him. He had been killed instantly. An examination of the Yamaha machine revealed no evidence of seizure or mechanical failure that may have caused the accident.

Mick Grant went on to win the race with Donny Robinson second and John Newbold, in his first TT meeting, took an excellent third place.

Kenny Blake was 32 years of age. He was a professional motorcycle racer by occupation and a resident of Strathalbyn, South Australia. He had considerable racing experience and success in Australia where he won several championships in 250cc, 350cc and 500cc events. He was a specialist of the Castrol Six Hours races, winning in 1973 when he rode solo, then again in 1974 with Len Atlee and 1977 teamed up with Joe Eastmore. On the Isle of Man, he had finished 13th in the 1978 Junior TT at 96.74mph. The following year he finished 12th in the Junior TT at 101.56mph, 8th in the Schweppes Classic Race at 107.36mph and 8th in the Senior TT at 106.08mph. In 1980 he took 4th place in the Junior TT at 101.42mph.

His funeral service was held in the Isle of Man and followed by committal at Douglas Borough Crematorium.

Alan Kenneth ATKINS

Alan Atkins pictured on the mountain section during the fateful 1983 Senior MGP

Unlike the previous day when mist and rain had forced the postponement of racing, conditions around the TT course on the afternoon of Friday 9th September 1983 were described as ideal for racing. Excellent news for the 100 competitors lined up along Glencrutchery Road in Douglas waiting to take part in the Senior Manx Grand Prix, the final race of the Diamond Jubilee meeting. Amongst them was Alan Atkins, riding a 347cc Yamaha machine bearing the race number 2. Three days earlier he had taken fourth place in the Junior Manx with a race average speed of 103.01mph.

At 3.00pm the flag dropped and the race commenced with the first two riders, Mick Noblett and Alan Atkins, setting off towards Bray Hill. The last man to leave the line was John McManus on his 1000cc Suzuki bearing the race number 112. The first man to complete the opening lap was Alan Atkins at 103.88mph. He continued straight through and was on his way down Bray Hill before Noblett crossed the line. However, on corrected time, it was Gary Radcliffe of Douglas who led the race from Chris Faulkner with Buddy Yeardsley of Laxey in third place and Alan Atkins holding fourth. The lead was to change several times during the race but by the end of the fifth lap, Nick Jefferies led the race by nine seconds from Faulkner while Alan Atkins had dropped down to twelfth place.

On his sixth and final lap of the race, Alan Atkins was seen approaching Milntown near Ramsey with another competitor, John McManus, directly ahead of him on the road. Then, as he began to negotiate the sweeping right hand bend the front wheel of his machine touched the rear wheel of the machine ahead of him. In an instant he was thrown from the Yamaha and struck the boundary wall of the house "Glen Royd" situated on the left side of Lezayre Road. Marshals went to his immediate assistance but there was nothing they could do for him. He had been killed instantly. John McManus had felt the collision with the rear of his machine and struggled for some distance to regain control of his machine. He stopped and pulled in to the side of the road and found that the left hand exhaust pipe of his machine was bent. He was unaware of the accident and assumed that he had touched a kerb or that the exhaust had dropped and caught the road surface. After securing the damaged exhaust he continued through Ramsey and up onto the mountain section of the course where, following reports of his exhaust system being loose, he was black flagged at the Bungalow and retired from the race.

Having taken third place on four previous occasions Nick Jefferies went on to win the race, his first success on the TT course. Buddy Yeardsley was second and Chris Faulkner third.

Alan Atkins was 28 years of age. He was a joiner by occupation and a resident of Tamworth, Staffordshire where he lived with his wife Ann and their two daughters, Charlotte aged 3 years and Laura aged four months. He was an experienced rider and had been a regular competitor on the Island since 1975, competing in no less than 14 races, during which time he had gained eight replicas.

His funeral service was held on Thursday 15th September and followed by interment at Amington Cemetery, Tamworth.

Roger John COX

Roger Cox and Colin Cowley prepare to take part in a practice session for the 1984 Sidecar TT

Dry roads, fine weather and clear visibility around the TT course on the morning of Tuesday 29th May 1984 provided perfect racing conditions for the competitors assembled at the Grandstand in Douglas waiting to participate in a practice session for the Sidecar Tourist Trophy Races. Amongst them were Roger Cox and his passenger Colin Cowley, riding a sidecar outfit powered by a 750cc Yamaha engine and bearing the race number 80. They were both newcomers to the TT course but had been racing together for two and a half years.

With the session under way the duo pushed off along Glencrutchery Road towards Bray Hill on their opening lap of the morning and safely made their way round the course to complete a lap that was well within the qualifying time. They continued past the Grandstand to commence their second lap and made their way through Union Mills, Greeba and on into the tricky Glen Helen section. With just under nine miles behind them they were seen approaching the tight right hand bend at Laurel Bank when the engine suddenly cut out. Cowley knelt upright in the sidecar and raised his left arm as the outfit free wheeled into Ebenezer Lane. Cowley stepped off the machine to examine the engine then indicated to Cox that the fuel pump was causing the problem. A few minutes later the outfit was rolled back onto the course and with a push from marshals they set off again. Almost immediately, Cowley had to raise his left arm again as other sidecars were passing but once it was clear they continued on their way.

Moments later, as they approached the right hand bend at Sarah's Cottage; Cowley leant over the right hand side of the outfit and put his weight over the rear wheel to prepare for the bend. However, as they went into the bend all three wheels lost adhesion with the road surface. The sidecar drifted across the road to the left and collided with the low earth bank then spun two or three times against the bank before disintegrating. Cowley was thrown over the bank and into undergrowth while Cox was thrown back into the roadway. The doctor on duty at that location went immediately to the two men and found Cox unconscious with serious injuries while Cowley had sustained fractures. Within a short time of the incident, an ambulance arrived on the scene and conveyed the gravely injured rider to the helicopter landing site 700 yards further along the course. He was then conveyed by helicopter to Noble's Hospital where he was admitted just after 7.10am. Cowley was taken to hospital by ambulance. Later that same day, following emergency surgery, Roger Cox was transferred by air ambulance to the neuro-surgical department at Walton Hospital, Liverpool but his condition slowly deteriorated over the following days and at 5.15am on Sunday 3rd June he succumbed to his injuries.

Roger Cox was 44 years of age. He was a mechanic by occupation and a resident of Brize Norton, Oxfordshire where he lived with his wife Anne and their two children, Sharon aged 14 years and Steven aged 12 years. They were all on the Island at the time of the accident. He was an experienced motorcyclist and began as a competitor in grass track and scrambles before progressing to sidecar racing. He was an extremely popular man who lived for motorcycles and always looked forward with excitement for each new racing season to start.

His funeral service was held on Friday 8th June and followed by committal at Oxford Crematorium.

David James MILLAR

Jimmy Millar at Ballaugh Bridge during practice for the 1984 Junior Classic MGP

With fine weather and dry roads around the TT course on the afternoon of Thursday 30th August 1984, conditions were almost perfect for racing, which was welcome news for the competitors gathered at the Grandstand in Douglas eager to take advantage of the sixth practice session for the Manx Grand Prix races. Amongst them was Jimmy Millar, riding a 350cc Aermacchi machine bearing the race number 89, which was entered in the Junior Classic Race to be held the following week. At the TT meeting several weeks earlier he had competed in the Historic 350cc Race and set the fastest lap of the race, 95.28mph, before finishing second to Steve Cull.

On receiving the signal to commence his opening lap he set off along Glencrutchery Road towards Bray Hill. then safely made his way round the course to complete his first circuit of the afternoon and without stopping, went straight through the start area to commence his second lap. He had safely negotiated his way through 21 miles of the course when, at about 4.20pm, he was seen approaching Pinfold Corner near Ramsey with another competitor, James Courtney from Dublin, a newcomer to the TT course, a short distance behind him. Courtney had been overtaken by Millar about one minute earlier and had decided to follow him in order to learn the lines taken by the more experienced rider.

Travelling at racing speed, Millar was on the correct racing line to negotiate the first right hand bend but on the exit of the corner his machine clipped the kerb on the left hand side of the road. He immediately lost control of the Aermacchi as it shot across the road to the right and collided heavily with the stone wall near to the house "Underhill". The unfortunate rider was thrown from his machine and came to rest in the middle of the road. The Aermacchi, having travelled a distance of 485 feet from the point where it first made contact with the kerb, had come to rest close to the wall on the right hand side of the road. Marshals went to the immediate assistance of the unfortunate rider and carried him to the side of the road but there was nothing they could do for him. He had been killed instantly. A split second after the accident had occurred James Courtney came upon the scene and stopped at a point just beyond where the fallen rider had come to rest but then proceeded when instructed to do so by a marshal at the scene.

John Kenneth Harding, Deputy Chief Scrutineer for the races, later examined the extensively damaged Aermacchi machine in the rear yard at Ramsey Police Station. He found no evidence to suggest that a mechanical failure had contributed to the accident.

Jimmy Millar was 38 years of age. He was a garage proprietor by occupation and a resident of Templepatrick, Ballyclare, Northern Ireland where he lived with his wife Jean and their two daughters Andrea and Cheryl. He was an experienced competitor on the TT course having first raced in 1977 when, riding an Aermacchi, he finished 49th in the Junior Manx Grand Prix. In 1983, again riding an Aermacchi, he took 4th place in the Junior Classic MGP with a race average speed of 89.91mph.

His funeral service was held in Northern Ireland and followed by interment at Carmavy Graveyard, Killead, Co. Antrim.

Sven Tomas ERIKSSON & Mats Urban ERIKSSON

Tomas Eriksson and Mats Eriksson

Only the bright setting sun would present problems around the TT course on the evening of Tuesday 28th May 1985, otherwise, the weather was fine and the roads were dry. Near perfect racing conditions for the sidecar competitors gathered at the Grandstand on Glencrutchery Road in Douglas waiting to take advantage of the second practice session for the International Sidecar Tourist Trophy Races to be held the following week. Amongst them were Tomas Eriksson and his passenger Mats Eriksson, his brother. They were riding an outfit bearing the race number 80 and powered by a 750cc Yamaha engine. As newcomers they were required to wear orange jackets over the top of their leathers to signify their inexperience on the TT course. During practice the previous day they had completed a lap at 87.64mph.

Shortly after 7.30pm, the two brothers set off towards Bray Hill followed a short time later by Robert Corkill and his passenger Paul Magee, riding an outfit bearing the race number 44 and also powered by a 750cc Yamaha engine. The two crews had safely negotiated their way through Union Mills, Ballacraine, Glen Helen and Kirk Michael village when, a short distance after Bishopscourt, Corkill came up behind the Eriksson brothers and had to reduce speed slightly as they were travelling much slower. A few seconds later, with the Eriksson's positioned towards the centre of the road; Corkill went to overtake them on the right as they approached the sweeping right hand bend at Alpine Corner. However, as he did so, they also moved over to the right and the two sidecars touched. In an instant the Eriksson's outfit veered to the left, mounted the footpath and collided heavily with the earth bank, disintegrating in a cloud of dust and debris before coming to rest on the footpath. Marshals went to the immediate assistance of the two men and found Tomas lying in the roadway close to the hedge on the right hand side of the road while Mats was found lying in the roadway close to the left hand kerb. There was nothing that could be done for them. They had both been killed instantly. Corkill, unaware of the serious nature of the collision, continued round the course to the Grandstand where he pulled in and after a brief discussion with Magee, reported the incident to the Clerk of the Course.

At Police Headquarters in Douglas the following day, Alan Verity the Chief Scrutineer, examined the red and white coloured sidecar outfit of Robert Corkill and found slight damage to the fibreglass on the left side of the fairing directly in front of the sidecar wheel. He then examined the extensively damaged sidecar outfit of the Eriksson brothers at Ramsey Police Station and found traces of red fibreglass on the exhaust system fitted on the right hand side. He found no evidence of mechanical failure on either sidecar likely to have contributed towards the accident.

Sven Tomas Eriksson, 26 years of age, was an engineer/mechanic by occupation and with several years racing experience. Mats Urban Eriksson, 30 years of age, was a welder by occupation. Both men were residents of Koping, Sweden where they lived with their parents. They had travelled to the Isle of Man from their home in Sweden via Denmark, Holland and England together with another brother, Svante Eriksson, who was part of their pit crew.

Their funeral service was held at Odensvi Kyrka (Church) in the small town of Koping and was followed by cremation.

Robert Gale VINE

Rob Vine leaves the start line to begin the fateful 1985 Senior TT

Buffeting winds were blowing across the mountain section of the TT course on the afternoon of Friday 7th June 1985 but the sun was shining and the roads were dry as 103 competitors lined up along Glencrutchery Road in Douglas waiting for the Senior Tourist Trophy race to commence. Amongst them was Rob Vine, riding a 500cc RG Suzuki bearing the race number 22. Earlier in the day, riding a Yamaha in the 750 Production Race he earned a bronze replica after finishing in eighth place with a race average speed of 102.84mph.

The flag dropped at 2.00pm and the first two riders left the start line to begin the race. Rob Vine was not long behind them and he safely made his way round the course to complete his opening lap with a time, which put him in 11th place. Joey Dunlop was leading the race from Klaus Klein, Roger Marshall, Mark Johns and Mick Grant.

Nine miles into his second lap of the race, Mick Grant sustained minor injuries when he lost control of his Suzuki at the Black Dub, the tricky left then right bends immediately after Glen Moar Mills. The fairing and petrol tank became detached from the machine as it somersaulted in the air. The debris was quickly removed from the roadway by marshals and cement dust was then scattered over the large spillage of fuel and oil. The yellow flag and oil flag were waved to warn approaching riders and a few had passed through the scene of the accident at a much reduced speed before Rob Vine appeared. He was alone on the road and acknowledged the flags by reducing speed then, after passing through the scene he began to accelerate and change gear as he came out of the right hand bend but as he did so his rear wheel stepped out to the left and the machine went from beneath him. Both rider and machine then slid along the road for about 100 yards before colliding heavily with a stone wall on the left. The unfortunate rider came to rest in the middle of the road while his machine disintegrated and scattered debris across the roadway. Marshals went to his assistance and carried him clear of the course and onto the footpath on the right hand side of the road where his helmet was removed but no signs of life could be detected. The emergency helicopter had been called and when it arrived at the scene Dr. David Stevens, the duty medical officer on board, certified that Rob Vine, his friend of six years, had probably been killed instantly.

Joey Dunlop went on to win the race and became only the second rider to win three TT races in a week. Roger Marshall finished in second place and privateer Mark Johns third.

Rob Vine, a single man, was 30 years of age. He was a garage proprietor by occupation and a resident of Dover, Kent where he lived with his parents. He was a very experienced rider who had made his first appearance on the Isle of Man in the 1977 Senior Manx Grand Prix. In the corresponding race of 1979 he finished 8th then topped that the following year with a 7th place in the Junior and 9th place in the Senior. He finished 5th in the 1981 Junior MGP and took second place in the 1982 Senior Manx Classic Race.

His funeral service was held at Douglas Borough Cemetery and followed by committal after which his ashes were returned to Kent for burial. His family later gave a generous donation to start the Rob Vine Memorial Fund for the provision of medical equipment at motorcycle and other sporting events on the Isle of Man.

Ian Graham OGDEN

Ian Ogden at Parliament Square, Ramsey during practice for the 1986 Senior TT

Although the roads around the TT course were damp on the morning of Wednesday 28th May 1986 the weather was fine and visibility was clear for the competitors gathered at the Grandstand in Douglas waiting to take part in the fourth practice session for the Tourist Trophy Races. Amongst them was Ian Ogden, riding a 500cc Suzuki machine bearing the race number 50 and entered in the Senior Race to be held on Friday 6th June.

After forty or fifty machines had set off along Glencrutchery Road towards Bray Hill, Egmont Wimmeder, a dental technician from Austria and a newcomer to the TT course, received the signal to commence his opening lap of the morning. He was riding a 750cc Harris Suzuki bearing the Formula I race number 96. On completion of his first lap, Wimmeder went straight past the Grandstand to commence his second lap of the morning.

Shortly before 6.00am, having made his way through Union Mills, Crosby and Glen Helen, Ian Ogden was seen travelling at racing speed along the straight section of road at Cronk y Voddy. He was in close company behind Egmont Wimmeder who had purposely positioned himself in the middle of the road so that other, more experienced, riders could overtake him. By this time the rising sun was just beginning to dazzle the riders on that section of the course. Then, as the two riders reached the apex of the right hand bend at the end of the straight, Ogden's front wheel suddenly slipped away to the left and his machine went down on it's side, just clipping the rear of Wimmeder's Suzuki before sliding along the road and colliding heavily with the stone built boundary wall of the house "The Old Parsonage". The unfortunate rider and his wrecked machine came to rest in the roadway where a police officer and marshals on duty near that location ran to his assistance and removed him to the side of the road but on examination they found there was nothing that could be done for him. He had been killed instantly. Wimmeder had only felt a very gentle push to the rear of his machine but this had not made him alter his line through the bend and looking back over his shoulder he saw Ogden's Suzuki spinning in the roadway. On rounding the next corner he had stopped and indicated to marshals that there had been an accident. He then continued round to complete the lap.

Alan Verity, Chief Scrutineer for the Auto-Cycle Union, later examined both machines. He found that although Ogden's machine was extensively damaged the engine still turned and the gears could still be selected. There was no evidence to suggest that a mechanical failure might have contributed to the accident. There was only very slight damage to the fibreglass moulding behind the seat on Wimmeder's machine.

Ian Ogden was 27 years of age. He was a civil servant by occupation and a resident of Ballasalla. He was an experienced competitor and on his debut on the TT course in 1982, riding a Suzuki, he won the Newcomers Senior Race at 96.28mph. In 1984 he finished second in the Senior MGP after setting the fastest lap of the race at 108.03mph. In the 1985 Senior MGP he again finished second with a race average speed of 102.27mph.

His funeral service was followed by committal at Douglas Borough Crematorium. A plaque in his name can be found on the memorial wall situated within the Borough Cemetery.

Alan George JERVIS

Dennis Holmes and Alan Jervis at the Bungalow during practice for the 1986 Sidecar TT

Weather conditions were fine on the morning of Friday 30th May 1986 as competitors gathered in the area of the Grandstand in Douglas, waiting to take advantage of the sixth practice session for the International Sidecar Tourist Trophy Races, the first of which was scheduled to be held at 5.00pm the following day. Amongst them were Dennis Holmes and his passenger, Alan Jervis, riding a blue and white coloured outfit bearing the race number 18 and powered by a 750cc Yamaha engine. During the week they had completed four laps of the course in total, one on Tuesday evening, two on Wednesday evening and one on the Thursday afternoon when they found that the machine was losing water.

Having rectified the fault on the machine their intention was to complete just one lap of the course to satisfy themselves that the problem had been dealt with. At about 6.15am, they set off along Glencrutchery Road and seconds later were seen travelling down Bray Hill at over 100mph. However, as they emerged from the dip at the foot of the hill onto Quarterbridge Road all three wheels left the ground for a split second then, on landing, the sidecar began to slide out of control. Veering to the right, the outfit mounted the footpath spun round and collided heavily with the boundary wall of a house then a lamp standard. It then continued, spinning along and across the road before coming to rest on the left hand footpath near to the junction with Selbourne Drive. Police Officers and Marshals on duty near that location went to the immediate assistance of the two men. Alan Jervis was found lying in the centre of the road and was carried into the driveway of the house "Tregenna" but there was nothing that could be done for him. He had been killed instantly. Dennis Holmes was found lying on the right hand footpath almost opposite Selbourne Drive and had sustained serious lacerations to his left knee. He was conveyed by ambulance to Noble's Hospital for treatment and never raced on the TT course again.

Following the accident, Alan Verity, Chief Scrutineer for the Auto-Cycle Union, examined the sidecar outfit. He found that the braking systems were working and there was no evidence of either the engine or gearbox having seized. Nothing was found to suggest that the accident had been caused by mechanical failure.

Alan Jervis was 37 years of age. He was a self-employed roof surveyor by occupation and a resident of Bignall End, Stoke-on-Trent where he lived with his wife Cynthia and their two young daughters. He had a wealth of racing experience and had first competed on the TT course during the 1985 TT meeting when he rode as passenger on a Yamaha powered outfit driven by Brian Wilson and they finished 24th in the Sidecar "A" Race and 37th in the Sidecar "B" Race. Dennis Holmes was also an experienced competitor and had become a regular at the TT since 1980 with his best result coming in 1983 when, with Steve Bagnall in the chair, he finished 8th in the second leg of the Sidecar Race. Having got together during the winter Holmes and Jervis began racing at the beginning of March 1986 and competed in many races both in the UK and Europe before travelling to the Isle of Man.

His funeral service, attended by a large number of mourners, was held at St. John The Baptist's Church (C of E), Ashley, Staffordshire on Monday 9th June and followed by interment.

Eugene Patrick McDONNELL

Gene McDonnell at the Gooseneck during the fateful 1986 Junior TT

Conditions were near perfect for racing on the morning of Wednesday 4th June 1986. The roads around the TT course were dry and visibility was clear on the mountain section, which was good news for the 72 competitors lined up along Glencrutchery Road in Douglas waiting to participate in the Junior Tourist Trophy Race. Amongst them was Gene McDonnell, riding a 250cc EMC machine bearing the race number 8. Two days earlier he had injured an ankle when he came off his machine during the Formula II race and could have withdrawn but had made the decision to take part in the race and had been passed as medically fit to compete.

The flag dropped at 11.00am and the race began with Steve Cull and Brian Reid being the first two riders away followed ten seconds later by Joey Dunlop and Graham Cannell. Thirty seconds after the race commenced it was the turn of Gene McDonnell to begin his race against the clock and he set off in company with Michael McGarrity. By the end of the opening lap Gary Padgett led the race from Brian Reid and Steve Cull.

During the third lap of the race, Brian Reid came off his machine at Ballaugh Bridge, sustaining a fractured collarbone and wrist. The rescue helicopter was summoned to the scene and landed in a field near to the bridge. Reid was placed inside and it took off again. At that moment, a pony, startled by the helicopter, bolted from it's paddock near to "Carmodil House" and jumped over a gate and onto the course directly in front of Gene McDonnell who was approaching Ballaugh Bridge at an estimated 140mph and had no chance of avoiding the animal, which was killed instantly. The unfortunate rider was thrown from the machine and came to rest on the forecourt of the garage situated on the left side of the road immediately before the bridge. His wrecked machine careered along the road and burst into flames on the same forecourt. Geoff Cannell of Manx Radio was broadcasting live from Ballaugh Bridge and his race commentary was cut short following the chilling words "Oh my god, there's been a terrible accident here". Marshals went to the immediate assistance of the rider but there was nothing they could do for him. He had been killed instantly. At the time of the accident he had been holding fourth place in the race.

Meanwhile, the race continued with Gary Padgett leading from Steve Cull and Phil Mellor, who set the quickest lap at 111.42mph. However, a two-minute pit stop at the end of the fourth lap put Padgett out of contention. Steve Cull went on to win the race with an average of 109.62mph with Phil Mellor second and Graham Cannell of Ballaugh in third place.

Gene McDonnell, a single man, was 24 years of age and just over a week away from his 25th birthday. He was a mechanic by occupation and a resident of Ballymena, County Antrim where he lived with his parents. He had three years racing experience and his debut on the Isle of Man was at the 1983 Manx Grand Prix when he finished 5th in the Junior Newcomers Race. In 1985 he won both the 250 & 350 races on the Billown Circuit at the Southern 100 motorcycle races. He was the Irish 350 road race champion and the previous month he had secured two excellent second places at the North West 200 in Northern Ireland.

His funeral service was held at Greenlough Parish Church, which was packed to overflowing as over two thousand friends and relatives paid their last tributes.

Andrew COOPER

Andy Cooper at the Bungalow during the fateful 1986 Senior TT

The Duke of Kent officially opened the new TT Grandstand on Friday 6th June 1986 then walked amongst and chatted to the many competitors awaiting the start of the Senior Tourist Trophy Race. Amongst them was former Manx Grand Prix winner, Andy Cooper, riding a GSXR 750cc Suzuki machine bearing the race number 52. Earlier in the week he had finished in 39th place in the Formula I Race with a race average speed of 104.66mph and 20th in the Production 750cc Race with a race average speed of 104.75mph.

At 2.30pm, the weather was fine and the roads were dry as the Duke of Kent flagged away the first rider before returning to the Grandstand. From the start it was Junior Race winner Steve Cull who led the field but his Suzuki expired at Ballaugh on the opening lap and with his retirement Trevor Nation found himself in the lead but by the Bungalow Roger Marshall had gone ahead and completed the lap in first place, just under one second ahead of Nation.

Andy Cooper completed his opening lap with an average speed of just under 107mph and without stopping continued past the Grandstand to commence his second lap. He had safely negotiated his way through to Ballacraine and into the tricky Glen Helen section when he was seen, alone on the road and travelling at racing speed, on the approach to the sweeping left hand bend known as Doran's Bend just after Ballig Bridge. Then, as he banked into the corner his machine suddenly went from beneath him, dropping onto it's left side. Both rider and machine slid along the road together before colliding heavily with the kerbing of the footpath on the right and were thrown into the trees and undergrowth beside the path. The unfortunate rider, his helmet having become detached, bounced back out onto the course and came to rest in the centre of the road while his wrecked Suzuki came to rest in amongst the trees. A police officer and marshals went to his immediate aid but there was nothing they could do for him. He had been killed instantly. It was found that his leathers were saturated in oil from the waist down.

The Suzuki was later examined by the Deputy Chief Scrutineer who found there was oil along the left side of the fairing and on both wheels. Closer examination revealed a hole in the oil cooler but he was unable to say if this had contributed to the accident.

After Trevor Nation ran out of fuel on the fourth lap and Roger Marshall lost time due to a stretched chain it was left to Roger Burnett (Honda) to take advantage and he went on to win with a race average speed of 113.98mph. Second place went to Geoff Johnson (Honda) and third place went to Barry Woodland (Suzuki).

Andy Cooper, a single man, was 32 years of age. He was a maintenance fitter by occupation, employed by Rolls Royce and was a resident of Mackworth, Derby where he lived with his parents. Described by his mechanic as an experienced rider who rarely took risks, it was thought that he had suffered only one accident in his twelve-year career when his machine seized during the 1985 Ulster Grand Prix and he sustained a broken arm. Riding a 347cc Yamaha in 1982 he had won the Junior Manx Grand Prix with a race average speed of 102.85mph.

His funeral service was held on 16th June and was followed by interment at Nottingham Road Cemetery, Derby.

Nigel HALE

Nigel Hale pictured at Quarterbridge during practice for the 1986 Lightweight Newcomers MGP

Conditions were fine on the evening of Wednesday 27th August 1986 and the roads around the TT course were dry, providing near perfect racing conditions for the competitors gathered at the Grandstand in Douglas waiting to participate in a practice session for the Manx Grand Prix. Amongst them was Nigel Hale, a newcomer to the TT course, riding a 250cc EMC machine bearing the race number 110, which was entered in the Lightweight Newcomers Race to be held the following week.

At lunch time that day he had taken some medication after complaining of a sore throat and suspected that he was developing the symptoms of influenza but by 6.00pm, just prior to the commencement of the session, he was cheerful and looking forward to practising.

When the session began he was one of the first riders to set off along Glencrutchery Road towards Bray Hill and safely made his way over the first nine miles of the course. Then, at about 6.25pm, he was seen travelling at racing speed and alone on the road as he approached the right hand bend at Sarah's Cottage just above Glen Helen but Marshals noted that he was on the wrong racing line for the bend, being on the right hand side of the road when he should have been over to the left. As a consequence, when he banked over to negotiate the bend his machine began to drift towards the hedge on the left. He appeared to realise his predicament and braked hard before attempting to "step off" the machine but both rider and machine went down then slid along the road together. The unfortunate rider collided heavily with the earth bank on the left and was then struck and crushed by his machine before they both bounced back into the roadway. The Marshals and a doctor on duty at that point went quickly to his aid and found he was unconscious and had stopped breathing. The doctor began immediate resuscitation procedures while waiting for medical assistance. Within five minutes of the call, the helicopter ambulance arrived on the scene and conveyed him directly to Noble's Hospital where he was admitted at about 6.45pm and placed in the Intensive Therapy Unit. However, without regaining consciousness and with his girlfriend at his side, he succumbed to his injuries at 1.30am the following morning.

Scrutineers later examined the EMC machine and found no evidence to suggest that the accident had been caused by a mechanical failure.

Nigel Hale, a single man, was 24 years of age. He was a mechanic by occupation and a resident of Knockmore, Lisburn, County Antrim where he lived with his girlfriend of eight years, Diedre Elizabeth Spruce. He had been riding motorcycles for approximately four years and for the previous two years had been competing in various road races in Northern Ireland. Just under two weeks prior to travelling to the Isle of Man he had taken part in the Ulster Grand Prix.

His funeral service was held in Ireland and followed by interment at Blaris New Cemetery, Blaris Road, Lisburn. His death came just thirteen months after his 19 year old brother, Geoffrey Hale, lost his life as the result of a road traffic accident in Ireland when his motorcycle was involved in a collision with a car.

Kenneth Patrick NORTON

Ken Norton at Ballacraine during practice for the 1987 Junior Newcomers MGP

Fine weather provided near perfect racing conditions on the evening of Tuesday 25th August 1987, the roads around the TT course were dry and visibility on the mountain section was clear. Welcome news for the competitors gathered at the Grandstand in Douglas waiting to take advantage of a practice session for the Manx Grand Prix. Amongst them was Ken Norton, a newcomer to the TT course, riding a Yamaha TZ 350cc machine bearing the race number 90 and entered in the Junior Newcomers Race to be held the following week. He had completed two laps of the course on this machine the previous evening without incident but chose to strip the engine and installed new pistons and rings. He had remarked to his mechanic Morgan Stewart that he was still unsure of the circuit and had a lot to learn.

At about 7.05pm he set off towards Bray Hill and safely negotiated his way round the course and on completion of his first circuit he continued straight through to commence his second lap of the evening. In the area of Sulby he was overtaken by a group of three machines, one of which was a Honda VFR750, ridden by newcomer Pete Searle. Ken Norton joined the group and tucked into Searle's slipstream as they continued through to Ramsey and up onto the mountain climb. At Waterworks Corner Searle backed off slightly after his footrest caught the road surface. Taking advantage of the situation Norton quickly overtook him then positioned himself in the slipstream of the Suzuki GSX-R being ridden by newcomer David Birtles. A short time later, following the sweeping left hand bend at Brandywell, Norton moved out from behind Birtles as if to overtake him on the inside of the slight right bend immediately before the 32nd Milestone. However, at that same instant, Birtles also moved across to the right, maintaining the correct racing line for the bend. Travelling at an estimated 130mph, Norton braked hard and the Yamaha stood up almost vertical on the front wheel, then, as the rear wheel came back down onto the road surface, the machine shot across the road, narrowly missing the rear wheel of the Suzuki and collided heavily with the grass bank on the left. The unfortunate rider was thrown from the machine and came to rest against the wire fencing on the right hand side of the road. His helmet had come off during the accident. Pete Searle, travelling close behind, narrowly avoided becoming involved as pieces of debris from the crashed Yamaha struck his machine. Marshals went to the immediate assistance of the fallen rider but there was nothing they could do for him. He had been killed instantly.

The "Arai" helmet, which had only been purchased the day after his arrival on the Island, was found to have sustained a severe blow to the rear lower edge and the securing strap had been almost pulled through the "D" ring fastening. The following day the severely damaged Yamaha was examined by the Chief Scrutineer and no evidence was found to suggest that the accident had been as the result of mechanical failure.

Ken Norton, a single man, was 32 years of age. He was an insurance broker by occupation and a resident of Bray, County Wicklow, Ireland. Although a newcomer to the Isle of Man he was a very experienced rider on the road circuits of Ireland.

His funeral service was held in Ireland on Monday 31st August and followed by interment at Springfield Cemetery, Bray.

Martin JENNINGS

Martin Jennings at the Gooseneck during the fateful 1987 Junior MGP

Conditions were ideal for racing on the afternoon of Tuesday 1st September 1987, the weather was fine, visibility was clear and the roads around the TT course were dry. Welcome news for the 94 competitors lined up along Glencrutchery Road in Douglas waiting to participate in the six lap Junior Manx Grand Prix. Amongst them was Martin Jennings, riding a 350cc Yamaha machine bearing the race number 73.

At 3.30pm the flag dropped and the race began with the riders setting off in pairs and at ten second intervals. Six minutes later it was the turn of Martin Jennings to begin his race against the clock and he set off towards Bray Hill on his opening lap. By the end of the first circuit Craig Ryding was leading from Mark Linton and Steve Hazlett. By the half way stage Ryding had built up a 30 second advantage over Hazlett and Mick Robinson was now in third place.

On completion of his fourth lap Martin Jennings pulled into the pits to refuel and gave the "thumbs up" sign to his pit attendant, Godfrey Ellis, indicating that he was happy with the machine. With the Yamaha refuelled he then set off again to commence his fifth lap of the race. At about 5.20pm, having safely made his way through Greeba, Glen Helen and Kirk Michael village, he was seen travelling at racing speed on the approach to Birkin's Bends at Rhencullen. However, on the exit of the second bend, the left hander, his machine drifted wide, mounted the grass bank on the right then struck a stone gate pillar, which was covered with straw bales, before colliding heavily with the gable end of the house "Cronk Steone". The unfortunate rider was thrown from the machine and came to rest on the opposite footpath just beyond the entrance to the house "Arenthrou". A police officer and marshals went to his immediate assistance but there was nothing they could do for him. He had been killed instantly. His wrecked machine came to rest at the entrance to "Arenthrou".

Chief Scrutineer David William Harding later examined the Yamaha machine and found that it had sustained severe impact damage. The tyre and inner tube were detached from the front wheel, which had completely collapsed. There were no signs of engine or gearbox seizure or any evidence to suggest that mechanical failure had contributed to the accident.

Craig Ryding went on to win the race with an average speed of 104.57mph, 16.8 seconds ahead of Steve Hazlett with Mark Linton completing the top three.

Martin Jennings was 39 years of age. He was a motor engineer by occupation and a resident of Camborne, Cornwall where he lived with his wife Lynn and their three children, Peter, Danny and Katherine. He was an experienced road racer who had made his first appearance on the Isle of Man at the 1984 Manx Grand Prix but he was forced to retire during the Newcomers Race. However, he did finish 43rd in the Senior Race. He returned again in 1985 and 1986, entering both Junior and Senior Races but retired during each race.

His funeral service was held at Heathcoats Social Club, Poole and followed by interment at Troon. As a memorial to Martin Jennings a bike run is held in Cornwall every year to raise money for charities and attracts several hundred participants.

Richard DUMBLE

Scott Renwick and Ricky Dumble ready to take part in a practice session for the 1988 Sidecar TT

Unlike the previous evening, when poor weather forced the cancellation of the practice session, the weather on the afternoon of Thursday 2nd June 1988 was fine and the roads around the TT course were dry. Near perfect racing conditions for the sidecar competitors congregating at the Grandstand on Glencrutchery Road in Douglas ready to take advantage of the afternoon practice session for the Sidecar Races, the first of which was to be held on Saturday 4th June. Amongst them were Scott Renwick and his passenger Ricky Dumble, riding an outfit bearing the race number 44 and powered by a 750cc Yamaha engine.

The pair had completed a total of two laps in previous sessions and had already achieved a qualifying time. They intended to make one circuit of the course at a steady rate just to complete the three laps they required for qualification to take part in the races.

At 3.15pm they pushed off from the grandstand to commence their opening lap of the afternoon and safely made their way through St. Ninians crossroads and down Bray Hill. However, as they emerged from the dip at the foot of the hill onto Quarterbridge Road the right hand side of the outfit began to lift as it veered to the right with the tyres squealing on the road surface. Both rider and passenger held on as the outfit mounted the footpath on the right and collided heavily with a boundary wall. At this point the two men and their sidecar disappeared in a cloud of dust and debris before coming to rest in the roadway near to the house "Tregenna". The outfit was lying upside down with the seriously injured Renwick lying alongside it. Dumble was lying in the road a short distance beyond the machine. He had also sustained serious injuries and was found to be unconscious initially but then began to come round. He kept repeating over and over again, " I should have listened to my wife". Both men were conveyed by ambulance to Noble's Hospital where, shortly after admission, Ricky Dumble succumbed to his injuries. Scott Renwick responded to treatment and survived the incident.

Alan Verity, Chief Scrutineer for the Auto-Cycle Union, later examined the sidecar outfit and he found that both engine and gearbox were free to turn, as were the three wheels. He discovered no evidence to suggest that a mechanical failure had contributed to this incident. However, he did suggest that the bigger sidecar outfits being used on the demanding TT course should have a chassis constructed of heavier tubular material.

Ricky Dumble was 30 years of age. He was a market trader by occupation and a resident of Oakley, Fife, Scotland where he lived with his wife Catherine. They had been married less than two years. He had been involved in motorcycle racing for twelve years, racing all over the United Kingdom and Europe. He had previous experience of the TT course, always as a sidecar passenger with only a two year break in 1984 and 1985. He had been teamed up with Scott Renwick for the previous eighteen months and they competed together at the 1987 TT meeting where, riding an outfit powered by a 750cc Yamaha engine, they finished 23rd in the Sidecar "A" Race at an average race speed of 91.87mph.

His funeral service was held at Holy Name Roman Catholic Church, Oakley at 10.15am on Saturday 11th June and followed by committal at Dunfermline Crematorium.

Kenneth Neil HARMER

Kenny Harmer pictured during practice for the 1988 750 Production TT

There were reports of damp patches on the roads around the TT course on the morning of Friday 3rd June 1988, which was not the best of news for the competitors assembled in the area of the Grandstand in Douglas waiting to take advantage of a practice session for the Tourist Trophy Races. Amongst them was Kenny Harmer, riding a Honda VFR750R machine bearing the race number 56 and entered in the 750 Production Race to be held the following afternoon.

The session commenced at 5.15am and five minutes later Kenny Harmer set off along Glencrutchery Road towards Bray Hill on his opening lap of the morning. Colin Gable who was riding a similar machine and entered for the same race followed him a few moments later. Gable had first noticed him earlier in the week when they completed two practice laps together and thought they were very well matched for speed, always being close together as they negotiated the course.

He was part way round on his first circuit when Gable caught up with him and stayed in close company for the remainder of the lap. On reaching the start area Harmer passed straight through to begin his second circuit of the morning and safely made his way round the course through to Ramsey and then onto the mountain climb. After rounding the corner at the Hairpin he began to accelerate away up the hill then glanced back and saw that Gable was less than a bike's length behind him. The road surface in this area was particularly damp in places, probably due to overhanging trees. Moments later he was seen approaching Waterworks Corner, which at racing speed is taken as two right hand corners, drifting wide on the first corner and then cutting in to take the second corner. However, as he banked over to negotiate the first corner his front wheel suddenly broke away to the left and the big Honda went from beneath him. The machine slid across the road, struck the left hand kerb then flew over the roadside fencing where it became suspended in the branches of a tree while the unfortunate rider was thrown against a metal signpost and his helmet came off. He came to rest on the footpath where marshals and the medical officer on duty at that location went to his immediate assistance but there was nothing they could do for him. He had been killed instantly.

Kenny Harmer was 37 years of age. He was an electrician by occupation and a resident of Charnock Richard near Chorley; Lancashire where he lived with his wife Sylvia and their two children Kurt aged 16 and Denise aged 9. He had made his TT debut in 1976 when he was passenger to Vince Winstanley and they finished 25th in the 1000cc Sidecar Race. He returned the following year as passenger to Trevor Youens but they were forced to retire during the second lap of the race. His first appearance on the TT course riding a solo machine was at the 1978 Manx Grand Prix when he finished 6th in the Senior Newcomers Race. One of his proudest racing moments came in 1984 when, after riding a Triumph Bonneville in the Senior MGP, he received the Ray Cowles Trophy, which was awarded to the best performance on a four stroke British machine. His best result on the Island came in 1987 when, riding a Honda, he finished 4th in the Senior MGP with a race average speed of 104.83mph.

His funeral service was held at Christ Church, Charnock Richard and was followed by interment.

Brian Joseph Andrew WARBURTON

Brian Warburton at Quarterbridge during the fateful 1988 Production TT

The weather was fine, the roads were dry and conditions were almost perfect for racing on the evening of Friday 3rd June 1988. Excellent news for the 99 competitors lined up along Glencrutchery Road in Douglas waiting to participate in the Production Tourist Trophy Race. Amongst them was the race veteran Brian Warburton, riding a Honda CBR600 machine bearing the race number 65. After an absence of several years he had yearned to race competitively over the TT course one more time and in order to do so he had misled the Auto-Cycle Union about his age. He was actually two years above the age limit of 55 years.

The race was split into two classes, the "C" class dominated by 600cc machines and the "D" class consisting of 250cc and 400cc machines. Shortly after 6.00pm the race began and just over five minutes later it was the turn of Brian Warburton to leave the start line to begin his race against the clock. He safely made his way his way round the course over the first two laps of the race then pulled into the pit lane to take on fuel.

With the tank replenished he set off again to commence his third lap and made his way through to Ramsey and up onto the mountain section where, at a point between Keppel Gate and Creg ny Baa, he was overtaken by Barry Woodland who was leading the "D" class of the race on his Yamaha FZR400R. He stayed in close company with Woodland through to the grandstand and remained with him as they commenced their fourth and final lap of the race. Having made his way through Union Mills and Glen Vine he overtook Woodland on the approach to the Highlander but then left his braking late going into the bends at Greeba Castle. He managed to negotiate the bends but then found he was on the wrong line going into the left hand bend at Appledene and as consequence he ran wide on the exit. His machine mounted the footpath and struck a wall before careering back across the road and colliding heavily with the stone wall on the left side of the road. The Honda disintegrated and Woodland had to brake hard in an effort to avoid the wreckage but some debris smashed into the left side of his machine, damaging the fairing and front brake disc. Brian Warburton came to rest in the roadway and was immediately attended to by a marshal. He had sustained serious injuries and was conveyed by helicopter to Noble's Hospital, where, despite surgical and resuscitation treatment for a period of two and a half hours, he succumbed to his injuries at 11.10pm that same evening.

Barry Woodland went on to win the Production "D" race from Graeme McGregor and Brian Reid. Brian Morrison won the Production "C" race by just three seconds from Roger Hurst with Steve Hislop in third place.

Brian Warburton was a garage proprietor by occupation and a resident of Stockport, Cheshire. He was married to Irene and had four daughters, Suzanne, Sharon, Sharman and Sara. He had considerable racing experience on the Isle of Man, having first raced on the TT course in 1957. In the 1965 Manx Grand Prix he finished 2nd in the Lightweight Race and 3rd in the Senior Race. He also finished 3rd in the 1969 Senior Manx Grand Prix.

His funeral service was held in the Isle of Man and followed by committal at Douglas Borough Crematorium.

Marco FATTORELLI

Franco Martinel and Marco Fattorelli at Greeba Bridge just moments before their fateful accident

Bright sunshine graced the Isle of Man on the evening of Tuesday 30th May 1989, the roads around the TT course were dry and visibility was clear on the mountain section. Almost perfect racing conditions for the sidecar competitors assembled at the Grandstand in Douglas as they prepared to take part in a practice session for the Sidecar Tourist Trophy Races, the first of which was to be held on Saturday 3rd June. Amongst them were the Italian duo of Franco Martinel and his passenger Marco Fattorelli, riding an outfit bearing the race number 60 and powered by a 750cc Yamaha engine. This was the second year they had raced together on the Island although Martinel had ten years experience of sidecar racing on the TT course.

Shortly after 7.35pm they set off along Glencrutchery Road towards Bray Hill on their opening lap of the evening and all was going well as they safely made their way over the opening six miles of the course and through the left hand bend at Greeba Bridge. Then, after passing the Hawthorn public house and on the approach to the next right hand bend Martinel glanced at his rev counter and noted that it was reading 10,000rpm, which was well below the maximum of 11,000rpm.

They negotiated the bend safely but then, on the short straight section of road approaching the next right hand bend at "Gorse Lea", the sidecar outfit glanced against the dry stone wall on the left and suddenly shot across to the opposite side of the road, mounting the footpath and colliding heavily with a wooden electricity pole before bouncing back into the roadway where it came to rest upside down. Martinel was trapped beneath the outfit initially but managed to crawl out. He then saw his passenger Marco Fattorelli lying motionless in the roadway and fearing for the safety of his friend he walked back along the course to warn approaching sidecar crews of the accident.

Within five minutes of the emergency call being received the rescue helicopter stationed at Creg ny Baa had arrived at the scene of the accident. However, there was nothing that could be done for the unfortunate competitor. He had been killed instantly. His bright blue and red coloured crash helmet had come off during the accident and was found lying in a field on the left hand side of the road.

An examination of the outfit by Alan Verity, Chief Scrutineer for the Auto-Cycle Union, revealed that the engine was free to turn and the gears could be selected. The spark plugs showed that the engine had been running well and had not seized. However, the steering damper was found to be loose in its clamp but there was no way of knowing if this occurred before or as a result of the accident.

Marco Fattorelli was 27 years of age and a single man although he was engaged to be married. He was a cycle mechanic by occupation and a resident of Via Verolengo, Turin, Italy. He was an experienced competitor and had competed with Martinel at the 1988 TT meeting but they were forced to retire in both Sidecar races.

His funeral service was held in Italy on Saturday 10th June and was followed by interment at the cemetery of Druento, a village in the district of Turin.

John Patrick David MULCAHY

1985 - John Mulcahy partnered with Steve Mills during the Sidecar TT

Brilliant sunshine, clear visibility and dry roads around the TT course on the evening of Tuesday 30th May 1989 provided ideal racing conditions for the sidecar crews gathered in the area of the Grandstand in Douglas waiting to participate in a practice session for the Sidecar Tourist Trophy Races the first of which was to be held on Saturday 3rd June. Amongst them were John Mulcahy and his passenger, Mark Beaumont, riding a sidecar outfit bearing the race number 44 and powered by a 1300cc Suzuki engine. Although Mulcahy had previous experience of racing on the TT course, Beaumont was a newcomer to the Island and this was to be the first time the pair had actually raced together. During the practice session the previous morning they completed one lap of the course then found that their machine had developed a slight oil leak and the decision was made to change the engine.

Shortly before 8.00pm they set off along Glencrutchery Road towards Bray Hill on their opening lap of the evening and began to negotiate their way round the course. On the approach to the 11th Milestone they overtook another outfit, number 64, ridden by John Geraint Roberts who had his wife Gillian as passenger. Then, on the exit of the left hand bend the wheel of the chair lifted and for a moment it appeared to Roberts that the sidecar would turn over so he reduced speed and dropped back. Roberts lost sight of them through Handley's Corner then caught a glimpse of them negotiating the following left hand bend and again the wheel of the chair was off the ground. He next saw them travelling well ahead and in the centre of the road on the straight section approaching the top of Barregarrow Hill when the outfit suddenly veered to the right, mounted the footpath and collided heavily with the grass bank before disappearing in a ball of dust and debris. Both rider and passenger were thrown from the outfit, Mark Beaumont came to rest on the footpath, he had been winded but was relatively unscathed. However, John Mulcahy had come to rest in the middle of the road with the outfit upside down and on top of him. Marshals went to his immediate assistance and lifted the sidecar from him. He was then carried to the side of the road where a police officer and a district nurse attempted to stabilise his rapidly deteriorating condition but without success. He died at the scene prior to the arrival of the rescue helicopter. Mark Beaumont later recalled that just prior to the accident he heard a noise, which he thought sounded like the chain had come off, a noise which marshals and spectators also heard.

An examination of the extensively damaged machine by the Chief Scrutineer Alan Verity revealed that the front wheel and forks were detached from the machine and an important part of the steering mechanism could not be found despite a thorough search of the accident scene and as such he was unable to verify that a mechanical failure had been a contributing element to the accident.

John Mulcahy was 37 years of age. Although single he was the father of one child, a daughter named Victoria. He was a mechanic by occupation and a resident of Newcastle upon Tyne. He made his first appearance on the TT course in the 1982 Sidecar Races and from that point on he became a regular TT competitor.

His funeral service was held at St. Ninians Roman Catholic Church, Edinburgh on Friday 9th June and followed by interment at Piercehill Cemetery, Edinburgh.

Philip Joseph HOGG

Phil Hogg at Ballaugh Bridge during practice for the 1989 Supersport 400 TT

Weather conditions were fine on the morning of Friday 2nd June 1989 and the roads around the TT course were dry. Ideal racing conditions for the competitors gathered at the Grandstand in Douglas waiting to take advantage of a practice session for the Tourist Trophy Races. Amongst them was Phil Hogg of Douglas and once the session commenced he set off and completed two laps on his OWO1 Yamaha Production 750cc machine. He then switched to his 250cc TZR Yamaha machine bearing the race number 93, which was entered in the Supersport 400 Race to be held the following week. Earlier in the week the engine of this machine had seized during a test run and it had been necessary for the mechanic to remove the barrel from the right hand side and fit a new piston, rings and gaskets.

Having set off from the grandstand Phil Hogg was unhappy with the running of the machine and pulled off the course at Union Mills, returning to the Grandstand via the back roads. The mechanic put the original jets back in and fitted softer plugs. He noted that the racing plugs were really "choked up" mainly due to the engine running rich. At about 6.35am, he set off from the start again and within minutes he was seen approaching Ballagarey Corner, Glen Vine with the engine of his machine misfiring but despite this he was still travelling very quickly. As he banked over to negotiate the sweeping right hand corner the engine cut out completely and the rear wheel locked up for a very short distance before the Yamaha went down. Both rider and machine slid across the road and collided heavily with the straw bales, which had been placed along the walls on the left side of the road. The unfortunate rider came to rest in the middle of the roadway. Marshals went quickly to his aid and found that he had neither pulse nor any sign of life. They desperately tried to resuscitate him whilst waiting for the rescue helicopter, which arrived on the scene of the accident within five minutes of being called but there was nothing that could be done him. He had succumbed to his injuries.

An examination of the Yamaha machine revealed that both cylinders had seized, both pistons were heat damaged and the right piston had a hole in the crown. There was no doubt that this engine failure had been the cause of the accident.

Phil Hogg, a single man, was 23 years of age. He was a joiner by occupation and a resident of Douglas. He began road racing in 1985 and made his debut on the TT course during the 1987 MGP when he finished second to Colin Gable in the Senior Newcomers race. In 1988 he made his first appearance at the TT, finishing 18th in the Production race. He also enjoyed success at the Southern 100 and had creditable placings at the Ulster GP before returning to the Isle of Man for the Manx where he finished 6th in the Junior race then went on to record the fastest lap in the history of the MGP when he achieved 114.02mph from a standing start on the first lap of the Senior Race but then crashed out of the race at Cronk ny Mona on the second lap and fractured his wrist.

His funeral service was held at St. Mary's Church on Wednesday 7th June and followed by interment at Douglas Borough Cemetery. Later that year, his family and friends provided the finance for the first Phil Hogg Motorsport Rescue Unit – an ambulance, converted to carry medical and rescue equipment for motorsport events, the Islands first MSA registered Rally Rescue Ambulance.

Glyn Philip MELLOR

Phil Mellor at Quarterbridge during the fateful 1989 Production 1300cc TT

The sun was shining brightly on the afternoon of Wednesday 7th June 1989 and the roads around the TT course were dry. Excellent news for the competitors lined up on Glencrutchery Road in Douglas waiting to participate in the 1300cc Production Tourist Trophy Race. Amongst them was race veteran Phil Mellor, riding an 1100cc GSXR K Suzuki machine bearing the race number 10. The previous Friday he had taken fourth place in the Supersport 600 race and on the Monday he finished ninth in the 750cc Production race.

The race commenced at 1.00pm with the riders being dispatched in pairs and at ten-second intervals. Phil Mellor began his race against the clock forty seconds later and left the start line with Mike Seward. Jamie Whitham, Mellor's Suzuki team mate, followed ten seconds later. Having made his way round the course, Mellor was just behind Seward as he crossed the line to complete his opening lap and was holding 7th position on corrected time. At the Quarterbridge on his second lap he had edged ahead of Seward but Jamie Whitham was now right behind them. Mellor made his way through to Ballacraine and moments later, at about 1.30pm, he was seen approaching Doran's Bend at full racing speed with Jamie Whitham now directly behind him and Seward just a few yards further back. Then, as he banked over to negotiate the sweeping left hand bend, his rear wheel began to slide away to the right and in an instant, despite his quick reactions in attempting to regain control; he was thrown from the Suzuki. Both rider and machine slid along the roadway and collided heavily with a dry stone wall on the right hand side of the road. A police officer and marshals went quickly to his aid and found that he had been gravely injured. He was placed on a stretcher and carried to a field adjoining the course, from where he was collected by the rescue helicopter and conveyed to Noble's Hospital where he was admitted at about 1.45pm. However, despite the best efforts of the medical staff, he succumbed to his injuries at 4.45pm that same afternoon.

Minutes after the accident, Jamie Whitham came off his Suzuki at Quarry Bends, directly in front of Mike Seward and Steve Henshaw. In attempting to avoid the fallen rider and machine the two riders collided and were thrown from their machines. Mike Seward sustained serious injuries but survived the incident. However, Steve Henshaw sustained fatal injuries. Whitham escaped relatively unscathed.

Dave Leach went on to win the race for the second year in succession. Nick Jefferies was second with Alan Batson in third place.

Phil Mellor was 35 years of age. He was a professional motorcycle racer by occupation and a resident of Shepley, Huddersfield where he lived with his wife Christine and their three month old son, Thomas. He was an experienced competitor having started racing in 1975 and had competed in more than 40 races on the TT course since his debut at the 1978 MGP when he won the Lightweight Newcomers Race. He had achieved three TT victories during his racing career; the 1983 350cc Junior TT, the 1984 250cc Production TT and the 1986 750cc Production TT.

A private funeral service was held on Tuesday 13th June and followed by committal. Two days later close to 500 relatives and friends attended a memorial service at St. Paul's Church, Marsh Lane, Shepley. Phil Mellor's Suzuki GB team mate Jamie Whitham read a lesson and TT commentator Fred Clark gave an address.

Steven HENSHAW

Steve Henshaw at Quarterbridge during the fateful 1989 Production 1300cc TT

Weather conditions on the afternoon of Wednesday 7th June 1989 were near perfect for racing as competitors entered for the 1300cc Production Tourist Trophy Race lined up along Glencrutchery Road in Douglas waiting for the race to commence. Amongst them was Steve Henshaw, an experienced competitor, riding a Yamaha FZR1000 machine bearing the race number 3. Just a few days earlier he had taken part in the Formula One TT and finished in 18th position with a race average speed of 111.46mph.

The race began at 1.00pm with Nick Jefferies and Brian Morrison being the first two riders away. Ten seconds later Steve Henshaw began his race against the clock and headed off towards the descent of Bray Hill. He was followed half a minute later by Mike Seward and Phil Mellor who in turn were followed ten seconds later by Mellor's Suzuki team mate Jamie Whitham. On completion of the first circuit, Dave Leach led the race from Nick Jefferies with Jamie Whitham third. Mike Seward was sixth and Phil Mellor seventh. Steve Henshaw recorded a lap time of 20.17 minutes and was holding 12th position in the race.

At Ballig Bridge, eight miles into the second lap of the race, Whitham was directly behind Mellor with Seward just a few yards further back when Mellor suddenly lost control of his machine as he negotiated Doran's Bend and sustained injuries that were to prove fatal.

Although close behind Mellor, Whitham was able to avoid becoming involved in the accident and continued racing. By Quarry Bends, he had passed Henshaw on the road but then, as he negotiated the first left hand bend, his machine began to slide from beneath him and he came off. At that moment Steve Henshaw and Mike Seward came upon the incident and were confronted with Whitham and his machine sliding along the road. They reacted quickly to take avoiding action but in doing so they collided and were thrown from their machines as they tumbled along the road and collided heavily with the dry stone wall on the right before rebounding back across to the other side of the road. Steve Henshaw came to rest against the left hand kerb and Marshals went to his immediate assistance but there was nothing they could do for him. He had been killed instantly. Mike Seward sustained serious injuries but survived the incident while Jamie Whitham escaped relatively unscathed.

Dave Leach went on to win the race for the second year in succession. Nick Jefferies finished in second place with Alan Batson taking third position.

Steve Henshaw was 35 years of age. He was a professional motorcycle racer by occupation and a resident of Jacksdale, Nottingham where he lived with his wife Val who was on the Island with him at the time of the incident. His first racing experience of the TT course was during the 1981 TT meeting when he secured creditable finishes in all three races he entered. In 1984 he suffered serious injuries in an accident at Glen Duff during practice for the TT but returned in 1986 and took 10th place in the Production A race.

His funeral service was held at St. Mary's Church, Jacksdale and followed by committal at Mansfield Crematorium. His ashes and racing helmet were later interred in the graveyard at St. Mary's Church.

Colin KEITH

Colin Keith at the Gooseneck during practice for the 1989 Senior Classic MGP

Weather conditions were fine on the evening of Tuesday 29th August 1989 and the roads around the TT course were dry, which was ideal for the competitors gathered at the Grandstand in Douglas waiting to take advantage of a practice session for the Manx Grand Prix. Amongst them, following a five year break from motorcycle racing, was Colin Keith, riding a 500cc single cylinder BSA machine fitted in a Ducati frame and bearing the race number 27, which was entered in the Senior Classic Race. The machine had been loaned to him by fellow competitor Robbie Allan and was capable of 125mph.

Once the session had commenced, Colin Keith headed off along Glencrutchery Road towards Bray Hill then safely made his way round the course and up onto the mountain section. He was being followed by Robbie Allan, having overtaken him earlier, and on rounding Brandish Corner he was about 300 yards ahead of him. On the approach to Hillberry Corner he overtook another competitor, who appeared to be touring, then banked over to negotiate the sweeping right hand corner. However, as he did so, his machine clipped the kerb on the right and went out of control. It shot straight across the road and crashed into the straw bales covering a wall on the left. The unfortunate rider was thrown into the air and came to rest on the left hand side of the road. Although initially knocked out he quickly regained consciousness but had sustained serious fractures to his left arm and leg. He was carried by stretcher to a nearby field then conveyed by helicopter to Noble's Hospital.

He remained in Noble's Hospital until Friday 8th September, when it was decided that he was fit enough to be transferred to a hospital nearer to his home, purely for a period of convalescence. He was conveyed by private aircraft and ambulance to the Royal Alexandra Hospital, Paisley, Scotland where he was admitted at about 3.00pm that day. He continued to show improvement until about 6.45pm on Sunday 10th September when he complained of feeling faint and collapsed. On finding no sign of a pulse medical staff began immediate resuscitation procedures but could not revive him. A post mortem examination later revealed that Colin Keith had died as the result of a massive pulmonary embolism.

A police vehicle examiner later examined the motorcycle at the home of Robbie Allan and found that the front wheel and forks had sustained damage. There were also scrape marks along the right hand side. The Ducati frame had been manufactured in 1965 and the BSA engine in 1972. He concluded that the machine had been in good mechanical condition prior to the incident at Hillberry.

Colin Keith was 47 years of age and a self taught motor mechanic by trade but worked as a die-caster with molten metals. He was a resident of Erskine, Scotland where he lived with his wife Jackie and their four children, Susan, Colin, Steven and David. He was an experienced competitor and a former Scottish Motorcycle Champion who had made his debut on the TT course at the 1974 Manx Grand Prix. He went on to win a total of three MGP replicas during 1978 and 1979.

His funeral service was held on Friday 15th September at Woodside Crematorium, Paisley and was attended by over two hundred mourners.

Ian STANDEVEN

Ian Standeven at Braddan Bridge during the fateful 1989 Junior MGP

Fine weather, clear visibility and dry roads around the TT course on the afternoon of Wednesday 6th September 1989, provided almost perfect racing conditions for the 89 competitors lined up along Glencrutchery Road in Douglas waiting to participate in the Junior Manx Grand Prix. Amongst them was Ian Standeven, riding a 347cc Yamaha machine bearing the race number 8.

The race began with the riders being dispatched in pairs and at ten second intervals. Thirty seconds after the first men had been sent on their way it was the turn of Ian Standeven to begin his race against the clock and he set off towards Bray Hill along with his starting partner Andy Bassett. He safely made his way round the course to complete his first circuit and on corrected time he was holding fourth place. On completion of the second lap Dave Montgomery led the race with a three second advantage over Mick Robinson. Stanley Rea was holding third position and Ian Standeven was maintaining his fourth place.

Having made his way through Greeba and Glen Helen, Standeven was fifteen miles into his third lap of the race, when he was seen coming out of Kirk Michael village and approaching Birkin's Bends at Rhencullen. Then, as he was negotiating the first right hand bend his machine began to run wide on the exit. Realising his predicament he braked hard, leaving a fifty foot tyre mark on the road surface, but his machine struck the kerb on the left, mounted the footpath and collided heavily with the straw bales covering the wall of the house "Laurel Dene". Both rider and machine then slid across the road before crashing into the grass bank on the right. A police officer and marshals went to his immediate assistance and found the unfortunate rider lying in the field beyond the grass bank. His helmet had come off during the accident and he had sustained serious injuries. Within twenty minutes the helicopter ambulance had conveyed him from Rhencullen to the playing fields at Ballakermeen School in Douglas where he was then transferred to an ambulance, which carried him the short distance to Noble's Hospital for emergency treatment.

Dave Montgomery went on to win the race with an average speed of 105.11mph and a forty two second advantage over Stanley Rea in second place. Third place went to Andy Bassett.

Three weeks following the accident and showing signs of recovery, Ian Standeven was transferred from Noble's Hospital by a special low level flight to Gloucestershire Royal Hospital, which was near to his home. However, two days after his arrival his condition suddenly deteriorated and on 29th September he succumbed to bronchial pneumonia.

Ian Standeven, a single man, was 39 years of age. He was a self employed builder by occupation and a resident of Stroud, Gloucestershire. As a regular competitor at the Manx Grand Prix since 1983 he would have had a good knowledge of the TT course.

His funeral service was held at Cheltenham Crematorium and his ashes were later interred beneath a horse chestnut tree at Lower Nash End Farm, Bisley, the home of his sister Penny and brother in law. As a point of interest, the tree had been grown from a conker taken from a tree planted by Ian when he was a young boy.

Gordon John SMYTH

John Smyth at Braddan Bridge during the fateful 1989 Senior MGP

Weather conditions were fine on the afternoon of Friday 8th September 1989, the roads around the TT course were dry and visibility was clear on the mountain section. Near perfect racing conditions for the 94 competitors lined up along Glencrutchery Road in Douglas waiting to participate in the six lap Senior Manx Grand Prix. Amongst them was John Smyth, riding an 1100cc Suzuki machine bearing the race number 17.

Once the race was under way it was not long before John Smyth set off towards Bray Hill and safely made his way round the course but had to make an unscheduled pit stop at the end of the lap because he was having a problem with his steering damper. After adjustments had been made he went off again to commence his second circuit. Nigel Barton was leading the race at the half way stage and he used his scheduled pit stop not only to refuel but also to change the rear wheel of his machine.

John Smyth also made a scheduled pit stop at the end of his third circuit and once his fuel tank was replenished he set off again to begin his fourth lap. He negotiated his way round the course and shortly after passing through Ramsey he overtook Trevor Burden, who then tucked in behind him on the mountain climb to take advantage of his greater experience of the course. A short time later, with Burden approximately 100 yards behind him, he was seen approaching the four right hand bends at the Verandah. He took the first two bends safely, straightened up momentarily, then leaned over to his right to negotiate the third bend but as he did so his right foot caught the road surface and as a consequence his rear wheel broke away and the machine dropped onto its right hand side. Both rider and machine then slid across the road and on striking the kerbstone on the left the Suzuki burst into a ball of flames as it cartwheeled over the grass verge and down onto the grassland below the road. The unfortunate rider was found lying in the grass and was unconscious. Marshals did what they could for him before he was conveyed by emergency helicopter to Noble's Hospital where he was admitted at 3.45pm but despite emergency medical treatment he succumbed to his injuries forty minutes later.

Nigel Barton went on to win with a race average speed of 111.53mph and a 45 second advantage over Allan McDonald in second place while Brad Ogden finished in third place. Trevor Burden went on to finish in 30th position.

John Smyth was 31 years of age. He was a Marine Engineer with the Isle of Man Steam Packet Company by occupation and a resident of Douglas where he lived with his wife Sharon; they had been married just six months. He had eight years racing experience and had made his debut on the TT course during the 1984 Manx Grand Prix when he finished 14th in the Junior Newcomers Race. He returned in 1985 and finished 16th in the Junior MGP. A crash at Greeba Castle during practice for the 1986 Senior MGP had left him with a pin in his right upper arm. In 1988 he finished 21st in the Senior Manx with a race average speed of 103.09mph.

His funeral service was held at All Saints Church and followed by interment at Douglas Borough Cemetery. Two years later, a marshal's shelter was built at the Black Hut in his memory and a memorial stone was unveiled by TT star Alan Jackson, a personal friend.

Bernard Henri TROUT

Bernard Trout at Ballaugh Bridge during the fateful 1990 Lightweight Classic MGP

Sunshine prevailed over the Isle of Man on the afternoon of Monday 3rd September 1990 and conditions were perfect for racing as 101 Manx Grand Prix competitors lined up along Glencrutchery Road in Douglas waiting to participate in both the Junior Classic and the Lightweight Classic races, which were being run simultaneously. Amongst them, competing in the Lightweight Race was Bernard Trout, riding a 250cc Ducati machine bearing the race number 119.

Once all the Junior machines had been dispatched from the start line the Lightweight Race commenced and it was soon the turn of Bernard Trout to set off towards St.Ninian's crossroads on his opening lap of the race. He safely made his way round the course to complete his first and second circuits, giving his pit attendant the thumbs up sign each time he passed the pit lane, indicating that all was going well. Concerned that he would not have sufficient fuel to complete the race, he pulled into the pits at the end of the third lap, then, with an additional half gallon of fuel in his tank he set off again to begin his fourth and final lap of the race. He safely made his way through Union Mills and Crosby then came upon the scene of an accident at Appledene where competitor Gerry Jenkins had sustained a dislocated hip after crashing his Greeves there a short time earlier. Having carefully made his way through the accident scene he continued with the race and moments later he was seen approaching Greeba Bridge. Then, on negotiating the left hand bend at the bridge he drifted wide on the exit and struck the kerbstone on the right. The unfortunate rider was immediately thrown from the machine and landed heavily in the roadway while the fuel that had spilled from the Ducati ignited and the entire width of the road became a mass of flames. Marshals and police officers went to his assistance and found his condition to be deteriorating rapidly. Within a few minutes, despite all efforts to resuscitate him, he succumbed to his injuries.

Later the same day, David William Harding, the Chief Scrutineer, examined the Ducati at Police Headquarters, Douglas and found that the fairing, fuel tank and seat had become detached from the machine. The exhaust pipe had broken away from the cylinder head and the megaphone was badly damaged. Both brakes were in working order and both tyres were still inflated. There was no evidence to suggest that a mechanical failure had contributed to this accident.

Bob Jackson, who had been the leading the race, was forced to retire at Ramsey during the third lap after his Suzuki developed an oil leak. His misfortune had allowed Marek Nofer to move into the lead and he went on to win the race with Alan Taylor second and Grant Goodings third.

Bernard Trout, a single man, was 35 years of age. He was a self-employed builder by occupation and a resident of Bournemouth. He had ten years experience of racing motorcycles and had competed in the previous two Lightweight Classic Manx Grand Prix Races. However, due to mechanical problems he had been forced to retire in both races.

His funeral service was held on 13th September and followed by committal at Medway Crematorium, Robin Hood Lane, Chatham, Kent.

Robert Kevin HOWE

Kevin Howe pictured during the fateful 1990 Senior MGP

Apart from a stiff breeze on the afternoon of Friday 7th September 1990, the weather was fine and the roads around the TT course were dry. Almost perfect racing conditions for the 94 competitors lined up along Glencrutchery Road in Douglas waiting to participate in the Senior Manx Grand Prix. Amongst them was Kevin Howe, riding a VFR750 Honda machine bearing the race number 99. He had last raced on the Island in 1984 but after watching the Senior Manx in 1989 he told a close friend that he just had to race again.

The flag dropped at 1.30pm and the race was under way with race favourites Brian Venables and Simon Beck being among the first to leave the start line. Eight minutes later it was the turn of Kevin Howe to begin his race against the clock and he set off towards Bray Hill. He safely made his way round the course to complete his first circuit and without stopping at the pits he commenced his second lap. Beck was leading the race by ten seconds from Venables with David O'Leary holding third place. On completion of his second circuit Kevin Howe pulled into the pits to refuel. There was no conversation between him and his attendants but he seemed calm as his visor and screen were cleaned. Then, with his fuel tank replenished he set off again to begin his third lap of the race and negotiated his way round the course for a third time. At this stage of the race Beck had increased his lead and was now over 30 seconds ahead of Venables who had Roy Anderson just five seconds behind him in third place.

Having made his way through Glen Helen, Ballaugh and Sulby, Kevin Howe was 22 miles into his fourth lap when he was seen travelling along Lezayre Road in Ramsey. He was in close company behind two other competitors as they approached Schoolhouse Corner and while the other riders were on the usual racing line he appeared to be slightly over to the left and as he banked over to negotiate the left hand bend his machine began to wobble then suddenly went from beneath him. Both rider and machine slid along the road and collided with the low boundary wall of "Ballaghennie House" on the right. The unfortunate rider came to rest on top of the wall while his machine came to rest in the lay-by outside the East Building of Ramsey Grammar School. A police officer and marshals went to his immediate assistance but there was nothing they could do for him. He had been killed instantly.

Simon Beck went on to win the race, setting new lap and race records. Brian Venables finished in second place with Roy Anderson taking third.

Kevin Howe, a single man, was 35 years of age. He was a miner by occupation employed by British Gypsum and was a resident of Penrith, Cumbria where he lived with his mother who, along with his girlfriend, had travelled to the Island to watch the race. His debut on the TT course was in 1982 when he came 5th in the Junior Newcomers MGP. The following year he finished 17th in the Junior Manx. After suffering mechanical failures at the 1984 MGP he made the decision to take a rest from racing. He was a keen sportsman and enjoyed rock climbing, squash and shooting. He had also experienced free fall parachuting.

His funeral service was held on Friday 14th September and followed by committal at Douglas Borough Crematorium. A memorial service was held on Tuesday 25th September at St. Andrews Church, Penrith.

Ian YOUNG

Ian Young pictured at Union Mills during practice for the 1991 Supersport 600 TT

Conditions were almost perfect for racing on the evening of Tuesday 28th May 1991. The roads around the TT course were dry and visibility was clear on the mountain section. In addition, an overcast sky was masking the setting sun which had been known to cause problems to riders travelling between Glen Vine and Ballacraine during evening practice sessions. This was all good news for the competitors who were gathering at the Grandstand in Douglas waiting to take advantage of a practice session for the Tourist Trophy races. Amongst them was Ian Young, riding a 600cc Honda machine bearing the race number 1 and entered in the Supersport 600 Race to be held on Wednesday 5th June. He had used the machine the previous evening and had experienced problems with the suspension but this had been attended to by a suspension specialist.

Shortly after 6.35pm, he set off along Glencrutchery Road towards Bray Hill on his opening lap of the evening and made good progress as he safely made his way through to Greeba Castle. He took the left and right hand bends and then accelerated away towards the section of the course known as Appledene where, travelling at racing speed, he negotiated the left hand bend and then the right but on the exit of the bend, for no apparent reason, he suddenly lost control of his machine and was thrown off. Both rider and machine slid diagonally across the road and collided heavily with a low stone wall on the left about twenty yards before the entrance to Greeba Kennels. The machine continued along the road for about 120 yards while the unfortunate rider came to rest in the middle of the roadway some twenty yards beyond the point of impact with the stone wall. Marshals quickly attended to him and carefully removed his crash helmet, giving first aid while they waited for the rescue helicopter, which arrived on the scene from Sulby Bridge within 7 minutes of being called. However, it was found that there was nothing that could be done for him. He had already succumbed to his injuries.

Alan Verity, Chief Scrutineer for the Auto-Cycle Union, later examined the Honda machine and despite the accident damage, the engine and gears were still free. There was no evidence to suggest that a mechanical failure may have contributed towards this accident.

Ian Young, a single man, was 27 years of age. He was a self-employed motorcycle courier by occupation and a resident of Billy Mill, North Shields. With ten years experience of racing motorcycles he was a competent and talented competitor. He had become a regular at the TT races and had recorded several top ten placings. His best results came in 1989 when he won four coveted silver replicas after finishing 7th in the Supersport 600 TT, 6th in the 750 Production TT, 5th in the Junior TT and 8th in the Senior TT with a race average speed of 113.68mph.

In 1990 he qualified fourth fastest for the Formula I Race at 118.46mph and during the actual race he was lying in fourth place at the end of the first lap. However, his race ended on his second circuit after a spill at the Black Dub from which he was fortunate to sustain no more than abrasions.

His funeral service was held at St. George's Church, Cullercoats on Tuesday 4th June followed by committal at Tynemouth Crematorium.

Petr HLAVATKA

Petr Hlavatka at Ballacraine during practice for the Formula One race at the 1991 TT

Conditions were ideal for racing on the evening of Wednesday 29th May 1991. The weather was fine and the roads around the TT course were dry, which was welcome news for the competitors gathered at the Grandstand in Douglas waiting to participate in a practice session for the Tourist Trophy Races. Amongst them was the Czechoslovakian rider, Petr Hlavatka, riding a two year old 750cc Suzuki machine bearing the race number 78, which had been entered in the Formula I Race to be held on Saturday 1st June. Although a newcomer to the TT course, he was one of Eastern Europe's top racing motorcyclists. He had been out on two previous practice sessions and had completed four official laps of the course.

Shortly after 6.30pm, with the session under way, Hlavatka set off along Glencrutchery Road towards Bray Hill on his opening lap of the evening. He safely made his way round the course and was within a mile of completing the lap when he was seen, alone on the road, travelling along the straight on the approach to the tight right hand bend at The Nook. However, instead of reducing speed and taking the normal racing line he attempted to go through the corner at full racing speed, showing no signs of braking or attempting to slow down. As a consequence, on the exit of the bend, he collided heavily with the earth bank on the left hand side of the road. Both rider and machine were thrown into the air and collided with the trunk of a large tree growing just inside the grounds of Government House. The Suzuki machine landed on top of the hedge while the unfortunate rider came to rest in the roadway. The police officer together with marshals on duty at that location went to his immediate assistance and found that his condition was serious. They did what they could for him while waiting for the helicopter ambulance, which arrived on the scene of the accident within five minutes of being called. The unfortunate rider was conveyed to Noble's Hospital and was admitted just over ten minutes after the accident occurred. However, despite all the efforts of the medical staff, he succumbed to his injuries in theatre at 10.00pm that same evening.

Petr Hlavatka was 43 years of age. He was a lorry driver by occupation and a resident of Zeravice, Czechoslovakia where he lived with his wife Nadezda and their three children, Tomas, Petra and Pavla. He had first taken up motorcycle racing in 1970 and as he became experienced he had taken part in International race meetings that were held in Eastern Europe. He became one of the top riders and was nominated for the Grand Prix CSSR.

His funeral service was held in Czechoslovakia and followed by interment at Zeravice Cemetery.

The following year, a blue speckled marble memorial stone and a small Czechoslovakian flag were placed on top of the hedge and at the base of the tree that was struck by the unfortunate rider. The land on which the tree is situated was within the grounds of Government House, the official residence of Sir Laurence Jones who held the position of the Island's Lieutenant Governor at that time. It was declared that as the memorial had been placed at the scene of a tragedy by people who care, it should remain there. However, in the interests of safety, the memorial was later removed to the inside of the hedge and mounted on a brick plinth.

Sadly, in July 1997, eighteen year old Tomas Hlavatka lost his life whilst motorcycle racing at the Most circuit in the Czech Republic. He was later buried alongside his father.

Francis DUFFY

Frank Duffy pictured during practice for the 1991 Ultra Lightweight TT

Conditions around the TT course were near perfect for racing on the afternoon of Thursday 30th May 1991. The roads around the TT course were dry and visibility was clear on the mountain section, which was good news for the competitors gathered at the Grandstand in Douglas waiting to take advantage of a practice session for the Tourist Trophy races. Amongst them was Frank Duffy, riding a 125cc Honda machine bearing the race number 69, which had been entered in the Ultra Lightweight race to be held the following week. During the Monday evening practice session he had completed two laps of the course on this machine and was fastest in his class. He completed a further two laps during the Wednesday morning session and was sixth fastest. The Honda had been purchased new at the start of the year and there had been no mechanical problems with the machine during practice.

At about 3.00pm, with the intention of completing two or possibly three laps of the course, Frank Duffy set off along Glencrutchery Road towards Bray Hill and had safely made his way through Union Mills, Glen Helen, Kirk Michael and Sulby when, just over twenty miles into his opening lap, he was seen, alone on the road and travelling at racing speed on the approach to the "S" bends at Kerrowmoar just after the Ginger Hall Hotel. He was on the usual racing line to negotiate the left hand bend but as he banked over, the front wheel of the Honda slid away to the right and he went down. Both rider and machine then slid along the road for about thirty yards before colliding heavily with the earth bank and hedge on the right before bouncing back into the roadway. Marshals went to his immediate assistance and quickly carried him to the side of the road where it was found that he was unconscious and had stopped breathing. Strenuous efforts were made to resuscitate him and he was carried to the helicopter pick up point situated nearby. Just over five minutes after receiving the call, the helicopter ambulance arrived at the scene and the medical officer onboard examined the unfortunate rider but sadly, it was found that he had succumbed to his injuries.

The Honda machine was later examined by Scrutineers at Police Headquarters in Douglas and was found to have sustained moderate damage. No evidence was revealed to suggest that a mechanical failure had contributed to this accident.

Frank Duffy was 28 years of age. He was a diesel fitter by occupation and maintained a fleet of plant machinery for a construction firm. Although a resident of Greenford in Middlesex at the time of his death he was born in County Monaghan, Eire. He had been riding competitively for about five years and his first appearance on the Isle of Man was at the 1988 Manx Grand Prix. Riding a Yamaha machine, he finished 10th in the Lightweight class of the Newcomer's Race and followed that result with 24th position in the Lightweight Race later in the week. He returned to the Island the following year with a Honda machine and finished 29th in the Lightweight MGP. In 1990 he made the decision to move on to the TT races and, riding a Honda, he competed in the Ultra Lightweight Race and finished in 7th place with a race average speed of 96.77mph.

His funeral service was held at the Sacred Heart Church, Aughnamullen, County Monaghan, Eire on Wednesday 5th June and followed by interment.

Roy ANDERSON

Roy Anderson at Creg ny Baa during the fateful Formula One race at the 1991 TT

Fine weather prevailed on the afternoon of Saturday 1st June 1991. The roads around the TT course were dry and visibility was clear on the mountain section, which was welcome news for the 55 competitors lined up along Glencrutchery Road in Douglas waiting for the Formula One Tourist Trophy race to commence. Amongst them was Roy Anderson, riding a 750cc Yamaha machine bearing the race number 34. Although making his TT debut, he was familiar with the course, having previously competed in the Manx Grand Prix and had taken third place in the 1990 Senior MGP with a race average speed of 109.89mph.

The race began at 2.00pm with Brian Morrison being the first man to leave the start line with the rest of the field being dispatched at ten second intervals. Five and a half minutes after Morrison had set off it was the turn of Roy Anderson to begin his race against the clock and he headed off towards Bray Hill and Quarterbridge Road. On completion of the second circuit Steve Hislop had set a new course record with a speed of 123.48mph and was now thirty seconds ahead of his Honda team mate Carl Fogarty.

On completion of his fifth lap, Roy Anderson made a scheduled pit stop at the Grandstand and told his pit crew that the machine was fine but he was having visibility problems due to insects plastered over the front of his visor. The visor was cleaned and he set off again to commence his sixth and final lap. At this time he was holding 14th position in the race. He safely made his way round the course through to Ramsey and then up onto the mountain section where, at about 4.05pm, he was seen alone on the road and travelling at racing speed on the approach to the right hand bend immediately before the Black Hut. He was on the usual racing line but as he banked over to negotiate the bend his right shoulder first caught a wooden fence post and then a concrete post. The unfortunate rider immediately lost control of his machine as it veered across the road and mounted a low grass bank before dropping into a culvert. At this point he was thrown from the machine and came to rest on the grass while the Yamaha rebounded back into the roadway. Marshals went to his immediate assistance and found his condition to be serious. Within 20 minutes of the accident, the gravely injured rider had been conveyed by helicopter and ambulance to Noble's Hospital where, despite emergency treatment, he succumbed to his injuries in theatre at 1.30am the following morning.

Steve Hislop went on to win the race from Carl Fogarty and Brian Morrison. Trevor Nation had actually finished in third place but was excluded for having an oversized fuel tank fitted to his machine.

Roy Anderson, a single man, was 39 years of age. He was an engineer by occupation and a resident of the village Boat of Garten near Aviemore, Invernesshire where he lived with his parents. He had been racing competitively for fifteen years and had raced for Scotland. He held the Production lap records at Newcastle and Silverstone and once won eight races in a row at a meeting in England. His first race on the Island was the 1989 Senior Newcomers MGP but he failed to finish.

His funeral service was held in Boat of Garten on Friday 7th June and followed by interment.

Paul Geoffrey ROME

Paul Rome at Keppel Gate during practice for the 1991 Junior MGP

The weather was fine and sunny on the afternoon of Thursday 29th August 1991, as competitors gathered at the Grandstand in Douglas ready to take advantage of a practice session for the Manx Grand Prix. Amongst them was Paul Rome of Laxey in the Isle of Man, riding a 250cc Yamaha machine bearing the race number 14 and entered in the Junior Race to be held the following week. During the previous evening's practice session he had just missed out on a 110mph lap by the small margin of 2.8 seconds.

The practice session commenced at 2.15pm with the riders setting off in pairs and at ten second intervals. Around twenty competitors had been dispatched before it was the turn of Paul Rome to head off along Glencrutchery Road towards Bray Hill on his opening lap of the afternoon. It was his intention to complete two laps of the course before stopping at the pits to refuel prior to going out again to complete a third lap. He quickly navigated his way round the course and up onto the mountain section where, in the vicinity of the Verandah, he passed the 750cc Suzuki being ridden by Eric Moore of Ramsey. A short time later, as he approached Brandish Corner he outbraked another competitor, Andy Jackson, and overtook him by going through on the inside of the left hand bend. He then made his way along the straight and through Hillberry Corner with Jackson about 100 yards behind.

By now he had caught up with another 750cc machine and on the sweeping left hand bend immediately following Cronk ny Mona he overtook this machine on the outside. However, in doing so he had to bank over so far that his rear wheel lost adhesion with the road surface and broke away to the right. The machine went down on its side, mounted the footpath on the right and collided heavily with the stone wall before rebounding back into the roadway in a cloud of smoke, dust and debris. Jackson narrowly avoided colliding with the crashed Yamaha but seconds later Eric Moore came upon the scene and as he began braking hard his machine went from beneath him. A police officer and marshals on duty at Signpost Corner immediately made their way to the scene of the incident and found Paul Rome lying in the roadway near to the kerb edge but there was nothing they could do for him. He had been killed instantly. Eric Moore had been thrown over the stone wall into an adjoining field and had sustained arm and leg fractures.

Andy Jackson went on to win the Junior Newcomers Race the following week and in the process he set a new race record with an average speed of 105.28mph.

Paul Rome, a single man, was 25 years of age. He was a clerk by occupation and a resident of Laxey where he lived with his parents. He had ridden motorcycles since he was sixteen years old and first started racing around the Jurby Circuit. He made his racing debut on the TT course during the 1985 MGP and from then on he became a regular at the meeting. In 1989, he competed in the 1300cc Production TT and finished in 27th position with a race average speed of 102.36mph. During the 1990 Junior MGP he escaped serious injury when he came off his machine at the bottom of Bray Hill.

His funeral service was held at Christ Church, Laxey on Thursday 5th September and followed by interment at Douglas Borough Cemetery.

Mark Andrew JACKSON

Mark Jackson at Creg ny Baa during the fateful 1991 Senior MGP

Conditions were ideal for racing on the afternoon of Friday 6th September 1991, which was excellent news for the 90 competitors lined up along Glencrutchery Road in Douglas awaiting the start of the Senior Manx Grand Prix. Amongst them was Mark Jackson, riding a Honda CBR 600F machine bearing the race number 47. This was his fourth appearance at the Manx and he knew the course well, having finished in all three of his previous races on the Island. During practice week he had been recording average lap speeds of around 101mph.

The race began at 1.00pm with the riders being dispatched in pairs and at ten second intervals. Just under four minutes later it was the turn of Mark Jackson to begin his race against the clock and he set off towards Bray Hill and Quarterbridge Road. However, barely twenty one miles into his opening lap he pulled in and stopped at Glen Duff because the seat of his machine had come loose. He lost valuable time in securing the seat and when he rejoined the race he was last on the road but he then made good progress and gradually made his way up through the field to a mid field position by the end of the fifth lap although he had been passed by the race leaders at this stage.

On his sixth and final lap of the race he had safely made his way through Glen Helen, Kirk Michael and Sulby when, at about 3.15pm, he was seen, alone on the road, approaching the fast left hand corner at Glentramman. He was travelling at racing speed and was on the usual racing line but then left it late to peel off into the corner, almost as if he had momentarily lost his bearings. Realising his predicament he suddenly sat upright and braked hard but was unable to avoid colliding heavily with the boundary wall of the house "Ballacree" situated on the right hand side of the road. He was thrown from the machine and came to rest on the left hand side of the road while his machine came to rest almost off the circuit in the entrance to the Churchtown loop road. Marshals and the doctor on duty at that location went to his immediate assistance and carried him to the relative safety of the pavement where his helmet was removed by the doctor who then gave medical aid while waiting for the rescue helicopter to arrive on the scene. The gravely injured rider was then conveyed to Noble's Hospital where, despite emergency surgery, he succumbed to his injuries at 6.20pm that same day.

Having led from the start, Tom Knight, who had dominated the practice sessions, went on to win and set a new race record with an average speed of 113.54mph. Alan Bennallick was second and Chris Hook third. All three men mounted on Honda machines.

Mark Jackson was 33 years of age and a precision engineer by occupation, employed at the Defence Research Agency, Malvern. He was a resident of Worcester where he lived with his wife Clare. His first racing experience on the TT course was during the 1987 Manx Grand Prix when he competed in the Senior Newcomers Race and finished in 13th place. He returned to compete in the Senior MGP in 1988 and again in 1989, recording creditable finishes in both races.

His funeral service was held at St. Lawrence's Church, Lindridge near Tenbury Wells and followed by interment. This was the second tragedy to hit the Jackson family as Mark's 18-year-old brother Paul lost his life in a motorcycle accident in 1973.

Manfred STENGL

Manfred Stengl at Creg ny Baa during the fateful 1992 Formula One TT

Fine weather prevailed over the Isle of Man on the afternoon of Saturday 6th June 1992 and with dry roads and clear visibility around the TT course the conditions were near perfect for racing. Welcome news for the forty seven competitors lined up along Glencrutchery Road in Douglas waiting to participate in the six lap Formula One Tourist Trophy Race. Amongst them was the Austrian race veteran Manfred Stengl, riding a 750cc Suzuki machine bearing the race number 52.

At 2.00pm the race commenced with Robert Holden being the first away, the following competitors starting at ten-second intervals. Eight and a half minutes later it was the turn of Manfred Stengl to begin and he safely made his way round the course for the first four laps, consistently lapping at times of just over 100mph. Then, having negotiated his way through to Ramsey and up onto the mountain section during his fifth lap of the race, he was seen, at about 4.00pm, approaching the 33rd Milestone. However, he was wide of the usual racing line and as a consequence the lower left side of his machine caught the road surface as he banked over to negotiate the sweeping left hand bend. He straightened up momentarily then tried to bank over once more but the machine grounded again and then suddenly stepped out to the right before crashing through the roadside fencing on the right. The unfortunate rider was thrown from the big Suzuki as it tumbled down the hillside and disintegrated. Marshals and two doctors went to his immediate assistance and found that he was still conscious but had sustained serious injuries. They did what they could for him while waiting for the helicopter ambulance, which arrived on the scene within a few minutes of being called. The gravely injured rider was conveyed to Noble's Hospital where he underwent emergency surgery but despite the best efforts of the medical staff he succumbed to his injuries in theatre later that evening.

Phillip McCallen, riding a 750 Honda, went on to win the race with a race average speed of 119.80mph. Steve Hislop, on the 588 NRS Norton, finished second with Joey Dunlop third.

Manfred Stengl, a single man, was 46 years of age. He was a resident of Salzburg, Austria where he worked as a local government officer. At the age of 17 he had taken part in the 1964 Winter Olympics held at Innsbruck and won the gold medal with Josef Feistmantl in the two-man Luge event. He made his debut on the TT course in 1984 and had become a regular at the TT, competing in many races over the mountain course.

His funeral service was held in Austria and followed by interment in the family grave at Salzburg "Kommunalfriedhof".

On Tuesday 30th August 1994, just over two years after his death, a marshal's shelter was erected in his memory at Keppel Gate, within sight of the point where Manfred crashed. His sister, Dr. Hannelore Salachner-Stengl, travelled to the Island to officially open the shelter and was accompanied by Manfred's father, Fritz Stengl, and his 11-year-old niece Katarina. Dr. Helmut Krackowizer, Chief of Austrian Motorcycling, also travelled to the Isle of Man for the occasion. The shelter contains two plaques, one in English and one in German, commemorating the distinguished international competitor.

Craig Sabell MASON

Craig Mason at Creg ny Baa during the fateful 1992 Junior MGP

Unlike the previous day when the inclement weather conditions had forced the postponement of racing, conditions were described as almost perfect for racing on the morning of Thursday 3rd September 1992. Visibility was clear and the roads around the TT course were dry, which was welcome news for the 102 competitors lined up along Glencrutchery Road in Douglas awaiting the start of the Junior Manx Grand Prix. Amongst them was Craig Mason, riding a 249cc Yamaha machine bearing the race number 55. During practice on this machine he had recorded an average lap speed of 109.61mph.

At 12 noon the flag dropped and the race began with the riders setting off in pairs and at ten second intervals. Four and a half minutes later it was the turn of Craig Mason to begin his race against the clock and he headed off towards the descent of Bray Hill. He safely made his way round the course and completed his opening lap with an average speed of 108.26mph, which placed him in eleventh position.

During his second lap, he had made his way through Union Mills, Greeba and Glen Helen when he was seen approaching Douglas Road Corner in Kirk Michael village with competitor Neil Cudworth directly ahead of him. Then, while negotiating the sweeping right hand bend, he overtook Cudworth on the inside and travelled ahead of him through the village to Rhencullen and Bishopscourt. Moments later, the two riders were seen negotiating the series of bends on the approach to Alpine Cottage at speeds of between 130-140mph when Mason touched the kerb on the left. His machine immediately shot across the road and collided heavily with the grass bank on the right hand side of the road. Cudworth applied his brakes as hard as he could but had no time to take avoiding action and he too crashed into the same grass bank. Both riders were thrown from their machines and came to rest in the roadway. By chance, two doctors from the helicopter ambulance, which was stationed just a few hundred yards away at Alpine Cottage, were watching the racing from the side of the road. Along with marshals they ran to the scene of the incident and quickly attended to the two riders. Neil Cudworth had sustained fractures to his right leg and left foot while Craig Mason's condition was critical, having sustained multiple injuries. Both men were conveyed by helicopter to Ballakermeen School playing fields then transferred by ambulance to Noble's Hospital where they were admitted within fifteen minutes of the accident occurring. Craig Mason underwent emergency surgery but despite the best efforts of the medical staff he succumbed to his injuries in the intensive therapy unit the following day.

David O'Leary of Wetherby, riding a 250cc Yamaha, went on to win the race with an average speed of 110.05mph. Second place went to Mark Baldwin of Bolton with Mick Robinson of Eastbourne third.

Craig Mason, a single man, was 32 years of age. He was an insurance consultant by occupation and a resident of Syston, Leicester. He made his debut on the TT course in 1990, finishing 4th in the Newcomers Lightweight race. He returned in 1991, finishing 16th in the Junior and 18th in the Lightweight, winning two replicas.

His funeral service was held on 12th September and followed by committal at Gilroes Crematorium, Leicester.

John JUDGE

John Judge at Creg ny Baa during the first lap of the fateful 1992 Junior MGP

The weather conditions on the morning of Thursday 3rd September 1992 were almost perfect for racing, unlike the previous day when inclement weather had forced the postponement of the races. The roads around the TT course were dry and visibility was clear on the mountain section, which was good news for the 102 competitors lined up along Glencrutchery Road in Douglas awaiting the start of the Junior Manx Grand Prix. Amongst them was John Judge, riding a Yamaha FZR 600cc machine bearing the race number 78.

At 12 noon the first men were sent on their way in pairs and at ten second intervals. Six minutes and twenty seconds later it was the turn of John Judge to begin his race against the clock and he set off towards Quarterbridge on his opening lap. He safely negotiated his way round the course and completed his first circuit with an average lap speed of 103.59mph, which placed him in 35th position.

At about 12.40pm, having made his way through Greeba, Glen Helen and Kirk Michael village, he was just over fourteen miles into his second lap when he was seen approaching Birkin's Bends at Rhencullen. However, he was not on the usual racing line, which is on the right hand side of the road whereas he was positioned in the centre of the road. As a consequence, he was too far over to the right on the exit of the bends and collided heavily with the straw bales and low stone wall outside the cottage "Cronk Steone", which is situated on the right at the top of Rhencullen Hill. The unfortunate rider was thrown against a wooden telegraph pole outside "Roadside Cottage" and came to rest in the driveway of "Rhencullen House" on the opposite side of the road with his wrecked machine lying nearby. Marshals went to his immediate assistance but found there was nothing they could do for him. He had been killed instantly. Seconds later, competitor number 76 Neil Myatt arrived at Birkin's Bends and acknowledged the yellow flags by applying his brakes and reducing his speed to 50-60mph but as he rounded the left hand bend he was confronted with several dislodged straw bales lying across the road directly in front of him. He was unable to take avoiding action and sustained a fractured leg when thrown from his machine after colliding with one of the bales.

David O'Leary of Wetherby, riding a 250 Yamaha, went on to win the race with an average speed of 110.05mph. Mark Baldwin of Bolton finished in second place with Mick Robinson of Eastbourne third. A total of 69 riders completed the race.

John Judge, a single man, was 33 years of age and a resident of Burnley, Lancashire. He was a mechanic by occupation and had been employed by Skipper of Burnley for about six years, specialising as a technician for rally and powerful cars. His passion for motorcycles began when he was 17 and he used his first bike to travel to and from work. He became interested in racing through friends and gradually moved up to faster and more powerful machines. His first appearance on the TT course was during the 1991 Manx Grand Prix but an injury to his wrist during practice prevented him from taking part in the races.

His funeral service was held at St John The Baptist Church, Padiham and followed by interment.

Stephen Laurence HARDING

Steve Harding at Quarterbridge during the fateful 1993 Supersport 600 TT

Conditions were ideal for racing on the afternoon of Wednesday 9th June 1993, the weather was fine and the roads around the TT course were dry, which was excellent news for the fifty eight competitors lined up along Glencrutchery Road in Douglas waiting to participate in the Supersport 600 Tourist Trophy Race. Amongst them was Steve Harding, riding a Yamaha FZR 600cc machine bearing the race number 61. Riding this machine during practice he had recorded an average lap speed of 98.18mph.

The four lap race commenced at 12.30pm and the first man to be flagged away was Simon Beck followed by Bob Jackson and then Joey Dunlop, all three mounted on Honda machines. With the riders setting off at ten second intervals it was exactly ten minutes after Beck had left the start line before Steve Harding was given the signal to begin his race against the clock and he set off with the intention of treating the race as a practice session in the hope of gaining a finishers award. He safely made his way round the course and completed his opening circuit with an average lap speed of 99.05mph, which placed him in 50th position.

During his second lap, he had made his way through Glen Vine, Crosby and Ballacraine when he was seen approaching Doran's Bend with competitor number 62 Peter Jarmann directly in front of him. The two riders negotiated the sweeping left hand bend and moments later they were seen approaching the right hand bend immediately before Laurel Bank but Harding was off the usual racing line for the bend and as a consequence he collided heavily with the rock face on the left. The unfortunate rider was thrown from his machine and came to rest in the roadway near to the kerb on the right hand side of the road while his wrecked Yamaha came to rest a short distance beyond him. Marshals went to his assistance and the helicopter ambulance arrived on the scene within five minutes of being called but there was nothing that could be done for him. He had been killed instantly.

Hector Gordon, Chief Scrutineer for the Auto-Cycle Union, later examined the Yamaha and found no evidence to suggest that a mechanical failure may have contributed towards the accident.

Having led from the start, Jim Moodie from Glasgow went on to win with a race average speed of 105.06mph. Bob Jackson from Windermere finished 22 seconds behind in second place with Simon Beck from Preston taking the final podium position. Moodie had also won the Supersport 400 race two days earlier.

Steve Harding, a single man, was 36 years of age. He was a technical illustrator by occupation employed at Marshall Aerospace and was a resident of Cambridge. His first appearance on the TT course was during the 1992 Manx Grand Prix when, riding a 600cc Yamaha, he finished 8th in the Junior Newcomers Race with a race average speed of 94.41mph. He was always meticulous when preparing his machine for racing and endlessly studied videos of the TT course before taking part.

His funeral service was held the following week and followed by committal at Cambridge Crematorium.

Kenneth John VIRGO

Ken Virgo above Waterworks Corner during the fateful 1993 Lightweight MGP

Visibility problems on the mountain section of the TT course on Friday 3rd September 1993 caused a two hour delay to the start of the Lightweight Manx Grand Prix. However, by late morning the weather conditions had improved and the roads were dry for the sixty four competitors lined up along Glencrutchery Road in Douglas in readiness for the start of the race. Amongst them was Ken Virgo, riding a 250cc Yamaha machine bearing the race number 17. Two days earlier he had escaped injury when he came off his machine at Glentramman during the first lap of the Junior Race. During practice his fastest lap speed was recorded at 103.53mph.

The race commenced at 12 noon with James Courtney being the first away. The following riders were sent off in pairs and at ten second intervals. Ninety seconds after Courtney had departed it was the turn of Ken Virgo to head off towards Quarterbridge on his opening lap of the race and he safely made his way round the course to complete his first circuit with an average lap speed of 103.51mph, which placed him in 19th position.

During his second lap, he had made his way through Union Mills, Greeba and Glen Helen when he was seen, alone on the road, approaching the bends at Handley's Corner. He was travelling at racing speed and was on the usual racing line to negotiate the first bend but at the last second the engine of his machine went silent. He immediately sat upright as he went through the left hand bend then attempted to negotiate the following right hand bend but drifted wide on the exit, crashing through the hawthorn hedgerow and colliding heavily with a wooden telegraph pole. Marshals went to his assistance and found he was showing no signs of life. Desperate efforts were made to resuscitate him while waiting for the helicopter ambulance, which arrived on the scene within five minutes of being called from Alpine Corner. However, there was nothing further that could be done for him, he had succumbed to his injuries.

The Yamaha was later examined but there was nothing found to suggest that the accident had been caused by a mechanical failure. Some witnesses at the scene of the accident suggested that the machine had slipped into neutral but this could only be speculated.

James Courtney from County Antrim went on to win the race with an average speed of 109.69mph. Twenty seconds behind in second place was Nigel Hansen of Banchory with third place going to Greg Broughton from Ramsey. James Courtney had also won the Junior race two days earlier.

Ken Virgo was 36 years of age. He was a self employed mechanic by occupation and a resident of Slimbridge, Gloucester where he lived with his fiancée, Sarah Ruth Bundy and their baby daughter. He was also the father to three children from a previous marriage. His first appearance on the Isle of Man was the 1987 Manx Grand Prix when he came third in the Lightweight Newcomers Race. In the 1992 Lightweight MGP he earned his second replica when, from a field of 74 riders, he finished in 8th position.

His funeral service was followed by committal at Gloucester Crematorium.

Robert Allen MITCHELL

Rob Mitchell at Ballaugh Bridge during practice for the 1994 Supersport 600 TT

Mist had formed on sections of the TT course on Thursday 2nd June 1994 and there was concern amongst race officials that the afternoon practice session for the Tourist Trophy Races would be disrupted, which was not the best of news for the competitors gathered at the Grandstand in Douglas. Amongst them was Rob Mitchell, riding a Yamaha FZR 600cc machine bearing the race number 33 and entered in the Supersport 600 race to be held the following Monday. During the Tuesday evening practice run he had recorded an average lap speed of 108.54mph on this machine.

Shortly after 2.00pm, just a few minutes later than scheduled, the session commenced. The sun was shining and the mist had now cleared as Rob Mitchell set off along Glencrutchery Road towards Bray Hill on his opening lap of the afternoon. He had safely made his way through to Ramsey and then onto the mountain climb when he was seen approaching the slight left hand bend immediately before the Gooseneck with four other riders in close company, two ahead of him and two behind. Suddenly and for no apparent reason, his machine went out of control. He tried hard to reduce speed and regain control of the machine but was unable to prevent it colliding heavily with the dry stone wall on the right hand side of the road. The unfortunate rider was thrown from the Yamaha and came to rest, unconscious, in the roadway. Marshals went to his immediate assistance and did what they could for him while waiting for the helicopter ambulance, which arrived on the scene just over five minutes after being called from Alpine Corner. The gravely injured rider was conveyed to the playing fields at Ballakermeen School in Douglas then transferred to an ambulance, which carried him the short distance to Noble's Hospital where he was admitted at 3.20pm. Despite intensive care his condition did not improve and on Monday 6th June he succumbed to his injuries.

His family gave consent for some of his organs to be donated and these provided a new lease of life to four other people. It was a source of comfort to his whole family to know that his organs were helping other people and that the manner in which he died was probably the way he would have wanted to go. He did not suffer, as he had been unconscious throughout.

Hector Gordon, the Chief Scrutineer, later examined the Yamaha machine and found no evidence to suggest that a mechanical failure had contributed to this accident.

Rob Mitchell was 30 years of age. He was a Caravan Site Proprietor by occupation and a resident of Aberdeen, Scotland where he lived with his wife Alison and their young son Peter, aged 7 years. He had been a keen motorcyclist for most of his life and by the age of 20 he had twice been crowned the North East scrambling champion. He had also won the 1993 Scottish 600 class championship, which had gone to the final race of the season. He made his debut on the TT course in 1993, when, riding a Yamaha FZR400 in the Supersport 400 TT, he finished 21st with a race average speed of 97.87mph. In the Supersport 600 TT he was forced to retire his Honda CBR600 at Ramsey Hairpin on the last lap of the race.

His funeral service was held at Kelman Memorial Church, Peterculter, on Monday 13th June at 11.00am and followed by interment at Drumoak Churchyard.

Edward Mark FARMER

Mark Farmer at Birkin's Bends during practice for the 1994 Formula One TT

Weather conditions were fine on the afternoon of Thursday 2nd June 1994. The roads around the TT course were dry and the mist on the mountain section that had threatened to disrupt the afternoon practice session for the Tourist Trophy races had lifted, which was welcome news for the competitors congregating at the Grandstand in Douglas. Amongst them was race veteran Mark Farmer and when the session commenced shortly after 2.00pm he set off round the course on the V & M Yamaha FZR 600, which had been entered in the Supersport 600 race, but he was unable to improve on the 116.89mph lap that he had achieved during the Tuesday evening practice session. As it turned out, this proved to be the fastest average lap speed for the class during the whole of practice week.

On his arrival back at the Grandstand he climbed aboard the revolutionary CRS Britten 1000cc machine bearing the race number 6, which was entered in the Formula One race to be held on Saturday 4th June. Riding the same machine the previous evening he had recorded an average lap speed of 118.21mph. He set off towards Bray Hill and safely made his way through the opening seven miles of the course to Ballacraine by which time he was being closely followed by Steve Hislop who was carrying a camera fitted to his machine, filming a lap of the course. Hislop remained in close company through Ballaspur, Ballig and Doran's Bend then slipped past him on the approach to the first right hand bend at Laurel Bank. Seconds later, whilst negotiating the bends at the Black Dub, just beyond the Glen Moar petrol station, Mark Farmer lost control of his machine and collided heavily with the grass bank on the left hand side of the road. The doctor on duty at that location went to him immediately but there was nothing that could be done. He had been killed instantly.

It had been speculated that engine seizure had led to the accident but an examination of the Britten by Hector Gordon the Chief Scrutineer for the ACU revealed no evidence to suggest that a mechanical failure had been a contributory factor in the incident.

Mark Farmer was 30 years of age. He was a professional motorcycle racer by occupation and a resident of Crawley, East Sussex where he lived with his fiancée Terrie Nolan. Like many of his fellow Ulstermen, he began his racing career on road circuits in Northern Ireland. His debut on the TT course was during the 1985 Manx Grand Prix when he finished 6th in the Senior Newcomers Race. The following year he made his first appearance at the TT and from thereon he became a regular at the meeting with perhaps his best results coming in 1992 when he came 5th in the Formula One, 6th in the Supersport 400 and 5th in the Senior with a race average speed of 118.32mph. He went on to win the 1992 British Supersport 400 championship. His last race on the Island was the 1993 Senior TT, riding an 888cc Ducati, he was lying in second place when he ran out of fuel at Hillberry during the second lap.

His funeral service was held in Northern Ireland at Drumcree Parish Church, Portadown, the hometown of his family and was attended by hundreds of mourners. On the coffin lay a family wreath together with a laurel wreath presented by fellow racer Joey Dunlop from his 125cc TT race win and another laurel wreath from Brian Reid who had finished second in the Junior TT. The floral tribute from his fiancée and a photograph of their dog Scottie were placed on the grave near the main entrance to the church.

Clifford Roy GOBELL

Cliff Gobell at Braddan Bridge during the fateful 1994 Senior Classic MGP

As forecast by the weathermen at Ronaldsway it was fine and bright on the afternoon of Monday 29th August 1994, leaving dry roads and good visibility around the TT course, which was excellent news for the 101 competitors gathered on Glencrutchery Road in Douglas waiting to participate in the Senior Classic Manx Grand Prix. Amongst them was race veteran Cliff Gobell, riding a 492cc Weslake machine bearing the race number 89. During practice his fastest lap on this machine had been achieved on the Thursday afternoon when he recorded an average lap speed of 91.87mph.

At 1.00pm the flag dropped and the race commenced with the riders being dispatched in pairs and at ten second intervals, Bill Swallow and Bob Heath being the first two away. Seven minutes and twenty seconds after their departure it was the turn of Cliff Gobell to begin his race against the clock and he set off towards Bray Hill on his opening lap. He had safely made his way through Glen Helen, Kirk Michael and Ballaugh when he was seen approaching Quarry Bends, at an estimated speed of 90-100mph, with another competitor, Heath Graham, marginally ahead of him on the road. At the first right hand bend he overtook Graham on the inside but this action put him off the usual racing line for the following bends and on the exit of the last right hand bend the Weslake drifted to the left, struck the kerb and mounted the footpath. The machine then veered diagonally across the road and mounted the grass bank on the right at which point both rider and machine crashed through the trees and undergrowth before coming to rest in the yard of a works depot situated on the exit of Quarry Bends. Heath Graham had been wearing a helmet video camera and the incident was recorded on film. Two race competitors, Paul Marks and Scott Richardson, who were not racing that day, had signed on as marshals and when the accident occurred they were positioned opposite the works depot. Both men went immediately to the scene and found the unfortunate rider lying behind one of the huts within the yard but there was nothing that could be done for him. He had been killed instantly.

Bob Heath, riding a Seeley, went on to win the race with an average speed of 103.41mph. Bill Swallow, also riding a Seeley, took second place and Bob Jackson, riding a Matchless, took the final podium position. Heath Graham continued his race but was forced to retire at Ballaugh Bridge on his last lap but gained a finish in the Junior Classic two days later. Paul Marks gained a finish in the Junior race but retired at Kirk Michael in the Senior. Scott Richardson also finished in the Junior then went on to gain a silver replica when he finished 22nd in the Senior.

Cliff Gobell, a single man, was 51 years of age. He was a self employed electrician by occupation and a resident of East Ham, London. He had a wealth of racing experience and made his debut on the TT course at the MGP in 1975. Over the years he had won several replicas and his best result came in 1985 when he finished second in the Junior Classic. Since 1991 he had been a regular competitor at the world famous Daytona meeting in America.

His brother Peter later stated that Cliff Gobell would be wearing his racing leathers when cremated in the City of London Cemetery, Manor Park and added that it was what he would have wanted as biking was his life.

Robert Paul FARGHER

Bob Munro and Paul Fargher at Braddan Bridge during the fateful 1995 Sidecar TT

Conditions were near perfect for racing on the afternoon of Saturday 3rd June 1995. The weather was fine, the roads around the TT course were dry and visibility was clear, which was welcome news for the 69 sidecar crews lined up along Glencrutchery Road in Douglas waiting to participate in the first leg of the Sidecar Tourist Trophy Races. Amongst them were Bob Munro and his passenger Paul Fargher, riding a bright red coloured outfit bearing the race number 31. The chassis of the sidecar had been built by Munro in 1993 and was powered by a 600cc Yamaha engine. Their best performance during practice had been recorded the previous evening, when they achieved an average lap speed of 96.79mph.

The race commenced at 5.00pm with Mick Boddice and his passenger Dave Wells being the first to leave the start line, followed ten seconds later by Rob Fisher and his passenger Boyd Hutchinson. Five minutes after the flag had first dropped, it was the turn of Bob Munro and Paul Fargher to begin their race against the clock and they set off along Glencrutchery Road towards Bray Hill on their opening lap. They safely made their way through Glen Helen and onto Cronk y Voddy where they overtook the outfit ridden by Artie Oates and Greg Mahon who then kept in close company behind them through Kirk Michael, Ballaugh and onto the Sulby Straight. Spectators positioned at the Ballabrooie housing estate saw them approaching and noticed that the fairing of their outfit was loose and scraping on the ground. Then, at an estimated 140mph, the sidecar suddenly veered sharply to the right and crashed through a hedgerow before colliding heavily with a tree. Both men were immediately thrown from the outfit. Bob Munro came to rest inside the confines of an electricity sub station while Paul Fargher came to rest near to the houses beyond the sub station. The two men were quickly attended to and the helicopter ambulance arrived on the scene within five minutes of the call but there was nothing that could be done for Paul Fargher. He had been killed instantly. Munro had sustained multiple injuries and was conveyed to Noble's Hospital for intensive treatment.

An examination of the sidecar outfit revealed that a bracket designed to hold the fairing to the frame of the outfit had broken due to poor brazing. A witness came forward after the incident and claimed that the outfit had clipped the kerb on the right in Crosby village just over four miles out from the start but this had not apparently caused the crew any concern as they continued without slowing down.

Rob Fisher & Boyd Hutchinson went on to win the race at an average speed of 106.47mph. Mick Boddice & Dave Wells finished in second place with Geoff Bell & Nick Roche in third position. Artie Oates & Greg Mahon retired at the pits on completion of their opening lap.

Paul Fargher was 31 years of age and the father of two children, Brendan and Glenn. He was a mason by occupation and a resident of Port St Mary. He had been riding together with Bob Munro for four years and during the 1994 TT races they finished 26th in the first race and 16th in the second race, which earned them a bronze replica.

His funeral service was held at Rushen Church on Friday 8th June and followed by interment.

Duncan Robert MUIR

Duncan Muir at Braddan Bridge during the fateful 1995 Junior MGP

Poor weather on the afternoon of Wednesday 30th August 1995 had forced a one hour delay to the start of the Junior Manx Grand Prix but by 1.50pm conditions had improved, which was good news for the 102 competitors lined up along Glencrutchery Road in Douglas waiting to participate in the race. Amongst them was Duncan Muir, riding a 600cc Honda machine bearing the race number 20. His fastest lap on this machine during practice had been recorded at 107.53mph.

At 2.00pm the flag dropped and the race commenced with the riders being dispatched in pairs and at ten second intervals. Roy Richardson and Greg Broughton were the first two away but as they left the start line Duncan Muir was having trouble starting his machine and at one point it appeared that he would be unable to take part in the race but the Honda eventually fired up and he was able to get away on time, heading off along Glencrutchery Road in company with his starting partner Brian Kneale. He safely completed his first circuit with an average lap speed of 108.36mph and was holding eighth position in the race. During his second lap he made his way round the course, through Ramsey and up onto the mountain climb, where, moments after rounding the tight right hand bend at the Gooseneck, he was seen travelling at racing speed and negotiating the fast left hand bend on the approach to Guthries. At this point the rear wheel of his machine suddenly stepped out to the right and he was thrown off, colliding heavily with a large wooden information board, which had been placed just over the wire fencing on the right. The board was there to advise riders of their position on the course. Marshals went to his assistance but there was nothing they could do for him. He had been killed instantly.

Christopher Mark Rowe, Chief Scrutineer, and his deputy, Harvey Garton, later examined the extensively damaged Honda machine and found no evidence to suggest that a mechanical failure had contributed to this accident.

Tony Duncan of Douglas went on to win the race with an average speed of 111.33mph. Second place went to Ricky Mitchell of Northern Ireland with Keith Townsend of Bishops Stortford taking third. Ian Kirk, one of the early contenders for the race had come off his machine at Bedstead Corner during the second lap and sustained serious injuries. Brian Kneale who had set off with Duncan Muir went on to finish the race in 30th place and earned a silver replica.

Duncan Muir, a single man, was 22 years of age. He was a motorcycle mechanic by occupation and a resident of Ballacaley Road, Sulby where he had lived since moving to the Island from the Midlands three years earlier. His first venture on the TT course was the 1994 Manx Grand Prix, winning the Senior Newcomers Race with an average speed of 106.87mph. Later that same week he took 12th place and a further silver replica in the Senior Manx Grand Prix with a race average of 105.51mph. His ambition had been to become a professional Grand Prix rider and TT Competitor.

His funeral service was held on Wednesday 6th September and followed by committal at Douglas Borough Crematorium.

Nicholas Edward Adam TEALE

Nick Teale pictured on his 250 Yamaha during the fateful 1995 Lightweight MGP

Although the weather forecast indicated that conditions would be dry and that any low mist on the mountain section of the TT course would lift before racing commenced at 10.00am on Friday 1st September 1995, the decision was made to delay the start of the Lightweight Manx Grand Prix to allow more time for the conditions to improve. Eventually, the 66 competitors began to line up along Glencrutchery Road in Douglas in preparation for the start of the race. Amongst them was Nick Teale, riding a 250cc Yamaha machine bearing the race number 84. During practice his fastest lap on this machine had been achieved on the Thursday afternoon when he recorded an average lap speed of 94.35mph.

When the race commenced the riders were set off in pairs and at ten second intervals with Greg Broughton and Alan Marshall being the first to leave the start line. Almost seven minutes later, it was the turn of Nick Teale to begin his race and he set off towards Bray Hill and Quarterbridge along with his starting partner John Lilley from Gloucester. He safely made his way round the course to complete his opening lap with an average speed of 101.46mph, which placed him in 29th position. An average lap speed of 104.65mph on his second circuit moved him up to 21st place and in contention for a silver replica.

During his third lap of the race he had negotiated his way through Crosby, Glen Helen and Kirk Michael when he was seen approaching Alpine Cottage near Ballaugh but he was not on the usual racing line for the sweeping right hand bend. Suddenly, he appeared to realise his predicament and sat upright, wrestling with the machine but was unable to prevent it mounting the footpath on the left before crashing through a thicket of trees. Marshals ran to his aid and found him lying in the undergrowth beneath the trees but there was nothing that could be done for him. He had been killed instantly.

Christopher Mark Rowe, the Chief Scrutineer for the races and his deputy, Harvey Garton, examined the extensively damaged Yamaha the following day and found no evidence to suggest that a mechanical failure had contributed to the accident.

Having led from start, Tony Duncan of Douglas went on to win the race with a race average speed of 111.10mph, adding to his victory in the Junior race two days earlier. Second place went to Chris Cannell of Laxey with Russell Henley of Nottingham taking third place.

Nick Teale, a single man, was 35 years of age and a resident of Wolverhampton. He was a former microbiologist at New Cross Hospital and was due to start a teacher training course at Wolverhampton University. He had been a spectator at the races on the Isle of Man since 1987 and this had inspired him to take up racing. He came 6th overall in the EMRA 125 championship in 1994 and had wins at Swinderby Airfield. Four days before the fateful race, riding a 600cc Kawasaki, he had finished 14th in the Junior Newcomers Race with a race average speed of 103.17mph, a performance that had earned him a coveted silver replica.

His funeral service was held at Bushbury Crematorium in Wolverhampton. His ashes were later interred at St. Michael's and All Angels Church in Tettenhall where his father was buried following his death in West Africa as a result of a car crash several years earlier.

Aaron James KENNEDY

Dave Kimberley and Aaron Kennedy at Braddan Bridge during practice for the 1996 Sidecar TT

Conditions were almost perfect for racing on the evening of Monday 27th May 1996. The roads around the TT course were dry and visibility was clear on the mountain section, which was welcome news for the competitors gathered at the Grandstand in Douglas waiting to take advantage of a practice session for the Sidecar Tourist Trophy Races. Amongst them were Dave Kimberley and his passenger Aaron Kennedy, riding a bright green coloured outfit bearing the race number 8 and entered in both Formula II Sidecar Races. The sidecar was based on a Trevor Ireson chassis and powered by a 600cc Kawasaki engine. Having been together for about a year, the pair had competed at a number of race meetings and while Kimberley had the experience of competing in four previous TT meetings Kennedy was a newcomer to the course.

At 8.05pm, they set off along Glencrutchery Road towards Bray Hill to commence their first lap of the meeting. The intention was to take it nice and steady having agreed to treat this first practice session as an opportunity for Kennedy to learn the course. As they accelerated away from the grandstand Kimberley glanced over his left shoulder to confirm that his passenger was correctly positioned on the outfit. They made their way through Quarterbridge and Braddan Bridge then on the way out of Union Mills, three miles out from the start, Kimberley once again had the opportunity to check that Kennedy was okay and as his passenger gave no indication of a problem he continued on through Glen Vine towards Crosby where the setting sun was low but not causing a problem to Kimberley as he had a tinted visor fitted to his helmet whereas Kennedy had a clear visor fitted.

Near to the church hall in Crosby, a spectator saw Kennedy adopt a kneeling position in the chair with his left hand behind him as if searching for a grab bar. At that moment he suddenly fell backwards off the outfit and slid along the road on his back for a distance of about 60 yards before colliding heavily with the kerbstone on the right hand side of the road. The spectator and a marshal quickly removed him from the roadway to the relative safety of the pavement and placed him in the recovery position but there was nothing more they could do for him. He had been killed instantly. Kimberley had continued through Crosby village, unaware of the incident until he felt the sidecar lift slightly as he negotiated the first left hand bend at Greeba Castle. He pulled in and stopped then walked back along the course to Greeba Castle where he was told that his passenger had fallen off at Crosby.

The sidecar was later examined by the Chief Scrutineer, Hector Gordon, at Police Headquarters in Douglas with particular attention being paid to the grips used by the passenger to hold onto the outfit. These were found to be clear of defect and in good order.

Aaron Kennedy was 26 years of age. He was a yardman by occupation and a resident of Shipston on Stour, Warwickshire where he had lived with his partner Julie Saunders for six years.

His funeral service was held at Chipping Norton Cemetery on Friday 7th June and followed by interment. The funeral procession from Shipston on Stour had included a large number of motorcyclists wishing to pay their last respects.

Robert Lorne HOLDEN

Rob Holden at Quarterbridge during practice for the 1996 Production TT

There were high winds blowing across the Isle of Man on the morning of Friday 31st May 1996 and damp patches on the roads around the TT course, especially under the trees, made racing conditions less than favourable. However, this had not deterred the competitors gathered at the Grandstand in Douglas waiting to take part in a practice session for the Tourist Trophy Races. Amongst them was Rob Holden, riding a 916 Ducati machine bearing the race number 5 and entered in the Production Race to be held the following Friday. Riding the same machine during the Wednesday evening practice run he had recorded an average lap speed of 113.32mph. That same evening, riding a Ducati Twin, he completed a lap with an average speed of 120.38mph to head the leaderboard for the Singles TT race. These lap times were not matched by any other rider during the actual races held the following week.

The first machines set off along Glencrutchery Road towards Bray Hill at 5.15am. Fifteen minutes later Holden received the signal to begin his opening lap of the morning and he safely made his way round the course through to Ballaugh where he overtook Michael Rutter on the Honda CBR900 Fireblade. Knowing of Holden's knowledge and experience on the TT course, Rutter decided to sit in behind him and on completion of the lap both riders went straight through the start area to commence their second circuit. By Ballacraine, Holden had pulled away and was a few seconds ahead of Rutter who had hoped to be closer to him through the tricky Glen Helen section of the course, keen to pick up some tips on lines. However, he was unable to gain a clear sight of him again after Ballacraine.

Moments later, Rob Holden was seen approaching the left hand bend immediately before the entrance to the Glen Helen Hotel and appeared to be on the usual racing line but his speed on the exit of the bend put him too far over to the right. He seemed to realise his predicament and braked hard but his machine continued in a straight line and struck the kerb on the right. At this point the unfortunate rider was thrown from the machine and came to rest in the middle of the roadway. Prompt action by marshals with yellow flags ensured that Michael Rutter was given sufficient warning and he was able to safely pass through the scene at a reduced speed. Marshals and a medical officer attended to the gravely injured rider and resuscitation efforts continued as he was carried on a stretcher to the helicopter landing site. The helicopter ambulance arrived on the scene within 10 minutes of being called but an examination carried out by the two doctors onboard revealed that he had succumbed to his injuries.

Rob Holden was 37 years of age and although married, he was separated from his wife Joanne. He was a storeman by occupation and although originally from Halifax, Yorkshire, he had emigrated to New Zealand as a teenager and was a resident of Wellington. With 20 years of racing experience he had been crowned New Zealand champion no less than 10 times. His first appearance on the TT course was in 1988 but it was not until 1994 that he landed a rostrum position when he finished 2nd to Jim Moodie in the Singles TT with a race average of 111.11mph. He went one better in 1995 and won the Singles TT with a race average of 110.79mph.

His funeral service was held at Old St. Paul's, Wellington, New Zealand on Friday 7th June and followed by committal.

Michael Anthony LOFTHOUSE

Mick Lofthouse at Signpost Corner during practice for the 1996 Lightweight TT

The weather was fine on the morning of Friday 31st May 1996, the roads around the TT course were dry and visibility was clear on the mountain section. Good news for the competitors gathered at the Grandstand in Douglas waiting to take advantage of a practice session for the Tourist Trophy Races. Amongst them was Mick Lofthouse, riding Dennis Trollope's 250cc Spondon Yamaha machine bearing the race number 4 and entered in the Lightweight Race to be held the following week. Two days earlier, on his Ultra Lightweight machine, he had unofficially put the 125cc lap record to over 110mph for the first time. His season was going remarkably well as he was lying second to Phelim Owen in the British 125 Supercup series and had won the 125cc race at the North West 200 in Northern Ireland prior to making his way to the Isle of Man.

Once the session had commenced, Mick Lofthouse set off along Glencrutchery Road towards Bray Hill on his opening lap of the morning and safely made his way round the course and through Sulby. Meanwhile, marshals at Pinfold Cottage, Lezayre had noted that the rising sun was beginning to affect the riders, some were slowing down and at least one held his hand up to shade his eyes. It was at this point that Mick Lofthouse, alone on the road and travelling at racing speed, emerged from the tree lined section of the course at Churchtown. He rounded the left hand bend at the entrance to Skye Hill onto the short straight before Pinfold Cottage then suddenly sat upright on the machine and veered sharply to the left, colliding with the kerb before mounting the footpath and crashing into a low hedge. The Yamaha continued through the hedge and came to rest in the field beyond while the rider was thrown back into the roadway, his helmet having come off during the incident. Marshals went quickly to his assistance and removed him from the road to the relative safety of the footpath but there was nothing more they could do for him. He had been killed instantly.

It was generally accepted that the rising sun had probably dazzled the unfortunate rider. No evidence was found to suggest that the Yamaha had suffered a mechanical failure.

Mick Lofthouse was 28 years of age. He was a professional racing motorcyclist by occupation and a resident of Oswaldtwistle near Accrington, Lancashire where he lived with his fiancée, Rosa Pirraglia. He made his debut on the Isle of Man TT course during the 1990 MGP, winning the Lightweight Newcomers Race with a race average speed of 100.89mph. Moving on to the TT in 1991 he notched up a creditable 12th place in the Supersport 400 race then, in 1992 he finished third behind the two Dunlop brothers in the Ultra Lightweight 125 TT. He suffered engine failure during the same race in 1993 and the following year he was lying second in the race when forced to retire at Sulby Bridge on the final lap due to the exhaust on his machine having snapped and become loose. In 1995 he led the Ultra Lightweight 125 TT for the first three laps despite sliding off his machine at Parliament Square on his second lap but during the final circuit he had been forced to cruise in from Windy Corner and saw his lead whittled away. However, on reaching the finish line he was being acclaimed as the race winner until Mark Baldwin came in to pip him by 0.6 of a second on corrected time.

His funeral service was held on the afternoon of Friday 7th June and followed by committal at Accrington Crematorium.

Stephen John TANNOCK M.B.E.

Steve Tannock at Braddan Bridge during the fateful 1996 Formula One TT

Fine weather prevailed over the Isle of Man on the afternoon of Saturday 1st June 1996 and with clear visibility and dry roads conditions were ideal for racing. Welcome news for the sixty one competitors lined up along Glencrutchery Road in Douglas waiting to participate in the six lap Formula One Tourist Trophy Race the start of which had been delayed for one hour. Amongst them was Steve Tannock, riding a Honda RC30 machine bearing the race number 80. Poor weather conditions had affected several sessions during practice week and although he had done reasonably well he did not achieve his qualifying time until the very last practice session on the Friday evening when he recorded an average lap speed of 105.97mph. He had also expressed concern to his brother that he was having difficulty adjusting to the machine, as it was a lot faster than what he was used to.

At 3.00pm the flag dropped and the race was under way with the riders being sent off individually and at ten second intervals. The last rider to leave was Steve Tannock and on receiving his starting signal he headed off towards St.Ninian's crossroads and Bray Hill on his opening lap. He safely negotiated his way round the course and completed his first circuit with an average speed of 105.12mph, which put him in 32nd position. Twenty two miles into his second lap he was seen travelling through the tree lined section of the course at Churchtown, Lezayre in close company with two other riders. Then, on the approach to the left hand bend immediately before Pinfold Cottage, he was overtaken by both riders and at that moment, for no apparent reason, he suddenly lost control of his machine, which veered to the left hand side of the road, mounted the footpath and collided heavily with a large tree. The Honda broke in two before coming to rest in the field beyond the trees while the unfortunate rider came to rest at the side of the road. Spectators and Marshals went to his immediate assistance but there was nothing they could do for him. He had been killed instantly.

Hector Gordon, Chief Scrutineer for the Auto-Cycle Union, examined the wrecked machine and found no evidence to suggest that a mechanical failure had contributed to the accident

Steve Tannock, a single man, was 40 years of age. He was a Disaster Relief Engineer by occupation and a resident of Bradford, West Yorkshire. He was an experienced racing motorcyclist having raced for fifteen years. His first venture on the Isle of Man TT course was at the 1994 Manx Grand Prix when, during the Senior Newcomers Race, he came off at Quarterbridge and was forced to retire. He fared much better in the Senior and completed the race with an average speed of 92.74mph. Moving on to the TT in 1995, he finished 12th in the Singles Race with an average speed of 96.61mph and gained a bronze replica.

His death came just a fortnight before he was due to receive an MBE at Buckingham Palace having been named in the 1995 Queen's Birthday Honours list in recognition of his services to humanity while employed in war torn Bosnia. The insignia was posted on to his parents on the 17th July 1996.

His funeral service was held at Douglas Borough Crematorium and his ashes were later scattered on the mountain section of the TT course overlooking the north of the Island.

John Clark GOW

Jack Gow at the Quarterbridge during practice for the 1996 Junior Classic MGP

Apart from the odd damp patch under the trees the roads around the TT course were mainly dry on the morning of Monday 19th August 1996, which was good news for the competitors gathered at the grandstand in Douglas waiting to take advantage of the second practice session for the Manx Grand Prix. Amongst them was race veteran Jack Gow, riding a 350cc Petty Manx Norton machine bearing the race number 7, which was entered in the Junior Classic Race scheduled to be held the following week. He had been out on the machine during the previous Saturday evening practice session but had not recorded a lap time.

Shortly after 7.00am, he set off along Glencrutchery Road towards St.Ninian's crossroads and safely negotiated his way round the course through to Ramsey then up onto the mountain section. A short time later he was seen approaching the bends at the 32nd Milestone and travelling at an estimated speed of between 80 and 90mph. He was on the usual racing line for the bends but as he rounded the last of the three left hand bends his rear wheel suddenly lost adhesion with the road surface. The Norton went broadside momentarily then went to the left, dropped into a roadside gully and collided heavily with the grass bank. The unfortunate rider was immediately thrown from the machine and came to rest in the roadway. Marshals went quickly to his aid and on finding his condition to be serious they did what they could for him until the arrival of the helicopter ambulance, which arrived on the scene within five minutes of receiving the call. The gravely injured rider was then conveyed to the playing fields at Ballakermeen School in Douglas where he was transferred from the helicopter to an ambulance, which then carried him the short distance to Noble's Hospital. On admission, at about 7.30am, it was found that he had sustained multiple internal injuries and his condition was critical. Despite extensive resuscitation measures, he succumbed to his injuries shortly after arriving at the hospital.

An examination of the relatively unscathed Norton machine by Scrutineer Chris Rowe revealed that it had been very well prepared for racing and nothing was found to suggest that a mechanical failure had been a contributory factor in this accident.

Jack Gow was 56 years of age and the father of four children Frances, Audrey, Lorraine and Jack. He was a garage proprietor by occupation and a resident of Errol, Tayside, Scotland where he lived with his wife Olive. He made his debut on the TT course in 1960, finishing 21st in the Lightweight 125 TT. Riding a variety of machines, he became a regular at the TT through to 1965 but with little success. However, he became Scottish Champion in 1965 and repeated that achievement in 1970. He returned to the Isle of Man in 1983 when the Classic Races were introduced at the Manx Grand Prix and riding a 350cc Aermacchi he took 6th place in the Junior Classic with a race average speed of 87.82mph. In 1993 he was crowned Scottish Classic Champion and that same year, riding an AJS, he finished 3rd in the Junior Classic with a race average speed of 95.66mph. The following year he took 4th place in the Senior Classic and had been holding 6th position in the Junior Classic when he was forced to retire on the Mountain Mile during the last lap of the race.

His funeral service was held on the afternoon of Monday 26th August and followed by committal at Dundee Crematorium.

Nigel James HADDON

Nigel Haddon at Signpost Corner during practice for the 1996 Senior MGP

The roads around the TT course on the morning of Monday 19th August 1996 were mainly dry apart from the odd damp patch under the trees, which was welcome news for the many competitors congregating in the area of the Grandstand in Douglas waiting to take advantage of a practice session for the Manx Grand Prix. Amongst them was Nigel Haddon, riding a 750cc Honda machine bearing the race number 22 and entered in the Senior Manx Grand Prix to be held the following week. He had been out on this machine the previous Saturday evening and recorded an average lap speed of 102.82mph.

During the course of the session Nigel Haddon set off along Glencrutchery Road towards the Quarterbridge. He safely negotiated his way round the course through to Ramsey and up onto the mountain section where visibility was down to 150 yards in places due to mist. Marshals on duty at the Black Hut saw him appear through the mist on the approach to the left hand bend, he was alone on the road and, in their opinion, travelling too quickly for the prevailing conditions. They then saw him sit upright on his machine as if he had suddenly lost his bearings and it quickly became obvious that he would be unable to negotiate the corner safely. On the exit of the bend the big Honda drifted wide and collided heavily with the grass bank on the right hand side of the road and the unfortunate rider was thrown from the machine. The marshals went to his immediate assistance and on finding his condition to be serious they did what they could for him until the arrival of the helicopter ambulance. However, just minutes earlier the helicopter had been called to another serious incident on the mountain involving race veteran Jack Gow and consequently there was a delay before it was able to attend. Within a few minutes of landing at the Black Hut the helicopter conveyed the unconscious and gravely injured rider to the playing fields at Ballakermeen School in Douglas. He was then transferred to an ambulance, which carried him the short distance to Noble's Hospital where it was found that he had sustained multiple internal injuries and his condition was critical. Despite extensive resuscitation measures, he succumbed to his injuries shortly after admission to the Casualty Department.

Chris Rowe, the Chief Scrutineer, later examined the Honda and found no evidence to suggest that a mechanical failure had played a contributory part in this accident.

Nigel Haddon, a single man, was 38 years of age. He was a motorcycle agent and tour operator from Cape Town, South Africa. Born in Reigate, Surrey, he had started motorcycle racing in 1978 at club and national level until 1983 when he emigrated to South Africa and began competing in the 750cc class. Away from the motorcycle scene, he had also raced powerboats and had driven a Lotus sports car in the classic series in South Africa. He made his debut on the TT course during the 1995 Manx Grand Prix when, riding a 599cc Honda, he finished 10th in the Junior Newcomers race with an average speed of 105.14mph and gained a silver replica. A few days later he gained a further silver replica when he finished 14th in the Senior MGP with a race average speed of 106.60mph.

His funeral service was held on 27th August and followed by committal at Douglas Borough Crematorium. A memorial service was held later at Kingswood Church, Reigate, Surrey where his ashes were interred.

Russell WARING

1996 - Russell Waring pictured at Parliament Square, Ramsey during the Ultra Lightweight TT

Fine weather, clear visibility and dry roads around the TT course on the morning of Monday 26th May 1997 provided ideal conditions for racing as competitors assembled in the area of the Grandstand in Douglas waiting to participate in the opening practice session for the Tourist Trophy Races. Amongst those taking advantage of an early opportunity to familiarise themselves with the TT course was Russ Waring, riding a Yamaha TZ 125cc machine bearing the racing number 44 and entered in the Ultra Lightweight TT to be held the following week. He had travelled to the Island determined to win a trophy in the 125cc class and was totally committed to achieving this result. The main dominating influence on his life for the previous three years was competing in the TT, which he loved.

When the time came, he set off along Glencrutchery Road towards Bray Hill together with another rider, a newcomer to the course, who was riding a much larger machine and by the time they reached the top of Bray Hill the other competitor was ahead of him. Being wary of the newcomer he was unable to pass until just after the left hand bend at the entrance to the Snugborough housing estate in Union Mills, a little more than two miles from the start. On the approach to the following right hand bend at the Railway Inn he was travelling at racing speed and on the usual racing line but as he peeled into the corner the front end of his machine slipped from beneath him and he went down. He slid across the road to the left and collided heavily with the high kerbing outside Glen View Cottages. Within twenty minutes he had been conveyed to Noble's Hospital by helicopter, being admitted at 5.50am suffering from serious hip and pelvic injuries. The following day he had recovered sufficiently enough to speak to a friend, Jonathon Owen, and explained to him that he had been concerned about the weather turning nasty at the end of the week and not having sufficient time to qualify. He had decided to try and qualify on Monday or Tuesday while the weather was good. Describing the accident, he stated that a novice rider had held him up and after passing him he was pushing the bike hard when the front end tucked underneath him and he stepped off. Over the next few weeks, although he had initially responded well to treatment, his condition gradually deteriorated and at 12.10am on Wednesday 18th June, he passed away in the ITU at Noble's Hospital.

A subsequent examination of the Yamaha machine by Hector Gordon, Chief Scrutineer for the ACU, revealed no mechanical defects likely to have contributed to the incident.

Russell Waring, a single man, was 34 years of age. He was a self-employed plasterer by occupation and a resident of Wing near Leighton Buzzard, Bedfordshire. His first racing appearance on the Island was at the 1995 MGP when he picked up two silver replicas. The first was awarded after he came 3rd in the Lightweight Newcomers Race with a race average speed of 105.48mph. The second came after he finished 8th in the Lightweight MGP with a race average speed of 105.84mph. Turning to the TT in 1996, he finished 22nd in the Lightweight Race with an average speed of 106.36mph and was awarded a bronze replica.

His funeral service was held at All Saint's Church, Wing near Leighton Buzzard on Tuesday 1st July and followed by committal. A memorial seat in his name was later placed outside the village hall in Union Mills.

Colin Christopher GABLE

Colin Gable on Quarterbridge Road during the fateful practice session for the 1997 Formula One TT

Despite the fine weather and dry roads around the TT course on the evening of Monday 26th May 1997 the glare from the setting sun was likely to be troublesome, which was not the best of news for those competitors gathered at the Grandstand in Douglas waiting to take advantage of the second practice session for the Tourist Trophy Races. Amongst them was race veteran Colin Gable, riding a 750cc Honda machine bearing the race number 17 and entered in the Formula One race to be held on Saturday 31st May. To combat the possible dazzling effects of the sun he had fitted a tinted visor to his helmet.

Departing from the grandstand shortly after 7.10pm, he had safely negotiated his way along the opening three miles of the course, through Quarterbridge, Union Mills and Ballahutchin Hill when he was seen approaching the right hand bend at Ballagarey Corner in Glen Vine. He was on the usual racing line and travelling at racing speed as he banked over for the bend but on the apex he leaned further over and on doing so his rear wheel suddenly stepped out to the left and he went down. The bright yellow Honda slid along the road, spinning in a shower of sparks, before colliding heavily with the straw bales positioned on the left hand side of the road just beyond the junction with the Ballagarey Road. Marshals immediately went to the assistance of the unfortunate rider and the helicopter ambulance arrived on the scene within minutes of being called but there was nothing that could be done for him. He had been killed instantly.

Marshals at the scene of the incident surmised that the very bright setting sun might have contributed to the accident although the rider had given no indication to suggest he was having trouble with the sun, nor had he slowed down.

Hector Gordon, Chief Scrutineer for the Auto-Cycle Union, examined the relatively unscathed Honda the following morning. The tyres were in good condition although there was some oil on the rear tyre. The front forks were damaged, consistent with a heavy impact on the right hand side. The brakes and clutch were operating and the wheels were free to rotate. The engine was free and all the gears could be selected. He found no evidence to suggest that a mechanical failure had been a contributory factor in this accident.

Colin Gable was 31 years of age. He was a design manager by occupation and a resident of Ravenstone, Leicestershire where he lived with his partner of six years, Sally Roberts and her daughter Sarah. He made his debut on the TT course during the 1987 Manx Grand Prix, winning the Senior Newcomers race with an average speed of 105.23mph and finishing one minute ahead of his friend Phil Hogg who, ironically, was killed at Ballagarey Corner, while practising for the 1989 TT. Third place man in that Senior Newcomers race was Al Dalton who was to lose his life in a motorcycle road traffic accident in Ormskirk, Lancashire in 1990. Colin turned to the TT the following year and from thereon became a regular at the event recording several top ten placings, which included third place in the 1995 Junior TT with a race average speed of 114.62mph. He had been crowned British 750cc Production Champion in 1988.

His funeral service was held on Wednesday 11th June at St. Michael and All Angels Church, Ravenstone, Leicestershire and followed by committal at Loughborough.

George Daniel SHIMMIN

Danny Shimmin rounds the Gooseneck during the fateful practice session for the 1997 Junior Classic MGP

Weather conditions across the Isle of Man on the evening of Saturday 16th August 1997 were fine and the roads around the TT course were dry, which was splendid news for those competitors assembled at the Grandstand in Douglas waiting to take advantage of the opening practice session for the Manx Grand Prix. Amongst them was race veteran Danny Shimmin, riding a 349cc Aermacchi machine bearing the race number 12 and entered in the Junior Classic Race to be held on Wednesday 27th August.

During the course of the session, Danny Shimmin set off along Glencrutchery Road towards Bray Hill on his first circuit of the meeting and safely negotiated his way round the course to record an average lap speed of 91.83mph, which was to prove the second fastest lap of the evening in that class. During his second lap, he had made his way through Union Mills and Crosby when he was seen approaching the bends at Greeba Castle, almost six miles out from the Grandstand. He took the left bend without problem but as he banked over for the right hand bend the Aermacchi went from beneath him and he went down. Both rider and machine then slid diagonally across the road and collided heavily with the straw bales covering a stone wall on the left. Marshals went to his immediate assistance and did what they could for him while waiting for the helicopter ambulance, which arrived on the scene within minutes of being called. The gravely injured rider was conveyed to the playing fields at Ballakermeen School in Douglas then transferred to an ambulance, which carried him the short distance to Noble's Hospital where he was admitted just over twenty minutes after the accident occurred. However, his condition failed to improve and he passed away shortly after midnight on the morning of Monday 18th August. There was much concern later when it was found that a ventilator used during his treatment had been assembled incorrectly. However, at his inquest a pathologist gave the opinion that this would not have contributed to his death.

An examination of the Aermacchi by scrutineers revealed that an oil leakage had contaminated the rear tyre of the machine and it was concluded that this would have caused loss of traction with the road surface.

Danny Shimmin was 50 years of age. He was a bus driver by occupation and a resident of Douglas where he lived with his partner Steph. He was an experienced and well travelled road racer having competed in Macau, Holland, Czechoslovakia, Portugal, Spain and Ireland. His first appearance on the TT course was at the 1965 Manx Grand Prix and from thereon he became a regular with top six finishes between 1971 and 1976 when, riding a 250 Yamaha, he won the Lightweight Race with a race average speed of 99.07mph and finished second in the Senior, just 1.4 seconds behind race winner Les Trotter. He then turned his attention to the TT races where he had been competing in the Production Races since 1970. By this time he was already very well known on the road racing circuits of Ireland and went on to win the MCUI 500 Classic Championship three years in a row, 1993, 94 and 95. In his last four rides at the Manx he had been placed in the top six and just a few weeks previous to his death he had taken fifth place in the Singles TT race.

His funeral service was held at St. Andrews Church, Douglas at 10.30am on Tuesday 26th August and followed by interment at Douglas Borough Cemetery.

Pamela Anne CANNELL

Pam Cannell at the Bungalow during practice for the 1997 Lightweight MGP

Sunshine graced the Isle of Man on the evening of Monday 18th August 1997, providing dry roads and clear visibility around the TT course. Ideal racing conditions for the competitors assembled at the Grandstand in Douglas waiting to take advantage of the third practice session for the Manx Grand Prix. Amongst them was Pam Cannell, riding a 250cc Yamaha machine bearing the race number 72 and entered in the Lightweight Race to be held the following week. During the Saturday evening practice session she had lapped the course at 91.28mph, an improvement of almost four minutes on her best lap time, which was recorded during her debut at the Manx in 1996.

The start of the session was delayed for a short time while a road sweeper dealt with an oil spillage on the road surface at Ballacraine. When practising commenced it was not long before Pam Cannell set off along Glencrutchery Road towards Bray Hill on her opening lap of the evening and she safely made her way round the course through Glen Helen, Kirk Michael and Ramsey before making the climb onto the mountain section. At around 6.45pm she was seen approaching the sweeping left hand curve at the Graham Memorial but was off the usual racing line and as a consequence she drifted to the right on the exit of the bend and her machine mounted the grass verge at the side of the road. It travelled along the verge for a short distance then began to cart wheel before bouncing over the wire fencing at the top of the bank. The unfortunate rider was thrown from the machine and came to rest near to the centre of the roadway. Marshals went immediately to her aid but there was nothing that could be done for her. She had been killed instantly.

Christopher Rowe, Chief Scrutineer for the Manx Motor Cycle Club later visited the scene of the accident and examined the Yamaha machine, which had only sustained minor damage. He found no evidence to suggest that a mechanical failure had contributed towards the incident.

Pam Cannell, a single woman, was 38 years of age. She was an Audit Accountant by occupation and a resident of Onchan in the Isle of Man. As an avid fan of motorcycle racing for many years, she used to marshal at local race meetings along with her close friend Monica Floding prior to them taking up the sport. Each progressed through the various gradings to earn their national ACU licences in time to make their debuts at the 1996 Manx Grand Prix. They set off together with start numbers 67 and 68 in the Lightweight Newcomer's Race and although they were well matched over the first two laps Pam was later forced to back off due to a holed exhaust system on her 250 Honda. They both went on to complete the race and received finisher's medals.

Racing most of the 1997 season in the United Kingdom, Pam kept her bike in England to save on travelling costs. She was a loyal and popular committee member of the Andreas Racing Association, always prepared to help out at local racing events whenever she wasn't competing herself.

Her funeral service was held at St. Jude's Church, Lezayre on Thursday 28th August and followed by committal at Douglas Borough Crematorium. Her ashes were later interred in the graveyard of St. Jude's Church.

Roger David BOWLER

Roger Bowler at Ballacraine during practice for the 1997 Senior Classic MGP

Operational difficulties connected with Noble's Hospital on Monday 18th August 1997 had resulted in the morning practice session for the Manx Grand Prix being cancelled by Neil Hanson, Clerk of the Course. However, the problem was resolved during the day and practising was back on schedule for the evening session, which was welcome news for those competitors congregating at the Grandstand in Douglas waiting to take advantage of the opportunity to familiarise themselves with the TT course. Amongst them was race veteran Roger Bowler, riding a 500cc Matchless machine bearing the race number 32 and entered in the Senior Classic Race to be held the following week.

There was a short delay before the session could commence as a road sweeping machine was operating on the course at Ballacraine in order to deal with an oil spillage on the road surface. Practising began once the road was cleared and after the first part of the session had ended it was the turn of the Classics and the first man away was Bob Heath on a 499 Seeley G50. A short time later, Roger Bowler set off along Glencrutchery Road towards Bray Hill on his opening lap of the evening and safely made his way round the course with an average lap speed of 85.99mph. Without stopping he commenced his second circuit and had made his way through Glen Helen, Kirk Michael and Ballaugh when, shortly before 8.00pm, he was seen approaching Quarry Bends with two other riders ahead of him on the road. He was on the usual racing line for the bends and travelling at racing speed but as he began to negotiate the first right hand bend his front wheel suddenly went from beneath him and he was thrown off. The unfortunate rider collided heavily with the stone wall on the right and was then struck by his machine. Marshals went to his immediate assistance and did what they could for him while waiting for the helicopter ambulance, which arrived on the scene within five minutes of being called. The gravely injured rider was conveyed to the playing fields at Ballakermeen School in Douglas then transferred to an ambulance, which carried him the short distance to Noble's Hospital. Despite the best of medical attention he succumbed to his injuries the following day.

Chris Rowe, Chief Scrutineer for the Manx Motor Cycle Club, examined the scene of the accident and found a slight tyre mark on the road surface. An examination of the Matchless revealed a slash in the front tyre, which may have been a contributory factor in the accident.

Roger Bowler, a single man, was 53 years of age. The former post office mechanic was a resident of Crawley, Sussex and had taken retirement five years earlier to dedicate his time to motor racing and studying computers for an Open University course. He was a very experienced racing motorcyclist and had ridden in the TT and MGP for 30 years with a number of excellent results, most notably being the 1972 Production 500 TT when, riding a Triumph T100T, he finished second with a race average speed of 92.09mph, just seven seconds behind the race winner, Stan Woods. Another notable ride was the 1979 TT when, riding a 600 Honda, he finished second to Alan Jackson in the Formula II Race with an average race speed of 99.67mph.

His funeral service was held in the Isle of Man on Wednesday 3rd September and followed by committal at Douglas Borough Crematorium.

Fergal Emmet NOLAN

Emmet Nolan on the start line for the fateful 1997 Senior MGP

Conditions were perfect for racing on the afternoon of Friday 29th August 1997, the weather was fine, visibility was clear and the roads around the TT course were dry. Welcome news for the 103 competitors lined up along Glencrutchery Road in Douglas waiting to participate in the Senior Manx Grand Prix. Amongst them was Emmet Nolan, riding a 750cc Yamaha machine bearing the race number 93. His fastest lap on this machine during practice was 96.70mph, which was achieved the previous Friday evening.

At 1.00pm the flag dropped and the race began with Roy Richardson and Keith Townsend being the first two away. Nearly eight minutes later it was the turn of Emmet Nolan to begin his race against the clock and he set off along Glencrutchery Road towards Bray Hill together with his starting partner and had safely made his way through Greeba, Ballacraine and Glen Helen when he was seen approaching Sarah's Cottage with another competitor ahead of him. He negotiated the tricky right hand bend then continued up Creg Willeys Hill but at Lambfell he came up close behind the rider in front very quickly and as they were both on the same racing line he had to brake hard to avoid a collision. His rear wheel lifted off the ground and began to twitch from side to side as he fought to maintain control of the machine but was unable to prevent it colliding with the earth bank on the right hand side of the road near to the farm entrance. The unfortunate rider was thrown from the machine and came to rest in the roadway. Marshals went to his assistance and did what they could for him while waiting for the helicopter ambulance, which arrived on the scene just over five minutes after being called. The unconscious and gravely injured rider was conveyed to the playing fields at Ballakermeen School in Douglas then transferred to an ambulance, which carried him the short distance to Noble's Hospital where he was admitted within twenty minutes of the accident occurring. He was rushed to the CT scan room but succumbed to his injuries a short time later.

There had been no suggestion that contact had been made with the other unidentified machine, which continued, the rider apparently unaware of the incident. An examination of the Yamaha machine revealed no mechanical defects likely to have caused the accident.

The initial race leader, Roy Richardson, retired on his third lap, leaving Gary Carswell of Maughold in the Isle of Man to go on and win the race with an average of 113.91mph, 25 seconds ahead of Keith Townsend in second place. Chris Hook completed the top three.

Emmet Nolan was 38 years of age. He was a plant fitter by occupation and a resident of Coachford, County Cork. He was a very experienced rider and had been competing for about 17 years not only on the Isle of Man, but also in America, the United Kingdom and the Continent. He made his debut on the TT course during the 1986 Manx Grand Prix when, riding a Honda, he finished 14th in the Senior Newcomer's Race. He returned in 1991 and rode a Yamaha in the Senior Manx but failed to complete the race. The following year he tackled the Senior Manx once more and, riding a Yamaha, finished in 45th place.

His funeral service was held in the church at Leighlin Bridge, County Carlow and followed by interment.

Michael John Ralfs CASEY

Mike Casey at the Quarterbridge during practice for the 1998 Lightweight TT

With dry roads and good visibility all around the TT course, conditions were near perfect for racing on the afternoon of Thursday 4th June 1998, which was good news for the competitors gathered at the Grandstand in Douglas waiting to take advantage of a practice session for the Tourist Trophy Races. Amongst them was Mike Casey, making a return to the TT course after missing the 1997 season as the result of an accident during the opening meeting at Jurby in which he sustained an injured knee cap, ankle and shoulder.

The first part of the session commenced at 2.00pm and he set off on the 600cc Honda machine, which had been entered in the Junior Race by Martin Bullock. He made his way round the course and returned to the Grandstand with an average lap speed of 111.34mph.

The second part of the session commenced at 3.05pm and this time he was riding his 250cc Honda machine bearing the race number 27 and entered in the Lightweight Race to be held the following Monday morning. On receiving his signal to proceed he moved off along Glencrutchery Road and quickly made his way through the left hand bend at St.Ninian's crossroads and down Bray Hill onto Quarterbridge Road. Having then negotiated Braddan Bridge, Union Mills and Ballahutchin Hill, he was three miles out from the start when he was seen on the approach to the sweeping right hand bend at Ballagarey in Glen Vine. Then, as he was travelling through the corner his machine clipped the edge of the kerbing on the apex and immediately veered off to the left. The unfortunate rider was thrown from the machine and collided heavily with a straw bale covering a gatepost in front of the house "Kufri". At almost the same instant he was hit by his machine before it struck the same gatepost and disintegrated, sending the fuel tank smashing into the roof of the house "Uplands" before falling back into the garden. A police officer and marshals went to his assistance and found him lying on the right hand side of the road near to the public telephone kiosk but there was nothing they could do for him. He had been killed instantly.

Scrutineers later examined the extensively damaged machine and found no evidence to suggest that a mechanical failure had contributed to the accident.

Mike Casey was 34 years of age. He was a marine engineer by occupation employed by the Isle of Man Steam Packet Company and a resident of Patrick where he lived with his wife Sandra. Mike had been racing motorcycles for more than fifteen years and made his debut on the TT course in the 1985 Manx Grand Prix when he finished third in the Senior Newcomers Race with a race average speed of 90.88mph. In 1993 he gained a silver replica after finishing 8th in the Senior Manx and another the following year after finishing 5th in the Senior. Success came in 1995, riding a Honda, he won the Senior Manx with a race average speed of 111.81mph and a ten second advantage over second place man Roy Richardson with Keith Townsend in third place. In 1996 he turned his attention to the TT Races, finishing 17th in the Formula One and 26th in the Junior.

His funeral service was held at Patrick Church near Peel on Tuesday 9th June and followed by interment. Several years later, at a point between the Mountain Box and the Black Hut on the mountain section of the course, a new shelter was built in his memory.

Jack George TRUSTHAM

Jack Trustham and Graham Harris at the Quarterbridge on their ill-fated TT Lap of Honour 1998

It was grey and overcast on the afternoon of Tuesday 9th June 1998 but the roads around the TT course were dry and visibility on the mountain section was clear. Good news for the large number of entrants gathered at the grandstand in Douglas waiting to participate in the TT Course Lap of Honour, which had been arranged to mark Honda's 50th Anniversary. Amongst them were Jack Trustham and his passenger, Graham Harris, riding a 1969 Imp Classic sidecar bearing the entry number 201 and powered by a 998cc engine.

On receiving the signal to commence they set off along Glencrutchery Road towards Bray Hill and had safely made their way through Crosby, Glen Helen and Barregarrow when they were seen approaching Douglas Road Corner in Kirk Michael village. They were alone on the road and travelling at approximately 50mph when, shortly before reaching the sweeping right hand corner, the outfit began to drift to the right then mounted and straddled the kerb of the footpath for a distance of about 15 yards before dropping back into the roadway. Jack Trustham made no reaction as the sidecar continued in a straight line across the road, mounted the footpath outside the house "Brynwood" and collided heavily with the straw bales covering the boundary wall. On impact with the bales both rider and passenger were thrown from the outfit. Marshals went to their immediate aid and found that Jack Trustham was showing no signs of life. Resuscitation attempts were commenced but without success. Graham Harris was unconscious and had sustained multiple injuries. The marshals did what they could for him while waiting for the helicopter ambulance, which arrived on the scene within two minutes of being called and conveyed the gravely injured man to Noble's Hospital.

The helicopter had already been airborne when called, having collected veteran rider Derek Minter from his spill at Glentramman. He had to be left at Douglas Road Corner for transportation to hospital by ambulance.

Jack Trustham, a retired solicitor, was 66 years of age. He and his wife Maureen, together with their son Edward, lived alternately between their homes in Hornchurch, Essex and Ballaugh in the Isle of Man. His first race on the TT course was the 1953 Junior Manx Grand Prix, when, riding an AJS machine, he finished in 39th place. He was to return to the MGP every year after that appearance through to 1970. Then in 1972 he appeared at the TT races, having moved from solo machines to sidecars and took 14th place in the 500cc race. He continued with the Sidecar TT races right up to his final race on the Isle of Man in 1977 after which he retired following a 25 year association with the TT course.

A post mortem examination revealed that he had died as a result of heart failure and therefore no inquest was held. He had been a fit and active man up until two years before his death when he suffered a minor heart attack.

His funeral service was held at St. Mary's Church, Ballaugh and followed by interment.

Charles Ian HARDISTY

Ian Hardisty at Ballaugh Bridge during the fateful 1998 Production TT

Fine weather prevailed on the morning of Friday 12th June 1998 leaving dry roads around the TT course and clear visibility on the mountain section. Near perfect racing conditions for the sixty three competitors lined up along Glencrutchery Road in Douglas waiting to participate in the three lap Production TT race. Amongst them was Ian Hardisty, riding a 750cc Kawasaki ZX7RR machine bearing the race number 66. On the previous Sunday afternoon he had competed in the Formula I race, which had been postponed on the Saturday due to adverse weather conditions and reduced from six to four laps. He finished in 25th place with an average speed of 103.49mph.

The race commenced at 10.45am with the riders being dispatched at ten second intervals and almost eleven minutes later, it was the turn of Ian Hardisty to begin his race against the clock. He set off towards Bray Hill and safely made his way round the course to complete his first circuit with an average lap speed of 107.44mph, which put him in 39th place. During his second lap, he had negotiated his way through Glen Helen, Kirk Michael and Sulby when, at about 11.30am, he was seen approaching the bends at Kerrowmoar but appeared to be off the usual racing line for the first bend. As a consequence, he drifted wide on the exit of the bend and collided heavily with the grass bank on the right. The unfortunate rider was immediately thrown from the machine and came to rest in the centre of the road. Marshals and a doctor on duty at that location went to his assistance and on examination could find no signs of life. Resuscitation procedures began even before he was carried by stretcher to the side of the road to await the arrival of the helicopter ambulance, which arrived on the scene within minutes of being called. Two doctors from the helicopter also tried resuscitation but all efforts proved to be in vain. He had been killed instantly.

Hector Gordon, Chief Scrutineer for the Auto-Cycle Union, later examined the relatively unscathed Kawasaki and found no evidence to suggest that a mechanical failure had been a contributory factor in the accident.

Jim Moodie went on to win with a race average speed of 119.19mph, giving Honda their 100th TT victory since their first appearance on the Island fifty years earlier. Nigel Davies took second and the final rostrum place went to Michael Rutter.

Ian Hardisty was 40 years of age, having celebrated his birthday on the Island just ten days earlier. He was a civil servant by occupation and a resident of Abergavenny, Wales where he lived with his wife Maria and their ten year old son Rhys. His first appearance on the TT course was during the 1995 Manx Grand Prix when he finished 7th in the Lightweight Newcomers race and then, in the Classic Lightweight Race, riding a 248cc Cowles Ducati he finished 11th and was awarded the Dick Linton Trophy for the Newcomer making the most meritorious performance during a Classic Race. He returned for the 1996 Manx Grand Prix and earned two silver replicas after finishing 42nd in the Junior and 16th in the Lightweight.

His funeral service was held on Tuesday 23rd June and followed by committal at Gwent Crematorium. His family had made it known that they felt it would be appropriate for any of his motorcycling friends to wear leathers at his funeral.

John Frederick HENDERSON

John Henderson on the mountain section during the fateful 1998 Senior TT

As forecast by the weathermen at Ronaldsway, the weather was fine and the roads were dry on the afternoon of Friday 12th June 1998 as seventy competitors formed up along Glencrutchery Road in Douglas waiting to participate in the Senior Tourist Trophy race. Amongst them, a day after his 42nd birthday was John Henderson, riding a 750cc Honda machine bearing the race number 63. Earlier that day, riding a Suzuki GSXR750 in the Production TT, he took 28th place with a race average speed of 108.86mph. On the previous Sunday he had finished 13th in the Formula I race with an average speed of 109.38mph.

The Senior race commenced at 1.15pm with the riders being dispatched at ten second intervals and just over ten minutes later it was the turn of John Henderson to begin his race against he clock. He set off towards Bray Hill and safely made his way round the course to complete his opening circuit with an average speed of 109.16mph, which put him in 53rd place. Recording an average of 111.74mph on his second lap he had moved up to 45th position and by the half way stage, having put in a lap of 109.54mph, he was up into 36th position. At the end if his fourth circuit he was holding 31st place and a lap of 109.97mph had helped to push him up into 29th position by the end of the fifth.

On his sixth and final lap of the race, he had safely negotiated his way through Glen Helen and Kirk Michael when he was seen travelling at racing speed on the approach to Birkin's Bends at Rhencullen. He appeared to be on the usual racing line as he took the right hander but then as he was rounding the following left hand bend his front wheel began to slide away to the right and he went down. Both rider and machine then collided heavily with the straw bales covering the corner of the house "Cronk Steone" situated at the top of Rhencullen Hill. Marshals went to his assistance and did what they could for him while waiting for the helicopter ambulance, which arrived on the scene within minutes of being called. The gravely injured rider was conveyed to Noble's Hospital where he was admitted within fifteen minutes of the accident occurring. However, despite emergency surgery and a prolonged period of intensive care, he succumbed to his injuries at 4.25pm on Saturday 27th June.

Hector Gordon, Chief Scrutineer for the Auto-Cycle Union, later examined the Suzuki and found no evidence to suggest that mechanical failure had played a part in this accident.

Ian Simpson of Dalbeattie went on to win the race by just 3.7 seconds from Bob Jackson of Windermere with the Irishman James Courtney coming home in third place.

John Henderson, a single man, was 42 years of age. He was a self employed draughtsman by occupation and a resident of Ross on Wye. He had been racing motorcycles for 20 years and had gained a wealth of experience on the TT course since his debut at the 1989 Manx Grand Prix when he finished 5th in the Lightweight Newcomers and 23rd in the Lightweight race. He moved up to the TT races the following year and finished 26th in the Junior. From thereon he became a regular on the TT course and had built up a collection of coveted replicas.

His funeral service was held in Douglas and followed by committal at Douglas Borough Crematorium. A memorial service was held later at St. Mary's Church, Ross on Wye.

Adam John WOODHALL

Adam Woodhall on the mountain section during practice for the 1998 Senior MGP

Other than blustery winds on the mountain section of the TT course on the afternoon of Thursday 27th August 1998 conditions were described as almost perfect for racing. The roads were dry and visibility was clear as competitors congregated in the area of the Grandstand in Douglas ready to take advantage of a practice session for the Manx Grand Prix, celebrating it's 75th anniversary. Amongst them was Adam Woodhall, riding a 996cc Suzuki machine bearing the race number 5 and entered in the Senior race to be held on Friday 4th September. His helmet, leathers and fairing were adorned with his customary bright pink spots.

Practising was due to begin at 2.00pm but there was a delay due to cars being left on the course at the Bungalow and Doran's Bend. Then, consent was given for an ambulance to cross the course into Ballanard Road and return. Therefore, it was shortly after 2.30pm when the session commenced and Adam Woodhall was one of the first riders to set off along Glencrutchery Road towards Bray Hill and Quarterbridge. Approximately five minutes later, having safely negotiated his way over the first seven miles of the course and through the right hand bend at Ballacraine he was seen approaching the left hander at Ballaspur with a much slower machine travelling directly ahead of him. On the exit of the bend he began to overtake on the left but at the same instant the other rider also moved to the left which forced him to move further over but as he did so his machine caught the roadside hedge and went out of control before colliding heavily with a stone gate pillar at the entrance to a field. The force of the impact caused the front of the Suzuki to disintegrate with the front wheel and forks becoming detached from the frame. The unfortunate rider was thrown and came to rest in the roadway just a few yards from the stone pillar. Marshals went to his assistance but there was nothing they could do for him. He had been killed instantly. Apparently unaware of the incident, the other competitor continued towards Glen Helen.

Chris Rowe, Chief Scrutineer for the Manx Motor Cycle Club, later examined the wrecked Suzuki and found no evidence to suggest that a mechanical failure had contributed to the accident.

When the Senior Race was held the following week, a number of riders had pink spots on their helmets, leathers and fairings in memory of Adam who was well known and respected by his fellow competitors.

Adam Woodhall was 33 years of age. He was a Sales Director by occupation, employed by the Natwest Bank. He was a resident of Bransford, Worcestershire where he lived with his partner, Gillian Basnett and his son Samuel. He had been racing motorcycles for fifteen years and made his debut on the TT course at the 1985 Manx Grand Prix when he finished 4th in the Senior Newcomer's race. From thereon he became a regular at the Manx and notched up a number of top ten finishes, gaining several replicas in the process. During the 1997 MGP he came 4th in the Junior with a race average speed of 110.73mph and 5th in the Senior with an average speed of 111.66mph.

His funeral service was held in the Isle of Man and followed by committal at Douglas Borough Crematorium.

Robert WINGRAVE

Rob Wingrave at Ballacraine during practice for the 1998 Senior Classic MGP

The weather was fine on the afternoon of Thursday 27th August 1998 and the roads around the TT course were dry, which provided almost perfect racing conditions for the competitors gathered at the Grandstand in Douglas waiting to take advantage of a practice session for the Manx Grand Prix, celebrating it's 75th anniversary. Amongst them was Rob Wingrave who had entered both the Junior and Senior Classic races to be held the following week.

The start of practising was delayed for half an hour before the first part of the session began shortly after 2.30pm. The Classic and Ultra Lightweight machines were allocated the second part of the session and when the opportunity came Rob Wingrave set off on his 350cc Norton and safely completed one lap of the course. He then mounted his 500cc Manx Norton bearing the Senior Classic race number 75 and set off along Glencrutchery Road towards Bray Hill. His fastest lap on this machine during practice had been set on the previous Saturday evening when he recorded an average speed of 90.36mph.

He had made his way through Quarterbridge then Braddan Bridge and was barely three miles into his lap when, at about 4.00pm, he was seen negotiating the right hand bend at the Railway Hotel in Union Mills but then as he approached the following sweeping left hander a marshal noted that he appeared to be off the usual racing line for the bend. As a consequence he drifted wide and at a point approximately twenty yards beyond the village post office, the Norton struck the kerb and mounted the footpath on the right. He struggled to regain control of the machine and did manage to steer it back off the footpath onto the roadway but at that point it veered diagonally across the road and collided with the boundary wall of the house "Greystones". The unfortunate rider was thrown from the machine and came to rest in the middle of the road. A police officer together with marshals went to his immediate assistance and within twenty minutes he had been conveyed by helicopter ambulance to Noble's Hospital where he underwent emergency surgery. There then followed a prolonged period of intensive care but his condition gradually deteriorated and at 2.00am on Saturday 12th September, he succumbed to his injuries.

Chris Rowe, Chief Scrutineer for the Manx Motor Cycle Club, later examined the relatively unscathed Manx Norton and found nothing to suggest that a mechanical failure may have contributed towards this accident.

Rob Wingrave was 54 years of age. He was a heating engineer by occupation and a resident of Rawledge near Farnham, Surrey where he lived with his wife Sam and their three children, Kate, Rebecca and Oliver. He had a wealth of racing experience and had enjoyed success in both moto-cross and trials riding. He made his debut on the TT course at the 1994 Manx Grand Prix and had competed in both the Senior and Junior Classic races from thereon, finishing in all eight races. His best result came in 1997 when, riding a Manx Norton, he finished in 24th place in the Junior Classic.

His funeral service was held in the Isle of Man and followed by committal at Douglas Borough Crematorium. A memorial service was later held in his local church in Rawledge where his ashes were interred.

Christopher EAST

Chris East at Ballaugh Bridge during the fateful 1998 Senior Classic MGP

Fine weather, dry roads and clear visibility around the TT course on the afternoon of Monday 31st August 1998 provided perfect racing conditions for the 88 competitors lined up along Glencrutchery Road in Douglas awaiting the start of the Senior Classic Manx Grand Prix. Amongst them was race veteran Chris East, riding a 496cc Matchless machine bearing the race number 19. His fastest lap on this machine during practice had been set on the previous Wednesday evening when he recorded an average speed of 92.12mph.

As a consequence of delays the race was reduced from four laps to three and when the flag eventually dropped the first two men left the start line to begin the race. A minute and a half later Chris East set off towards Bray Hill along with his starting partner Bud Jackson. He safely made his way round the course to complete his opening lap with an average speed of 95.40mph, which put him in 15th position.

Having made his way through Union Mills, Ballacraine and Glen Helen on his second circuit he was seen approaching the sweeping right hand bend at Douglas Road Corner in Kirk Michael village. He was travelling at racing speed and on the usual line but as he was negotiating the bend his rear wheel suddenly stepped out to the left and he was thrown off, colliding with the straw bales covering the wall by the gateway of the house "Tamarisk". Unfortunately, his machine followed and struck him before rebounding back into the roadway. Marshals and medics went to his immediate assistance and did what they could for him while waiting for the helicopter ambulance, which arrived on the scene within three minutes of being called. He was conveyed to the playing fields at Ballakermeen School in Douglas then transferred to an ambulance, which carried him the short distance to Noble's Hospital where he underwent a considerable period of intensive care. However his condition slowly deteriorated as he failed to respond to treatment and at 12.05pm on Saturday 19th September, almost three weeks after the accident, he succumbed to his injuries.

An examination of the Matchless revealed that the rear wheel and tyre were contaminated with oil that had come from a chain oiler pipe and it was possible that this oil spillage may have been a contributory factor in this accident.

Bob Heath from Walsall went on to win the Senior Classic Race with a 15 seconds advantage over Bill Swallow in second place. Third position went to Tony Myers.

Chris East was 55 years of age. He was an insurance consultant by occupation and a resident of Malvern, Worcestershire where he lived with his wife Wendy. Between 1965 and 1974 he had raced in the Manx Grand Prix and had completed all but one of nine races with the best result coming in 1972 when he finished 12th in the Senior Manx. He returned in 1987 to compete in the Classic Races and from thereon he became a regular, completing all but one of twelve races prior to the 1998 meeting with his best results coming in 1989 when he finished 7th in the Senior Classic and 1995 when he finished 9th in the Senior Classic.

His funeral service was held in the Isle of Man on the afternoon of Friday 25th September and followed by committal at Douglas Borough Crematorium.

Bernadette Johanna Hermana BOSMAN - SAALBRINK

Helmut Lunemann and Bernadette Bosman on their fateful practice lap for the 1999 Sidecar TT

Dry roads and clear visibility around the TT course on the evening of Monday 31st May 1999, provided ideal racing conditions for the competitors gathered at the Grandstand in Douglas waiting to take advantage of a practice session for the Sidecar Tourist Trophy races. Amongst them were Helmut Lunemann and his Dutch passenger Bernadette Bosman riding a sidecar outfit powered by a 600cc Yamaha engine and bearing the race number 40. Having decided not to take advantage of the morning practice session, this was to be their first outing on the TT course together. Lunemann, 62 years of age and from Germany, had competed at the TT since 1967, riding solo machines until 1979 when he switched to sidecars. Bernadette, although experienced in motorcycle racing, had never competed on the Isle of Man before. The couple had met about twelve months earlier and had competed together just once before, at a meeting in Belgium approximately two weeks prior to the TT festival.

Shortly after 8.00pm the first of the sidecars set off along Glencrutchery Road towards Bray Hill on their opening lap and it was soon the turn of Lunemann & Bosman to head off on their first lap of the meeting and with the intention of completing two laps of the course. As they travelled through Union Mills, three miles out from the start line, Lunemann felt the sidecar go light momentarily as they rounded the left hand bend near to the petrol station but it settled down again and they continued towards Glen Vine.

Just over thirteen miles into the lap they were seen approaching Douglas Road Corner in Kirk Michael village. They safely negotiated the sweeping right hand bend but moments later, as they rounded the slight right hand bend outside the Mitre Hotel, Bernadette lost her grip and fell from the outfit. The unfortunate competitor then struck a stone wall just beyond the forecourt of the Isle of Man Bank on the left hand side of the road, before coming to rest in the roadway opposite the public telephone kiosk. A police officer and marshals went to her immediate assistance but there was nothing they could do for her. She had been killed instantly.

Unaware of the tragedy, Lunemann continued and on the straight section of road following Ballaugh Bridge he once again felt the sidecar go light momentarily. Due to his riding position he was unable to see the chair fully and believed that Bernadette was kneeling closer to the centre of the unit and out of his view. In Sulby Village he saw a black flag being waved and it was at this point he saw that Bernadette was no longer with him. He stopped at Sulby Bridge where a Travelling Marshal informed him what had happened.

Bernadette Bosman (nee Saalbrink), a married woman, was 40 years of age. She was a headmistress by occupation and a resident of Lelystad, Holland where she lived with her husband Peter Bosman who was on the Island with her. Although she had no children of her own, she was involved with the care of under privileged and handicapped children in Europe.

Her funeral service was held on Thursday 3rd June and followed by committal at Douglas Borough Crematorium. One of her favourite sites on the Isle of Man was the Spooyt Vane Waterfall near Kirk Michael and her ashes were later scattered there. A memorial seat was placed at that location, overlooking the waterfall.

195

Simon Anthony BECK

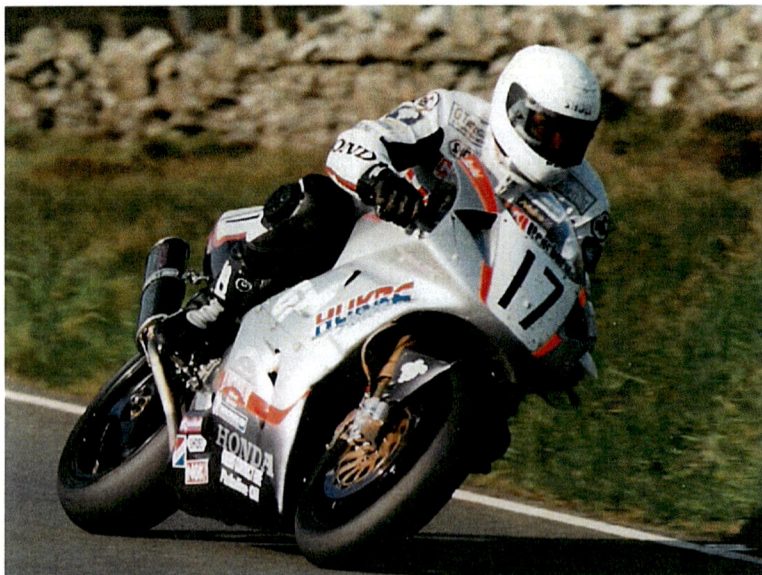

Simon Beck on the mountain section during practice for the 1999 Formula One TT

The roads around the TT course were dry on the evening of Tuesday 1st June 1999 and visibility was clear on the mountain section, which provided almost perfect racing conditions for the competitors gathered at the Grandstand in Douglas waiting to take advantage of a practice session for the Tourist Trophy races. Amongst them was former Manx Grand Prix winner Simon Beck, riding a 750cc Honda RC45 machine bearing the race number 17 and entered in the Formula I race to be held on Saturday 5th June.

Once the session had commenced it was not long before he set off along Glencrutchery Road towards Bray Hill and safely made his way round the course to complete his opening circuit of the evening with an average speed of 119.16mph, which was to be the fastest lap of any class that evening. After a few adjustments were made to his machine he set off again to commence his second lap and made his way through to Ramsey and up onto the mountain section where he was seen approaching the sweeping left hand bend at the 33rd Milestone. He was travelling at racing speed and on the usual racing line but as he negotiated the bend his rear wheel suddenly lost traction with the road surface and despite his attempts to regain control of the machine he was thrown off, coming to rest on the grassland below the road. Marshals went to his aid and did what they could for the gravely injured rider while waiting for the helicopter ambulance, which arrived on the scene just over five minutes after being called. He was conveyed to the playing fields of Ballakermeen School where he was to be transferred to an ambulance but when the helicopter landed it was found that the unfortunate rider had succumbed to his injuries.

Hector Gordon, Chief Scrutineer for the Auto-Cycle Union, later examined the crash damaged Honda and found no evidence to suggest that the accident may have been caused as the result of a mechanical failure.

Simon Beck was 30 years of age. He was a professional motorcycle racer by occupation and a resident of Leyland, Lancashire where he lived with his partner of two years, Lesley Beveridge. He made his debut on the TT course at the 1988 Manx Grand Prix when he came 4th in the Senior Newcomers race. He returned the following year and finished 13th in the Senior MGP but glory was to come in 1990 when he won the Senior Manx setting a new race record of 110.57mph and a new lap record of 113.30mph. He then turned his attentions to the TT and in 1993 he finished 3rd in the Supersport 600 race. In 1995 he finished third in the Formula I race with an average speed of 116.67mph. Following injuries sustained from a crash at the North West 200 races in Ireland he missed the 1996 TT. However, he returned in 1997 and finished 3rd in the Production Race, 5th in the Senior Race and 9th in the Formula I Race during which he recorded an average lap speed of 122.71mph. In 1998 he finished 4th in the Formula I race with a speed of 117.82mph.

Hundreds of mourners gathered to pay their last respects at his funeral service, which was held at St. Ambrose Parish Church in Moss Lane, Leyland at 11.00am on Monday 14th June.

A memorial plaque was later affixed to the roadside wall at Westwood Corner, which was one of his favourite sections of the course.

196

Terence FENTON

Mark and Terry Fenton pictured during the fateful 1999 Sidecar TT

Conditions were near perfect for racing on the afternoon of Monday 7th June 1999. The weather was fine, the roads around the TT course were dry and visibility on the mountain section was clear. On Glencrutchery Road in Douglas there were 68 sidecar outfits lined up as their crews prepared to take part in the second of the two Sidecar Tourist Trophy races. Amongst them were Mark Fenton and his passenger, Terry Fenton, his father, riding a sidecar outfit bearing the race number 53 and powered by a Honda CBR600 engine. In the first race, held two days earlier, they had finished in 21st place with a race average speed of 98.49mph.

At 1.15pm the flag dropped and the three lap race began with Dave Molyneux and his passenger Craig Hallam being the first to be sent on their way. They had won the first race on the Saturday and were clear favourites to win again. Over eight minutes later it was the turn of Mark and Terry Fenton to begin their race against the clock and they set off towards Bray Hill. Having safely negotiated their way round the course they completed the first circuit with an average speed of 98.76mph, which put them in 25th position. By the end of the second lap they had moved up into 23rd position having attained an average lap speed of 100.61mph.

On their third and final lap of the race they had made their way through to Ramsey and up over the mountain section when they were seen approaching Hillberry Corner, barely two miles from the finish line. Then, as they were negotiating the sweeping right hander, the outfit clipped the kerb on the apex of the bend and as a consequence it veered diagonally across the road before colliding heavily with the straw bales covering the boundary wall of the house "The Beeches". On impact the sidecar disintegrated and both competitors were thrown into the roadway. A doctor and a police officer immediately attended to them while marshals cleared the debris that had been strewn across the course. On examination it was found that nothing could be done for Terry Fenton. He had been killed instantly. Mark Fenton had been knocked unconscious but came round before being conveyed by the helicopter ambulance to Noble's Hospital where he was detained for three days.

The extensively damaged sidecar outfit was examined later and no evidence was found to suggest that a mechanical failure had been a contributory factor in this accident.

Terry Fenton, a married man, was 56 years of age. He was a joiner by occupation and a resident of Carlton, near Goole, North Yorkshire where he lived with his wife Sandra. They had three children, Colin, Jane and Mark. He had acted as passenger to Mark for the previous five years and was an experienced competitor, racing regularly at meetings in the United Kingdom. They enjoyed success in 1998, winning the Best National Newcomers Award, finishing 10th in only their second season in the British Sidecar Championships despite entering only half the races. Terry, the oldest passenger in the championships was also honoured with an outstanding achievement award by the sport's governing body. They made their TT debut in 1998 and did well during practice. However, on the opening lap of the Sidecar "B" race they were forced to stop and make adjustments on Bray Hill but despite the disappointment they continued and completed the race.

His funeral service was held on Friday 18th June and followed by committal at York Crematorium.

Stuart Hunter MURDOCH

Stu Murdoch at Braddan during the fateful 1999 Junior 600 TT

The weather was fine, visibility was clear and the roads around the TT course were dry on the afternoon of Wednesday 9th June 1999, which provided near perfect racing conditions for the 68 competitors assembled on Glencrutchery Road in Douglas waiting to participate in the Junior 600 Tourist Trophy Race. Amongst them was Stu Murdoch of New Zealand, riding a brand new Honda CBR600 machine bearing the race number 80. His best practice lap on this machine had been achieved on the Thursday afternoon when he recorded an average speed of 107.63mph.

At 1.15pm the flag dropped and the race began. First man away was Chris Heath who had escaped serious injury after crashing at the bottom of Barregarrow during practice week. The following riders were dispatched at ten second intervals and just over 13 minutes later it was the turn of Stu Murdoch to begin his race against the clock and he set off towards Bray Hill. He safely made his way round the course and completed his opening lap with a speed of 106.54mph, which put him in 50th position. On completion of his second circuit he had moved up to 44th position having recorded a speed of 108.65mph, which was 12 seconds inside his best practice time.

On his third lap of the race, he had made his way through Union Mills, Crosby and Greeba Bridge when he was seen approaching the sweeping right hand bend at Gorse Lea. He was travelling at racing speed and on the usual racing line but as he was negotiating the bend his machine clipped the kerb on the right and immediately went out of control. He quickly sat upright as he fought to regain control of the Honda but was unable to prevent it colliding heavily with a low stone wall and trees on the left hand side of the road. On impact the machine burst into flames and disintegrated as it tumbled along the road. Spilled fuel from the crashed machine ignited and the whole width of the road was covered in flames. The unfortunate rider came to rest in the roadway and was quickly attended to by marshals but there was nothing they could do for him. He had been killed instantly.

Hector Gordon, Chief Scrutineer for the Auto-Cycle Union, examined the wrecked Honda and found no evidence to suggest that a mechanical failure had contributed to this accident.

Jim Moodie, from Glasgow, went on to win with a race average speed of 118.11mph, 19.4 seconds ahead of David Jefferies in second place with Iain Duffus taking third.

Stuart Murdoch was 33 years of age. He was an electrician by occupation and a resident of Dunedin, New Zealand where he lived with his partner Cherie Wells. He had first raced on the Island in 1997, gaining a finishers award in the Junior TT with a race average of 106.31mph. He returned in 1998 but sustained injuries in a crash involving three machines at the top of Barregarrow on the Thursday of practice week and was unable to take part in the races the following week.

As the result of a chance remark to his partner during their time together, it was arranged that he would be late for his own funeral service which was held in Dunedin on Friday 18th June with more than 350 mourners attending. The service was followed by committal.

Martin John SMITH

Martin Smith on the mountain section during the fateful 1999 Senior MGP

The Isle of Man was bathed in sunshine on the afternoon of Friday 3rd September 1999 and conditions around the TT course were ideal for racing, which was excellent news for the competitors lined up along Glencrutchery Road in Douglas waiting to participate in the Senior Manx Grand Prix, the final race over the TT course before the new millennium. Amongst them was Martin Smith, an experienced MGP competitor, riding a Honda CBR600 machine bearing the race number 10. Two days earlier, riding the same machine in the Junior Manx, he had finished in 11th place with a race average speed of 110.32mph, a performance that earned him a coveted silver replica.

At 1.00pm the flag dropped and the race was underway with Colin Breeze being the first to set off. Forty seconds later it was the turn of Martin Smith to begin his race against the clock and he headed off towards the top of Bray Hill accompanied by his starting partner, the Irish rider Uel Duncan. He safely made his way round the course to complete his opening circuit with an average speed of 112.32mph, which put him in 11th position.

He recorded an average speed of 113.45mph on his second lap and was holding 8th position as he pulled into the pits to refuel. He took a cold drink and once his fuel tank had been replenished he set off again to commence his third lap of the race. Having made good progress through Crosby, Ballacraine and Glen Helen he was seen approaching the sweeping left hand bend at Westwood Corner just before Kirk Michael village with the 750 Yamaha of Dean Nelson, race number 6, directly ahead of him. As the two riders began to negotiate the bend it appeared that Martin Smith was attempting to pass Nelson on the outside but in order to do so he was banked over so far that the left side of his machine was scraping the road surface. Suddenly, the Honda went from beneath him, sliding across the road before mounting the footpath on the right and colliding heavily with the hedgerow just beyond the house "Westwood". The unfortunate rider came to rest in the roadway near to the point of impact with the hedge. Marshals went to his immediate assistance but there was nothing they could do for him. He had been killed instantly.

Harvey Garton, Chief Scrutineer for the Manx Motor Cycle Club, later examined the crash damaged machine at Police Headquarters in Douglas and found no evidence to suggest that a mechanical failure had contributed to this accident.

Having led from the start, Colin Breeze, riding a 750cc Kawasaki, went on to win the race with an average speed of 115.10mph and just 5.7 seconds ahead of Alastair Howarth with Keith Townsend in third place. Dean Nelson finished in 8th position.

Martin Smith was 36 years of age. He was a diesel mechanic by occupation and a resident of Oldsbury near Birmingham where he lived with his partner Paula Luton and their nine year old son Luke. He had been a regular competitor at the Manx Grand Prix since 1987 and had won several replicas.

His funeral service was held at Long Lane Methodist Church on Tuesday 14th September and followed by committal at Powke Lane Crematorium.

Stephen Philip WOOD

John Macaskill and Stephen Wood at Ballacraine during practice for the 2000 Sidecar TT

Fine weather, clear visibility and dry roads around the TT course on the evening of Monday 29th May 2000 provided ideal racing conditions for the competitors gathered at the Grandstand in Douglas waiting to take advantage of a practice session for the Sidecar Tourist Trophy Races. Amongst them were John Macaskill and his passenger, Stephen Wood, riding an outfit powered by a 600cc Yamaha engine and bearing the race number 46. The two men had been racing together for three years and while Macaskill had previous experience of racing sidecars on the TT course Wood was a newcomer. However, they had travelled to the Island the previous September to enable Wood to familiarise himself with the circuit.

Once the session was under way they set off along Glencrutchery Road towards the top of Bray Hill and safely made their way round the course through to Ramsey where, shortly after leaving Parliament Square they were seen travelling up May Hill at racing speed. Then, as they approached the left hand corner at "Whitegates" the outfit hit a bump in the road, which put them off the usual racing line to negotiate the bend. John Macaskill had a split second to make a decision and he chose to take the slip road bearing off to the right. However, Stephen Wood had already positioned himself for the left hand bend and was unprepared for the outfit suddenly turning right into Claughbane Road. The unfortunate passenger was thrown from the outfit and collided heavily with a large wooden notice board, which had been placed at the roadside to give approaching riders advance warning of the bend. He came to rest in the garden beyond the sign where marshals and a police officer went to his assistance. Meanwhile, Macaskill had continued for a short distance along the slip road and turned into the entrance of the house "The Garth" at which point he discovered that his passenger was missing. He ran back along the road to the corner to find his friend being attended to. The gravely injured competitor was placed on a stretcher and carried back down May Hill to the Coronation Park where the helicopter ambulance had landed. Further emergency medical assistance was given before he was conveyed from the scene but sadly, when the helicopter landed on the playing fields at Ballakermeen School, near to Noble's Hospital, in Douglas, it was found that he had succumbed to his injuries.

Hector Gordon, Chief Scrutineer for the ACU, examined the sidecar outfit later and found no evidence to suggest any mechanical failure or defect had contributed to this accident.

Stephen Wood was 40 years of age and a Systems Operator by occupation. He was a resident of Newcastle-upon-Tyne where he lived with his partner Jane and their three children, Amy aged nine, Ben aged three and Mikey aged two. The two men had arrived on the Island on Saturday 27th May and took part in the opening practice session later that evening. However, on their first lap the machine developed mechanical problems and they were forced to retire at the 11th Milestone. During the morning practice session on Monday 29th May, the two men were again among those taking part and went on to record an average lap speed of 82.70mph on their opening lap but were forced to retire during their second lap after they ran out of fuel at Glen Auldyn near Ramsey.

His funeral service was held in St. Mary's RC Church, Great Lime Road, Forest Hall at 10.00am on Tuesday 6th June and followed by committal at Whitley Bay Crematorium.

Christopher David ASCOTT

Chris Ascott at Ballacraine during practice for the 2000 Lightweight 400 TT

Visibility was clear and the roads around the TT course were dry on the evening of Tuesday 30th May 2000, leaving almost perfect racing conditions for the competitors congregating at the Grandstand in Douglas waiting to take advantage of a practice session for the Tourist Trophy races. Amongst them was Chris Ascott, riding a Kawasaki ZXR400 machine bearing the race number 72 and entered in the Lightweight 400 race to be held the following week. He had completed one circuit during the previous Saturday evening session and a further three on the Monday evening with the fastest lap being recorded as 97.24mph.

Once the session began he did not have long to wait before setting off along Glencrutchery Road towards Bray Hill on his opening lap of the evening and safely negotiated his way round the course back to Douglas with an average lap speed of 97.89mph. Without stopping he continued through the start area to commence his second circuit and made his way through the Glen Helen section and on towards Kirk Michael. Then, at about 7.30pm, he was seen, in close company behind three other riders, approaching the bends at Cronk Urleigh, just beyond the 13th Milestone. On reaching the first right hander the riders ahead of him reduced speed slightly in order to negotiate the bends but he left his braking a fraction too late and his front wheel touched the rear wheel of the machine directly in front of him. He immediately sat upright and braked hard but was unable to avoid colliding with the trees on the left. The unfortunate rider was thrown from his machine and came to rest in the roadway where marshals went to his aid and on finding no signs of life they began resuscitation efforts while waiting for the helicopter ambulance, which arrived on the scene less than five minutes after being called. However, it was found that there was nothing more that could be done for him. He had been killed instantly. The other rider had continued unscathed, probably unaware of the tragedy behind him.

Hector Gordon, Chief Scrutineer for the Auto-Cycle Union, later carried out an examination of the wrecked Kawasaki and found no evidence to suggest that a mechanical failure may have contributed towards this accident.

Chris Ascott, a married man, was 36 years of age and a Production/Warehouse Manager with SKF Engineering. He was a resident of Wingrave near Aylesbury, Buckinghamshire where he lived with his wife Sue and their eight year old son, Jamie. He was an experienced racing motorcyclist and had been crowned East Midlands Racing Association Champion in 1998. On the Isle of Man he had competed in the Ultra Lightweight TT in 1999 when he finished 24th and had also competed in the North West 200 races in Ireland for three years. In addition to motorcycle racing he was also active in other sports such as skiing and sailing.

His funeral service was held on Monday 12th June and followed by committal at Amersham Crematorium. A memorial plaque was later attached to the roadside wall of Cronk Urleigh Lodge situated near to the scene of the accident.

Later in the year a cheque for £2,500, which had been raised in his memory by family and friends, was presented to the accident and emergency unit of Noble's Hospital. The money was to be used to purchase a volumetric infusion pump, a critical item of equipment used for treating patients who had sustained multiple injuries.

Raymond HANNA

Ray Hanna at Ballaugh Bridge during practice for the 2000 Lightweight 250 TT

Apart from the possibility of the rising sun being troublesome between Kirk Michael and Ramsey on the morning of Wednesday 31st May 2000 conditions around the TT course were described as almost perfect for racing, which was welcome news for the competitors gathered at the Grandstand in Douglas waiting to take advantage of a practice session for the Tourist Trophy Races. Amongst them was the race veteran Ray Hanna, riding a Yamaha TZ250 machine bearing the race number 30 and entered in the Lightweight 250 race to be held the following Monday. Riding the same machine during practice the previous evening, he had recorded an average lap speed of 102.48mph.

Practising commenced at 5.15am with the first part restricted to the larger machines. Then, at 6.05am it was the chance of the smaller machines and during this period Ray Hanna set off along Glencrutchery Road towards the top of Bray Hill and had safely made his way through Union Mills, Glen Vine and Crosby when he was seen approaching the bends at Greeba Castle, just five miles into his opening lap of the morning. He negotiated the first left hand bend then banked over for the following right hander but as he did so the front wheel of the Yamaha suddenly went from beneath him and he went down. The unfortunate rider slid along the road, past the entrance to Greeba Castle and collided with the straw bales covering the stone wall on the left side of the road. At almost the same instant, he was struck by his machine, which had slid along the road behind him and at this point his helmet came off. He came to rest in the roadway alongside the straw bales while his machine came to a stop on the opposite side of the road along with his helmet. Marshals went to his immediate aid but found there was nothing they could do for him. He had been killed instantly.

Later that same morning, Hector Gordon, Chief Scrutineer for the ACU, examined the Yamaha and found impact damage to the front wheel and fork assembly. The throttle was free to operate, all gears could be selected and the engine was free. Nothing was found to suggest that a mechanical failure might have contributed towards the accident.

Ray Hanna was 49 years of age and the father of two daughters, Amanda and Petula from his previous marriage. He was a loom fitter by occupation and a resident of Tandragee, County Armagh, Northern Ireland where he lived with his long term partner, Sandra. He was described as a father figure to many of the sport's competitors and was renowned for his kind nature and readiness to help those in need. He had achieved an impressive record during a race career spanning 30 years, winning the Irish Road Racing 200cc championship in 1998 and 1999. During the 1990's he recorded three victories in the 200cc at his home track, the Tandragee 100. He had a wealth of experience on the TT course having made his debut during the 1984 TT and in 1986 he produced possibly his best result on the course when he finished 12th in the Lightweight 250 TT. He went on to take 13th place in the 1994 Ultra Lightweight TT and then in the 1999 Lightweight 250 TT he finished in 18th position with a race average speed of 106.22mph, just missing out on a bronze replica.

His funeral service was held at Tandragee Free Presbyterian Church on Sunday 4th June and followed by interment at Seagoe Cemetery. With over five hundred mourners attending the church service, extra seats had to be provided outside the church.

Leslie WILLIAMS

Les Williams in Kirk Michael village moments before his fateful accident in the 2000 Production TT

Wet weather conditions prevailed across the Isle of Man on Friday 9th June 2000 and the Production Tourist Trophy race scheduled to commence at 10.45am was postponed until late in the afternoon when the Clerk of the Course, announced that the race would begin at 4.30pm and be reduced from three laps to two. Not the best of news for the 59 riders competing in the race as they lined up along Glencrutchery Road in Douglas. Amongst them was Les Williams, riding a Honda VTR1000-SP1 machine bearing the race number 34. During the Wednesday morning practice session, he achieved an average lap speed of 111.58mph on this machine.

The roads were still wet when the flag eventually dropped and local resident Richard "Milky" Quayle was the first to set off towards Bray Hill followed ten seconds later by Nigel Davies from Llanelli. Five and a half minutes after Quayle started it was the turn of Les Williams to begin his race against the clock and he set off on his opening lap of the race. Despite the poor conditions he made good progress and by Kirk Michael village he had passed three other riders. However, less than two miles further along the course, having negotiated the bends coming in to Ballaugh village, he was seen travelling along the straight section on the approach to the bridge when his front wheel suddenly went from beneath him and the Honda dropped onto its right hand side. The unfortunate rider slid across the wet road along with his machine and collided heavily with a stone wall on the right. He came to rest on the roadway immediately outside the car showrooms on the left side of the road while his machine eventually came to a stop on Ballaugh Bridge. Marshals and police officers went quickly to his aid and did what they could for him while waiting for the helicopter ambulance, which arrived on the scene within five minutes of being called. The gravely injured rider was conveyed to the playing fields of Ballakermeen School in Douglas then transferred to an ambulance, which carried him the short distance to Noble's Hospital where, despite the best efforts of the medical staff, he succumbed to his injuries at around 12 noon the following day.

Hector Gordon, Chief Scrutineer for the ACU, later examined the relatively unscathed Honda and found no evidence to suggest that a mechanical failure was responsible for the accident.

With conditions at their worst on the mountain section of the course, several riders pulled in and retired at the end of the first lap. David Jefferies, riding a Yamaha R1, went on to win with an average speed of 98.58mph. Richard Quayle finished second with Michael Rutter taking third place.

Les Williams, a single man, was 41 years of age. He was a Quantity Surveyor by occupation and a resident of Ormskirk, Lancashire where he lived with his mother Edith and brother Chris. His first appearance on the TT course was at the 1997 Manx Grand Prix when he finished 4th in the Junior Newcomers Race. He returned in 1998, finishing 10th in the Junior Race and 11th in the Senior. In 1999 he finished 4th in the Junior and was lying 5th in the Senior when he was forced to retire at Creg ny Baa on the last lap of the race.

His funeral service was held in Ormskirk Parish Church at 11.00am on 19th June and was followed by interment.

Donald Kenneth MUNRO

Kenny Munro at Braddan Bridge during his fateful practice lap for the 2000 Junior MGP

Conditions were described as near perfect all round the TT course on the evening of Saturday 19th August 2000, which was good news for the competitors gathered at the Grandstand in Douglas waiting to take part in the opening practice session for the Manx Grand Prix. Amongst them was Kenny Munro, riding a Honda CBR600 machine bearing the race number 15 and entered in the Junior race to be held on Wednesday 30th August.

Although scheduled to commence at 6.15pm there was a delay due to a road traffic accident at Ballig Bridge prior to roads closing. Eventually the first part of the session commenced at 7.00pm and this was restricted to Classic, Newcomers and Ultra Lightweight machines. Then, at 7.30pm the second part of the session began and during this period Kenny Munro set off along Glencrutchery Road towards the top of Bray Hill on his opening lap of the meeting. In the paddock he had told his girlfriend Catherine Whittaker that his intention was to complete two steady laps of the course. He had safely made his way through Glen Helen and Ballaugh when he was seen approaching Sulby Bridge with Derek Heron close behind him. An oil spillage on the bridge had been covered with cement dust and to avoid riding through the dust he moved over to the left while Heron moved to the right. As he accelerated away from the bridge he was still marginally ahead of Heron but moments later as he negotiated the left hand bend at the Ginger Hall Hotel his helmet caught the iron railings on the left. As a consequence his machine straightened up and veered across the road to the right, mounted the footpath and collided with the hedge. The unfortunate rider was thrown against a road sign and came to rest on the footpath while his machine rebounded back into the roadway and struck Heron's machine. Fortunately, Derek Heron was able to maintain control but, in a state of shock, he pulled in and retired a short distance beyond the point of the incident. Marshals went to the immediate assistance of the gravely injured rider and did what they could for him while waiting for the helicopter ambulance, which arrived on the scene just over five minutes after being called. He was conveyed to the playing fields at Ballakermeen School in Douglas then transferred to an ambulance, which carried him the short distance to Noble's Hospital where he was admitted at 8.10pm, less than 20 minutes after the accident occurred. However, despite the best efforts of the medical staff, he succumbed to his injuries 25 minutes later.

Harvey Garton, Chief Scrutineer for the Manx Motor Cycle Club, later examined the Honda and found no evidence to suggest that a mechanical failure had contributed to this accident.

Kenny Munro was 45 years of age. He was a motorcycle mechanic by occupation and a resident of Burscough, Lancashire where he lived with his mother Edna. Married twice, he was the father of two daughters, Stacey aged 16 and Stephanie aged 9. He had considerable racing experience during the 1980's but had then retired from the sport. However, he returned to motorcycle racing in 1999 and made his debut on the TT course at the Manx Grand Prix, finishing second to Ryan Farquhar in the Senior Newcomers race then later in the week he finished 19th in the Senior Manx.

His funeral service was held in Burscough Parish Church at 1.30pm on 29th August and followed by interment. A poignant feature of this tragedy was that his elder brother Roddy had also lost his life years earlier after the motorcycle he was riding collided with a van in 1971.

Colin Derrick DANIELS

Colin Daniels turning into Parliament Square, Ramsey during practice for the 2002 Production 600 TT

Following the cancellation of the Tourist Trophy races in 2001 due to the foot and mouth epidemic, racing was back on the Island in 2002 and on the evening of Monday 27th May the weather conditions were almost perfect for racing as riders prepared for the third practice session of the meeting. Amongst them was Colin Daniels, riding a 600cc Suzuki machine bearing the race number 88 and entered in the Production 600 race to be held on Friday 7th June. He had been out on this machine during the practice session that morning and on the Saturday evening, completing two laps in each session with his best average lap speed being recorded at 103.35mph on the Saturday.

The roads closed at 6.00pm and fifteen minutes later the first of the competitors were sent on their way round the course. Just a handful of riders had left before Colin Daniels set off along Glencrutchery Road towards the top of Bray Hill on his opening lap of the evening. However, less than 25 seconds later he was seen fighting to regain control of the Suzuki, which had suddenly developed a "tank slapper" half way down Bray Hill, but his efforts were in vain as the machine went down on its side. Both he and his machine then slid diagonally across the road, mounted the footpath on the right and collided heavily with the low garden wall of the house "Cronk Aash". Following impact with the wall, momentum carried the unfortunate rider along the footpath and across the road junction before he crashed into the wooden fence fronting the garden of number 1, Port-e-Chee Avenue. He came to rest on the footpath by the fence and was quickly attended to by spectators and police officers who did what they could for him while waiting for an ambulance to arrive on the scene. The gravely injured rider was then conveyed to Noble's Hospital where, despite immediate resuscitation procedures, he succumbed to his injuries at around 6.45pm that same evening.

Chief Scrutineer, Harvey Garton, later examined the Suzuki machine at Police Headquarters, Douglas. The tyres were brand new before the session and neither the engine nor gearbox had seized. No evidence was found to suggest that a mechanical failure had been a contributory factor in this incident.

Colin Daniels was 42 years of age. He was an electrician by occupation and a resident of Stockport where he lived with his wife Yvonne and their two children, Scott aged 23 years and Leanne aged 18 years. Having ridden motorcycles from a very young age he had only taken up racing in the mid 1990's, competing on circuits near his home and at Mallory Park. He made his debut on the TT course in the 1998 Manx Grand Prix, finishing 8th in the Senior Newcomers race on a 600 Suzuki with a race average speed of 99.37mph, which earned him a coveted silver replica. Later that same week he was awarded a further replica after he finished 47th in the Senior Manx with a race average speed of 104.14mph. Returning the following year, he finished 56th in the Junior Race and 32nd in the Senior, gaining another silver replica. In 2000 he earned two further replicas after taking 23rd place in the Junior MGP and an outstanding 7th place in the Senior with a race average speed of 111.71mph.

Over 300 mourners attended his funeral service, which was held at St. Thomas's Church, Hillgate, Stockport at 11.45am on Wednesday 5th June and followed by committal at Stockport Crematorium.

Shane Maurant ELLIS

Shane Ellis leaves Parliament Square, Ramsey during practice for the 2002 Senior Newcomers MGP

Weather conditions were almost perfect for racing on the morning of Monday 19th August 2002 as competitors gathered at the Grandstand in Douglas waiting to participate in an untimed practice session for the Manx Grand Prix. Amongst them, fulfilling a lifetime ambition to compete on the TT course was Shane Ellis, riding a 1000cc Aprilia machine bearing the race number 7 and entered in the Senior Newcomer's race to be held the following Monday morning. Two days earlier, he had ridden this machine during the opening practice session, which had also been untimed and although he was able to attain high speeds on the lower parts of the course he had to slow to around 30mph on some areas of the mountain section due to thick mist and damp roads.

The roads closed at 5.55am and practising commenced at 6.10am. During the course of the session Shane Ellis set off along Glencrutchery Road towards Bray Hill on his opening lap of the morning. Being a newcomer to the Island he was obliged to wear a bright orange jacket over the top of his leathers during practice, which indicated his inexperience on the course. He had safely made his way through Union Mills, Crosby and Greeba when he was seen approaching the sharp right hand bend at Ballacraine with three other competitors in close company behind him. He was immediately ahead of Les Turner, riding a 600cc Yamaha bearing the Junior race number 92 as all four riders rounded the corner and headed along the short straight section of road towards the sweeping left hand bend at Ballaspur. Seconds later, with Turner almost up alongside him, he began to negotiate the bend and at that moment the two machines collided. Both machines immediately went out of control and crashed into the trees on the right hand side of the road. The wrecked Aprilia rebounded back into the roadway and into the path of the following two riders, Gail Musson and Andy Russell, but they managed to avoid the debris and continued on their way round the course. Marshals went to the immediate assistance of the fallen riders and found them lying in the grass field beyond the trees along with the extensively damaged Yamaha but there was nothing that could be done for them. They had both been killed instantly.

The two machines were later examined at Police Headquarters in Douglas by official scrutineers and no evidence was revealed to suggest that the accident had been caused due to a mechanical failure.

Shane Ellis was 39 years of age and the father to two children. He was a Photo Journalist by occupation and a resident of Chesterfield. His partner, Lydia Cooper, received a letter from him on the morning of the accident and stated later that this was to be his last race before they married and settled down. Several years earlier Shane, a former paratrooper, had been involved in a near fatal crash which left him with a broken neck and wheelchair bound for a considerable length of time but he recovered from his injuries and returned to the sport that he loved. Earlier in the season he had competed in the Northwest 200 and the Dundrod 150 races in Ireland.

His funeral service was held at Newstead Village Hall on Monday 2nd September and was followed by interment at Kingsway Cemetery, Kirkby with a guard of honour formed by the Kirkby branch of the Royal British Legion.

Leslie James TURNER

Les Turner in Parliament Square, Ramsey during practice for the 2002 Senior MGP

Reports of almost perfect weather conditions across the Isle of Man on the morning of Monday 19th August 2002 provided welcome news for the large number of competitors gathered at the Grandstand in Douglas waiting to take advantage of the second untimed practice session for the Manx Grand Prix. Amongst them was Les Turner, riding a 600cc Yamaha machine bearing the race number 92 and entered in the Junior race to be held the following week. On the Saturday evening two days earlier he had taken part in the opening practice session and this had given him the opportunity to test his other machine, a 750cc Suzuki, which had been entered in the Senior race.

The roads closed at 5.55am and practising commenced at 6.10am. During the practice period Les Turner set off along Glencrutchery Road towards Quarterbridge on his opening lap of the morning. He had safely made his way through Braddan, Glen Vine and Gorse Lea when, with seven miles of the course behind him, he was seen approaching Ballacraine with Shane Ellis, a newcomer riding a 1000cc Aprilia, immediately in front of him. Behind them were two other riders, Gail Musson and Andy Russell, both on smaller capacity machines. After taking the tight right hand corner he accelerated away and up towards the sweeping left hander at Ballaspur. Seconds later, he was almost alongside Shane Ellis as they began to negotiate the bend but it quickly became obvious that they were both taking the same racing line, he braked hard and tried to cut back behind the Aprilia but was unable to avoid a collision. In an instant, the two machines went out of control and crashed into the trees on the right hand side of the road. The wrecked Aprilia rebounded back into the roadway and across the path of Musson and Russell but fortunately they were able to avoid the debris and continued on their way round the course. Marshals went to the assistance of the two fallen riders and found them lying in the grass field beyond the trees along with the extensively damaged Yamaha but there was nothing that could be done for them. They had both been killed instantly.

Scrutineers later examined both the Aprilia and the Yamaha at Police Headquarters in Douglas and found no evidence on either machine to suggest that a mechanical failure had contributed towards the accident.

Les Turner, a single man, was 31 years of age. He was a self employed landscape gardener by occupation and a resident of Orpington, Kent. He started motorcycle racing in 1996 and competed at all the top circuits in the UK but it was at Brands Hatch where he won his first Powerbike race in July 1999, the first of seven trophy wins at the track. He added two more victories in the Powerbike and Supersport series at Brands Hatch in 2000. However, like many others, he ranked the Isle of Man among his most favourite racing venues and made his debut on the Island at the Manx Grand Prix in 2000. Riding a 600cc Honda he finished 12th in the Senior Newcomer's race with a race average speed of 101.58mph.

A measure of his popularity was emphasised when a one minute silence was held as a mark of respect for him at the Brands Hatch and Snetterton race meetings the following Monday.

His funeral service was held on Thursday 5th September and followed by committal at Falconwood Crematorium, Eltham, London.

Philip Richard HAYHURST

Philip Hayhurst at Ballacraine during the fateful 2002 Ultra Lightweight MGP

Unlike the previous day when the forecast of bad weather had forced the postponement of racing, conditions on the morning of Saturday 31st August 2002 were almost perfect for racing as the 54 competitors for the four lap Ultra Lightweight Manx Grand Prix lined up along Glencrutchery Road in Douglas waiting for the race to commence. Amongst them was Philip Hayhurst, riding a 124cc Yamaha machine bearing the race number 87. During practice his fastest average lap speed on this machine had been achieved on the Wednesday evening when he recorded 92.73mph.

Shortly after 10.15am the race began with Paul Corrin of Onchan being the first of the competitors to set off towards the top of Bray Hill. Just under three minutes later it was the turn of Philip Hayhurst to begin his race against the clock and he safely made his way round the course to complete his first circuit with an average speed of 91.41mph, which put him in 39th position. On completion of his second lap he pulled into the pit lane where his wife, Jenny, refuelled the Yamaha. He had recorded a lap average of 92.28mph and had moved up two places. With the fuel tank replenished he set off again to commence his third lap and had made his way through to Lezayre Road in Ramsey when he was seen approaching the left hand bend known as School House Corner. He was alone on the road and travelling at racing speed as he leaned over to negotiate the corner but as he did so the machine suddenly went from beneath him and he went down. The unfortunate rider and his machine then slid along the road before colliding heavily with the earth bank beside the gateway of the house "Ballaghennie". Marshals went to his immediate assistance and found him lying in the roadway. He was quickly carried to the side of the road but there was nothing that could be done for him. He had been killed instantly.

Scrutineers examined the Yamaha later the same day and found no evidence to suggest that a mechanical failure had contributed to this accident.

Setting a new race record average speed of 105.00mph, Alan Bennie went on to win the race just six tenths of a second ahead of Paul Corrin with Andy Russell taking third place.

Philip Hayhurst was 45 years of age and the father of Louise, aged 20 years. He was a welder by occupation and a resident of Milnthorpe, Cumbria where he lived with his wife Jenny. He had first raced on the Isle of Man at the Manx Grand Prix in 2000 when he finished 18th in the Junior Classic race which earned him a coveted silver replica. Later the same week he finished 24th in the Lightweight Race.

His funeral service was held at Preston Patrick Parish Church at 1.15pm on Monday 16th September and followed by committal at Lancaster Crematorium.

The day after the incident, his brother, Andrew Hayhurst, travelled to the Isle of Man to make necessary arrangements. While on the Island Andrew learned that his partner, Pamela Graham who lived with him in Sedburgh, had been involved in a serious road traffic accident in Cumbria. She had been driving her Mitsubishi Shogun when it left a country road and plunged into Killington Lake. Although pulled from the submerged vehicle by two police officers she died several hours later in Lancaster Infirmary.

Alan David JEFFERIES

David Jefferies at Union Mills during practice for the 2003 Formula One TT

Conditions were near perfect for racing on the afternoon of Thursday 29th May 2003, the roads around the TT course were dry and visibility on the mountain section was clear, which was welcome news for the competitors assembled at the Grandstand in Douglas waiting to participate in a practice session for the Tourist Trophy Races. Amongst them was nine times TT winner David Jefferies, riding a Suzuki GSX-R1000 machine bearing the race number 1 and entered in the Formula One race to be held on Saturday 31st May.

The session commenced at 1.45pm and it was not long before he set off towards Bray Hill and safely made his way round the course to complete his first circuit of the afternoon with an average lap speed of 125.20mph, then, without stopping, he embarked on his second lap. Meanwhile, minutes earlier, Daniel Jansen had been passing Marown Church when his 1000cc Suzuki suffered a major engine failure and left a large cloud of smoke in his trail as he coasted into Crosby village then pulled onto the footpath outside "Crosby Villas". Adam Nowell, the rider directly behind him, later stated that he had been left covered in oil but was able to carry on and complete his lap. A marshal began walking back along the course towards the church looking for signs of oil spillage or debris and had found none when David Jefferies appeared, travelling at an estimated 160mph and about 20 yards behind his Suzuki team mate Adrian Archibald. They had just passed the church hall and were negotiating the slight kink going into Crosby when the rear wheel of David Jefferies machine suddenly stepped out to the right. He had no chance to regain control of the machine and collided heavily with a stone wall on the right hand side of the road. The big Suzuki then tumbled across the road and struck a telegraph pole, which snapped, bringing a telephone wire down into the road. Marshals went to the assistance of the unfortunate rider but there was nothing they could do for him. He had been killed instantly. Adrian Archibald had experienced no difficulties in that area and had continued round the course unaware of the tragedy that had occurred behind him. A short time later, Jim Moodie, attempted to pass through the debris at a greatly reduced speed but was injured when the dislodged telephone wire was drawn across his neck. He was admitted to Noble's Hospital and kept overnight before being discharged the next day.

Following conflicting opinions that oil on the road surface had been the cause of the accident the Coroner of Inquests later determined that the evidence certainly suggested there might well have been oil on the road when the accident occurred.

David Jefferies, a single man, was 30 years of age. He was a professional motorcycle racer by occupation and a resident of Baildon, Yorkshire. He made his debut on the TT course in 1996, finishing 10th in the Production TT, 16th in the Junior and 16th in the Senior. From thereon he became a regular at the meeting and in 1999 he won the Formula One, Production and Senior races. He repeated that magnificent performance the following year, winning the Production, Junior and Senior races then, in 2002 he recorded a further three victories, winning the Production 1000, Formula One and Senior races taking his total to nine TT wins.

His funeral service was held on Friday 13th June at St. Peter's Church in Shipley, West Yorkshire where loudspeakers relayed the service to the hundreds of mourners gathered outside. The service was followed by a private ceremony at Nab Wood Crematorium.

Peter Karl JARMANN

Peter Jarmann on Glencrutchery Road preparing to take part in the 2003 ACU lap of honour

On the evening of Monday 2nd June 2003, the weather was fine and the roads were dry, almost perfect conditions for the large number of riders gathered at the grandstand on Glencrutchery Road in Douglas waiting to take part in the ACU lap of honour. There was an original entry list of 135 riders. Amongst them was Peter Jarmann from Switzerland riding a 1964 Bultaco TSS 250 machine bearing the entry number 71. Earlier that day, riding a Kawasaki 400 machine, he had competed in the Lightweight 400 Race and finished in 9th position with a race average speed of 102.49mph.

The parade commenced at about 6.15pm, three hours later than scheduled because of delays to racing during the earlier part of the day. Several machines had been dispatched from the start line before Jarmann received his signal to commence his parade lap. Alongside him on his right was Jim Weeks riding a 1972 Suzuki T500 machine bearing the entry number 31. Jarmann accelerated away faster and pulled slightly ahead but Weeks quickly caught up and passed him but as he did so he missed a gear, which allowed Jarmann to go slightly ahead again. Then, as they travelled through St. Ninians crossroads, at an estimated 80-100mph, the rear wheel of the Bultaco suddenly locked and Jarmann was thrown from the machine. Either he or his machine struck Jim Weeks on the left shoulder but it was not a heavy blow and Weeks was able to maintain control of his Suzuki as he continued his descent of Bray Hill. The unfortunate Peter Jarmann slid along the road on his back, mounted the footpath on the right hand side of the road and collided heavily with the boundary wall of 63 Bray Hill before coming to rest lying face down in the centre of the road. The Bultaco machine came to rest at the edge of the roadway outside 47 Bray Hill. Spectators, marshals and police officers quickly attended to him but he showed no signs of life. Continual resuscitation attempts were made before he was conveyed by ambulance to Noble's Hospital where, at 6.40pm it was confirmed that he had succumbed to his injuries.

An examination of the Bultaco machine by Chris Rowe, Deputy Chief Scrutineer revealed that the engine had suffered a "cold seizure" which is caused when the engine is not up to working temperature and there is a partial seizure of the piston and cylinder due to uneven cooling.

Peter Jarmann, a single man, was 46 years of age. He was a motorcycle shop proprietor by occupation and lived in Uzwil, Switzerland. He had been racing motor cycles all over Europe for many years and had first competed on the TT course in the Isle of Man during the 1991 MGP when, riding a 750 Honda, he took part in the Newcomers Race and finished in 14th place. His association with the TT races began in 1994 and from thereon he became a regular visitor with his best result coming during the 1999 Lightweight 400 TT when he finished in 9th place. He was a very experienced competitor at the Southern 100 races on the Billown Circuit in the Isle of Man and had in fact raced the Bultaco there during the Pre TT Classic races just a few days before his accident.

His funeral service took place at 2.00pm on Friday 13th June and was followed by committal at Douglas Borough Crematorium.

Martin FARLEY

Martin Farley at the Gooseneck during the fateful 2003 Senior Newcomers MGP

With the announcement from the Clerk of the Course that conditions were just about perfect for racing on the morning of Monday 25th August 2003, the competitors entered in the Manx Grand Prix Newcomers Race began to line up along Glencrutchery Road in Douglas. Amongst those taking part in the Senior Class of the race was Martin Farley, riding a 599cc Yamaha R6 machine bearing the race number 40. He had completed 14 laps on this machine during practice, achieving his best average lap speed of 110.74mph on the Friday evening.

All competitors were informed that during the first lap of the race there would be oil flags displayed on Bray Hill and at Parliament Square in Ramsey, otherwise the roads around the TT course were dry and visibility was clear on the mountain section. At 10.15am the flag dropped and the race commenced with the Irishman Alex Donaldson being the first away. The remaining riders followed in pairs and at ten second intervals. Just over three minutes later it was the turn of Martin Farley to begin his race against the clock and as his starting partner, Clive Williams, was posted as a non-starter he was alone as he set off towards Bray Hill. He safely made his way round the course and completed his opening lap with an average speed of 111.28mph, which placed him in 6th position, just 26 seconds behind the race leader. On completion of his second circuit he pulled into the pit lane to refuel and having recorded an average lap speed of 111.86mph he had now moved up into 5th place. By the end of his third lap he had maintained his race position with an average speed of 110.27mph.

During his fourth and final lap of the race, he had made his way through Crosby, Glen Helen and Kirk Michael when he was seen, alone on the road and travelling at racing speed, approaching the sweeping right hand bend at Alpine Corner. However, observers noted that he was not on the usual racing line to safely negotiate the bend and at the last moment he appeared to realise his predicament but by then he had no chance of taking the bend. In an instant, the machine mounted the footpath on the left and collided heavily with the straw bales covering the boundary wall of Alpine Cottage. The unfortunate rider was thrown over the wall and through trees before coming to rest in the garden of the house while his Yamaha flew high into the air and came to rest on the right hand side of the road on the exit of the bend. Along with marshals, the doctor from the helicopter ambulance stationed at Alpine went to his assistance but there was nothing that could be done for him. He had been killed instantly.

Harvey Garton, Chief Scrutineer for the Manx Grand Prix, later examined the Yamaha and found no evidence to suggest that a mechanical failure had contributed towards this accident.

Ian Hutchinson from Bingley went on to win the race with an advantage of just 2.8 seconds over Jonathon Ralph who had led for the first three laps. Alex Donaldson took third place.

Martin Farley was 36 years of age. He was a maintenance engineer by occupation and a resident of Wakefield where he lived with his wife Julie and their two young children, Louise and Callum. After a long absence from the sport he made a return to motorcycle racing in 2002, competing at circuits such as Croft and Scarborough.

His funeral service was held at Lawnswood Crematorium, Leeds on Thursday 11th September.

Serge Henri Pierre Le MOAL

Serge Le Moal at the Quarterbridge on his fateful lap during practice for the 2004 Ultra Lightweight 125 TT

Although it had been raining on the morning of Saturday 29th May 2004 and thick mist covered the mountain section of the TT course, conditions had slowly improved throughout the day and by 6.00pm the roads were dry and the mist had been replaced by blue skies. However, there was a stiff breeze blowing in from the southwest but overall it was good news for the competitors gathered at the grandstand in Douglas waiting to take advantage of the opening practice session for the TT races. Amongst them was the Frenchman, Serge Le Moal, a newcomer to the TT course, riding a five year old 125cc Honda RS machine bearing the race number 18 and entered in the Ultra Lightweight 125 TT to be held on Monday 7th June.

Since his arrival on the Island on Wednesday 26th May he had experienced problems with his road bike and had to borrow a machine in order to familiarise himself with the course but still only managed to complete one full circuit on open roads prior to the start of practising.

Shortly after 6.15pm the first of the riders were sent on their way and Serge Le Moal followed a short time later. As a newcomer he was obliged to wear an orange jacket over his leathers to indicate his inexperience on the TT course. He made his way along Glencrutchery Road towards the top of Bray Hill then through to the Quarterbridge where he was seen to travel wide as he negotiated the slow right hand bend. Moments later he was seen approaching Braddan Bridge at full racing speed with the 400cc Kawasaki of Manfred Vogl close behind him. However, he was positioned on the left hand side of the road whereas he should have moved over to the right in order to negotiate the first of the two bends. Without reducing speed he continued straight on until the last second when he suddenly realised his situation and dropped the machine onto it's left hand side but it was too late, both rider and machine slid across the road, mounted the footpath on the right and collided heavily with straw bales covering a stone wall. The unfortunate rider came to rest at the side of the road while his machine came to a stop in the centre of the road ten yards beyond him. He was barely two miles from the grandstand and probably only just over a minute into his first ever official lap of the TT course. Marshals, together with the crew of the Phil Hogg Motorsport Ambulance, which was stationed nearby, went to his aid and found his condition to be serious. The gravely injured rider was conveyed by ambulance to the newly opened Noble's Hospital in Braddan, a short distance from the scene of the accident. However, upon his admission at 6.37pm it was found that he had succumbed to his injuries.

The Honda motorcycle was later examined at Police Headquarters, Douglas and nothing was found to suggest that the accident had been as the result of a mechanical failure.

Serge Le Moal was 44 years of age. He was a self employed carpenter by occupation and a resident of Lamballe, France where he lived with his wife Lydie and their young daughter. He was also father to two older daughters from a previous marriage. He had been racing motorcycles of various sizes on circuits for five years and had been a regular competitor in the French Open Championships.

His funeral service was held in St. Brieuc, France on Wednesday 16th June and was followed by committal. His ashes were later interred in the cemetery at Planguenoual, Cotes D'Armor.

John Paul COWLEY

Glyn Jones and Paul Cowley at White Gates during practice for the 2004 Sidecar TT

Despite the threat of rain on the evening of Wednesday 2nd June 2004 the weather had remained fine and the roads around the TT course were dry, providing almost perfect racing conditions for the competitors gathered at the grandstand in Douglas waiting to take advantage of a practice session for the Sidecar Tourist Trophy races. Amongst them were Glyn Jones and his passenger Paul Cowley riding an outfit powered by a 600cc Yamaha engine and bearing the race number 17. During practice on the Monday evening Paul had escaped injury after falling from the outfit at Ramsey Hairpin then on the Tuesday evening they had been forced to retire following a collision with another sidecar.

Prior to the Wednesday evening session the crews were issued with a written notice urging them to take extra care following a higher than usual number of incidents and particular concern was expressed at the number of passengers who had fallen from their outfits. Three passengers had fallen out on Monday and a further two on Tuesday.

The session commenced shortly after 8.00pm and the pair set off along Glencrutchery Road towards the descent of Bray Hill. They had safely negotiated their way as far as Ballacraine when they were black flagged for what was thought to be a suspected puncture but having made a thorough check of the outfit, together with the Travelling Marshal, no fault was found and they were allowed to continue. They went on to complete their opening lap and having recorded an average lap speed of 96.83mph they stopped at the grandstand where the sidecar was checked over and both men had a drink of water before setting off again. They had safely made their way through to the tricky Glen Helen section of the course when they were seen approaching the bends at the Black Dub, nine miles into their second lap of the evening. As they rounded the first left hand bend Paul switched his position from the left side of the outfit over to the right in readiness for the following right hand bend but as he did so he lost his grip and fell from the sidecar. He then collided heavily with the grass banking on the left before coming to rest, unconscious, in the centre of the road. A doctor and marshals who had been stationed in the location of the Black Dub quickly attended to the unfortunate competitor and did what they could for him while waiting for the helicopter ambulance, which arrived on the scene just over five minutes after being called. The gravely injured rider was conveyed to Noble's Hospital, Braddan where he was admitted at 9.35pm but despite the best efforts of the medical staff he succumbed to his injuries ten minutes later. Unaware of what had happened Glyn Jones had continued along the course but once he realised that his passenger was no longer with him he pulled in and stopped just before Sarah's Cottage.

Paul Cowley was 22 years of age and had formerly spent four years in the Royal Air Force where he worked as a gas turbine engineer, helping to build jet engines for Tornado fighters. Although originally from the Isle of Man he was a resident of Lincolnshire where he lived with his partner, Teresa Jefferey who was pregnant with their first child, He was also a stepfather to Teresa's five year old daughter Sophie. He was an experienced sidecar passenger and in 2003 had taken part in the British Sidecar Championships with driver Ian Ashley.

His funeral service was held at 1.15pm on Friday 18th June and followed by committal at Douglas Borough Crematorium. His daughter, Shauna, was born on 11th October 2004.

Colin Stewart BREEZE

Colin Breeze at Ballacraine during the fateful 2004 Formula One TT

As predicted, the thick mist that covered the Snaefell Mountain Road earlier in the day had cleared by the afternoon on Saturday 5th June 2004, which was good news for the competitors lined up along Glencrutchery Road in Douglas awaiting the start of the Formula One race. Amongst them was Colin Breeze, riding a 1000cc Suzuki GSXR machine bearing the race number 22 and on which he had achieved a lap speed of 120.01mph during practice.

At 2.00pm the flag dropped and the race was underway. Three minutes later it was the turn of Colin Breeze to begin his race against the clock and he set off towards the top of Bray Hill then safely made his way round the course to complete his first circuit with an average lap speed of 119.59mph, which put him in 16th position. On completion of his second lap he pulled into the pit lane to refuel. An average lap speed of 119.63mph had helped to move him up two places on the leaderboard. Nothing was said between him and his pit crew, which indicated to them that he had no concerns about the machine. With his tank replenished he set off again and had safely negotiated his way through Ballacraine, Kirk Michael and Ballaugh when he was seen approaching Quarry Bends, almost 18 miles into his third lap. He was alone on the road and travelling at racing speed. He took the first right hander then banked over to negotiate the following left hander but on doing so his machine touched the kerbstone on the left generating a shower of sparks. The rear wheel lifted into the air momentarily and the machine began to slide sideways before tumbling across the road and colliding heavily with the hedge on the right. The unfortunate rider parted company from the machine and came to rest against the kerb on the left hand side of the road. Marshals went to his immediate assistance but there was nothing they could do for him. He had been killed instantly.

Harvey Garton, the Chief Scrutineer, later examined the Suzuki machine and found no evidence to suggest that a mechanical failure had contributed to this accident.

John McGuiness went on to win with a race average speed of 125.38mph; just less than twenty seconds ahead of Adrian Archibald in second place while third spot went to Bruce Anstey of New Zealand.

Colin Breeze was 44 years of age and the father of two children from a previous marriage. His girlfriend, Kay Georgina Sanderson, was on the Island when the accident occurred. He was an IT Technician by occupation and a resident of Kibworth, Leicestershire. His debut on the TT course came during the 1990 MGP when he finished 5th in the Senior Newcomers Race. After a long absence, he returned to the Manx in 1997 and finished 10th in the Senior with a race average speed of 110.63mph. In 1998 he took 2nd place in the Senior then in 1999 went one better, winning the Senior Manx Grand Prix with a race average speed of 115.10mph and raising the lap record for the Manx to 117.48mph. Following this success he turned to the TT races, gaining excellent results in the seven races in which he had competed.

His funeral service was held at St.Wilfrid's Church, Kibworth at 12.15pm on Friday 18th June. Loudspeakers were set up outside to relay the service to the hundreds of mourners who could not get into the packed church. After the service, his coffin was carried from the church to the strains of "Always Look on the Bright Side of Life". The service was followed by committal at Kettering Crematorium.

Gavin Lee FEIGHERY

Gavin Feighery at the Quarterbridge during practice for the 2004 Senior Newcomers MGP

Strong winds were blowing across the mountain section of the TT course on the evening of Saturday 28th August 2004 but otherwise the weather was fine, the roads were dry and visibility was clear, providing near perfect conditions for the competitors gathered at the Grandstand in Douglas waiting to take advantage of the final practice session for the Manx Grand Prix. Amongst them was Gavin Feighery, riding a 600cc Suzuki machine bearing the race number 12 and entered in the Senior Newcomers Race to be held on Monday 30th August. On the opening practice session the previous Saturday he and the other Newcomers were given a one lap escorted tour of the course under the control of Travelling Marshals, a new idea that was being introduced for the first time. During the week he gradually increased his lap times and on the Friday evening he had recorded an average lap speed of 112.14mph.

Shortly after 7.15pm he set off along Glencrutchery Road towards Bray Hill on his opening lap of the session and had then safely made his way round the course, through Ramsey and up onto the mountain climb where he was seen approaching the sweeping left hand bend at the Mountain Box in close company behind fellow newcomer Niall Scollan. He positioned himself as if to overtake on the right but at that same moment Scollan moved to the right in preparation to negotiate the bend. In that instant, the wheels of Gavin Feighery's Suzuki went onto the grass verge and he was immediately thrown from the machine as it went out of control, tumbled across the grass and crashed through the windows of the marshal's shelter. Inside the building at that time was David Higgs, another newcomer who had retired a short time earlier, and he narrowly escaped serious injury, as did the flagman who had been positioned just outside the shelter. Both men went to the assistance of the unfortunate rider who had come to rest in front of the building and found that he was unconscious. They did what they could for him prior to the arrival of the helicopter ambulance, which arrived on the scene just over five minutes after being called. The gravely injured rider was then conveyed to Noble's Hospital, Braddan where, on his arrival, he was taken to theatre for emergency treatment then admitted to the Intensive Care Unit but his condition slowly deteriorated and he succumbed to his injuries in the early hours of Sunday morning 29th August.

Harvey Garton, Chief Scrutineer for the Manx Grand Prix, later examined the Suzuki and found no evidence to suggest that the accident had been as the result of a mechanical failure. Niall Scollan went on to compete in the Newcomers Race two days after the accident and finished in 22nd place but David Higgs was a non-starter.

Gavin Feighery, a single man, had celebrated his 21st birthday just three weeks earlier. He was a resident of Braddan and employed as a Television Editor with Greenlight Television in the Isle of Man. He joined the company on leaving school and as the youngest member of staff he became known as the "Pesky Kid" a nickname that he used later when he created his own race team, Pesky Kid Racing. His motorcycle racing career began in April 2001 and he became a regular competitor at Jurby and on the Billown Circuit. He also competed on short circuits in England such as Brands Hatch and Cadwell Park.

His funeral service was held at Braddan Church on the morning of Tuesday 7th September and followed by committal at Douglas Borough Crematorium.

Thomas Tegid McSeveney CLUCAS

Tommy Clucas at the Ginger Hall during the fateful 2004 Junior MGP

The weather was fine on the afternoon of Wednesday 1st September 2004 and the roads around the TT course were dry with just a slight breeze blowing across the mountain section. Good news for the competitors lined up along Glencrutchery Road in Douglas waiting for the Junior Manx Grand Prix to commence. Amongst them was Tommy Clucas, riding a Honda CBR600RR machine bearing the race number 1. Following his performances in 2003 and having set the fastest lap during practice week he was the firm favourite to win the race.

As he made his way to the start line he had a few words with Chris Kinley, broadcasting live for Manx Radio, then put on his distinctive helmet and wheeled the Honda to the line. At 1.15pm the flag dropped and with no starting partner he was alone as he set off towards Bray Hill. He safely made his way round the course to complete his opening lap with an average speed of 120.28mph, shattering the existing lap record and leading the race by eleven seconds from Davy Morgan. On pulling into the pit lane to refuel at the end of his second circuit he had increased his lead to twenty seconds with Dean Sylvester now in second place. With the tank replenished, screen cleaned and his visor replaced he set off again. Once again he made his way round the course and as he passed the grandstand to begin his fourth and final lap he was recorded as travelling at 146.0mph. Having then made his way through Union Mills, Glen Helen and Kirk Michael he was approaching Ballaugh Bridge when clouds of smoke suddenly began pouring from the Honda just a moment before it went out of control. The unfortunate rider was thrown from the machine and collided heavily with the straw bales covering the railings on the right hand side of the bridge. As he fell back into the road he was struck by his machine. Marshals and medical officers went to his immediate aid and found his condition to be serious. They did what they could for him while waiting for the helicopter ambulance, which arrived on the scene within five minutes of being called. The gravely injured rider was conveyed to Noble's Hospital in Braddan where he underwent emergency surgery before being transferred to the Intensive Therapy Unit. However, at 9.23pm that same evening, with his family by his side he succumbed to his injuries.

Harvey Garton, Chief Scrutineer for the Manx Grand Prix, later examined the Honda and discovered evidence of mechanical failure. There was a hole in the engine crankcase, which had been caused by the failure of the left hand conducting rod.

With a race average speed of 118.13mph, Dean Sylvester of Stanstead went on to win the race with Davy Morgan thirteen seconds behind in second place and Seamus Greene third.

Tommy Clucas, a single man, was 36 years of age. He was a stores supervisor with the Manx Electricity Authority and a resident of Peel. In his younger years he had been a top footballer in the Isle of Man and had gone on to represent the Island at International level. He began his racing career in April 2000 and had gained a wealth of experience at circuits all over Great Britain. During the 2003 Manx Grand Prix he had been leading both Junior and Senior races before mechanical failures forced his retirement from each race.

Hundreds of mourners attended his funeral service, which was held at St German's Cathedral, Peel on 14th September and followed by committal at Douglas Borough Crematorium.

Anders Joakim KARLSSON

Joakim Karlsson at the Quarterbridge during practice for the 2005 Supersport Junior TT

Although many points around the Isle of Man were bathed in sunshine on the evening of Monday 30th May 2005, it was dull and overcast in Douglas. However, the roads around the TT course were dry, which was welcome news for the large number of competitors gathered at the Grandstand in Douglas ready to participate in the second practice session for the Tourist Trophy races. Amongst them was Joakim Karlsson from Sweden, riding a 1000cc Suzuki GSXR machine bearing the race number 77 and entered in the Superbike Race to be held on Saturday 4th June. Two days earlier, using his 600cc Suzuki, he had taken part in the opening practice session of the meeting, which was untimed. This was to be his first time out on the bigger machine and as a newcomer he was obliged to wear an orange jacket over his leathers to indicate his inexperience on the TT course. He had entered all five of the solo races listed for the meeting.

The format for the Tourist Trophy races had changed significantly from previous years as there were no two-stroke machines featured and the Formula One and Production races had gone. These were replaced by three new races. Superbike, for machines over 750cc up to 1000cc; Superstock, for machines over 600cc up to 1000cc; and Supersport, for machines over 400cc up to 750cc.

The practice session commenced shortly after 6.15pm and it was not long before Joakim Karlsson set off along Glencrutchery Road towards Bray Hill on his opening lap of the evening and his first timed lap of the meeting. He negotiated his way through Ballacraine and the tricky Glen Helen section before descending Barregarrow Hill. Then, shortly after rounding the sweeping left hand bend at Westwood he was seen approaching Douglas Road Corner in Kirk Michael village. However, it appeared that he was travelling too fast for the right hand bend and on realising his predicament he began to brake hard, his rear wheel locked up momentarily before the machine went down on it's side. Both rider and machine then slid along the roadway before colliding heavily with the gate pillars either side of the driveway leading to the house "Brynwood". The unfortunate rider came to rest on the driveway of the house with his Suzuki machine lying nearby. Marshals went to his immediate assistance but there was nothing they could do for him. He had been killed instantly.

Harvey Garton, Chief Scrutineer for the races, later examined the Suzuki machine at Police Headquarters in Douglas and was unable to find any evidence to suggest that the incident was related to any mechanical failure.

Joakim Karlsson was 39 years of age and father to a daughter aged 7 years. He was a mechanic by occupation and a resident of Habo, Jonkoping, Sweden where he lived with his partner, Pernilla. He began motorcycle racing in 1983 but retired from the sport in 1990. However, after an absence of fourteen years he made the decision to begin racing again and in addition to competing at events in Scandinavia he made his real road race debut at the Ulster Grand Prix in 2004. During the winter, together with fellow Swedish rider, Christer Miinin, they spent four days on the Island as guests of the Mike Hailwood Foundation.

His funeral service was held at the beautiful and unique timber built Church in Habo, Sweden on the afternoon of Tuesday 21st June.

Leslie Ronald HARAH

Les Harah and Paul Sanderson at the Bungalow during the fateful 2005 Sidecar TT

Intermittent rain showers crossed the Isle of Man on Saturday 4th June 2005 and left wet roads around the TT course together with thick mist on the mountain section. These conditions left the race officials with little option but to delay the start of racing several times throughout the afternoon. Eventually, the TT Superbike Race was postponed to the following day but the roads remained closed in the hope that the Sidecar Tourist Trophy Race could be held later in the day. By 5.30pm the weather had cleared and the roads were beginning to dry out, prompting the decision to start the race at 6.00pm, which was excellent news for the sidecar crews as they began to line up along Glencrutchery Road waiting for the race to commence. Amongst them were Les Harah and his passenger Paul Sanderson riding an outfit bearing the race number 53 and powered by a 600cc Yamaha engine.

The race started with Dave Molyneux and Daniel Sayle being the first to leave the line. Just over eight minutes later it was the turn of Les Harah and Paul Sanderson to begin their race against the clock and they set off towards the descent of Bray Hill. They then negotiated their way round the course and completed their opening lap at an average speed of 91.88mph, which put them in 48th position. On their second circuit of the course they made their way through to Lezayre Road in Ramsey, then made the slow right hand turn into Parliament Square before accelerating away towards the left hand bend leading into Queens Pier Road and the mountain climb. However, whilst negotiating the bend it is thought that the wheel of the sidecar clipped the kerbstone on the left as the outfit suddenly veered sharply across the road, mounted the footpath and struck the frontage of Raymotors Garage. The outfit then collided heavily with the straw bales covering the boundary wall of the houses situated on the right before coming to rest on the footpath. Marshals went to the assistance of the two men and found Sanderson lying beside the outfit having sustained relatively minor injuries. However, Les Harah was unconscious, still astride the machine and slumped over the fuel tank. He was placed on a stretcher and carried a short distance along the road to the Coronation Park where he was transferred to the helicopter ambulance, which then conveyed him to Noble's Hospital where, shortly after admission, it was found that he had succumbed to his injuries.

Nick Crowe and Darren Hope went on to win the race following the retirement of race favourites Dave Molyneux and Daniel Sayle during the second lap.

The sidecar outfit was later examined at Police Headquarters in Douglas and no evidence was found to suggest that a mechanical failure had contributed to the accident.

Les Harah was 53 years of age. He was an electrician and builder by occupation and a resident of Brough, East Yorkshire where he lived with his partner, Barbara Failey. His two children, Lee and Anna were grown up and he was a grandfather to Olivia and Jacob. He had a wealth of experience racing sidecars and had competed in seven TT races since 2000.

More than 300 mourners attended his funeral service, which was held at Haltemprice Crematorium in Willerby near Hull at 1.30pm on Wednesday 15th June. As he had requested, the Christmas carol Silent Night was played during the service along with the song It Takes Two by Marvin Gaye and Kim Weston.

Ian SCOTT

Gus Scott at Braddan Bridge during the fateful 2005 Senior TT

The sun had begun to break through the clouds on the morning of Friday 10th June 2005 as competitors collected their machines from the holding area at the grandstand in Douglas and moved them onto Glencrutchery Road in readiness for the start of the six lap Senior Tourist Trophy race, the concluding competition of the meeting. Amongst them was Ian "Gus" Scott, a newcomer to the TT course, riding a 1000cc Honda CBR machine bearing the race number 45. During practice he had recorded an average lap speed of 112mph on this machine on which he was carrying his original race number 25. At his own request, race officials had moved him down the starting list to number 45.

In the days preceding this race he had competed in four other races, the Superbike TT, Supersport Junior TT 'A', Supersport Junior TT 'B' and Superstock TT. He finished in all four and earned a bronze replica in the second Supersport race.

The race commenced at 10.45am, Ryan Farquhar being the first to leave the line with the following riders starting at ten second intervals. A little over seven minutes later Gus Scott began his race against the clock and set off towards Bray Hill. He safely made his way round the course to complete his opening lap with an average speed of 116mph, which placed him in 33rd position. Without stopping, he passed the grandstand to begin his second circuit, making his way through Ballacraine and the tricky Glen Helen section of the course before entering Kirk Michael. As he was travelling through the village a situation was unfolding a short distance ahead of him. Keith Stewart had pulled in to the left side of the road at the front of the petrol station because an air duct had become loose on his machine. At this point, a race marshal, April Bolster, who had been observing from the front garden of her home, began to make her way across the road towards Keith Stewart but in doing so she crossed directly into the path of Gus Scott who would have been travelling in excess of 130mph. He had no chance of avoiding her and a high speed collision occurred. The unfortunate rider was thrown from his machine and came to rest in the roadway beyond the petrol station while Mrs Bolster had come to rest on the footpath opposite her home. Marshals went to the two casualties and on finding no signs of life resuscitation attempts were made while waiting for the helicopter ambulance, which arrived on the scene within five minutes of being called but there was nothing more that could be done. Both had been killed instantly.

John McGuiness, a close friend of Gus Scott, went on to win the race unaware of the tragedy that had cost his friends life until after the trophy had been presented to him. He added later that Gus and he had been great mates with the late David Jefferies.

Gus Scott, a single man, was 40 years of age and the father of Yasmin, his ten year old daughter. He was a freelance journalist by profession and a resident of Kendal in Cumbria. He had a wealth of experience on a variety of machines and had competed at Scarborough and the Southern 100 in the Isle of Man many years earlier. He had also become a regular at Macau where he took a 4th place finish in 2002.

His funeral service was held at St. Oswald's Church, Burneside near Kendal on Tuesday 21st June and followed by interment.

Geoffrey Brian SAWYER

Geoff Sawyer at the Quarterbridge during practice for the 2005 Senior Classic MGP

Blue skies and sunshine graced the Isle of Man on the evening of Wednesday 24th August 2005, unlike the previous evening when inclement weather conditions had forced the cancellation of the scheduled practice session for the Manx Grand Prix races. Now, with dry roads around the TT course together with excellent visibility on the mountain section conditions were almost perfect for racing, which was welcome news for the large number of competitors gathered at the Grandstand in Douglas waiting to take advantage of the fourth scheduled practice period. Amongst them was race veteran Geoff Sawyer, riding a 500cc Matchless machine bearing the race number 37 and entered in the Senior Classic Race to be held on the afternoon of Monday 29th August. Riding the same machine during practice two days earlier he had recorded an average lap speed of 87.91mph. Competing in the 2004 Manx Grand Prix he had finished 12th in both the Senior Classic Race and the Junior Classic Race.

Les Doherty the Practice Controller, advised the competitors on the conditions around the course and warned that they might encounter problems from the setting sun on certain parts of the course. At 6.16pm, just one minute later than scheduled, practising commenced with a mixture of Ultra Lightweight and Classic machines taking part. A short time later it was the turn of Geoff Sawyer to set off along Glencrutchery Road towards the daunting descent of Bray Hill then safely negotiated his way round the course to complete his opening lap with an average speed of 84.19mph. Then, having made his way through Quarterbridge and Braddan Bridge, he was less than three miles into his second lap of the evening when he was seen approaching the right hand bend by the Railway Hotel in Union Mills. He was on the usual racing line for the bend but as he banked over his rear wheel suddenly stepped out to the left and the machine went from beneath him. Both rider and machine slid along the road, mounted the footpath on the left and collided heavily with the straw bales covering the boundary wall of the two cottages situated at that location. The unfortunate rider came to rest on the footpath and marshals who went to his assistance found his condition to be critical. He was placed on a stretcher and carried to the Strang Road then transferred to an ambulance, which conveyed him the short distance to Noble's Hospital. However, a short time after his admission it was found that he had succumbed to his injuries.

The badly damaged Matchless was later examined at Police Headquarters in Douglas and no evidence was found to suggest that a mechanical failure had contributed to the accident.

Geoff Sawyer was 55 years of age and an interpreter by occupation, specialising in French and German. He was a resident of Ipswich in Suffolk where he lived with his partner Kath Moore. He had a wealth of racing experience and made his debut on the TT course during the 1988 Manx Grand Prix when, riding a Matchless, he finished 33rd in the Senior Classic Race with an average speed of 82.12mph then, riding a Rotax, he finished 45th in the Lightweight Race with an average speed of 88.53mph. From thereon he raced regularly in both the Manx Grand Prix and the TT. Over the years he had competed in more than sixty races over the TT course and became the recipient of a number of coveted replicas.

His funeral service was held on the afternoon of Thursday 8th September and followed by committal at York Crematorium, Middlethorpe, North Yorkshire.

John William LODER

John Loder pictured during practice for the 2005 Senior Classic MGP

The weathermen at Ronaldsway forecast cloudy skies with occasional outbreaks of rain for the Isle of Man on the evening of Friday 26th August 2005 and this proved to be correct as a heavy shower passed over the Grandstand on Glencrutchery Road in Douglas at around 5.30pm. With reports of rain falling on parts of the TT course the news was not good for the large number of competitors congregating in the area of the Grandstand waiting to participate in the penultimate practice session for the Manx Grand Prix races. Amongst them was the race veteran John Loder, riding a 496cc Nourish Seeley machine bearing the race number 3 and entered in the Senior Classic Race, which was to be held on the afternoon of Monday 29th August. Riding this same machine on the opening practice session the previous Saturday he had recorded an average lap speed of 94.88mph. His achievements of finishing 2nd in the Senior Classic Race at the 2003 and the 2004 Manx Grand Prix meetings had marked him as a potential race winner this year.

Following a brief delay due to a fuel spillage on the course, the first part of the session commenced at 6.37pm with a mixture of Ultra Lightweight and Classic machines taking part. As the light was failing early it was decided that the duration of the practice period would be reduced by 15 minutes and the Roads Open car would be dispatched at 7.55pm. Several riders, expecting the worse, opted to go out in their oversuits. The lack of adhesion on the road surface was experienced by a number of riders whose machines went into slides as they released the clutch on setting off. A short time later it was the turn of John Loder to head off along Glencrutchery Road towards Bray Hill and Quarterbridge Road on his opening lap of the evening. He safely negotiated his way round the course through Glen Helen, Ballaugh and Ramsey before starting the climb onto the mountain section of the course. A short time later he was seen approaching the sweeping left hand bend at the 33rd Milestone where the warning flag indicating "Lack of Adhesion" was being displayed. Accordingly, he was travelling slower than full racing speed but then, as he was banked over to negotiate the bend his rear wheel stepped out to the right as it crossed the double white lines in the centre of the road and despite his best efforts he was unable to regain control of the machine before it went from under him. Both rider and machine slid across the roadway and down onto the grassland on the right. Marshals went to the assistance of the unfortunate rider but found there was nothing that could be done for him. He had been killed instantly.

Scrutineers later examined the Seeley machine at Police Headquarters in Douglas and found no evidence to suggest that a mechanical failure had contributed to the accident.

John Loder was 56 years of age. He was an accounts manager by occupation and a resident of Kings Heath near Birmingham where he lived with his wife Diane and their two children, Joanna aged 19 and William aged 20 who had been on the Island with his father for the races. He had a wealth of racing experience and had made his debut on the TT course in 1979 when he finished 3rd in the Senior Newcomers Race. He went on to compete in over forty races on the Isle of Man TT course, receiving a number of replicas in the process.

His funeral service was held on the afternoon of Tuesday 13th September and followed by committal at the Robin Hood Crematorium in Birmingham.

Edwin Arthur BYERS

Eddie Byers at Ballaugh Bridge during the fateful 2005 Junior Classic MGP

Although the sun was shining across most of the Isle of Man on the morning of Wednesday 31st August 2005, there was thick mist clinging to the mountain section of the TT course, which left the Clerk of the Course for the Manx Grand Prix with little option but to announce a delay to the start of the four lap Junior Classic race scheduled to begin at 10.15am. Not the best of news for the 66 competitors gathered at the grandstand in Douglas waiting to participate in the race. Amongst them was race veteran Eddie Byers, riding a 350 7R Seeley machine bearing the race number 58. Two days earlier, riding a 496cc G50 Seeley machine, he had earned a coveted replica after finishing 10th in the Senior Classic Race with a race average speed of 96.99mph

Whilst waiting for the mist to lift, conditions on the lower sections of the course had deteriorated and rain showers had left wet roads. However, by 11.15am the mist had started to lift and the wet roads were beginning to dry. With this information, the decision was made to start the race at 11.30am and machines were moved from the holding area onto Glencrutchery Road where they were lined up in readiness for the start of the race. Chris McGahan and Wattie Brown were the first two away with the following riders setting off in pairs and at ten second intervals. Almost five minutes later it was the turn of Eddie Byers to begin his race against the clock and he left the start line in company with newcomer Richard Wright from Onchan, riding a 346cc Honda. Having safely negotiated his way round the course he completed his opening lap with an average speed of 90.46mph and was lying in 24th place. He completed his second circuit with an average lap speed of 90.57mph and had moved up five places to 19th. On his third lap of the race, having safely negotiated his way round the course, through Glen Helen, Kirk Michael and Ramsey then up onto the mountain climb, he was seen approaching the tricky double bend at the 27th Milestone, just beyond Guthries Memorial. Then, on passing through the bends he lost control of his machine and collided heavily with the stone banking on the left. The unfortunate rider was thrown from the machine and came to rest in the roadway where a marshal went to his aid but found there was nothing that could be done for him. He had been killed instantly.

Scrutineers later examined the Seeley at Police Headquarters in Douglas and found no evidence to suggest that a mechanical failure had contributed to this accident.

Chris McGahan from Douglas went on to win the race with second place going to Tony Cawte of Crosby. The final podium position went to Dave Madsen-Mygdal of Douglas.

Eddie Byers was 56 years of age and the father of a grown up daughter, Kelly. He was a motor technician by occupation and a resident of Stondon Massey, Essex. He had a wealth of racing experience and made his debut on the TT course during the 1984 MGP when, riding a Suzuki, he won the Senior Newcomers Race with a race average speed of 95.72mph. He went on to compete in over 25 races over the famous Isle of Man circuit including one venture to the TT races in 1987 when he took part in the Production TT Race.

His funeral service was held on Tuesday 20th September and followed by committal at Chelmsford Crematorium.

Barry Tim JOHNSON

Tim Johnson at the Gooseneck during the fateful 2005 Junior Classic MGP

Thick mist enveloped the mountain section of the TT course on the morning of Wednesday 31st August 2005 and even though the sun was shining on the rest of the course race officials for the Manx Grand Prix were left with little option but to announce a delay to the start of the Junior Classic race. Not the best of news for the participating competitors gathered at the Grandstand in Douglas. Amongst them was Tim Johnson, riding a 349cc Aermacchi machine bearing the race number 17. Two days earlier, riding a 500cc Velocette Venom, he had taken part in the Senior Classic Race and despite having to make two stops for mechanical adjustments, he finished in 18th place with a race average speed of 91.40mph, just missing out on adding a silver to his collection of ten coveted replicas.

By 11.30am the mist had cleared and the race began. Eighty seconds later it was the turn of Tim Johnson to begin his race against the clock and he set off along Glencrutchery Road then safely negotiated his way round the course to complete his opening circuit with an average speed of 96.51mph, which put him in 6th place. Then, an average lap speed of 97.52mph on his second lap helped to move him up into 3rd place. On completion of his third lap, putting in an average lap time of 97.96mph, he had maintained his race position. During the course of his fourth and final lap of the race he made his way through to Ramsey where it was shown that he was holding third position and was just seven seconds behind second place man Tony Cawte. On leaving Ramsey he made his way up onto the mountain section and was seen travelling at racing speed on the approach to the left hand bend at the Black Hut, less than ten miles from the finish line. Just ahead of him, travelling at a much slower speed was competitor number 78, Harvey Swetnam, riding a Seeley and as a late starter he was still on his third lap of the race. Tim Johnson positioned himself to pass the slower machine on the right and was committed to the manoeuvre when Swetnam began to move across the road, heading for the small car park on the right hand side of the bend and in doing so he blocked Johnson's path. Realising his predicament Tim Johnson braked hard then in an effort to avoid a collision with the Seeley he stepped off the Aermacchi and slid along the road with his machine before mounting the grass bank on the right and colliding heavily with a metal road sign. The unfortunate rider came to rest just inside the entrance to the car park and a marshal went to his immediate assistance but there was nothing that could be done for him. He had been killed instantly. Swetnam had come to a stop within the car park and was unharmed.

Chris McGahan from Douglas went on to win the race. Second place went to Tony Cawte of Crosby and the final podium position went to Dave Madsen-Mygdal of Douglas.

Tim Johnson was 51 years of age and the owner of a building renovation company. He was a resident of Winkleigh, Devon where he lived with his partner of 31 years, Jane Pereira. He had a wealth of racing experience and made his debut on the TT course in 1989 when he rode a 1954 BSA A10. It is believed that at the time of his death he held the outright lap and race records for Velocettes on the TT course having achieved an average lap speed of 95.57mph and an average race speed of 94.82mph in the Senior Classic race at the 2002 MGP.

His funeral service was held in the paddock at his home in Devon on the afternoon of 23rd September and followed by a private service at Barnstaple Crematorium.

John Paul BOURKE

John Bourke at the Creg ny Baa during the fateful 2005 Junior MGP

Low clouds covered the high grounds of the Isle of Man at dawn on Thursday 1st September 2005 but, as forecast by the weathermen at Ronaldsway, they slowly lifted throughout the morning and were replaced with sunshine. Welcome news for the 96 competitors gathered in the area of the grandstand in Douglas waiting to participate in the four lap Junior Manx Grand Prix, which had been postponed the previous day due to adverse weather conditions. Amongst them was John Bourke, riding a 600cc Suzuki machine bearing the race number 85. During practice he had recorded an average lap speed of 101.19mph on this same machine.

When the roads closed at 11.30am attendants were active in the pit lane making preparations for the pit stop that was to be made during the race. Then at 12.15pm, with reports of dry roads and clear visibility around the course, the flag dropped and the race was underway with the riders setting off in pairs and at ten second intervals. Seven minutes later it was the turn of John Bourke to begin his race against the clock and he set off along Glencrutchery Road in company with his starting partner Chris Woods of Dumbarton. He then safely negotiated his way round the course and completed his opening lap with an average speed of 103.53mph, which put him in 69th position. On completion of his second circuit he pulled into the pit lane to refuel and having recorded an average speed of 103.85mph he had moved up two places. With his tank replenished he set off on his third lap and had made his way down Bray Hill then through Quarterbridge and Braddan Bridge when he was seen approaching the Railway Hotel at Union Mills in close company behind Andrew Timbrell, race number 77, who had started the race 40 seconds ahead of him. Then, as the two riders prepared to negotiate the right hand bend outside the hotel the front wheel of John Bourke's machine came into contact with the rear wheel of Timbrell's machine. As a consequence, both machines went out of control and continued straight on into the Lhergy Cripperty Road junction before colliding heavily with the straw bales covering the boundary wall of a cottage. Marshals went to the immediate assistance of the two men and found there was nothing they could do for John Bourke. He had been killed instantly. Andrew Timbrell had sustained serious injuries and was conveyed to Noble's Hospital where he lay in a coma for five days before recovering.

Harvey Garton, Chief Technical Officer for the races, later examined the two machines and found no evidence to suggest that a mechanical failure had contributed to this accident.

Ian Patterson from Weardale went on to win the race with an average speed of 118.02mph. Seamus Greene of Letterkenny finished second and John Burrows of Dungannon third.

John Bourke was 37 years of age. He was an Information Technology Technician by occupation and a resident of Clondalkin village near Dublin where he lived with his partner Ann. He had a wealth of racing experience and had made his debut at the Manx Grand Prix in 2004 when, riding a 750cc Suzuki, he finished 14th in the Senior Newcomers Race with a race average speed of 99.53mph and was awarded a coveted silver replica. Later in the week he took part in the Senior Manx and recorded a creditable race average speed of 100.70mph.

His funeral service was held at the Church of the Immaculate Conception in Clondalkin on Tuesday 13th September, followed by committal at Newlands Cross Crematorium, Dublin.

Donavon Geoffrey LEESON

Don Leeson at the Gooseneck during the fateful 2005 Ultra Lightweight MGP

Friday 2nd September 2005, the concluding day of the Manx Grand Prix meeting and the Isle of Man was bathed in sunshine. The roads around the TT course were dry and visibility on the mountain section was clear. Almost perfect racing conditions for the competitors gathering in the area of the grandstand on Glencrutchery Road in Douglas waiting to take part in both the Lightweight and Ultra Lightweight Races which were to be run concurrently. Amongst those entered for the four lap Ultra Lightweight was Don Leeson, riding a 400cc Honda machine bearing the race number 100. Two days earlier, riding a 247cc Suzuki, he had finished 5th in the Lightweight Classic Race with a race average speed of 83.98mph.

At 10.15am the flag dropped and the Lightweight Race commenced. Three minutes later the Ultra Lightweight Race began but there was some confusion at the start line as John Richards had been inadvertently set off alongside the last man in the Lightweight, which left Graham Taubman to head off alone. Five minutes later it was the turn of Don Leeson to begin his race against the clock and he set off towards Bray Hill in company with his starting partner John Harrison. He then safely made his way round the course to complete his opening lap with an average speed of 94.08mph, which put him in 47th position. Without stopping he passed the grandstand then once again made his way round the course and on completion of his second circuit he pulled into the pit lane to refuel having recorded an average speed of 95.36mph, which had helped to move him up one place. With his tank replenished and visor cleaned he set off again to begin his third lap. Having made his way through Glen Helen, Kirk Michael and Ballaugh he was seen approaching Quarry Bends near Sulby but then, as he was negotiating the bends, he drifted wide on the exit of the second left hander, mounted the grass bank on the right then crashed through trees and undergrowth before coming to rest in an adjacent maintenance yard. Marshals went to his immediate assistance but there was nothing they could do for him. He had been killed instantly.

Harvey Garton, Chief Technical Officer for the races, later examined the wrecked Honda and found no evidence to suggest that a mechanical failure had contributed to this accident.

The race had continued and Paul Corrin went on to win after race leader Graham Taubman fell from his machine at Glen Helen on the final lap. Alan Oversby finished second with Maria Costello taking third place and becoming the first female solo rider to finish on the podium at either the TT or Manx Grand Prix.

Don Leeson was 57 years of age and the father of two daughters, Donna and Jennifer. He was a carpenter by occupation and a resident of the historic market town of Corwen in Wales where he lived with his partner Jay. He had a wealth of racing experience and was Secretary of the Vintage Japanese Motorcycle Club. His first race on the Isle of Man TT course was in the 1995 MGP when, riding a Suzuki, he competed in the Lightweight Classic Race and finished in 16th place. He went on to compete in the Manx Grand Prix several times after his debut and was a regular finisher, picking up seven finishers medals.

His funeral service was held on the afternoon of Thursday 15th September and followed by committal at Pentrebychan Crematorium in Wrexham.

Jun MAEDA

Jun Maeda at the Quarterbridge on his fateful practice lap for the 2006 Superstock TT

The Isle of Man was bathed in bright sunshine on the evening of Monday 29th May 2006 although there was a cold northwesterly wind blowing across the Island. With dry roads and clear visibility around the TT course conditions were almost perfect for the competitors assembling on Glencrutchery Road in Douglas waiting to participate in the second practice session for the Tourist Trophy races. Amongst them was the Japanese rider Jun Maeda, riding a 1000cc Honda Fireblade machine bearing the race number 12 and entered in the Superstock Race to be held on Monday 5th June. Having been unable to take advantage of the first practice session on the Saturday evening this was to be his first outing on the course since his excellent performances in the races the previous year.

Watching proceedings was a party of Japanese dignitaries, including the Governor of Tokyo, Shintaro Ishihara and the Mayors of Miyakejima and Hachojojima Islands, who were on the Isle of Man to see if real road racing could be promoted in their homeland. In their honour it was decided that Jun Maeda would be allowed to head the field away then, shortly after 6.15pm, the flag dropped and he set off towards Bray Hill. He had safely made his way through Quarterbridge then Braddan Bridge when he was observed travelling through Union Mills. However, he was not travelling at racing speed and appeared to be touring as he began the climb on Ballahutchin Hill towards Glen Vine. Moments later, competitor Carl Rennie, riding a 1000cc Kawasaki ZX10 was seen negotiating Union Mills at full racing speed with another rider Seamus Greene, riding a 1000cc Suzuki GSXR close behind him. As they were climbing the hill Rennie caught a glimpse of something to his right and instinctively moved over to the left. At that instant Seamus Greene was suddenly confronted with Jun Maeda travelling slowly and directly in front of him. He had no time to avoid a heavy collision and the impact left the roadway covered in oil and debris from the two machines. Marshals went to the aid of the unfortunate riders and did what they could for them until they were conveyed by helicopter ambulance to Noble's Hospital a short distance away in Braddan. The practice session was immediately stopped to allow the scene of the accident to be cleared.

The following day Seamus Greene, winner of the 2005 Senior Manx Grand Prix, was transferred to the Neurological ward of Walton Hospital in Liverpool where he was to undergo further intensive treatment. Jun Maeda remained in Noble's Hospital until Thursday 1st June and was then transferred to a specialist orthopaedic hospital in Manchester. However, despite initial signs of improvement following emergency surgery his condition slowly deteriorated and he succumbed to his injuries at 11.17pm on Monday 5th June.

Jun Maeda, a single man, was 38 years of age. (Born: Tokyo 6th November 1967) He was a professional racing motorcyclist and journalist by occupation and a resident of Kyoto, Japan. He made his TT debut in 1997 and steadily improved his times over the following years until 2005 when he took four top ten finishes and recorded a lap time of 124.78mph in the Senior Race, which elevated him to the 12th fastest competitor on the TT course.

At the request of his family his remains were cremated at Blackley Crematorium, Manchester on Monday 12th June. His ashes were then returned to Japan for interment. A memorial service was held in Kyoto on the afternoon of Sunday 25th June.

Terry John CRANE

Terry Crane at Ballacraine during his fateful practice lap for the 2006 Lightweight MGP

Apart from the gusty winds blowing across the Isle of Man the weather conditions were fine on the evening of Monday 21st August 2006. Visibility was clear on the mountain section of the TT course and the roads were mostly dry other than a few damp patches under the trees. Unlike the previous Saturday when mist and rain had disrupted the opening practice session for the Manx Grand Prix and only a few newcomers managed a lap of the course under escort. Therefore, for most of the competitors congregating at the Grandstand in Douglas it would be their first time out for this meeting. Amongst them was Terry Crane, riding a 250cc Honda machine bearing the race number 14 and entered in the Lightweight Race to be held on Friday 1st September. He had lost his right leg in a racing accident and had a pedal clip of the type favoured by cycle racers fitted to the right side of his machine to harness his false leg.

Just five minutes later than scheduled, the session commenced at 6.20pm with Dick Cassidy, the Chief Travelling Marshall, being the first away. He was escorting five newcomers who had been unable to participate in the untimed lap of the course on the Saturday. Twenty minutes later, the session opened for Classic, Newcomers and Ultra Lightweight machines. Then, at 7.25pm, it was the turn of the Senior, Junior and Lightweight entrants to take advantage of the practice session, which included Terry Crane and he set off along Glencrutchery Road towards Bray Hill and Quarterbridge on his opening lap of the meeting. Having safely negotiated his way round the course through to Ramsey he then began the climb up onto the mountain section.

Meanwhile, at the 33rd Milestone, competitors Geoff Hand and Michael Dunlop had both retired their machines near to that location and were sat together watching the remainder of the practice session when they saw Terry Crane approaching the sweeping left hand bends. Then, as he banked over to negotiate the first of the bends the front wheel of his machine suddenly went from beneath him and he slid across the road to the right before coming to rest on the grassland below the road. Marshals, together with the two competitors, went to the assistance of the unfortunate rider and found his condition to be serious. Within a short time he was conveyed by helicopter to Noble's Hospital where he was admitted to the intensive therapy unit but despite specialist treatment he succumbed to his injuries later that evening.

Scrutineers later examined the crash damaged Honda at Police Headquarters in Douglas and found no evidence to suggest that a mechanical failure had contributed to this accident.

Terry Crane was 46 years of age and the father of two sons, Dave and Adam. He was a farmer by occupation and a resident of Santon in the Isle of Man where he lived with his wife Maria. He had a wealth of racing experience and made his debut on the TT course during the 1988 Manx Grand Prix when, riding a Suzuki, he competed in the Senior Newcomers race and finished 16th with a race average speed of 91.44mph. He did not return again until 2002 and from thereon he became a regular at the Manx, picking up four finishers medals. Over the years he had made a number of appearances on the Billown Circuit in the south of the Island.

His funeral service was held at St. Peter's Church, Church Langton, Leicestershire on Tuesday 12th September and followed by committal at Kettering Crematorium.

Marc Robert RAMSBOTHAM

Marc Ramsbotham at Braddan Bridge during the ill fated 2007 Senior TT

Exceptionally large numbers of race enthusiasts positioned themselves around the TT course on the morning of Friday 8th June 2007, the final day of the Centenary TT meeting. The Island was bathed in sunshine, the roads were dry and apart from a few pockets of mist on the high ground conditions were almost perfect for racing as competitors lined up along Glencrutchery Road in Douglas waiting to participate in the six lap Senior Tourist Trophy race. Amongst them was Marc Ramsbotham, a newcomer to the TT course, riding a 1000cc GSXR Suzuki machine bearing the race number 72. Despite sustaining an elbow injury following a spill at Waterworks on the Monday of practice week he had gone on to compete in the Superbike race on Monday 4th June finishing 46th with a race average speed of 112.45mph. The following day he finished 42nd in the Superstock race with an average speed of 114.18mph.

At 10.45am the race commenced with Michael Rutter being the first away. The remainder of the field followed at ten second intervals and almost twelve minutes passed before it was the turn of Marc Ramsbotham to begin his race against the clock. He completed his opening lap with an average speed of 116.15mph and was lying in 49th place then an average speed of 117.53mph on his second circuit helped to move him up into 40th place. His race continued with excellent lap times and by the end of the fourth lap he had moved up into 33rd place with an average lap speed of 118.64mph. On commencing his fifth lap he made his way round the course through to Ramsey then began the climb up onto the mountain section. Moments later, as he banked over to negotiate the right hand bend at the 26th Milestone he came into contact with several wooden fence posts situated at the roadside. He was thrown from the machine as it then careered across the road, mounted the grass bank on the left and ploughed through a group of spectators and marshals before coming to rest back in the roadway. The unfortunate rider had been killed instantly. Race spectator Dean Jacob aged 33 died at the scene. Another spectator Gregory Kenzig aged 52 was conveyed by helicopter to Noble's Hospital but died shortly after admission. Two marshals, Hilary Musson aged 60, a former TT competitor, and Janice Philips aged 50 had sustained serious injuries and were airlifted to Noble's Hospital. Both survived the incident.

Having led from start to finish, John McGuiness went on to win the race but his record breaking lap of 130.35mph was overshadowed by the tragic incident on the mountain. Guy Martin finished second with Ian Hutchinson taking the final podium position.

Marc Ramsbotham was 34 years of age. He was a self employed commercial fitter by occupation and a resident of the small village Spooner Row near Wymondham, Norfolk where he lived with his wife Sarah and their two young daughters, Beulah aged 13 years and Bronwyn aged 11 years. Having taken up motorcycle racing in 1998 he had secured some excellent results but was plagued with injuries sustained in the sport. In 2006, he took to road racing and returned top performances at Scarborough and the Ulster Grand Prix. Just before travelling to the Isle of Man he had won 3 out of 4 races at Scarborough.

On Thursday 5th July a horse drawn hearse carried him to Wymondham Abbey, Norfolk where more than 500 mourners attended his funeral service.

Also Remembered

All competitors, race officials and spectators who have sustained life changing injuries during these race meetings and especially those who have lost their lives.

Do not stand at my grave and weep,

I am not there, I do not sleep.

I am in a thousand winds that blow,

I am the softly falling snow.

I am the gentle showers of rain,

I am the fields of ripening grain.

When you awaken in the morning's hush

I am the swift uplifting rush

Of quiet birds in circling flight.

I am the soft stars that shine at night.

Do not stand at my grave and cry,

I am not there, I did not die.

ACKNOWLEDGMENTS

Since beginning my research I have been assisted by many people and I would like to show my appreciation by including their names in this book.

Michael Brown; Walter Radcliffe; Peter Curtis; Susan Cain; Roger Sims and the library staff at the Manx Museum; Bill Snelling; Ann Smith; Pamela Austin; Audrey Bradford; Janette Edwards; John Drapkin; Eddie Menday; Donald Pilling; Tony Wright; Gordie Moore; Tessa Dudley; John R E Pirie; John M Pirie; Karl Schleuter; Roy Thomas; Kerry Bradford; Frank Jones; John Van Tilburg; Sarah Amato; Doris Drinkwater; Anita Westfield; Herbert Bent; Patricia O'Driscoll; Ian Huntley; Victoria Crow-Cook; Edna Stephen; Geoff Evans; Mr G.M.F. Sandys-Winsch; David Butler; Lottie Watters; Laura Bradford; Janice Harper; Mr J. Antram; Gordon Meehan; Hylton Pratt; Paul & Jan Robinson; Tony Baitup; Dorothy Armstrong; Peter Chapman; Eddie Christian; Peter Collis; Robert & Helen Finch; Pete Twentyman; Peter Platt; Ron Hardy; Jill Locke; Ted & Margaret Heaney; Christine, Nathan & Aalish Evans; David Swann; Alan Tricoglus; Roger Nevin; Wyn Evans; Des Evans; Jeff Gawley; Gordon Quirk; Joan Corbett; Elaine Small; Anne Hudson; Dr David Stevens MBE; Marco Vasille; Des Founds; Val Henshaw; Jackie Keith; Billy Gallaway; Penny Smith; Doris Jackson; Mike Teale; James Tannock; Mrs Waring; Maureen Trustham; Edward Trustham; Rosa Saalbrink; Glynne Shearman; Arnie Withers; Helen Mason; Mike O'Connor; Will Loder; Jane Pereira; Darren Bradford; Charlie Howland; Brian Teare; Arthur Moore; John Heaney; Mike Stott; Rachel Lloyd-Jones; David Bradford; Paul Hayes; Kurt Harmer; Graham Dalling; Shaun Brown; Jenny Simmonds; Graham Holloway; Brian Screen; Jane Skayman; Monica Clark; Daniel Bradford; Alice Wilson; Steve Hampson; Russell Lee; Eddie Radcliffe; Barry Ramsey; Eric Sloane; Richard Faragher; Dave Evans; Terry Cringle; Annie Gale; Ralph Crellin; Roy Cowin;

I would particularly like to thank the following people who have not only supplied the excellent photographs used in this book but also gave consent for them to be used. I am extremely grateful.

Bill Snelling of Fottofinders - amulree@mcb.net
Michael Brown Collection
Mike Yiend -
John Watterson – Isle of Man Newspapers
Dave Kneen - www.manxphotosonline.com
Manx National Heritage -
Simon Lee - themanxpicturebox@talk21.com
Mortons Media Group Ltd -
National Motor Museum Beaulieu - www.motoringpicturelibrary.com
Chris Wood - www.speed-images.co.uk
Bill Dale - isleofmanphotos@manx.net
Kris Clay - www.isleofmanphotographs.com
Albert Lowe -
Eddy Richardson -